BY DAVE MARSH

Born to Run: The Bruce Springsteen Story

The Book of Rock Lists

Elvis

Before I Get Old

EDITED BY DAVE MARSH

The Rolling Stone Record Guide

The New Rolling Stone Record Guide

FORTUNATE
SON

FORTUNATE SON

SON

Criticism and Journalism by America's Best-Known Rock Writer

DAVE MARSH

Random House   New York

Copyright © 1985 by Duke and Duchess Ventures, Inc.

All rights reserved under International and Pan-American Copyright Conventions. Published in the United States by Random House, Inc., New York, and simultaneously in Canada by Random House of Canada Limited, Toronto.

Library of Congress Cataloging in Publication Data

Marsh, Dave.
Fortunate son.

1. Rock music—Addresses, essays, lectures. I. Title.
ML3534.M38 1985   784.5'4   84-42509
ISBN 0-394-72119-5

Manufactured in the United States of America

Designed by Jo Anne Metsch

98765432

First Edition

Grateful acknowledgment is made to the following for permission to reprint previously published material:

Almo Music Corp.: Lyrics excerpted from "Missin' Twenty Grand." © 1982 Almo Music Corp. (ASCAP). Words by David Lasley. All rights reserved. International Copyright secured.

Bema Music Co.: Lyrics excerpted from "My Town," by Michael Stanley Gee. Copyright © 1983 by Bema Music Co. and Michael Stanley Music Co. All rights reserved.

CBS Songs: Lyrics excerpted from "Louis Quatorze" © 1981 April Music Ltd. (PRS). Words by Malcolm McClaren. Music by David Barbarossa, Lee Gorman, Matthew Ashman. Rights in U.S.A. administered by Blackwood Music, Inc., 49 East 52 Street, New York, NY 10022. All rights reserved. Used by permission.

Chappell & Co., Inc.: Lyrics excerpted from "Follow That Dream," by Ben Weisman and Fred Wise. Copyright © 1962 by Gladys Music. All rights administered by Chappell & Co., Inc. (Intersong Music, Publisher). International Copyright Secured. ALL RIGHTS RESERVED. Used by permission.

Creem Magazine: The following articles originally appeared in *Creem Magazine*, and are © Creem Magazine: "The Teenage Dreams of Billy Levise" (originally, "Put the Bacon on the Paper, So's the Grease'll Run Off"), 1969; "Bob Seger: Doncha Ever Listen to the Radio," 1971; "Iggy in Exile," 1973; "The Daring Young Men and the Flying Chimpanzees," 1972; "Gary Glitter—Garbage Rock Comes of Age," 1972; "Crazy 'Bout the La-La," 1970; "MC5: Back on Shakin' Street," 1972; *"Some Time in New York City,"* 1971; "Rudy Martinez Returns," 1970; "Elements of Style," 1973.

Dreena Music & Dan Daley Music: Lyrics excerpted from "Still in Saigon," by Dan Daley. 1981 Dreena Music and Dan Daley Music.

Gear Publishing Co.: Lyrics excerpted from "Against the Wind," "Heavy Music," and "2 + 2 = ?," by Bob Seger.

Jondora Music: Lyrics excerpted from "Who'll Stop the Rain." © 1969 Jondora Music.

MCA Music: Lyrics excerpted from "Was I Right or Wrong," words and music by Gary Russington and Ronnie Van Zant. © Copyright 1978 by Duchess Music Corporation and Get Loose Music. Rights Administered by MCA MUSIC, A Division of MCA, INC., New York, NY. Used by Permission. All Rights Reserved.

MPL Communications, Inc. and Wren Music Co.: Lyrics excerpted from "Well All Right" by Norman Petty, Buddy Holly, Jerry Allison and Joe Mauldin. © 1958 MPL Communications, Inc. and Wren Music Co. Used by permission.

Straight Arrow Publishers, Inc.: The following articles by Dave Marsh: "I Call and Call and Call on Mick," *Rolling Stone* # 195, September 11, 1975. By Straight Arrow Publishers, Inc. © 1975. "Frampton: Packaging Pays Off," *Rolling Stone,* November 18, 1976. By Straight Arrow Publishers, Inc. © 1976. "Do You Wanna Dance," *Rolling Stone,* 1976. By Straight Arrow Publishers, Inc. © 1976. "Paperback Writer," *Rolling Stone* # 219, July 28, 1977. By Straight Arrow Publishers, Inc. © 1977. "Hey Rocky What's a Punk," *Rolling Stone* # 234, March 10, 1977. By Straight Arrow Publishers, Inc. © 1977. "Kick Out the Jams," *Rolling Stone,* 1977. By Straight Arrow Publishers, Inc. © 1977. "How Great Thou Art" (Elvis Presley Obituary), *Rolling Stone* # 248, September 22, 1977. By Straight Arrow Publishers, Inc. © 1977.

Excerpts from *The New Rolling Stone Record Guide,* edited by Dave Marsh with John Swenson. A Random House/Rolling Stone Press book. Copyright © 1979 by Rolling Stone Press. "Sly and the Family Stone," from *The Rolling Stone Illustrated History of Rock & Roll,* edited by Jim Miller, a Random House/Rolling Stone Press book. Copyright © 1980 by Rolling Stone Press. All rights reserved. Reprinted by Permission.

Warner Bros. Music: Lyrics excerpted from "Thank You for Talking to Me Africa." © 1972 Mijac Music. All rights reserved. Used by permission.

For my parents,
O.K. and Mary Marsh

Foreword

I n addition to common authorship, these pieces are linked by two themes. Throughout they focus, at first instinctively and later more consciously, on rock music as a form of culture for the uncultured, and particularly as a means of expression for those to whom more rigorously credentialed channels are denied. As one consequence, the audience and the performer are almost always linked in my writing, through their changing relationships to the ideals and ideas that the music expresses and represents.

Secondly, the later articles and essays operate from an increasing conviction that, while rock acquires important dimensions of its meaning through social interaction and through its use by the audience for specific purposes, the music is a self-sufficient mode of expression. That is, rock performers over the past twenty-five years have struggled toward and have occasionally actually achieved one of the most interesting and valuable postwar popular arts, and one that is (for all its British influence and attraction) at best uniquely American. To make a lengthy case for rock as art is not only sententious but probably pointless and unquestionably futile. But it does seem important to me that rock is able to stand on its own terms in expressing what the individuals who speak through it need to say. As a result, there's almost nothing here in favor of rock's hyphenated forms (jazz-rock, etc.), since they are mostly created by those who think that the music is in need of some sort of elevation (the descendants of those who hoped to render jazz "symphonic"?), nor any of the theatrical mismatches with which the music is often encumbered, since snobbery is not unknown even in Hollywood and on Broadway. And, God knows, rock and roll does incite the snobs.

As an anthology, *Fortunate Son* is intended to portray the development of certain ideas over a long period of time. Consequently, some of what's said here isn't what I'd now say and a lot of it isn't said the way I'd say it now. On the other hand, revisions for the sake of clarity have been made with a free hand and certain small amounts of reorganization and cutting

have been done, under the assumption that a clearly and cogently expressed idea is more valuable than an authentically fuzzy one. The places
where I've censored myself for fear of embarrassment are all too obviously
infrequent. The embarrassment is all mine; the malicious glee belongs to
whoever will have it.

Contents

Introduction

I

This old town is where I learned about lovin'
This old town is where I learned to hate
This town, buddy, has done its share of shoveling
This town taught me that it's never too late
                    —Michael Stanley, "My Town"

When I was a boy, my family lived on East Beverly Street in Pontiac, Michigan, in a two-bedroom house with blue-white asphalt shingles that cracked at the edges when a ball was thrown against them and left a powder like talc on fingers rubbed across their shallow grooves. East Beverly ascended a slowly rising hill. At the very top, a block and a half from our place, Pontiac Motors Assembly Line 16 sprawled for a mile or so behind a fenced-in parking lot.

Rust-red dust collected on our windowsills. It piled up no matter how often the place was dusted or cleaned. Fifteen minutes after my mother was through with a room, that dust seemed thick enough for a finger to trace pointless, ashy patterns in it.

The dust came from the foundry on the other side of the assembly line, the foundry that spat angry cinders into the sky all night long. When people talked about hell, I imagined driving past the foundry at night. From the street below, you could see the fires, red-hot flames shaping glowing metal.

Pontiac was a company town, nothing less. General Motors owned most of the land, and in one way or another held mortgages on the rest. Its holdings included not only the assembly line and the foundry but also a Fisher Body plant and on the outskirts, General Motors Truck and Coach. For a while, some pieces of Frigidaires may even have been put together in our town, but that might just be a trick of my memory, which often confuses the tentacles of institutions that monstrous.

In any case, of the hundred thousand or so who lived in Pontiac, fully half must have been employed either by GM or one of the tool-and-die shops and steel warehouses and the like that supplied it. And anybody who earned his living locally in some less directly auto-related fashion was only fooling himself if he thought of independence.

My father worked without illusions, as a railroad brakeman on freight trains that shunted boxcars through the innards of the plants, hauled grain from up north, transported the finished Pontiacs on the first leg of the route to almost anywhere Bonnevilles, Catalinas and GTOs were sold.

Our baseball and football ground lay in the shadow of another General Motors building. That building was of uncertain purpose, at least to me. What I can recall of it now is a seemingly reckless height—five or six stories is a lot in the flatlands around the Great Lakes—and endless walls of dark greenish glass that must have run from floor to ceiling in the rooms inside. Perhaps this building was an engineering facility. We didn't know anyone who worked there, at any rate.

Like most other GM facilities, the green glass building was surrounded by a chain link fence with barbed wire. If a ball happened to land on the other side of it, this fence was insurmountable. But only very strong boys could hit a ball that high, that far, anyhow.

Or maybe it just wasn't worth climbing that particular fence. Each August, a few weeks before the new models were officially presented in the press, the finished Pontiacs were set out in the assembly-line parking lot at the top of our street. They were covered by tarpaulins to keep their design changes secret—these were the years when the appearance of American cars changed radically each year. Climbing *that* fence was a neighborhood sport because that was how you discovered what the new cars looked like, whether fins were shrinking or growing, if the new hoods were pointed or flat, how much thinner the strips of whitewall on the tires had grown. A weird game, since everyone knew people who could have told us, given us exact descriptions, having built those cars with their own hands. But climbing that fence added a hint of danger, made us feel we shared a secret, turned gossip into information.

The main drag in our part of town was Joslyn Road. It was where the stoplight and crossing guard were stationed, where the gas station with the condom machine stood alongside a short-order restaurant, drugstore, dairy

store, small groceries and a bakery. A few blocks down, past the green glass
building, was a low brick building set back behind a wide, lush lawn. This
building, identified by a discreet roadside sign, occupied a long block or
two. It was the Administration Building for all of Pontiac Motors—a
building for executives, clerks, white-collar types. This building couldn't
have been more than three-quarters of a mile from my house, yet even
though I lived on East Beverly Street from the time I was two until I was
past fourteen, I knew only one person who worked there.

In the spring of 1964, when I was fourteen and finishing eighth grade,
rumors started going around at Madison Junior High. All of the buildings
on our side of Joslyn Road (possibly east or west of Joslyn, but I didn't
know directions then—there was only "our" side and everywhere else)
were about to be bought up and torn down by GM. This was worrisome,
but it seemed to me that our parents would never allow that perfectly
functioning neighborhood to be broken up for no good purpose.

One sunny weekday afternoon a man came to our door. He wore a coat
and tie and a white shirt, which meant something serious in our part of
town. My father greeted him at the door, but I don't know whether the
businessman had an appointment. Dad was working the extra board in
those years, which meant he was called to work erratically—four or five
times a week, when business was good—each time his nameplate came to
the top of the big duty-roster board down at the yard office. (My father
didn't get a regular train of his own to work until 1966; he spent almost
twenty years on that extra board, which meant guessing whether it was safe
to answer the phone every time he actually wanted a day off—refuse a call
and your name went back to the bottom of the list.)

At any rate, the stranger was shown to the couch in our front room. He
perched on that old gray davenport with its wiry fabric that bristled and
stung against my cheek, and spoke quite earnestly to my parents. I recall
nothing of his features or of the precise words he used or even of the tone
of his speech. But the dust motes that hung in the air that day are still
in my memory, and I can remember his folded hands between his spread
knees as he leaned forward in a gesture of complicity. He didn't seem to
be selling anything; he was simply stating facts.

He told my father that Pontiac Motors was buying up all the houses in
our community from Tennyson Street, across from the green glass building, to Baldwin Avenue—exactly the boundaries of what I'd have described as our neighborhood. GM's price was more than fair; it doubled
what little money my father had paid in the early fifties. The number was
a little over ten thousand dollars. All of the other houses were going, too;

some had already been sold. The entire process of tearing our neighborhood down would take about six months, once all the details were settled.

The stranger put down his coffee cup, shook hands with my parents and left. As far as I know, he never darkened our doorstep again. In the back of my mind, I can still see him through the front window cutting across the grass to go next door.

"Well, *we're* not gonna move, right, Dad?" I said. Cheeky as I was, it didn't occur to me this wasn't really a matter for adult decision-making —or rather, that the real adults, over at the Administration Building, had already made the only decision that counted. Nor did it occur to me that GM's offer might seem to my father an opportunity to sell at a nice profit, enabling us to move some place "better."

My father did not say much. No surprise. In a good mood, he was the least taciturn man alive, but on the farm where he was raised, not many words were needed to get a serious job done. What he did say that evening indicated that we might stall awhile—perhaps there would be a slightly better offer if we did. But he exhibited no doubt that we would sell. And move.

I was shocked. There was no room in my plans for this . . . rupture. Was the demolition of our home and neighborhood—that is, my life—truly inevitable? Was there really no way we could avert it, cancel it, *delay* it? What if we just plain *refused to sell*?

Twenty years later, my mother told me that she could still remember my face on that day. It must have reflected extraordinary distress and confusion, for my folks were patient. If anyone refused to sell, they told me, GM would simply build its parking lot—for that was what would replace my world—around him. If we didn't sell, we'd have access privileges, enough space to get into our driveway and that was it. No room to play, and no one there to play with if there had been. And if you got caught in such a situation and didn't like it, then you'd really be in a fix, for the company wouldn't keep its double-your-money offer open forever. If we held out too long, who knew if the house would be worth anything at all. (I don't imagine that my parents attempted to explain to me the political process of condemnation, but if they had, I would have been outraged, for in a way, I still am.)

My dreams always pictured us as holdouts, living in a little house surrounded by asphalt and automobiles. I always imagined nighttime with the high, white-light towers that illuminated all the other GM parking lots shining down upon our house—and the little guardhouse that the company would have to build and man next door to prevent me from escaping our lot to run playfully among the parked cars of the multitudinous employees. Anyone reading this must find it absurd, or the details heavily derivative of bad concentration-camp literature or maybe too influenced by the Berlin Wall, which had been up only a short time. But it would be a mistake to dismiss its romanticism, which was for many months more real to me than the ridiculous reality—moving to accommodate a *parking lot*—which confronted my family and all of my friends' families.

If this story were set in the Bronx or in the late sixties, or if it were fiction, the next scenes would be of pickets and protests, meaningful victories and defeats. But this isn't fiction—everything set out here is as unexaggerated as I know how to make it—and the time and the place were wrong for any serious uproar. In this docile midwestern company town, where Walter Reuther's trip to Russia was as inexplicable as the parting of the Red Sea (or as forgotten as the Ark of the Covenant), the idea that a neighborhood might have rights that superseded those of General Motors' Pontiac division would have been regarded as extraordinary, bizarre and subversive. Presuming anyone had had such an idea, which they didn't—none of my friends seemed particularly disturbed about moving, it was just what they would *do*.

So we moved, and what was worse, to the suburbs. This was catastrophic to me. I loved the city, its pavement and the mobility it offered even to kids too young to drive. (Some attitude for a Motor City kid, I know.) In Pontiac, feet or a bicycle could get you anywhere. Everyone had cars, but you weren't immobilized without them, as everyone under sixteen was in the suburbs. In the suburb to which we adjourned, cars were *the* fundamental of life—many of the streets in our new subdivision (not really a neighborhood) didn't even have sidewalks.

Even though I'd never been certain of fitting in, in the city I'd felt close to figuring out how to. Not that I was that weird. But I was no jock and certainly neither suave nor graceful. Still, toward the end of eighth grade, I'd managed to talk to a few girls, no small feat. The last thing I needed was new goals to fathom, new rules to learn, new friends to make.

So that summer was spent in dread. When school opened in the autumn, I was already in a sort of cocoon, confused by the Beatles with their paltry imitations of soul music and the bizarre emotions they stirred in girls.

Meeting my classmates was easy enough, but then it always is. Making new friends was another matter. For one thing, the kids in my new locale weren't the same as the kids in my classes. I was an exceptionally good student (quite by accident—I just read a lot) and my neighbors were classic underachievers. The kids in my classes were hardly creeps, but they weren't as interesting or as accessible as the people I'd known in my old neighborhood or the ones I met at the school bus stop. So I kept to myself.

In our new house, I shared a room with my brother at first. We had bunk beds, and late that August I was lying sweatily in the upper one, listening to the radio (WPON-AM, 1460) while my mother and my aunt droned away in the kitchen.

Suddenly my attention was riveted by a record. I listened for two or three minutes more intently than I have ever listened and learned something that remains all but indescribable. It wasn't a new awareness of music. I liked rock and roll already, had since I first saw Elvis when I was six, and I'd been reasonably passionate about the Ronettes, Gary Bonds, Del Shannon, the Crystals, Jackie Wilson, Sam Cooke, the Beach Boys and those first rough but sweet notes from Motown: the Miracles, the Temptations, Eddie Holland's "Jamie." I can remember a rainy night when I tuned in a faraway station and first heard the end of the Philadelphia Warriors' game in which Wilt Chamberlain scored a hundred points and then found "Let's Twist Again" on another part of the dial. And I can remember not knowing which experience was more splendid.

But the song I heard that night wasn't a new one. "You Really Got a Hold on Me" had been a hit in 1963, and I already loved Smokey Robinson's voice, the way it twined around impossibly sugary lines and made rhymes within the rhythms of ordinary conversation, within the limits of everyday vocabulary.

But if I'd heard those tricks before, I'd never understood them. And if I'd enjoyed rock and roll music previously, certainly it had never grabbed me in quite this way: as a lifeline that suggested—no, insisted—that these singers spoke *for* me as well as to me, and that what they felt and were able to cope with, the deep sorrow, remorse, anger, lust and compassion that bubbled beneath the music, I would also be able to feel and contain. This intimate revelation was what I gleaned from those three minutes of music, and when they were finished and I climbed out of that bunk and walked out the door, the world looked different. No longer did I feel quite so powerless, and if I still felt cheated, I felt capable of getting my own back, some day, some way.

Trapped

II

It seems I've been playing your game way too long
And it seems the game I've played has made you strong
— Jimmy Cliff, "Trapped"

That last year in Pontiac, we listened to the radio a lot. My parents always had. One of my most shattering early memories is of the radio blasting when they got up—my mother around four-thirty, my father at five. All of my life I've hated early rising, and for years I couldn't listen to country music without being reminded almost painfully of those days.

But in 1963 and 1964, we also listened to WPON in the evening for its live coverage of city council meetings. Pontiac was beginning a decade of racial crisis, of integration pressure and white resistance, the typical scenario. From what was left of our old neighborhood came the outspokenly racist militant anti–school busing movement.

The town had a hard time keeping the shabby secret of its bigotry even in 1964. Pontiac had mushroomed as a result of massive migration during and after World War II. Some of the new residents, including my father, came from nearby rural areas where blacks were all but unknown and even the local Polish Catholics were looked upon as aliens potentially subversive to the community's Methodist piety.

Many more of the new residents of Pontiac came from the South, out of the dead ends of Appalachia and the border states. As many must have been black as white, though it was hard for me to tell that as a kid. There were lines one didn't cross in Michigan, and if I was shocked, when visiting Florida, to see separate facilities labeled "White" and "Colored," as children we never paid much mind to the segregated schools, the lily-white suburbs, the way that jobs in the plants were divided up along race lines. The ignorance and superstition about blacks in my neighborhood were as desperate and crazed in their own way as the feelings in any kudzu-covered parish of Louisiana.

As blacks began to assert their rights, the animosity was not less, either. The polarization was fueled and fanned by the fact that so many displaced Southerners, all with the poor white's investment in racism, were living in our community. But it would be foolish to pretend that the situation would have been any more civilized if only the natives had been around. In fact the Southerners were often regarded with nearly as much condescension and antipathy as blacks—race may have been one of the few areas in which my parents found themselves completely in sympathy with the "hillbillies."

Racism was the great trap of such men's lives, for almost everything could be explained by it, from unemployment to the deterioration of community itself. Casting racial blame did much more than poison these people's entire concept of humanity, which would have been plenty bad enough. It immobilized the racist, preventing folks like my father from ever realizing the real forces that kept their lives tawdry and painful and forced them to fight every day to find any meaning at all in their existence. It did this to Michigan factory workers as effectively as it ever did it to dirt farmers in Dixie.

The great psychological syndrome of American males is said to be passive aggression, and racism perfectly fit this mold. To the racist, hatred of blacks gave a great feeling of power and superiority. At the same time, it allowed him the luxury of wallowing in self-pity at the great conspiracy of rich bastards and vile niggers that enforced workaday misery and let the rest of the world go to hell. In short, racism explained everything. There was no need to look any further than the cant of redneck populism, exploited as effectively in the orange clay of the Great Lakes as in the red dirt of Georgia, to find an answer to why it was always the *next* generation that was going to get up and out.

Some time around 1963, a local attorney named Milton Henry, a black man, was elected to Pontiac's city council. Henry was smart and bold— he would later become an ally of Martin Luther King, Jr., of Malcolm X, a principal in the doomed Republic of New Africa. The goals for which Henry was campaigning seem extremely tame now, until you realize the extent to which they *haven't* been realized in twenty years: desegregated schools, integrated housing, a chance at decent jobs.

Remember that Martin Luther King would not take his movement for equality into the North for nearly five more years, and that when he did, Dr. King there faced the most strident and violent opposition he'd ever met, and you will understand how inflammatory the mere presence of Milton Henry on the city council was. Those council sessions, broadcast live on WPON, invested the radio with a vibrancy and vitality that television could never have had. Those hours of imprecations, shouts and clamor are unforgettable. I can't recall specific words or phrases, though, just Henry's eloquence and the pandemonium that greeted each of his speeches.

So our whole neighborhood gathered round its radios in the evenings,

family by family, as if during wartime. Which in a way I guess it was—
surely that's how the situation was presented to the children, and not only
in the city. My Pontiac junior high school was lightly integrated, and the
kids in my new suburban town had the same reaction as my Floridian
cousins: shocked that I'd "gone to school with niggers," they vowed they
would die—or kill—before letting the same thing happen to them.

This cycle of hatred didn't immediately elude me. Thirteen-year-olds
are built to buck the system only up to a point. So even though I didn't
dislike any of the blacks I met (it could hardly be said that I was given the
opportunity to *know* any), it was taken for granted that the epithets were
essentially correct. After all, anyone could see the grave poverty in which
most blacks existed, and the only reason ever given for it was that they liked
living that way.

But listening to the radio gave free play to one's imagination. Listening
to music, that most abstract of human creations, unleashed it all the more.
And not in a vacuum. Semiotics, the New Criticism and other formalist
approaches have never had much appeal to me, not because I don't
recognize their validity in describing certain creative structures but because they emphasize those structural questions without much consideration of content. And that simply doesn't jibe with my experience of
culture, especially popular culture.

The best example is the radio of the early 1960s. As I've noted, there
was no absence of rock and roll in those years betwixt the outbreaks of
Presley and Beatles. Rock and roll was a constant for me, the best music
around, and I had loved it ever since I first heard it, which was about as
soon as I could remember hearing anything.

In part, I just loved the sound—the great mystery one could hear welling
up from "Duke of Earl," "Up on the Roof," "Party Lights"; that pit of
loneliness and despair that lay barely concealed beneath the superficial
bright spirits of a record like Bruce Channel's "Hey Baby"; the nonspecific
terror hidden away in Del Shannon's "Runaway." But if that was all there
was to it, then rock and roll records would have been as much an end in
themselves—that is, as much a dead end—as TV shows like *Leave It to
Beaver* (also mysterious, also—thanks to Eddie Haskell—a bit terrifying).

To me, however, TV was clearly an alien device, controlled by the men
with shirts and ties. Nobody on television dressed or talked as the people
in my neighborhood did. In rock and roll, however, the language spoken
was recognizably my own. And since one of the givens of life in the
outlands was that we were barbarians, who produced no culture and basically consumed only garbage and trash, the thrill of discovering depths
within rock and roll, the very part that was most often and explicitly

degraded by teachers and pundits, was not only marvelously refreshing and exhilarating but also in essence liberating—once you'd made the necessary connections.

It was just at this time that pop music was being revolutionized—not by the Beatles, arriving from England, a locale of certifiable cultural superiority, but by Motown, arriving from Detroit, a place without even a hint of cultural respectability. Produced by Berry Gordy, not only a young man but a *black* man. And in that spirit of solidarity with which hometown boys (however unalike) have always identified with one another, Motown was mine in a way that no other music up to that point had been. Surely no one spoke my language as effectively as Smokey Robinson, able to string together the most humdrum phrases and effortlessly make them sing.

That's the context in which "You Really Got a Hold on Me" created my epiphany. You can look at this coldly—structurally—and see nothing more than a naked marketing mechanism, a clear-cut case of a teenager swaddled in and swindled by pop culture. Smokey Robinson wrote and sang the song as much to make a buck as to express himself; there was nothing of the purity of the mythical artist about his endeavor. In any case, the emotion he expressed was unfashionably sentimental. In releasing the record, Berry Gordy was mercenary in both instinct and motivation. The radio station certainly hoped for nothing more from playing it than that its listeners would hang in through the succeeding block of commercials. None of these people and institutions had any intention of elevating their audience, in the way that Leonard Bernstein hoped to do in his *Young People's Concerts* on television. Cultural indoctrination was far from their minds. Indeed, it's unlikely that anyone involved in the process thought much about the kids on the other end of the line except as an amorphous mass of ears and wallets. The pride Gordy and Robinson had in the quality of their work was private pleasure, not public.

Smokey Robinson was not singing of the perils of being a black man in this world (though there were other rock and soul songs that spoke in guarded metaphors about such matters). Robinson was not expressing an experience as alien to my own as a country blues singer's would have been. Instead, he was putting his finger firmly upon a crucial feeling of vulnerability and longing. It's hard to think of two emotions that a fourteen-year-old might feel more deeply (well, there's lust . . .), and yet in my hometown expressing them was all but absolutely forbidden to men. This doubled the shock of Smokey Robinson's voice, which for years I've thought of as falsetto, even though it really isn't exceptionally high-pitched compared to the spectacular male sopranos of rock and gospel lore.

"You Really Got a Hold on Me" is not by any means the greatest song

Smokey Robinson ever wrote or sang, not even the best he had done up to that point. The singing on "Who's Loving You," the lyrics of "I'll Try Something New," the yearning of "What's So Good About Goodbye" are all at least as worthy. Nor is there anything especially newfangled about the song. Its trembling blues guitar, sturdy drum pattern, walking bass and call-and-response voice arrangement are not very different from many of the other Miracles records of that period. If there is a single instant in the record which is unforgettable by itself, it's probably the opening lines: "I don't like you / But I love you . . ."

The contingency and ambiguity expressed in those two lines and Robinson's singing of them was also forbidden in the neighborhood of my youth, and forbidden as part and parcel of the same philosophy that propounded racism. Merely calling the bigot's certainty into question was revolutionary —not merely rebellious. The depth of feeling in that Miracles record, which could have been purchased for 69¢ at any K-Mart, overthrew the premise of racism, which was that blacks were not as human as we, that they could not feel—much less express their feelings—as deeply as we did.

When the veil of racism was torn from my eyes, everything else that I knew or had been told was true for fourteen years was necessarily called into question. For if racism explained everything, then without racism, not a single commonplace explanation made any sense. *Nothing* else could be taken at face value. And that meant asking every question once again, including the banal and obvious ones.

For those who've never been raised under the weight of such addled philosophy, the power inherent in having the burden lifted is barely imaginable. Understanding that blacks weren't worthless meant that maybe the rest of the culture in which I was raised was also valuable. If you've never been told that you and your community are worthless—that a parking lot takes precedence over your needs—perhaps that moment of insight seems trivial or rather easily won. For anyone who was never led to expect a life any more difficult than one spent behind a typewriter, maybe the whole incident verges on being something too banal for repetition (though in that case, I'd like to know where the other expressions of this story can be read). But looking over my shoulder, seeing the consequences to my life had I not begun questioning not just racism but all of the other presumptions that ruled our lives, I know for certain how and how much I got over.

That doesn't make me better than those on the other side of the line. On the other hand, I won't trivialize the tale by insisting upon how fortunate I was. What was left for me was a raging passion to explain things in the hope that others would not be trapped and to keep the way clear so that others from the trashy outskirts of barbarous America still had a place to stand—if not in the culture at large, at least in rock and roll.

Of course it's not so difficult to dismiss this entire account. Great revelations and insights aren't supposed to emerge from listening to rock and roll records. They're meant to emerge only from encounters with art. (My encounters with Western art music were unavailing, of course, because every one of them was prefaced by a lecture on the insipid and worthless nature of the music that I preferred to hear.) Left with the fact that what happened to me did take place, and that it was something that was supposed to come only out of art, I reached the obvious conclusion. You are welcome to your own.

1

*Can't Forget
the Motor City*

Introduction

Just the other night I was chastised by my wife for being so obsessed with my origins in Michigan that I spoke of the place as if it existed on another planet. She said that in her opinion there was a good chance that I should never have left. And in some ways Detroit may be on a different planet from New York and the subliterary life, and in many others I never have left it, or to state the facts more correctly, it has never left me.

Detroit had no rock and roll aesthetic, exactly. Rhythm and blues is at the center of everything discussed here and of almost everything that the area has produced musically, but of what American music scene is that not true? (Nashville, I suppose, but name another.) So this chapter doesn't pin down my musical background, nor is it an end to a discussion of my home-boy prejudices and favorites. Instead, what this section offers is a beginning, my beginnings—impressions, allusions, old friends whose importance I know how to describe if not explain.

The Teenage Dreams of
Billy Levise

The first time I met Mitch Ryder was in the back room of the book and record store cum head shop where I was working in the summer of 1969. He had a girl on his lap, had the cheekbones of a Cherokee and the tan to go with them, and was cordial as could be. Introduced to me as Billy, he seemed like nothing more than a nice guy. When

I later asked who he was, I was told "Mitch Ryder." I would not have been more awestruck if the answer had been Billy Budd.

Ryder was a genuine rock legend—a great singer whose records were exciting and unforgettable and one of the few white singers who had soul credibility. In those days, two years away from the charts already qualified him as a legend from the mists of the unchronicled past. And at nineteen, just beginning to work at Creem, I had met very few—if any—musicians whose names would have rung a bell east of Lake Erie.

Ryder's presence in the head shop wasn't as inexplicable as I thought. He was managed by the owner, Barry Kramer, who was also the proprietor of Creem. So we began to see each other frequently, since Ryder's band rehearsed in the loft above the magazine's offices. The music was great, though the thunderation made it hard to write and almost impossible to talk on the phone. So we began a bantering, mock hostile relationship that continues, from time to time, to this day.

Ryder's comeback was somewhat abortive. He got the full complement of the Wheels back together for one night—Sunday, September 17, at a sparsely attended "pop festival" in Sarnia, Ontario. Even so, the reunion might have gained some notice had it not occurred on the final night of the Woodstock Festival. Yet I was there, and it was as hot as anything you could have hoped to hear in Max Yasgur's muddy field. Hotter, since the Wheels were more intense and funky than 90 percent of the acts on the Woodstock bill.

The Detroit/Memphis Experiment flopped. It wasn't a bad record, but it lacked the very intensity that should have been its hallmark. (It does contain a fine reading of Otis Redding's "Direct Me.") Thereafter, Ryder did form a band, called Detroit, around himself and Badanjek. That group made only one album, an excellent set that came closer to R&B energy than the Stax effort, but it also failed to sell for a dismaying variety of reasons: lack of promotional clout, less than scintillating production, flabby arrangements.

Ryder has spent the past few years recording off and on, mostly in Germany, where he remains a name. Most of these records were marred by his nostalgia for the excesses of late sixties hard rock, the acid-etched era that his handlers had shut him away from. Indulging himself in this way, Ryder made several records in the late seventies and early eighties that sounded dated when they were new. Yet he remains an able, inevitably soulful singer, and his writing has grown more and more honest through the years. Though much of what he says in this story—originally titled "Put the bacon on the paper so's the grease'll run off," which will give you some idea of our unhip defensiveness in the late sixties—ought to be taken with several grains of salt, his 1978 "comeback" record, How I Spent My Vacation, contains several brutally revealing confessions of his sexual and other confusions during his stint at the top.

Mitch's only recent shot at American success came in 1983, when John Cougar Mellencamp produced Never Kick a Sleeping Dog. Despite a memorable rendition of Prince's "When You Were Mine," it didn't sell. But it demonstrated that Ryder still has talent, and my feeling is that he'll be around, on the fringes if not in the center of things, for a while yet. Like the rhythm and blues singers upon whom he cut his teeth, he gets more wily as he matures.

Without Mitch Ryder and the Detroit Wheels (or for that matter, Billy Lee and the Rivieras), none of the other music that emerged from Detroit and shook up rock so thoroughly would have been even imaginable. With the sole exception of Bob Seger, he's the most influential white performer that the city has produced; literally everyone looks up to him. So his story deserves its pride of place here. "The Teenage Dreams of Billy Levise" is the oldest piece collected in Fortunate Son, not so much because I'm thrilled with the way it's written as because Billy's story is an admonitory classic of rock and roll, a summation of what happened to innocents who ventured forth at a certain time from a certain place.

The first rocker a lot of Detroiters can remember making it, one that we could relate to as a hometown representative, was Mitch Ryder. "Jenny Take a Ride" is one part field holler, one part shitkicker stomp, but the only place that medley could have fused so firmly was in Detroit, blighted factory center of urban America. It was an honest synthesis, marrying Buddy Holly and Little Richard, white man's rock and black man's R&B, and it ran through "Devil with a Blue Dress On/Good Golly Miss Molly," "Shake a Tail Feather" and "Sock It to Me."

But Ryder dropped from sight a couple of years ago, and it was commonly assumed that his success had been a fluke. It wasn't until he began appearing again around town that he shattered the stereotype of the ass-kicking greaser. He played free concerts in the park, and he played *rock and roll*! So Mitch Ryder has made his comeback in the most literal way. "We had to return to Detroit to find what we'd lost in New York."

In the fifties, the midwestern rock scene was primarily beer parties, wedding receptions and DJ hops. The only constant access to rock and roll music anyone had was through the radio. One of those radio shows came out of the bent frequencies of the ozone from Nashville. In Michigan, you could hear it only at night—usually very stormy nights. "The disc jockey's name was John R. He played Little Richard records and I bought my first copy . . . I could see white girls react to it, white girls who had never heard a spade sing before," Ryder recalls.

Having confirmed that traditional teenage affinity for the seductive properties of rock, Ryder and his junior high school friend, Joe Kubert, started a band, The Tempest. Mostly, Kubert remembers, it played weddings, with a lineup that included vocal, accordion, bass, guitar, drums and sax. Ryder remembers "playing 'What'd I Say' in fifty different versions. We'd be booked on weekends into the Sheraton Cadillac for thirty dollars a night for weddings."

Like most bands of its type, the Tempest quickly disintegrated. But also like many such groups, a couple of musicians came out of it. Mitch and Joe decided to continue together; they were the only ones who'd ever seen the Tempest as more than a weekend gig.

Mitch was even more serious than Joe. He spent the next couple of years "drifting through downtown Detroit, singing and living with spades. Doing my whole trip that way." He remembers the old R&B haunts, clubs like the Village and the Tantrum, listening to Ahmad Jamal at the Minor Key. Fronting a group of black musicians called the Peps, he became a regular at the Village. "We sang whatever the number one rhythm and blues tune was at the time. I used to do a whole lot of Smokey [Robinson] things back then, 'cause I had a high range. I used to sing at all these black parties that they'd have down at the Gold Room of the 20 Grand." The 20 Grand was the baddest black nightclub of them all. For anyone, let alone a white kid, to be allowed to sing there was an honor. But the blacks were impressed that the white kid, who called himself Billy Lee (a contraction of his true name, William Levise), could sing R&B so effectively. "They'd say things like, 'My, you sing nice. And so white, too.'"

Unlike many of his peers, Ryder doesn't ever feel that he was hung up on the myth of what Norman Mailer called the "White Negro." "Since I grew up in Detroit, it's something I'm familiar with," he says. "I used to sing in all the gospel churches with my father. For two years, we'd go there. All these things are stuff that I exposed myself to because of my love for a certain type of music."

Just turned sixteen, Ryder decided to head for the glory of the West Coast and the possibility of a recording contract. Like most sixteen-year-old kids' dreams, from fire engines to the Haight, the reality was much crueler than the fantasy. "My folks gave me the bread to go, and it was really like a lot of bread for them to give me at the time," Ryder remembers, a bit amazed at his own audacity and naiveté. "But they believed in me."

Billy headed straight for RCA Victor. "They wanted to know how come I didn't have any tapes. I didn't know where else to go, but I wanted to make it look good, so I stayed in my hotel an additional five days and used up all the money. Afraid to go out in the streets for fear I'd get lost."

But Billy refused to let the fantasy die there. He kept on singing, grubbing out the little jobs in bars and teen clubs, *wanting* to make it. He ended up auditioning again, this time for Motown. "There was some sort of weird dude called Eddie Holland playing piano there. They had about five rooms in this old renovated house and they were just starting to get some hits with Smokey. Holland and Gordy liked the way I sang but they said, 'We need original material.' And sent me off."

The Peps got an audition with Mrs. Thelma Gordy for her Tamla label and actually signed with her, but for various reasons—mostly economic—Ryder split. On his own, he returned to the scene of whatever triumphs he'd known, the Village. Shortly he began headlining there. "They even painted my name on the front of the building."

The name was Billy Lee and the Rivieras, a crazy group of greasers who were one of the progenitors of the entire Detroit rock scene: MC5, Stooges and all the rest.

The Village was a spawning ground for other Detroit groups—most notably the Four Tops—but Ryder was its first success. A month after his break from the Peps, he signed a contract with the Reverend James Hendricks' Carrie label, a rhythm and blues/gospel company. Ryder's first record was a song called "Fool for You" on that label.

It was now 1963. Graduating from high school, Ryder and Kubert decided to split to Florida for a midwinter holiday. It was while they were there that the Beatles exploded across the States, with a whirlwind effect that sent Mitch and Joe right back to Detroit, once more pursuing their music vigorously.

But they were still having trouble finding serious, compatible musicians. "Nothing really happened," says Mitch, "so I went back to work at the Village. I was packing them in when three guys came in one night to be the backing group, 'cause the other band didn't show up."

The other three, known already as the Rivieras, were guitarist Jim McCarty, drummer John Badanjek and bassist Earl Elliott. With the addition of Kubert as rhythm guitarist, and Mitch singing, the Detroit Wheels had been formed. For the time being, they simply merged their names, becoming Billy Lee and the Rivieras, prime motivators in shaping a Detroit sound far removed from the superslickness of Tamla/Motown.

The band practiced and gigged together for six months, then, with typically teenage naiveté, decided to do a record. But for that, they needed front money. They turned to Gabe Glantz, owner of the Village and later proprietor of that palace of psychedelic delight, the Grande Ballroom. "He offered us a ridiculous contract that we never signed," Mitch says. "But we got the money out of him anyway because Teddy Martine [a bizarre singer/drag queen then a fixture on the local scene] liked me very much and talked Glantz into financing us." The label was Bryan Hyland's Hyland Records; the tune was the rock standard "Do You Wanna Dance?" "Dave Prince [a disc jockey at WXYZ] used to play the record. He was the only jock in the world who'd play the record."

So the Rivieras went through the starvation period that leads to either stardom or oblivion. They played weddings, bar mitzvahs and a lot of free hops. "I remember driving all the way to Grosse Ile for WKNR, the new super station, and not even getting gas money." Mitch says.

WXYZ had become involved with a teen dance and drink club called the Walled Lake Casino, thirty odd miles north of Detroit. Dave Prince was a DJ at the Casino; through him, Billy Lee and the Rivieras became regulars there. During the early sixties, the Casino was *the* place to go on weekends, and all the Ruben and the Jets plastic American pathos in the world could be located there.

"It got to the point where our popularity was so massive that we started drawing two and three thousand kids every night we appeared. One night Smokey Robinson and the Miracles got pissed off 'cause the Casino used to have these little cards they'd give out; there was one with his appearance on it, and we got equal billing. We went through a whole scene with him 'cause we'd never had any hits, and he was upset."

Mitch remembers the Casino as the prototypical teenage hangout. "Kids would just be walking around. There would be a big mass in the center, either watching or rapping, and then you'd have a thousand people going around in a big slow circle clockwise around the room. Cruising. The girls would sit on the side and wait to get picked up, and you'd have about three or four hundred of them who'd nail themselves at the side of the stage, waiting for our performance." Largely drunk, the crowd came to see a show that was as high energy and crazed as anything the Stooges ever perpetrated.

"The chicks didn't have to throw themselves at us; we threw ourselves at them. We used to take our shirts off and yell and scream and dance. McCarty would switch from guitar to drums and Johnny would jump off the piano and we'd shake together, jump in each other's arms, do flips and splits. We'd scream and sing and I'd do the knee drop. I did that knee drop continuously for six years till I went to the doctor and he told me I had bone splinters. I asked him how James Brown was doing it and he said, 'He wears knee pads.' Blew my mind."

But the group was still dissatisfied with its progress. At the height of their popularity, Billy Lee and the Rivieras could pack three thousand a night into the Casino. But they were so frustrated in their attempts to expand their reputation that Ryder himself tried to enlist in the Army three times. "Too young, they told me, come back when you're eighteen. But by the time I was eighteen, I was hip to 'em and they had to come after me." They were turned away by the bone splinters in his knee. As it was, one member, Earl Elliott, had to leave the group right after its second hit in order to do time in the Army.

Ryder remains defensive about the Casino. "We made the Casino, that's the only reason Lee Alan ever hyped us." Alan was perhaps the area's most popular jock at the time, and to a lot of kids, it looked like he'd created the Rivieras. The truth may have been the opposite.

Again the Rivieras made a demo tape, but this time they gave it to Prince, who in turn sent it to a former Detroiter then working in the New York music business, Bob Crewe. Crewe had already had hits with "Silhouettes" by the Rays, "La Dee Dah" by Billy and Lillie, and the Four Seasons' whole string. Crewe liked the tape and sent them train fare to New York.

"The first time we went to New York, we took a train out. What's that one, the Grand Central? It was like the biggest thrill 'cause I was leaving. I had just gotten married a month before and it was like a whole scene from a World War II flick," says Mitch.

"We got to New York the next morning and the sun was out, after all night in the train, and we were just amazed at the buildings. Said, 'God, are we super! Came all this way, they must really want us!' Because, you see, we hadn't gotten the recognition in Michigan that we needed for our starving egos."

But no matter how bad Detroit had been, New York was infinitely worse. "We couldn't get any gigs 'cause nobody liked the Detroit sound at the time. So we lived at 71st and Broadway, what they now call Needle Park, for six months. We used to sit up and listen to people get mugged on the streets and kill time fighting cockroaches," Badanjek remembers.

The few gigs they could get were held in the remote Jersey swamplands; they had no rehearsal hall, so they practiced in the hotel rooms. "We used to set up the amplifiers at night and scare the Puerto Ricans," said Badanjek. "Make spaceship sounds and warn them of impending raids and things."

"The noise didn't bother them"—Ryder laughs wryly—" 'cause we were on the fourteenth floor and the people on the thirteenth floor were all nice people—deaf and dumb, it was like a Puerto Rican convalescent home."

Crewe didn't help the band get jobs; he offered them "advance money," one of the oldest ruses in the record-business handbook. "We were happy to take it at that point. We were all living on about forty dollars apiece a week. Paying our rooms and then I'd send about fifteen dollars home each week."

Six months after their arrival in New York, in the early part of 1966, the group finally saw the inside of a recording studio. "We just did a stereo tape—two tracks. Crewe said, 'Play some of the songs you do in your show.' " As a result, the tape consisted primarily of "Beatles hits or whatever came out of our heads at the time." That meant a synthesis of the rhythm and blues Ryder had learned in the streets of Detroit and the rock and roll that was beginning to blossom from the Rivieras' Anglo-American peers.

It took Crewe six months to get around to listening to the tape. "This is how his glorious career as our producer started: We were running the tape and listening to the tunes and all of a sudden he said, 'It's a hit!' He ran in and overdubbed a tambourine on it and put it out." What Crewe released turned out to be the group's first hit, "Jenny Take a Ride," a medley of the old Chuck Willis blues, "C. C. Rider" (originally composed by Ma Rainey) and Little Richard's "Jenny Jenny," with an emphasis in energy and wildness upon the latter.

"That's the genius of Bob Crewe basically, his ability to hear a song. No matter how little effort he puts into it, he's got an ear.

"But he wasn't involved in the music *at all* on the hits, not until the Dynavoice label, 'What Now My Love' and all those things. Everything at the beginning was all McCarty's brainchild and mine—whatever we put together with the group. The whole concept of medleys was ours too. If you want a different opinion, though, I'm sure you can contact Bob Crewe in New York. He'll be glad to give you one."

"Jenny Take a Ride" broke in December 1965 under the name Mitch Ryder and the Detroit Wheels. The name change was made for a number of reasons. Crewe felt Billy Lee and the Rivieras sounded too country and western and there was already another group called the Rivieras, who had a hit with "California Sun," in early 1964. "We all volunteered names— one was going to be Mike Rothschild. So we went through the phone book and picked out Mitch Ryder. Somewhere in Manhattan right now there's a guy telling everybody that he's Mitch Ryder and they're all laughing at him. In all actuality, though, he is Mitch Ryder. Detroit Wheels didn't take much inspiration after that."

It was right after Thanksgiving, 1965. The Wheels were playing a gig in Massena, New York, which as Ryder notes, "is right under Cornwall, Canada. They called us up on the phone and said 'You have a hit.' It broke Philly at the same time it hit in Detroit."

The flip side of "Jenny" was "Baby Jane (MoMo Jane)," a drug lyric combined with rhythm and blues—probably the first time for that particular combination. But the focus of Ryder's music was mostly on sensuality. "The drug songs will go down quick," he commented at the time. "Those are temporary, but sex is permanent.

"It's becoming an art today to try and slip something by the censors [that's the program directors of the radio stations]. The hipper the lyrics are, the hipper the kids have to be to catch them." Ryder had the insight to see that exactly what's happening today would eventually occur: that the rock audiences would begin to take such lyrics for granted—even expect them—because of the correspondence to their own experiences and desires.

The Wheels sound was then directly involved with the body; at its best, it damn near compels dancing. "In the early days, a lot more boys would come to our concerts than girls," Ryder recalls. "Because we were doing things that they wanted to do to their girlfriends but couldn't 'cause they didn't have the guts."

The earliest rock stars, especially Ryder's main influence, Little Richard, were as crotch-oriented as any of today's stars. But those original singers, erotic as they were, were mostly black men, while the audience was the sexually repressed white teenager. "I sort of became an acceptable substitute for Little Richard," Ryder admits. "I did it out of a deep desire to become what Little Richard was to me: free and sexual and animal." Mitch says that he has sometimes become so involved in his shows that he's had orgasms right on stage.

And that's the premise of "Jenny" and the Ryder hits that followed—that rock and roll was still body music. If anything, rhythm and blues—the way they found it—is even more erotic. And the best way to experience that eroticism is live, because you can't get it all down on tape and anyway, nobody would broadcast it if you did.

After "Jenny" made the charts, the Wheels immediately began touring. "We were gigging all over for $1,000 a night, right after working for $350 a *week.*" During the next year, Mitch Ryder and the Detroit Wheels were a major attraction on such tours and programs as the Dick Clark Caravan of Stars, the Murray the K events at the Brooklyn Fox, as well as on TV's *Shindig!* and *Where the Action Is*.

In England, "Jenny" took the country by storm, especially the music world. Ryder had captured the essentials of soul music in a way that singers like Eric Burdon had been struggling for years to achieve. "We beat them to it," Mitch says. "As a matter of fact, Eric Burdon had a 'C. C. Rider' due for release, and when mine came out, it blew his whole fucking thing. He waited another year to put his out." It appears on *Animalization;* the song made the American Top Ten late in 1966. But in the Animals version, Burdon interpolates the line, "Jenny take a ride now, heh heh heh," as a tribute to the Wheels. He and Ryder were later to become very close. One of the highlights of Ryder's career came when the Animals were performing at the Schaefer Music Festival in Central Park in the summer of 1966. Mitch showed up for the Animals set and was all but raped in the front row until he got up and jammed with the Animals in a set that culminated in a Ryder/Burdon duet on an extended "C. C. Rider."

Ryder's next few singles—"Little Latin Lupe Lu," "Takin' All I Can Get" and "Breakout"—were good records, but they did progressively less well commercially. These records actually got some R&B airplay, at that time an extremely rare occurrence for white performers. But in general, Ryder thinks, the Wheels were becoming too black-sounding. "We were getting heavier and heavier into blues, but people weren't getting in on it with us."

Troubles began developing, centering on Crewe's plan to have Ryder go solo. There were also personality conflicts between Ryder and McCarty, a brilliant but moody guitarist. McCarty and the often equally moody Ryder didn't see eye to eye on some things both considered important, including business matters more than music. So Crewe and the band's manager, Allan Stroh (a Crewe associate), did their best to get the band to split up. McCarty was the first one gone.

The culmination of the Wheels' time together came during the recording sessions, where Mitch's other hits—"Devil with a Blue Dress On/ Good Golly Miss Molly," "Sock It to Me," "Too Many Fish in the Sea," "Shake a Tail Feather," "Joy"—were cut. The group had by then become deeply involved in the burgeoning Greenwich Village rock scene and invited Michael Bloomfield, Barry Goldberg and several others to the sessions. According to Ryder, "McCarty walked out because he was pissed at Crewe. Crewe was belittling Bloomfield and things like that. We'd be sitting in the studio trying to work things out and Crewe would come swishing out; he'd start demanding that we play these corny, weird lines.

This is where he started imposing himself. He actually believed that he was responsible for the music we were making."

Although the Wheels' hits were far from any of the other hits Crewe had ever made, he and Stroh had decided to make Ryder into a pop star of such proportions that he could play in movies and Vegas main rooms —become a "respectable entertainer." Stroh finally convinced Ryder that the Wheels should be discarded; Ryder is despondent when he recalls it. "I busted the group up," he says, as though confessing a mortal sin. "I forced it on 'em." "Devil" had just become another million seller; "Sock It to Me" was about to be released. It was Christmas 1966, a year after "Jenny Take a Ride," and it was all but over.

Ryder regards being rent from his band as the beginning of his career's downfall. "From that point until now, it's just been nothing but financial burden and troubles for me. Misunderstandings and trying to get rid of the whole mess."

There were still hits, but all of them came from that last session with the Wheels. Then in late 1967 Crewe released a song called "What Now My Love." The change was incredible. Previously, Ryder had been playing and recording with a minimal four- to six-piece group. Now he was touring with at least ten, occasionally as many as sixteen musicians. The recording sessions were done with orchestras. "I walked into that session one day and saw sixty musicians sitting there, ready to play. So I asked Crewe who was paying for it all. He said, 'You are.' I just said, 'I don't believe this.' He came back with 'Don't worry, it'll be a hit.' "

Bloomfield did appear on some of the *What Now My Love* album sessions, but he finally grew completely exasperated with Crewe and walked out. "At that point, I realized that it wasn't my head that was fucked up. It was Crewe's," says Ryder. But he was locked into the plan.

Ryder's show band was a failure primarily because Mitch could never accept the glitter and shuck required to make it work. "The concept was to present rock and rhythm and blues in a very plastic manner . . . so you could take it into a Vegas main room. We had costumes and lighting and swirling discs; fantastic, incredible makeup and garb, but the show never came off. My managers took every penny I had and sunk it into the show. I used to have four and five costumes that cost a thousand dollars apiece. People would show up just to see the trappings, the bullshit."

Ryder couldn't and perhaps wouldn't let it work. He was wed to the idea of being a rocker, and he wanted the credibility that the British groups and his friends in the Village were garnering. He wanted a group, an entity he distinguishes from a mere band. "The whole thing was a disaster 'cause I refused to put myself into it. I'm sure I could have brought it off if I would've worked with it, but I just couldn't—I didn't feel comfortable. I tried to put myself into it in a group way, but it just never happened."

There were a variety of other reasons why the show band failed. One was the inability of the other players to relate to the show in anything other than a mercenary manner. The sound couldn't really grow because the band members were working a job. "There wasn't a lick of creativity in the two years I toured with the big show," Mitch complains. "It was like a paying job for 'em. There was no incentive . . . They were just whores, money whores."

And the show didn't lend itself to Ryder's raw, primitive R&B style—it was designed for superslickness. Yet the show band years weren't altogether degrading. For instance, one of the band's first gigs was headlining Murray the K's 1967 Easter Show at the RKO 58th Street theater in New York. "The Cream were booked fifth on that bill," Mitch says. "It wasn't until then that I realized how important the Wheels were—Clapton asked what Jimmy was doing. I was headlining, with Wilson Pickett. But that was all based on what I'd done with the Wheels, and they weren't there to reap any of the benefits."

So Ryder dropped from sight just when he should have been consolidating his successes. Instead, he spent 1967 hassling out his difficulties with Crewe. The records began bombing; even though they'd been done with the Wheels, "they weren't singles material," Ryder now thinks. The road show was on the skids, the money was shrinking, and the musicians weren't going to stick unless they got paid. "We were making incredible bread at one point—$12,000 for a one-hour show in West Virginia, I think. But the show band became incredible to work with, because there would be weekends when the most we'd be making was $1,500. And these guys would demand their $250 salary that they'd been receiving, and also wanted their transportation paid. And they wanted it every week, whether they worked or not."

Coupled with this were the financial problems with Bob Crewe. The Wheels saw no money—Badanjek said he never received a cent from recording, not even the session money that the union contract demands be paid. Ryder didn't fare much better. "I was with Bob Crewe and I must have sold six million records," he says. "I received two things from him: a $15,000 advance (which is nowhere near six million records, especially since I had part of the writing royalties) and a $1,000 royalty check. Sure, I got the gig money, but that's nothing to do with him—he still got his 10 percent anyway."

By mid-1968, the second year of the show band, Ryder was through with Crewe. "He started putting out the shit he wanted me to record. The first year I'd recorded those things, but the second year I wouldn't touch 'em."

Thoroughly disillusioned, nearly bankrupt, Ryder dismantled the show. He moved to rid himself of the Crewe organization.

The next problem was finding a compatible producer. Fortunately, Dot had recently bought Stax/Volt Records in Memphis. Steve Cropper, lead guitarist of Booker T. and the MGs and one of soul's most important writer/producers, was available to work with Ryder.

"It would do several things, solve several problems. First, it would raise me to the heights of any artist trying to record R&B. [Stax had never before recorded a white vocalist, even though half its session band was white.] And it would be a commercial success, which would eliminate my financial problem and enable me to reach a position where I could get something happening again musically in my own mind."

So in June of 1969, Ryder journeyed to Memphis and the Stax studios on McLemore Avenue. The idea for the album was to attempt to strike a balance between Ryder's wild power and the taut instrumental work of the MGs—thus the title *The Detroit/Memphis Experiment*.

The album, not yet released, is exactly that, a one-shot attempt to achieve something new, based on fundamentally sound principles. Ryder's energy combined with the MGs' funk points in the same direction as Sly Stone's new music.

But that's not Ryder's conception of his music; it's just an acceptable compromise. The real plan is to re-form the Detroit Wheels. Two of the original Wheels, Kubert and Badanjek (the latter one of the most influential rock drummers ever), are with his band now. Ryder also has Detroit pianist Boot Hill, part of the Commander Cody coterie, and a trumpet and tenor sax. The sound will be closer to contemporary white rhythm and blues—Joe Cocker style. That sound certainly hasn't stood still in the two years since Ryder left the scene; if anything, it has mushroomed beyond anyone's expectations. Aware of this, Ryder is confident of regaining success. The teenage lust for rock and roll hasn't yet left him. He's only twenty-four.

"All I know is what I've gone through: rock and roll with the Rivieras, rhythm and blues with the Wheels, big band with the show. And now the Stax record, which I'm sure will be as successful as the first two, simply because it's got an energy people can closely relate to."

There's still that age-old dream. And though the perils that the Byrds defined in "So You Wanna Be a Rock and Roll Star" are genuine, they can also be overcome. Once you've been there, at any rate, it's the last line that reverberates: "Don't forget what you are / You're a rock'n'roll star." Mitch Ryder knows. Like the Beatles, he'd

like to get back. There's a good chance that he will. Which speaks
well for the dreams of thirteen-year-olds.

Creem, 1969

Doncha Ever Listen to the Radio?

*More than any other performer, Bob Seger symbolized the heartland
rock that grew up in Detroit and spread throughout the Midwest in
the late sixties and through the seventies. The great stars of Motown
were black and kept themselves isolated in any event. Mitch Ryder
and the Detroit Wheels were, as we've seen, swept into the black hole
reserved for American rockers who stuck their necks out before the
British conquest of the charts (and concomitant redefinition of credibility) was completed. The MC5 and the Stooges were psychedelic
eccentrics who had vision and excitement but lacked chops and mass
appeal.*

*But Seger is, in his way, as wholesome and sincere as it's possible
for a genuine rock and roll genius to be. When he finally hit his stride,
beginning in the late seventies with his* Live Bullet *album, America
concurred: "Night Moves," "Rock and Roll Never Forgets," "Old
Time Rock & Roll" and "Feel Like a Number"—among his other
hits—were the best Top Forty rock of their era.*

*It says something scary about the wastefulness of the rock industry
that it took Seger so long to make himself heard; the records he made
in the first ten years of his career aren't that much more polished than
the string of successes beginning with the anthemic "Night Moves."
It's significant, though, that that song, and many of his others, scored
by looking over their shoulder—talking about rock and its audience
in just the terms for which Seger is praised in this piece. The sad part
is that by the time his music hit the airwaves, looking over his shoulder
meant literally "Lookin' Back." That he's kept rocking, in and out of
fashion (and sometimes by the skin of his teeth—see section four,
"Don't Let Me Down") is a tribute to both tenacity and talent.*

This sometimes hysterical story is from the period just before he formed the first version of the Silver Bullet Band, his first completely professional group, and arrived at the foundation of the sound for which he's become famous. (Incidentally, he used a horn—Alto Reed's saxophone—and he made it rock.)

1.

ITEM: In the last seven years, Bob Seger has had ten Top Ten records in Detroit.

ITEM: Of those ten, three have sold over 50,000 copies.

ITEM: One of them, "Heavy Music," sold 66,000 copies in Detroit alone, *despite* the company that issued it folding as it was breaking into the national charts.

ITEM: In November 1969, during the Vietnam War Moratorium, the largest antiwar demonstrations ever held, disc jockeys all over the country began playing a (then) two-year-old Seger single, "2 + 2 = ?," which is one of the most powerful antiwar songs ever recorded. Sales spurted, but Seger's record company failed to reissue the single speedily.

ITEM: Of all the records Seger has released, not one has ever reached higher than No. 17 on *Billboard's* charts.

ITEM: No Seger single has ever been played on the radio in San Francisco, Los Angeles or New York.

QUESTION: If Bob Seger is so good, why haven't you ever heard of him?

The contradiction in trying to write about an unknown quantity in rock and roll is readily apparent. Because we're basically dealing with popular music, an essential criterion for judging any performer's importance has to be record sales. How many people are aware of this music? Has it reached us?

That's not to say that all great rockers sell lots of records. But it's undeniable that a singer means more to everyone when he has hits, if only because we've then invested something in him. He's no longer a private interest; he's become a public passion.

So Bob Seger is a paradox; he's been heavily influential in Michigan, yet means nothing elsewhere. He's not a Van Dyke Parks woodwork pest, but he's also not a John Fogerty, even though he should be, because his songs are that good and they're cut from the same mold.

No one has yet figured out his odd track record, but what's even stranger than his lack of sales is that no one has picked up on Seger's songwriting. In the age of songwriter worship, Seger is a rare commodity, as good in his own way as Fogerty, Robbie Robertson or Carole King, a mere cut below Dylan and Chuck Berry in his ability to push a sensibility out there and define it. But there haven't even been many cover versions. And the few there were have been "terrible," according to Seger himself. "Mostly they were European and they were awwwwwwful. It seems like the only people who do my stuff are these really off-the-wall cats who are lookin' for really off-the-wall stuff. I always wanted to see Joe Cocker doing 'Ramblin' Gamblin' Man,' but instead I get this terrible version of 'East Side Story' by the St. Louis Union, produced by Tony Clarke [of the Moody Blues]. A kitchen sink production thing—it's really funny; it was terrrrrrible."

Someday, though, one of Bob Seger's songs will burst out of the charts and then watch out! Cause he does know what it's all about, and given the chance, he'll set everyone wobblin'.

2. East Side Story

Seger's string of remarkable singles and perverse luck began in 1965, a magic year for the Beatles, Britain and America's sense of The Rock.

Seger had been in a few bar bands and received an invitation to Vegas but decided to stick around Michigan. He and his band, the Last Heard, went into a thimble-sized Motor City recording studio around that time, to cut a song that he'd written called "East Side Story."

The record was released on Hideout Records, owned by a local entrepreneur named Punch Andrews, who controlled a string of teen clubs called the Hideouts. Andrews went on to become Seger's manager, but at the time, he was making their record as much to hype attendance at his clubs as anything else. (A number of other performers—Glenn Frey, Suzi Quatro—cut their first discs for Hideout.) The phenomenon wasn't uncommon locally—booking agent/manager Jeep Holland also ran his A-Square Records in Ann Arbor and had several local smashes with the Rationals ("I Need You," and their legendary white soul version of "Respect") and the SRC (a knockoff of Cream's Skip James' ruination, "I'm So Glad").

Unquestionably, the teen-club scene was extremely different in ambience and everything else from the later ballroom daze, much less the theater and arena venues of today. For example, Seger and his group played half a hundred different clubs in Michigan, Ohio, Illinois and Indiana. Many were franchise joints: Hideouts, Crow's Nests, Hullabaloos. These clubs were forums for unsophisticated music and lifestyle—rock culture in the raw. Teenagers danced and drank to bands who did the same when they weren't onstage. It was egalitarian good fun, even if it was rarely brilliant musically. Out of such scenes came some of the great American bands: the Detroit Wheels, the Young Rascals, Creedence Clearwater, Grand Funk Railroad, the pantheon of sixties punk. It was peer-group rock, played for an audience that often consisted of kids you'd run into the next Monday morning in high school hallways. Bands who went through the teen-club mill were left with far fewer pretensions than their younger brothers who came up through the ballrooms.

For all of that, "East Side Story" was a remarkably progressive record. The fuzztone is strong and full; the wall-of-sound Seger and coproducer Doug (Fontaine) Brown threw up behind the powerful vocal had a charge of echo and energy not unlike punk's version of Phil Spector's Wall of Sound; the lyric was a full-fledged narrative, about a broken love affair, a heist, a casualty.

Seger once told me that the song was based on a true story. Now he hedges a bit. "It's true, there was a love affair that was broken up for that reason [because the boyfriend became a thief], but there wasn't a death involved. That just came in because I was very involved with . . . uh . . . nineteen-year-old emotional extravaganza."

"East Side Story" escapes the traditional death-rock mold because Seger is essentially a moralist. His Johnny Brown isn't just a rebel; he was a burglar. "East Side Story" is therefore ultimately closer to "Staggerlee" or Robert Mitchum's "Thunder Road" than to "Leader of the Pack" or "Tell Laura I Love Her." But because Seger is a moralist and was devoted to melodrama, Johnny Brown had to die. It's the same kind of attitude that has led Seger to speak of the ethics of the counterculture more frequently than any other important songwriter—and which has led him to speak of it quite critically of late.

"East Side Story," good as it was, had to be released three separate times before Cameo/Parkway, the Philadelphia label that originally specialized in dance hits but was making a foray into garage-band rock and roll, picked it up for national distribution. (Cameo signed a number of top Detroit and Michigan groups in that period, including the Rationals, Terry Knight and the Pack [later Grand Funk] and ? and the Mysterians, thanks to its A&R man, Neil Bogart.) The Cameo release made a little noise in what came to be the usual Seger markets: the upper Midwest, Florida, Boston, Washington, D.C. But it never got big enough anywhere outside Detroit to spread.

Seger's second single, "Persecution Smith," a blatant Bob Dylan cop, was the perfect folk-rock knockoff—it sounds like a particularly demented outtake from *Bringing It All Back Home*. Sloppily executed as it is, it still expressed very well the sense of collective alienation and pure fear the rock audience was beginning to feel.

"Persecution Smith" was a heavily drawn figure closer to P. F. Sloan's "Eve of Destruction" character than anything in Dylan. Maybe he was a parody of such characters. "That was the first time that I tried to write about the long-hair thing," Seger says. Seen in that light, "Persecution Smith" is an interesting artifact in which rock and roll, on the verge of becoming self-conscious, finds itself steeped in paranoia: "He's here, he's there, he's *everywhere,*" Seger sings of his personal gremlin, "He's found up town and underground / In Watts, Californ-ya, you know who he was with . . ."

Seger *was* heavily influenced by Dylan. "I used to know all these Dylan tunes, but I never, ever played 'em," he says. "I'd just sing 'em to myself. Fantastic lyrics. I never really understood any of the lyrics, and I'm not sure what a lot of them *meant,* but the images and the words seemed to conjure up a feeling that somehow made sense." It was Seger's ability to grasp what everyone else was feeling and transmute it into a song that is both an eccentric tribute to Dylan and a parody of him that makes "Persecution Smith" exciting and valuable even now.

But this was all just a part of Seger's dues-paying. What came next revealed him in full bloom.

3. Heavy Music

Everyone who heard it was incredulous. No one had ever put it that way before, but suddenly the phrases seemed to have been there all the time. And the music that punched the message home said the same thing, just as effectively.

That's true of a lot of songs, from "Like a Rolling Stone" to "Get Back." "Heavy Music," Bob Seger's third single, strikes the same way. Its musical power abets its lyric, so that together they're improbably strong.

"Persecution Smith" was self-conscious because it made an assumption about its audience. "Heavy Music," like only a few of the best rock and roll records, speaks self-consciously about rock and roll itself: about the music and what it means. With a thundering bass line and a sudden chant, it rocks out of a tinny transistor speaker, *proclaiming* itself. Its opening lines ("Doncha ever listen to the radio / When the big bad beat comes on") are as magically rhetorical as anything ever written. Of course you do—otherwise you wouldn't have heard *this.*

Like "Who Put the Bomp," "Heavy Music" asks the questions that every other song about rock and roll has tried to answer, from the Coasters' "Baby That Was Rock and Roll" to the Velvet Underground's "Rock and Roll." And Seger expresses this so perfectly that the song could still be a hit today. It hasn't lost a drop of the magic it possessed in 1966. It's a pure hit—so simple it's almost primal.

Such songs echo through rock history. Chuck Berry sang "Gotta be rock and roll music," and the Beatles echoed "Get back, Jo Jo!" Eric Burdon defined who in "Monterey," while the Guess Who, Johnny Kidd and the Who said why with "Shakin' All Over." And in times of peril, there have been songs like "It Will Stand" and "Rock and Roll Is Here to Stay." Two years ago, Fleetwood Mac stepped to the stage and sang, "This is the rock / We've been talking about." Gentle but true.

It can be an invitation ("C'mon over baby, whole lotta shakin' goin' on"), a challenge ("Get back, Loretta!") or a threat ("Roll over Beethoven and tell Tchaikovsky the news"). Sometimes it's just a stone-cold, drop-dead-in-your-tracks pronouncement that a new phase has dawned:

> Doncha ever feel like goin' insane
> When the drums begin to pound
> Ain't there ever been a time in your life
> You couldn't believe what the band is puttin' down

Seger was talking "heavy music," all right, but it must be remembered that no one had thought to call it that before. Though the song may never have reached your backyard, it was Bob Seger who coined the phrase that sums up everything since Zep unzipped and the Jeff Beck Group zapped us right in the guts with a whole new sound. That sound was what the Who and the Yardbirds had been implicitly promising but never quite defined. Seger put his finger on it and the result was 60,000 sales almost immediately, a remarkable number in a local market, even one as large as this. You could hardly walk anywhere without hearing "Heavy Music," and every time you got into the car, you practically had to keep one foot on the dash to keep it from driving you right through the windshield.

Then it disappeared. Just stopped. Friends from out of town responded that they'd "never heard of it" when we asked, even though they too whooped it up when they finally did. Suddenly it was hard to find copies even back home.

Given the heralded and inherent Motor City chauvinism, we were almost glad it was our secret, a password akin to "Kick Out the Jams!" But the mystery remained pungent: What happened? How did *this one* fail to take off?

"A lot of people really misconstrued it," Seger says of his magnum opus. "That was a song about the music but a lot of people thought it was a song about music and *sex*, the two together. There was nothing sexual in it, it was simply read in by a lot of program directors. The part about goin' deeper." (The song has a lengthy middle section in which Seger chants the words "Goin' DEEP-AH!" in progressively more frantic tones.)

"We just jammed it down in Columbus, we got into this jam about 'deeper,' and I really dug the jam. We happened to be taping that night, and then I went home and wrote the song around it.

"It was really weird . . . It was like going in as . . . well, you know. I don't know, there were complaints about it when it was first played on *Swingin' Time* [a local TV show]. Until, of course, it got out of hand and then they couldn't help but play it. Even then, they said, 'You know, you better go in and rerecord that tail end, put something different on the tail, because no one's ever gonna play it.'

"But it wasn't a matter of no one playing that one—it was a matter of the product being cut off.

"That was our biggest record," Seger continues. "Sixty-six thousand and it's still sellin'. When you can find it. Which you can't, hardly, anymore.

"What happened was, it got into the 70s in *Billboard* and then died. [Actually the song spent five weeks on *Billboard*'s Bubbling Under the Hot 100 chart, never reaching any higher placement than 103.] But that was because Allen Klein—yes, that Allen Klein—bought Cameo-Parkway and the stock soared over the next two weeks. And then the federal government shut the company down. The stock went from two to seventy, so the company was literally shut down; I didn't even find out until a couple of years later what happened to that record. But that's what happened."

4. Ramblin' Gamblin' Man

At least that got Cameo, which as Seger puts it "wasn't exactly a major label," out of the way. "We got a release from Cameo," says Seger. "They'd never paid us a cent for any of the records. So we said, 'Okay, keep your money and give us a release.' So we got a release." Meantime, Capitol had made its move on Detroit, signing up all the old Cameo acts, eventually including Seger.

Seger's output at Capitol has been even more prolific and just as good. Two of his seven Detroit Top Ten records have sold more than 50,000 copies. "Ramblin' Gamblin' Man," his second Capitol single, made number 17 in *Billboard*, again without airplay in New York or California.

The first Capitol single was a magnificent antiwar rocker, "2 + 2 = ?" It's a screamer that lays things out simply and unequivocally. Seger almost croons the opening lines over a throbbing bass note, and the song builds as his singing picks up urgency. Finally the song is topped off with a zooming, Brian Jones–style guitar that sounds a warning note for everyone who heard the call and refused:

> And you stand and call me upstart
> Ask what answer can I find
> I ain't sayin' I'm a genius
> Two plus two is on my mind.

From the first verse, one might think it was nothing more than a rehash of Dylan's "Master of War," but Seger once more pulls his listeners in with a reversion to teenage mythology—telling the story of a high school friend ("just an average, friendly guy") who dies in the Vietnamese mud while his girlfriend sits and cries back home, understanding nothing but the pointlessness of his death.

Detroit made the song a hit, but in 1966 the rest of the country wasn't ready to hear antiwar rock on the radio. When the roles were reversed in November 1969—when millions of people, having figured out that it was the war, not the antiwar movement, that was causing the national blight and hundreds of thousands marched on Washington alone—disc jockeys by the dozen began to play the song. Capitol agreed to rerelease it. But they moved too slowly and the momentum was lost (a nice metaphor for what's later happened to the antiwar movement itself), so Seger's chance was again blown.

"Ramblin' Gamblin' Man," Seger's second Capitol single, is much like a Creedence Clearwater tune—say, "Travelin' Band," a thunderous spoof on the rock and roll star's macho stud routine. It's probably Seger's best song to date, but it's not quite as raw as his earlier sides.

The first Seger album, *Ramblin' Gamblin' Man*, included both Capitol singles when it was released in January 1967. There were a couple of other tightly written songs, and a few quasi-experimental extended tracks that are mostly dreck. Capitol squeezed one more single from the record, the impossibly trendy "Love Needs to Be Loved," cut from the same cloth as "All You Need Is Love" and "We Love You." But when the band starts rocking on that post-Beatles chorus, you can't help but love it. With philosophical aphorisms floated—and sometimes sailing—all over the place, it sounds like a John Lennon period piece.

But it wasn't until early 1969 that "Love Needs to Be Loved" hit the airwaves. Meantime, Seger had been changing his band—including the name of the group, which was now the Bob Seger System.

Seger had also come to the conclusion that he couldn't sing and play guitar at the same time. "That was the first time that I decided that," he says. "So we got this guitarist named Tom Neme. And then Neme came up with all these songs that he wanted to do. At that point I was really tired. I wanted to quit. That was when I enrolled in college—no, I wasn't going to be a criminologist, that was just a joke at the time—and I was goin' to school. I was waiting for [the band] to do this album, and then I would quit."

As a result, though the *Noah* album is called a Bob Seger System record and it's Bob alone who appears on the cover, Seger now says, "I didn't have anything to do with that album. I wrote 'Noah,' the song, and one or two others, a lot of it during that long break between albums. 'Noah' is about that: 'Lay back, you've had your fun. Let them do it for a while.' That's what the album's about, too. How they blew it."

But by the time the album cover was being prepared, Seger was already reconsidering. "The first album was trio, this album is more in many respects. It's more sound, it's more guts, it's more soul and it's more *conflict,* " he wrote in the liner notes. "Seger will always be Bob Seger, any change must come from the System and Tom Neme." In the photo on the back cover, the band appeared full face. Seger was visible only in a mirror.

After the record was released, he immediately fired Neme and went back to playing guitar himself. (Neme's songs lent new weight to the term inconsequential.) "Noah" hit locally again, but not as big as some of the others. Meanwhile, the band was disintegrating and several more personnel changes were transpiring. The new band, stripped down to a quartet, prepared a third album, *Mongrel*, released in the fall of 1970. It's a brilliant record, every song tough and to the point. "The whole idea was the mongrel, the American of any nationality who grows his hair long and tries to sink into a culture," Seger says.

Mongrel's commentary on that culture isn't exactly fawning. "Highway Child," one of the best tunes on the album, sums up: "I been so high my mind were fried . . . I'm so damned apathetic I can't believe I'm free."

In its own way, *Mongrel* speaks about America as clearly as *The Band*, and its music is surely as exciting. The album is an unfound classic—or maybe just a period piece. But if it is only a period piece, it's one from *our* era. Here is the counterculture, in all its strength and folly. "Evil Edna" confronts the new sexual mores and walks away amazed. Yet even here Seger's moralism cuts through. Edna dies, even though she's sounder than those who'd condemned her. "That's a song not so much about groupies as the sexual ethics of the very young," Seger says. He also notes that "Evil Edna" was conceived as a warning to one of his friends, who condemned women for violating the double standard.

"Leanin' On My Dream," though, makes the most pointed comment about what's wrong in this version of America. It sets up a typical Seger situation, the singer being dragged toward protest against his will, seeing the recruiter for the movement on TV just after he's spurned his offer, then receiving his own draft notice and hitting the picket line himself. As a battler against apathy, Seger knows no equal, and he gets away with a lot because he's so damn funny about it.

But even *Mongrel,* as good and relatable as it was, couldn't break Seger out of Detroit. In November 1971 he struck again with another local hit, "Lookin' Back." It's one of his best songs, the same commentary as *Mongrel* but distilled to a three-minute single. Cut at the album sessions, it takes the full blast of long-hair paranoia—"You hit the street / You feel 'em starin' "—but once again, all that anyone does about it is sit around and watch the TV. "Lookin' Back" is a criticism of both the "straight" culture and the counterculture community.

But once more, "Lookin' Back" refused to rise nationally. Despite hitting in Houston as well as the usual spots, it didn't rise above No. 97 in *Billboard*.

5. Brand New Morning

"It's weird," Seger says, " 'Lookin' Back' is one of our biggest hits in Detroit—it's as big as 'Gamblin' Man,' sold around 50,000 copies.

"You know, 'Gamblin' Man' was a No. 1 record here. It sold about 40,000 copies in Detroit, another 10,000 elsewhere. 'Lookin' Back' didn't get any higher than No. 3 here, and the reason is, they can't take it any higher because it isn't a national hit. It just doesn't look right."

"Lookin' Back" is his eleventh single in the past seven years that's hit the Top Ten in Motown but flopped nationally. Yet Seger refuses to blame his record company. "I don't really know that much about the business side of it, and I must say in the record company's defense that we have had notoriously rotten [live] shows for the last couple years. Or not consistently rotten, but on and off, you know?"

At present, Seger is involved in enough projects to make the head swim. He broke up the System as soon as *Mongrel* was completed, then played solo for six to eight weeks, which resulted in an acoustic album, *Brand New Morning*. The title is not self-descriptive.

Then Seger hooked up with Dave Teegarden and Skip Van Winkle, the Motor City's favorite transplanted Okies. (They hit with "God Love and Rock and Roll" in 1970.) The trio billed itself as STK (Van Winkle's real name is Knape) and played gigs as a three-part concert: Seger solo, Teegarden and Van Winkle together, then all three for a rock and roll set. Finally, they dropped all but part three, added guitarist Mike Bruce (late of Bobby Bland's Revue) and began to record. They're planning on a Teegarden single; an STK single, "If I Were a Carpenter," on which Seger sings lead; and a new Seger single.

"STK is a lack of direction. Like, if I had my way, it'd be all rock and roll and my tunes, too. And if Dave had his way, it'd be all soul, and if Michael had his, it'd be all blues. And if Skip had his, it would just be a two-man group. So we've agreed to a cut-off date at the first of the year, unless things change drastically."

Meantime, Seger is preparing an all-new group, teaching the new players his material and getting ready to make a record with *them*. "It'll be a big band. No horns, though. I *hate* horns. A rock and roll band, because that's basically all I know. That's the only thing I can construct well. But maybe three guitars, bass, drums, keyboard and a lotta singers."

The STK experience has meanwhile had one invaluable consequence. "I used to hate performing. I got to the point where I wanted to have a really big album, so I could get off the road and just sit and write and create like the Beatles did when they went off the road. But since I've been with Skip and Dave, I've come to dig performing more than I ever have in my life. Maybe that's why I haven't been writing much, because I've been concentrating on the show."

Meanwhile, Hideout is reportedly considering buying back the Cameo masters and releasing them as an album called *Bombs Away*. Seger isn't overly enthusiastic about the idea, saying he wouldn't want such a hit ("It's old-fashioned"), but Punch Andrews is. And just think the record could even include that immortal 1967 Christmas ditty, "Sock It to 'Em Santa": "Sock it to 'em Santa, you know where it's at / Sock it to 'em, Santa, I want a baseball bat!"

Finally, there's the matter of whether Seger's songs are really definitive. "I don't know," he says a little warily. "I care, sure I care. But I've said a lot about the long-hair thing. I said it all on *Mongrel*. 'Lookin' Back' was conceived mostly as about people like Agnew, you know, but in the last year, I haven't felt quite so smart as I did then."

Neither does anybody else, I suppose. But it's nice to have someone around who can articulate even our stupidity and make us dig it. I don't know how to make it happen, but here's hoping everyone outside Detroit gets to hear Bob Seger do that—and real soon. 'Cause he knows what he's talking about.

Creem, 1972

Iggy in Exile

Though my love for music this ruggedly noisy has somewhat abated with age, there's no doubt that, when it was released, Raw Power *was everything I claimed for it. Though the Stooges withered away from the usual punk-rock diseases (dope and despair), they were maybe the one hometown band that I felt closest to in the Vietnam years—the one group that knew that the guns were pointed at them, also, and made music that reflected the utter futility you had to feel in the face of that fact. And Iggy Pop (née Stooge) knew what he was about, as any of the reporters and critics he shrewdly manipulated can assure you. His 1983 biography,* I Need More, *is a surprisingly accurate, if also self-serving, account of those years between the inaugural shows of the Stooges and his mid-seventies European dalliance with David Bowie. After that, I lose track.*

Raw Power *also represents the height of my attempt at* Creem *to create a high-energy prose style that paralleled the raw nerve and giddiness of the best of the city's radical rock. For me, the style eventually seemed like a dead end, though Lester Bangs of course made more consistent and certainly greater use of it. "Iggy in Exile" remains my own review in that style that I actually like, despite the fact that it's more windy than pithy.*

Raw Power is the best high-energy album since *Kick Out the Jams*, and it sometimes makes me think that Iggy and the Stooges could kick their ex–Big Brothers' butts in the right kind of alley.

I can't believe this is the same group that made the Stooges' first two albums. No longer the band you love because they put out so much despite their limitations, this version of the Stooges is tremendously powerful, and with the aid of skillful production, the noise-raunch power tremble of complete ecstasy that *Kick Out the Jams* hitherto represented all by itself is finally fully realized IN THE STUDIO. Consider that, boob-a-la—it's like staging an air raid on Hanoi in Grauman's Chinese Theater.

Iggy kicks it loose from the beginning. The guitar charge is just like the old Five's guitar work, tremendous bursts of apocalyptic interstellar energy, limited only by contemporary technology and harnessed to a strong, if unsteady, backbeat. Bassist Ron Asheton pulls down the sound, melding it into something almost earthly, while the rest of the band accelerates so hard and so fast that if Iggy wasn't the singer, you'd wonder whose record this was. It's like they OD'd Pete Townshend on Quaalude and acid, forced him into a 1965 time warp and made him keep all the promises he made in "Can't Explain."

By the time the second song, "Raw Power," comes on, you're startled, so busy trying to figure out what this meta-metamorphosis portends that you can't quite believe that the record is doing it all by itself, so you look around the floor but no, not there. Then Iggy screams, "Raw Power got a healin' hand / Raw Power can destroy a man," which for once isn't a call to the demiurges who guard rock'n'roll to come out and visit us (i.e., bail out the singer)—no, this is an irrefutable statement of fact. Like the songs on the first Stooges record, which had titles like "No Fun," "Real Cool Time," "Little Doll" and "I Wanna Be Your Dog," "Raw Power" is just the eye of the Ig roving around the street, putting down what he sees, not mincing words or trying for fluidity but letting it ooze, rough and uh, raw, splat, screeeeee: "You're alone and you've got the shakes / So've I, baby, but I got what it takes." And "Raw Power," so help me God, begins with an authentic belch, a true-to-life burp—which is, like farting, a form of *truly* raw power. And it goes like this: urgggllllppppp. I swear.

Now comes the part for people who never liked the Stooges. (Whatever Stooges fans think of such folks, they *are* all but legion.) "Give Me Danger" is the real Iggy ballad, the one Mr. Pop kept threatening us with when he did tunes like "Ann, My Ann" and "Dirt." But this Iggy ballad is one where you can't make out the lyrics because of the guitars, which is okay because these guitars are as luminous as Jimi Hendrix jamming with John Fahey. The playing is by James Williamson (who replaces Ron Asheton). You won't believe it until you hear it, and even then it might take you a week: that's how long it took me, even after seeing them live in London last summer.

Now, this is the part that you won't believe at all (as if you're gonna believe me when I tell you how great this record is, anyway), but after a while you look at the titles and you begin to wonder what is this record *about?* Now, I'm not saying that Iggy has made the first dementoid concept album or some avuncular nonsense like that, I'm just going to tell you what this album is about and you can believe it or not:

> Raw Power *is what happens if you watch the Vietnam War live on TV every night, and that is the central fact of the culture in which you live for ten years (or more).*

Look at these titles: "Hard to Beat" (Kissinger'd buy that, even); "Search and Destroy," for which no explanation is necessary; "Death Trip," ditto; "Penetration," a sort of behind-the-lines excursion . . .

Maybe Iggy was imagining—it's a big maybe but what the fuck—that he didn't beat the draft after all. In fact he went to Vietnam and got his legs and arms shot off and came back a crippled, quadriplegic junkie who got himself atomic-powered prosthetic limbs and set out to avenge the destruction he'd endured. And the way he does it is to write a song about how he got fucked up, see, with these lines:

> I'm the world's most forgotten boy
> The one who searches and *destroys*

And then singing about his fantasy after he got shot, his dream while he almost bled to death, which is that Madame Diem showed up and sucked him off and fucked him in ways he hadn't thought possible: "Love in the middle of a fire fight."

Now you might think this is totally ridiculous, and you're absolutely right, but that's what this album makes me think about—and I ain't even told you about the long songs yet.

Everyone talks about how we need a band that can hold this decade in the palm of its hand and spitshine and polish it, but the Stooges just come out and do that, and with their feet they dance a merry little gallows jig, too. *Raw Power* is like a great James Bond novel that never got written, but its concepts are all sketched in here. Like, when the Stooges play their own version of "St. James Infirmary," called "I Need Somebody," where Iggy is bad as Howlin' Wolf pounding Mick Jagger on the head with a forty-pound stack of Yma Sumac records.

And all the while Iggy just keeps singing in his best Frank Sinatra voice (the one he uses to sing "Shadow of Your Smile" when the amps blow up in the middle of a set). He isn't singing "I need somebody, too," either; any dorkoid in the world could sing about how lonely we all are. He's singing about how he needs somebody to . . . do something so unspeakable you couldn't (*he* couldn't) imagine what it even is or how to do it, if you knew.

Then "Death Trip," a nightmarish reworking in no uncertain terms of Jim Morrison's "Moonlight Drive" fetish. Real-ly. Death to the death culture and all that rot, as David Bowie taught him to say. Iggy immerses himself in all the rage of being fucked up and more appropriately, fucking YOURSELF up that anyone can imagine, and then he sings, as in a love song:

> I'm with you and you with me
> We're goin' down in history

And he ain't talking about a blow job, either, he's talking about going down like Hitler, like Rasputin, like every mangled dictator and dog-eared mass murderer there ever was, if you'll just come right along on his little death trip—here, step inside. Stab, stab.

I'm tempted myself. Only a truly diabolical mind could have made the best album of the seventies, of course, and Iggy apparently has it because he's summed everything up and it took him only nine songs to do it. And he didn't have to write any songs about being/not being/wishing he were cosmic or a star or some bullshit.

Step inside the Fun House, home of the O Mind, and we will all have a real cool time, AC/DC and Raw Power alike.

Creem, 1973

Missin' Twenty Grand

This piece speaks for itself, I hope, for between it and the thrill of listening once again to David Lasley's music, I feel inescapably reconnected to the very beginning of this story—my version of the songs he sings, I guess.

Yes, we was funky, boys and girls
Singin' up in the clouds
Four years away from twenty—
but grand and very proud, always
hopin for some action
From the latest, hottest local station
—David Lasley

As you may know, I'm not ordinarily in the habit of touting solo albums
made by James Taylor's backing singers. On the other hand, David Lasley
is certainly the most soulful backup singer Taylor's ever had, and the only
one whose solo album, *Missin' Twenty Grand*, owes a greater debt of
inspiration to Smokey Robinson than to Bob Dylan.

To me, Lasley's record is immediately marked as one of the finest of this
year, if only for its artful combination of falsetto soul singing and reflective,
confessional songs, supported by tight, funky, sophisticated but always
light-handed arrangements, refreshing after so much wooden white funk
on both shores of the Atlantic this season. Not to mention much adult
good humor: I defy any human of any sexual persuasion who has ever
cohabited with a fellow post-adolescent not to appreciate Lasley's deadpan
account of his dealings with his "Roommate," the usual unfaithful dead-
beat slob.

The emotional center of *Missin' Twenty Grand* is the same stretch of
inner city Detroit where my inaugural critical outpost, *Creem*, resided
until 1972. It's a small piece of land, maybe a couple of square miles, from
Third Street down around Selden and Alexandrine, a spot that makes the
Bowery look cozy, up to Motown's Hitsville studios on West Grand Boulevard and then west maybe as far as the Twenty Grand Lounge itself. The
Twenty Grand was the finest nightclub in the city, the place where I
(among many others) first heard the likes of Bobby Bland and Wilson
Pickett sing. So Lasley's liner notes (from which the introductory quota-
tion to this piece is taken), his album title and certainly his best song,
"Third Street," evoke for me more than just a place—they are also a part
of an age and of my coming of age.

Lasley has perfectly rendered those first moments when a kid from a
small town, a suburb, even (in his own case) a farm, was pulled into the
urban center, drawn by the wigged-out rhythm and blues or rock'n'roll of
the day, and encounters the genuine demimonde—not the stuff they show
on TV, but the authentically bizarre places and characters who always
inhabit such areas. "Met my first drag queen at fifteen / Didn't know until
I was sixteen," Lasley sings, and the spaces between those lines—between

the seeing and the knowing—and his eerily confident falsetto establish an encounter that's universal.

Other people went through the same thing in different ways and different towns. My own version of Third Street was whiter and more druggy, less gay and thuggy, but close enough for me to recognize Mrs. Brown, the crone who swiped Lasley's sound and sold it back to him for a quarter a play on the jukebox, and even the asshole who picks a fight with the kid weeping at the counter of the all-night café.

Yet there's something specifically Detroit about all this, or at least about the particular way in which it returns to haunt all those it touched. There's something that connects Lasley's liner notes, with their frank innocence, with the compulsion of ex-Eagle Glenn Frey to mention his Motor City roots prominently on his first solo album, something shared, I suspect, by George Clinton, Iggy Pop, David and Donald Was, Bob Seger, Ron Banks, Mitch Ryder, Commander Cody—all those who escaped. In a way, it might be nothing more than the memory of those who didn't.

Or maybe I just feel that way because I've also been listening to some of that forgotten crowd again, on a bootleg compilation called *Michigan Brand Nuggets*, annotated with the kind of in-jokes that are usually the province of New Yorkers who don't know that Soupy Sales really got his act together on WXYZ. This new *Nuggets*—the title is a glancing nod at Lenny Kaye's original punk rock sampler—features seven tracks by Bob Seger (including the notorious "Ballad of the Yellow Beret" and the hilarious "Sock It to 'Em, Santa") and five by the MC5, which alone would be good reason to seek it out. Seger was all along one of rock's great voices and one of its best synthetic songwriters, while the Five were the quintessential punk rockers, granddaddies of the Dolls and Sex Pistols, and to this day the most cataclysmically exciting noise-rockers I've ever seen.

If *Michigan Brand Nuggets* contained only those songs, though, it wouldn't be worth that much more than a footnote. There's nothing among Seger's early songs that comes close to "Ramblin' Gamblin' Man," which is still legitimately available from Capitol. And the Five's "Borderline"/"Lookin' at You" isn't worth nearly as much as "Kick Out the Jams," their devastating debut which Elektra recently reissued at a bargain price.

What moves me about the new *Nuggets* is the amount of forgotten talent scattered across the two discs, from the goofy one-shot doo-wop of Tim Tam and the Turn-Ons' "Wait a Minute" to the incipient folk rock of Southbound Freeway's "Psychedelic Used Car Lot Blues" to the full-throttle growl of the Woolies' "Who Do You Love." There is a story behind every one of these records and what happened to the people who made them: One of the Turn-Ons is now a booking agent; Larry Miller, who was in the Freeways, went on to become the first hip FM disc jockey in Detroit and San Francisco; the Woolies emerged as Chuck Berry's favorite backing band. Or take the four tracks by the Rationals, a band whose spirit was very close to David Lasley's—they played white soul with aching intensity and had a great lead vocalist, Scott Morgan. When you realize that Morgan cut the gorgeous, impassioned version of Chuck Jackson's "I Need You" when he was only about fifteen, the fact that he didn't go on to become a star seems utterly unfathomable.

It isn't only the ghost of wasted opportunity and unrecognized talent that haunts these Detroit memories (though I assure you that if Scott Morgan had been a New Yorker his name would be as revered in the Village as, say, Danny Kalb's). So much of the music from that time and place, not only the midsixties white garage-band stuff collected on *Nuggets* but also a good deal else, from Little Willie John to Was/Not Was, is imbued with the spirit of an eccentric brand of freedom, in which the continual, blues-based quest for the magic of self-invention is tied to an equally ceaseless willingness to start from scratch. This is what links Berry Gordy and the MC5, Mitch Ryder and George Clinton, Iggy Pop and Smokey Robinson; and it's what unites "I'll Try Something New" with "Kick Out the Jams" and "One Nation Under a Groove" with "I Wanna Be Your Dog." That and a sense of struggle, because there's no place I know where the fragile process of self-invention through music could possibly be more difficult than in those industrialized streets back home.

I don't mean to exaggerate this quality. Nonetheless, it's as fundamental and unavoidable in Detroit music as the touch of the idyllic and pastoral that enters all of San Francisco's music, even that of such regional rebels as John Fogerty and Sly Stone. And it is just this kind of regional accent that we're losing now; the new regional centers springing up select their styles off the rack of internationalized forms so much alike that I, at least, can't recognize any spiritual or emotional difference between them.

To the sort of music fan who doesn't make much distinction between a nation controlled by Ronald Reagan and one controlled by slightly less inhumane types, such distinctions may be altogether too fine to matter very much. But to me they're the difference between making one's way in the world and spending that life trapped. And ultimately this is the quality that draws me most wholeheartedly to David Lasley and *Missin' Twenty Grand*, which is dedicated "to the children of the world with hope that in my lifetime we may all know a world that does not perceive a boy or girl, a man or a woman by the color of their skin."

That may be the ultimate statement of what it means to be a white kid singing soul. And it links explicitly with David Lasley's allusions to gayness and its consequences, which are scattered throughout the album and expressed more vividly and certainly more proudly than any others I've ever heard in pop music. Without them, this would be sensuous and gorgeous music. With them, *Missin' Twenty Grand* becomes as overwhelming as an unexpected call from an old friend.

Musician, 1982

2

*Stardom and Its
Consequences*

Introduction

The idea here is simple: Stardom *has* consequences. And if that isn't a revelation, it isn't something you can very easily learn from reading the run-of-the-mill entertainment reportage in which our society is daily deluged. The idea that fame and success don't always work out so well is embedded in pop mythology, but the idea that this process is complex is not. "Lonely at the top" is not just a cliché; it's thought to be the sum and substance of the whole deal. Yet, as these portraits show, what making it does to people—at least the kind of people who become rock and soul performers—is diverse, unpredictable and quite fascinating.

The Daring Young Man and the Flying Chimpanzees/ Call to A.R.M.S.

This story catches one of my favorite bands, Rod Stewart and the Faces, in early 1972. It was an auspicious time, since Stewart was just then trying to create a follow-up to his first hit single, "Maggie May." His solo success had outstripped the group's, creating inevitable tensions, a situation only slightly alleviated by the fact that the current Faces LP, A Nod's as Good as a Wink (To a Blind Horse) *contained their first American hit, "Stay with Me," a rousing Chuck Berry style rocker clearly depicting the fuck 'em and forget 'em philosophy of campaigning rock stars.*

The staff of Creem *spent a lot of time with the Faces in their early*

*days in the States—around 1970. It was fairly common for the group
to spend its leisure time partying at Creem's headquarters, which also
happened to be the living quarters of most of the staff. Since Detroit
was the first place in America where the Faces were a live success, such
visits were fairly frequent in those days. As a result, this story may
reveal an almost excessive familiarity with the band.*

The last week of April, the American Retreaders Association shared the
Executive Inn in Louisville, Kentucky, with a collection of dwarfs, freaks,
dope dealers, high-wire acts, aerial motorcyclists, a few journalists, and a
couple of rock and roll bands.

This is the Rock & Roll Circus . . . Sideshow. The Main Event takes
place only once each evening, and that's what we're here for. Step right
this way, friends, and have a look inside:

In the center ring, for your enjoyment, ladies, gentlemen and children
of all ages, we present an act beyond mortal belief. This evening only,
flown DIRECT from London, England, the Rock & Roll Rooster and
his famous friends, the nimble, amazing Briton-chimpanzees! See them
walk and strut and kick out the very jams you've come to witness! Watch as they tread a path 'cross stages braver men have feared
to tread.

Please direct your attention to the center ring, ladies and gentlemen,
and welcome:

ROD STEWART AND THE FACES!

In the cavernous hallways of the inn, it is cool and dark. The Faces
haven't yet arrived to add specific tension to its plush plastic comforts. The
rooms are filled with much veneer; the carpets bear a design of sorts; the
bathrooms are immaculate, without even the shadow of a ring in the tub.

The Faces arrive around 4:00 P.M. By five it's time to eat dinner in the
Colonial Bar and Grill, a spacious room filled with a sense of chintz royalty.
At a back table sit Billy Gaff, the Faces manager; Ronnie Lane, their bass
player who also writes and sings; publicist Pat Costello; photographer Peter
Hujar; and the Creem team. Costello is verbose. Hujar is reserved in a way
that only a New Yorker confronting the hinterlands can be reserved. Gaff
is hyper, the paragon of British rock management. Tonight the pressure's
on for him: tickets for the show haven't sold well in advance, and he's
worried that they'll be playing to a half-empty house. Lane is quiet, re-

served in the way that only a professional British rock star can be reserved.

"Well," he says, "what are *you* doing here?"

The band was supposed to know we were coming . . . Oh fuck . . .

Gaff is bubbling over. He raves about the quality of the food. Then with
a swoop of his fork he begins to describe his plans for upping ticket sales
tonight. "I don't understand it. Tickets just aren't moving. Did you see
the plane I hired? Had a streamer behind it to advertise the show. And
we did TV spots."

Enter the Rock and Roll Rooster. He's bedecked in a white suit which
epitomizes British punque. He is sunburnt and angular, looking very tall
and very lean. Rod Stewart bends, the way he sways like a sapling onstage,
to whisper for a moment to Gaff. He leaves quickly. Momentarily Gaff and
Lane follow. Unconstrained, Costello and Hujar begin to regale us with
the previous day's debauch in Clemson, South Carolina.

"I can't understand it," says Hujar, who's not especially familiar with
rock and roll persons. "Why would anyone destroy something just to
destroy it?

"They expect to have to pay for it, too. Which is okay, I guess, but even
if you had the money . . ."

There is a story about the previous day, which was spent lounging on
a Clemson beach. The band had decided to cut a boat loose from its
moorings—just to cut it loose. No ulterior motive, nothing personal; just
something to do.

There are also stories about: broken lamps; groupies fucked with bana-
nas; two members of the band who wanted adjoining rooms and, not
receiving them, created a suite themselves by bashing through a wall. Bills
for hotel damages were averaging $250 a day.

"But why?"

Well . . . theater? Decadence? Fun? Assertion of success?

"Naw," says Charley Auringer, *Creem*'s ace photographer. "It's the old
biker idea. It's *class*. Like, it's class to be totally outrageous. Piss in your
best friend's living room. It's just . . . *it's total gross-out."*

The Louisville arena is so large that if more tickets aren't sold, there will
be severe problems, including about 300 percent too much natural echo.
But the place begins to fill up nicely as the recently re-formed Free open
the show. By the end of their brief, monotonous set, the house is about
half full, with customers still coming in.

During Free's set, the Circus proper sets up. Behind the stage, and to the side of it, high wires are strung. The trapeze act, a crew of Chileans, is to go on first. It isn't much. One of the connections is missed and the trouper falls—but he's back on the swing in a second, and you're left with the feeling that the fall is a setup.

Louisville is the tour's fourth stop, but this is the first night that the circus has been presented in its entirety. According to the Faces, most of the arenas have restrictive fire laws or inadequate facilities. (It's hard not to wonder why someone didn't investigate a little more thoroughly before booking the tour.)

But in any case, the circus isn't what anyone came to see. As with so many things connected to rock these days, the kids know and accept that the circus is bogus but entertaining. Not engrossing, but a good backdrop against which to smoke dope and drop Quaaludes.

Most of all, the circus is depressing, because there isn't anything remotely rocking about it. This is nuclear family entertainment for audiences used to nuclear explosion performances. The only thing that comes close to that is the finale, a demented La Chinoise.

The motorcycle high-wire act over, out walks Princess Fong. She looks thirtyish; she's about as tall as Yoko but more intriguingly proportioned. She is wearing a kimono.

Suddenly, yet with ceremonial dignity, she is yanked aloft by her two-foot pigtail. As La Chinoise is suspended from the ceiling, one has time to ponder the reality of her hair. But on the other hand, if it isn't hers— it's a wig or a fall—then what's the *wig* attached to?

It's that sense of inscrutability that makes La Chinoise so wonderfully sexy and mysterious. There's no way to tell if she's truly as beautiful as she seems, or if it is really only what amounts to "her fog, her amphetamine and her pearls."

Nevertheless, there is awe upon the crowd as she is pulled up, up, up, while a spotlight dazzles her in its glow. Thirty feet up, maybe a bit higher, La Chinoise does a kip up, then "skins the cat" and drops down so that she is again suspended "only by the hair on her head," and the real attraction begins. One by one she drops a couple of dozen varicolored kimonos that plummet below, to the arms of a waiting stagehand. And she is fully revealed, in a two-piece outfit that yet leaves much to the imagination.

La Chinoise is lowered back down, to thunderous applause, then goes back up for a cup of tea, which isn't yet in the cup. She balances the silver tray and pours the tea, without a moment's hesitation, none of the cheap near-miss/false-start theatrics of the trapeze act, none of the save-the-hit-for-last cheap shots of Free. In her own way, La Chinoise is as talented, as professional, as engrossing as the Faces.

The Faces came out, as they always do, and simply plugged in and started to blow. Rod leaned over, touched the mike and the situation immediately exploded. In less than fifteen seconds, the center section of the crowd powered its way past the guards and into the shell in front of the stage where the circus acts had performed. The cops wisely didn't make a move to stop them.

The Faces had never played Louisville before. Like many British acts, they avoided the South, the weakest American market for such music. But it didn't seem to matter, as this audience reacted as if they'd been waiting for their show for years.

The band was full on from the beginning. No shucking and jiving, no stopping to tune up, no delays. The sound was almost perfect: each instrument could be heard clearly, MacLagan's organ and Kenney Jones' powerful drumming coming through especially well, especially in light of the way those instruments have often been buried in the past.

The Faces work perfectly with Rod. It is not a mistake to say that they couldn't make it without him, I suppose, but it's also not a mistake to think that Rod couldn't make it as well as he does without the band.

Ron Wood: "At the beginning it's [husky whisper] 'C'mon, Rod.' But by the end [he chirps], 'Hey, they all got it on!' "

In the middle of the set, they're settling into a groove that could carry the show to only a middle height. Then the band breaks into the crusher. Stewart steps to the mike, allowing himself one of his rare grins and begins to sing as Wood plays the lyrical guitar introduction. "Wake up, Maggie, I think I . . ." Rod sings. But before the rest of the line is out of his mouth, the stage is covered with bodies. Perhaps two hundred actually make it to the apron of the stage, so that the musicians have very little room, forcing Rod to stop his Groucho walk with the mike. The uninitiated experience an intuitive fear.

"Aren't you scared?"

Wood: "Naw, man. They came but they just stayed there."

MacLagan: "They probably would get really silly, but they don't want to hurt you, they just want to be close and be part of the party."

Wood: "I did feel a few fingers on the knee last night . . ."

Even knowing how good "Maggie May" is, the live arrangement is so perfectly textured, it's arranged so beautifully, the whole dynamic of the situation is so right that it's hard to believe. Here is a dimension of interplay between "star" and band that's altogether rare. The music is skillfully made, but not tight or constricted.

The circus is malarkey next to Stewart bounding across the stage Groucho style or crooning into the the mike like an obscene parody of Bing Crosby; Wood with all the perfectly timed and casually choreographed moves of the best British guitarists; Lane tromping about like a drunken sailor. MacLagan and Jones don't do much, but they provide a backbeat that's an essential backdrop for the show.

The Faces' show is so finely tuned that it even works where once it was weakest: on the songs when Stewart hands the vocal mike to Ronnie Lane.

Lane is a good singer, but he's not Stewart, and always before, it has always seemed that his spot was designed primarily to give Rod a break. No more. His songs were always good, and his ideas about how to present them are fine. Best of all, Lane mocks himself so well you're never sure how serious he is—more than he's giving away, quite often, but never quite as much as he could be, given the quality of his songs.

Rod: "I'm not a natural songwriter . . . like Ronnie Lane [brief snicker]. Well, he is. Songs flow out of him. It's a struggle for me. I'm lucky to get one a month."

Lane: "Generally, to the layman in the street, we're always going to be Rod's backup band. But to anyone who takes a little interest, the truth will be obvious."

They're into "Losin' You" now. It is thundering just as nicely as "Maggie May," luring the kids into crawling farther and farther onto the stage, pushing more and more of them up there.

When Rod takes a breather, turns his back to the audience and gets a drink, you can see the strain. It's not a pretty sight—not quite surliness or anger, just weariness and tension.

Rod: "There's too much work . . . It's draining on the brain all the time. Fucking writing songs and getting them together . . . I don't know, maybe I'm just lazy, but it seems like too much work."

"There wasn't the pressure there before 'Maggie May' or Every Picture that there is now. If they actually want a record by a certain day, I suppose they must have it. That's the drawback—if I could finish the album when I wanted to, it'd be all right."

"Losin' You" is the "last" number, but even though it goes on for the best part of ten minutes, there's never any possibility that the show could end there. The band couldn't get out of the arena with their necks without a couple of encores.

"Is it the public?"

Rod: "No, they don't ask me when I'm gonna bring an album out. They just presume. But it's affecting me health. And there isn't any break, because we've got to start working on the group's album when this one's done."

The encore is "Stay with Me," and amazingly, it's the best number of the concert: Wood is astounding on slide guitar. At the end, Rod kicks out twenty footballs (which are actually what we call beach balls, but football's a different game in Britain). Then it's over. About an hour later, the crowd disperses. Then the band jams past what's left of the mob into a pair of limousines that carries it back to the hotel.

It's only eleven o'clock. The evening's fun has just begun.

At the hotel, everyone settles into the coffee shop. The result is less a meal than a drama. In the corner, crunched in between several others but acting removed from everyone, sits Rod Stewart, looking even more dour than usual. The rest of the band hasn't yet arrived.

As they straggle in, the coffee shop grows more and more boisterous. Orders are taken with the usual confusion of a forty-year-old waitress trying to cope with the wishes of a pack of twenty-five-year-old hippies. Dozens of cups of coffee are demanded, bunches of sandwiches, and a pair of fruit salads, because they have whole strawberries. Stewart settles for bacon and eggs.

The rest of the Faces bound in one and two at a time, surrounded by fans and groupies, if there's a distinction. Each musician strolls to a seat in a pair of back-to-back booths. The siege of the Executive Inn is on. Jeff Franklin, the Faces' booking agent, begins to toss certain items of his meal at other members of the entourage. The adjoining booth is, by the rules of rock etiquette, required to respond in kind; certain escalations are built into the deal. On and on it goes, with gleeful bellows of outrage whenever a particularly excellent or appropriate hit is scored. It's all becoming a bit messy when the proprietress steps in: *"If you boys don't stop throwing food RIGHT NOW, I'm going to make all of you clean it up yourselves!"*

"Oh, we'll stop right away, mum," assures Stewart as he sticks one of his enormous, bony-fingered hands in front of his face and tosses a bite straight into the back of MacLagan's head.

But after that it really does settle down, as though the imposition of some form of adult conscientiousness into the proceedings removes their zest. One fan says, "We got a party in room 13xx." So Lane, MacLagan, Wood and some others head up there.

The room seems hidden in the hallways of the inn. When we finally locate it, only one of the three downer-freak occupants is there, and he's asleep in bed. We're about to leave when his female partner shows up. (The third has been pulling Wood's coat sleeve all evening, while looking as if he's about to puke or pass out, babbling incoherently about how great the Faces are.)

The 'ludette opens the door of the room and we enter. From the chest of drawers she pulls one of the most massive assortments of pills I've ever seen: "Let's see . . . we got some Quaalude, some mescaline, a little acid. Anybody want some speed?"

Suddenly we notice that only four of us are present. "Hey," someone asks, "where's everyone else?"

"Oh, there are three or four guys in the bathroom," she says gleefully. "Uhhh . . . maybe you oughta look inside."

Water is seeping under the bathroom door. Ms. 'Ludes looks inside. Someone has stopped up both tub and toilet and water is pouring out. We look at one another and race from the room, giggling. "Well," one of us laughs, "I guess we know who was *there*."

Upstairs, Rod leads a pack of boys and girls around and around the second-floor corridors. He looks slightly drunken, although it might just be that he's adopted the same awkward/agile stance he uses onstage. Of the band, only Lane is with him. The others have retreated to their rooms for some rest.

Stewart doesn't look like he's having much fun. Aside from the hour or so he spent onstage, he has smiled only once or twice all evening, opened up verbally only when he was given pictures of himself performing with former Temptation David Ruffin.

In front of the elevator is a colonial credenza. Stewart half stumbles over it and dumps it over and it clatters to the floor. Suddenly the elevator doors open and three huge cops emerge. "Y'all better just get on back to yer rooms. And if you ain't registahed, ya better git *out*."

Jeff Franklin pulls the sheriff over to the side. "Listen, if you arrest Rod [who has been giving him some lip], these kids are gonna take this place apart. Now, we'll get everyone out of the hotel and you don't need to worry anymore."

And that makes it a night.

The next day, the Faces and I talk while they prepare to get on a plane heading even farther south. The band is jovial, even the abnormally reticent Kenney Jones climbing up to a ledge near the ceiling to shoot some photos. (Kenney, the rest of the band claim, "doesn't know what city he's in until the day after we get there. He doesn't like to travel.")

Everyone turns up but Rod. We go through all the motions of the interview, but it's not enough to meet expectations.

Oddly, it was Rod and the group's management who had made such a big deal of the group being included in all the stories about Stewart. Maybe because of his involvement with the ill-fated Jeff Beck Group, which died in a clash of egos, or maybe just instinctively, Stewart knows he needs this band.

He's not well equipped for stardom. We talked for a while a little later in the day, but he seemed more depressed and moody than any other time I've ever seen him.

As an afterthought, I asked about his marriage. "I'm not." How'd the rumors get started? "Probably because I got engaged . . . Don't know why the fuck I did that."

The rest of the band are sympathetic. Lane offers, "He probably feels more responsibility if the show's going wrong than, say, I would. I'd probably just turn around and say, 'Oh, fuck it,' you know."

It's that sort of drive that has made Rod Stewart one of the biggest rock stars of the moment. But it's also the kind of thing that's driving him crazy.

On the way to the airport, he stared out the window of his limousine.

"Well, would you prefer that it just were . . . over?"

A long pause. He sucked in his breath and then almost exploded: *"No. Christ, no."*

Creem, 1972

The Faces did hold together, largely thanks to their hit with "Stay with Me." And while Stewart's follow-up album didn't contain another "Maggie May," "You Wear It Well" did make No. 13.

Yet the Faces were already beginning to disintegrate. The sordid high life depicted in this story and Stewart's complete usurpation of the spotlight drove Ronnie Lane from the group by the end of 1973. In late 1974, Ron Wood began playing with the Rolling Stones, and though he returned for one last tour with Faces late the next year, Stewart, then going Hollywood in a big way through his lover, Britt Eklund, was clearly ready to move along. His solo success in late 1976 with "Tonight's the Night" sealed his move to a completely solo career.

These partings were bitter. Though no one seemed angry with the ever-chipper Wood for teaming up with his crony and idol Keith Richards and the Stones, the rest of the group very much resented Stewart's success and what were interpreted as his lordly airs. In the beginning the Faces had perhaps the greatest camaraderie of any band I've ever been around, but by the end they were factionalized and spatting constantly.

Yet my idea that they needed one another was not as wrong as it seems at first blush. Rod Stewart, of course, is now an international sex symbol attracting the most piratical gossip columnists, thanks partly to his relationships with Eklund and Alana Hamilton, but also producing a string of increasingly trivial hits that reached its nadir with 1978's "Do Ya Think I'm Sexy," a song so sleazy that even his staunchest supporters (like me) gave up on him. By the mideighties Rod's association with the glitzy Hollywood scene had robbed him of whatever was left of his rock credibility. Nor did he seem a happy man, as his marriage to Hamilton concluded in messy, highly publicized separation. In the end, even though he played the role to the hilt, Rod Stewart really wasn't cut out for that kind of celebrity.

Ron Wood remained a Rolling Stone, and on the group's early 1980s concert dates, he made sure to include his old Faces mate, Ian MacLagan, as keyboardist. Wood apparently was cut out to be a pop star of the first magnitude, though he seemed to have aged badly by the mideighties. Mac, living quietly in Southern California, seemed content, with his wife, the former Kim Moon, and their children providing a stable domestic base from which to do occasional concert tours as a sideman while playing frequently on other people's records.

There was a brief attempt at the end of the decade to re-form the Small Faces, as the group had been known before the arrival of the tallish Stewart and Wood. But original member Steve Marriot had blown his voice out in the heavy rocking Humble Pie, and without a front man the group couldn't get off the ground a second time. Drummer Kenney Jones was left holding the bag for most of the new debts —he was able to pay them off, he later said, only when he was asked to join the Who upon the death of Keith Moon. Jones remained a member of that group until Pete Townshend announced its disbandment at Christmas 1983.

Ronnie Lane was first to leave, and briefly it seemed as if he might get away with the most of any of the old gang. He invested his earnings with the Faces in a mobile studio, which a number of his friends (notably the Who) used for their recordings, and toured England with a real Rock and Roll Circus—a traveling gypsy tent show. But a combination of tax problems and lack of a sensible support structure for experiments such as the Circus left him broke at the end of two years. At the same time, Lane's health began to deteriorate. He found that he suffered from the same degenerative muscle disease, multiple sclerosis, that had killed his mother. A few friends—notably Glyn Johns, Eric Clapton and Pete Townshend—attempted to tide him over, and Lane made some fairly desperate searches for a cure. But it wasn't until he was virtually immobilized, in late 1982, that much could be done. At the end of 1983, Eric Clapton and Wood, among others, organized an all-star British rock revue which toured both America and England to raise funds, not for Lane personally but for the treatment center that helped relieve some of his pain.

Watching the final performance of that tour inspired these thoughts. You're forgiven for noticing much aging among both subjects and author.

The importance of the Call to A.R.M.S. (Action Research for Multiple Sclerosis) benefit, which ended its American tour at Madison Square Garden December 8 and 9, was anything but immediately obvious. After all, its three principal performers—Eric Clapton, Jeff Beck and Jimmy Page—had spent the better part of a decade avoiding revelations or (to be less polite) going through the motions. In fact, the most intriguing question was how anybody had been able to persuade such a troupe of dinosaurs —including two and a half Rolling Stones, a member of the Who, two partners in the celebrated Grease Band and assorted lesser lights—to play for a Cause in the first place.

A big part of the attraction was Ronnie Lane, a musician admirable not only for the spunky way in which he has coped with MS but also for his courage in dropping out of the big-time rock rut years before that became a fashionable thing to do. But A.R.M.S. was something more and other than a tribute to Lane's personality, which has always been at least as ornery and irascible as sweet and generous. Ronnie is one of the wittier, wiser characters in rock, and his suffering has been—and will be—immense and expensive. But that's not the secret of the A.R.M.S. show, either.

The crowd's motivation, on the other hand, was easier to discern and more instructive. Again, it had little to do with Lane's music, which is hardly well known in Britain, let alone over here. (His *Rough Mix* album with Pete Townshend is the best known, and a few other solo LPs may be available on import. All contain gently rocking, folkishly insightful music that's well worth the investment.) But most of the crowd at the Garden shows was too young even to remember Ronnie's tenure in the Faces, which he quit in 1973.

The crowd went nuts, not when Lane appeared during the encores, but when Jimmy Page stuck his wan face out from behind the speakers downstage left around 10:00 P.M. The reception was as tumultuous as any ever heard for Presley or the Stones. And when Page sidled into his instrumental version of "Stairway to Heaven," it was impossible to forget that Led Zeppelin was the most wildly popular British band of the seventies. Playing his great hit, Page toyed with all sorts of ghosts —not the least those of his old band and its deceased drummer, John Bonham—and boy, did he look the part: gray as a piece of overcooked steak.

Indeed, one of the most revealing contrasts of the evening was between Page and Jeff Beck, who in the twenty years since the Yardbirds have not changed even the way their hair isn't combed, and poor Pete Townshend, shambling around backstage, looking fit but nerve-racked, a guy who's leaped aboard so many bandwagons that he seems to have forgotten who he started out to be.

There's a meaningful measure of the British idea of rock in that comparison, more so because the similarities among these guitar greats is more striking than their differences. Each in his own way has attempted to deny the passage of time as a method of attaining eternal youth. For Townshend, this has meant continually going where the young hipsters go (which is especially wearing when they're heading in multiple directions). For Page and Beck, it has meant refusing to budge very far from the habits and mannerisms of their own youth. Either way, this trio is an incarnation of the "Hope I die before I get old" ideology of British rock. (An ideology with stronger tentacles than those who call these men dinosaurs imagine. Consider the Jam's self-immolation.)

Among other things, this ideology of Youth Rampant is where the silly concept that rock is meaningful only to the young commences. In essence, it's a denial of aging and death. And it's possible to argue that it has been maintained for so long because the central community of British rock— the stars themselves—has yet to face an adult death. British rock performers don't ever die at work or in plane crashes on the way to work. They expire in sports car wrecks and swimming pools, are electrocuted in the bath, dope or drink themselves to death. No one has yet had to watch a patriarchal figure like Muddy Waters go down from the simple ravages of time. There is a difference in these modes of dying, even in the observing of them.

But Ronnie Lane's death will not be a glamorous shock, and no one will be able to write it off as the product of prolonged adolescent indulgence, either. Most likely Ronnie Lane will die at the hand of a cruel disease. As everyone who watched him proceed to the mike at the Garden now knows, it already makes his every movement agonizing. On that stage, the performers were working for A.R.M.S. and for their mate, but I think many were also coming to terms, for the first time in their own work, with the true awfulness of dying, with the fact that they themselves are growing old.

So it makes sense that the pointmen of this expedition were Ronnie Lane and Eric Clapton, the two British rock musicians who *have* come to some kind of terms with death. Clapton was fixated upon it from the beginning—it was the source of the terror he loved in Robert Johnson's voice. In one sense, Clapton has let the knowledge that there's no escape turn him into a British Boz Scaggs, wearing beautiful silk suits and singing tailored humbuggery like "Wonderful Tonight." But no Clapton show can ever be without its bit of blues, and when he turned it on that night, with a fine rendition of Muddy's "Sad Day," he showed that he has forgotten nothing.

Ronnie Lane's music has been suffused with melancholy and mortality since his latter days with the Faces. (It could be one reason he had to quit that high-spirited group.) Certainly, knowledge of death infects all of the songs on *Rough Mix*, made when he already was partly incapacitated by MS. Like Townshend, Lane is a follower of Meher Baba, and his religiosity, rather than driving him into deep conservatism as it has with too many of his peers, seems to have sparked a generous, humble acceptance that strikes me as absolutely ancient.

And so it was that, even as Ronnie was making me cry with the last two songs he may ever sing on a stage, his own "April Fool" and Leadbelly's "Goodnight, Irene," I was hearing another tune in the back of my head. It was "Annie," the one he and Clapton wrote together for *Rough Mix*, and it is of course a meditation on eternity and death. That is, it's a prayer and I leave you with its last, most shining verse, not only as a tribute to the great spirit of Ronnie Lane, but in that very spirit:

Hear the children, they call, Annie,
Every leaf must fall, Annie,
God bless us all, Annie,
Wherever we'll be.

Record, 1984

Gary Glitter:
Garbage Rock Comes of Age

In a way, this piece seems a strange prophecy of the future as promised and, sadly, delivered by MTV. In the rush of amazement that televised rock has been commercially successful in the United States in the early eighties, the role that TV has long played in creating British and other European pop stars has too often been ignored.

Also ignored, of course, is the absolutely unwholesome exploitation these video stars represent. There is little difference between Gary Glitter and Duran Duran, in my estimation, save that Glitter's clunky sexuality was perceived as unthreatening while Duran Duran's exotica strikes a later, perhaps more cosmopolitan generation as enticing (but still, not dangerous). Cute and cuddly boys are always a prime commodity at one end of the rock spectrum. Not surprisingly, Glitter made a comeback attempt at the end of the early eighties British mini-invasion.

When the curtain comes up, the band are already there, pumping out a fuzzy, semi-atonal, rhythmically confused version of left-field fifties music. They're swathed in silver lamé, sparkling against hot white super-troopers, lights designed for stardom. There are six of them, guitar, bass, drums, keyboard, two horns. The crowd—which inhabits the space between Jethro Tull sophisticates and not quite Slade teen footballers—is berserk, mostly with impatience.

The guitar punches into one more chorus of the dog-eared riff, and then the white light goes blue. The glitter curtain parts ever so slightly, and down a Bette Davis staircase comes a figure out of a rock fantasy. Trussed in a black cape, with two orange feathers sticking up like the wings of an angel, Gary Glitter is an imposing if ridiculous figure. He looks like a vaudeville mortician.

Glitter's act is pure TV, a bopper fantasy without parallel. "He only does everything David Bowie would do if he thought it would make him successful," says the friend sitting next to me at London's Palladium. And it's true. Gary Glitter carries everything just a little bit further; even his name trudges the boundaries of the blatant.

Unlike Elvis, who hands his cape to an aide as though expecting the imminent announcement of his own coronation, Glitter tosses both cape and feathers to hordes of juvenile girls (few boys, surprisingly enough for bottom-level glam-rock). Gary Glitter's relationship to the King is just that: the same thing, only tackier. Where Elvis does cornball send-ups of his rock and roll hits as an act of patrician humility, Gary Glitter does lousy, puerile versions of fifties rock hits because he—or his management or someone—knows it doesn't matter. Grace, coordination, even talent are superfluous; the essence is the star. Not even the persona of the star, particularly, just the star. Ready made for a TV-bred crowd of eight- to sixteen-year-olds who don't remember Elvis or Little Richard and don't care about David Bowie. ("Too intellectual," I'm sure, and that's fair enough.)

Gary Glitter does remember, of course, because he is neither eight nor sixteen. He is probably about thirty-five, though he claims to be twenty-eight. Does it matter? "I look pretty young, but I'm just backdated," as the man says. I'm twenty-two, but tonight I feel forty.

Once the cape comes off, Glitter stands in a silver-spangled lamé jumpsuit unbuttoned at the chest, three-inch clog-soled shoes, arms outstretched as if to boast about his paunch. He dances with a certain lack of rhythm that's found only in those who want to be rock stars with true desperation. His vocal range is something less than a single note, one that croaks and wobbles on its way to the PA, then is further distorted until it amounts to something like a song. Not really music, maybe, but who cares?

Sophisticates in Britain are starting to like Slade. The line is that they're good musicians, and it may well prove the downfall of the Wolverhampton shredders, just as similar acceptance by the rock intelligentsia did in Grand Funk. For once admitted into the realm of the aesthetically acceptable, what good is a rock and roll star, anyway? This is especially true of teen stars, as both Glitter and Slade seem to be. There is nothing more boring than your younger brother's favorite rock star—except your older brother's favorite rock star.

Meantime, Glitter has raised his arms out in something approaching a parody of crucifixion, thrown back his head and in a semi-stifled snort/ shout hollered: "Do yer wann' *touch* me?" A lone pair of knickers—that's British for female undergarments—floats up to the stage in response, while three hundred screaming weenyboppers attempt to perform the suggested act by leaning, squealing, over the orchestra pit.

Behind me, two eight-year-olds, faces and hair covered in testimonial glitter, are berserk. In all other directions, there is exhilaration and ecstasy. Glitter is churning out tunes now, like a Rube Goldberg parody of a rock star. Wind him up and his audience wets its pants. I love it—with some reservations.

Gary Glitter raises the demon inside me which longs to become a manager, producer or some similar Svengali. What you could do with Glitter in the U.S.! Put him on teen dance shows coast to coast, cover him in glitter and rush him through the streets, maybe even add him to a soap opera. Accentuate the zomboid.

"Rock and Roll Part Two," which is Gary's only American hit (he's had others in Britain), sounds like lobotomized Yardbirds. It was too good to be true when he turned out to be the harbinger of a look halfway between two of my favorite movies, *Privilege* and *Creation of the Humanoids*. In the former, a P.J. Proby style rock star, who performs in a cage, sings in a sadistic whine and finally beats the shit out of the tormentors—in the seats and backstage, too—who have made him the vile object he now is. In the end, he becomes a Christian leader. The part was played—well, I think—by Paul Jones, Manfred Mann's original lead singer.

Creation of the Humanoids is Andy Warhol's favorite movie, and Gary Glitter might like it, too, since he is living proof that a society of totally mechanized humans is not only viable but probably just around the corner. Put two bolts in the sides of Glitter's neck and paint a flat landscape on the backdrop and you'd think you were watching a pop music animation of the Munsters.

All I can say afterwards is that he must be incredible on TV. Glitter goes the Monkees one better. Not only is he the totally manufactured star, but his *entire life* is an updated situation comedy satyricon. In the middle of an interview with members of an American press junket—flown over to witness his London triumph at the Palladium, the cornerstone of England's music hall tradition—in walks his MOTHER! She is tiny, gray, eighty. She has seen the slightly androgynous concert. She crooks her finger. "I want to talk to you." Later, we find out that she thoroughly enjoyed the program. Just wanted a few minutes alone with the boy.

Glitter fielded the most absurd questions with ease, stumbling over only those which were a bit too American. "Is there any place you'd draw the line . . . to satisfy your audience?" I blurted at one point. Glitter looked as if I was from Mars.

He does a better fuck scene with the guitarist than David Bowie. He's more crassly huggable than Marc Bolan. More good times ("Let's watch some football after the show!") than Slade. More rock and roll loving than the Beatles. More *sincere* than Cliff Richard. Less subtle than even the Rolling Stones.

It's just that he's terrible. Not the worst act I've ever seen, certainly not the worst musician. He's just awful. It'd be funny even if you didn't know that the audience doesn't know, even if you didn't suspect that Glitter himself doesn't know.

Creem, 1973

Frampton: Packaging Pays Off

Here's a bit of cynical, altogether accurate theorizing on one of the more pathetic cases of seventies rock stardom. Peter Frampton was talented—he was a fine guitarist, if not much of a songwriter, and not more lacking in ideas than any other pop face of his time. He was also cute, and this misled a manager hungry for Hollywood into thinking Peter was capable of becoming a matinee idol.

Ultimately that means that Frampton was twice cursed by the processes of fame. First, in order for Frampton to become successful, more emphasis was placed upon his visage than his skills. And then, because the movies are big-time and rock and roll is supposed to be lowlife, he was forced out of playing music at all and flung into one of the worst movies of all time. How would you like to have played the lead in Sgt. Pepper's Lonely Hearts Club Band, *the emptiest pop spectacle ever created?*

Exaggerated commercialism and the attendant media furor dealt one blow to his credibility; the movies finished him off. He re-

*mains at best an object lesson in how talent is squandered in the
modern world.*

Nearly six million people have purchased *Frampton Comes Alive!*, a two-
record album of substantially the same performance Peter Frampton gave
at the three nights of shows he recently performed at Madison Square
Garden. I'd like to speak to those who haven't succumbed to his wiles, if
either of you is interested.

Frampton's two-hour-plus show is divided into discrete acoustic and
electric segments. The material is drawn exclusively from his four studio
albums, with the exception of a few new acoustic numbers and a couple
of borrowings from other artists: Junior Walker's "Roadrunner," done in
medley with Stevie Wonder's "Signed, Sealed, Delivered, I'm Yours."
Frampton's musical showstopper is "Show Me the Way," in which he
plays his guitar through a voice-bag device, which Stevie Wonder pioneered and which sounds a little more human than the standard wa-wa
pedal. The most effective showstopper, and the one really worthwhile
moment not included on the LP, comes when Frampton removes his shirt
and straps an electric guitar over the resultant bare chest. The house went
nuts at this and various other appropriate moments throughout the show.

What's really curious is the success of Frampton and his album, which
is now the biggest-selling live album and the biggest-selling double album
in history.

Frampton is neither an excellent melodist nor an exceptional lyricist; his
guitar work is competent but no more; his showmanship is equally unex-
ceptional. He is perhaps preternaturally cute, but judging from the Garden
crowd, he's not playing exclusively for teenage women. On the other hand,
he has no glaring flaws in any of these areas.

Like no other rock star before him, Frampton's appeal frustrates analysis. If his stardom were of the dimensions of, say, Deep Purple's—nice
competent nonentity—this would be bearable. But the magnitude of his
success, both live and on record, begs for explanation.

If there is an answer, it most likely lies in market engineering. Frampton's career is a triumph of the packaging formula record companies,
booking agents and managers have developed since Cream. It's no accident that his booking agent, Frank Barsalona, developed Led Zeppelin and
the Who and most of the other heavyweight English acts of the late sixties,
nor that Frampton's personal manager, Dee Anthony, developed Emerson, Lake and Palmer, Joe Cocker, Ten Years After and Humble
Pie.

Indeed, if there's anything about Frampton which is extraordinary, it is his sheer diligence: it could almost be argued that every show he worked in four years of solid touring has paid off in a specific number of album sales. Here's a formula act to beat all the rest, and make the Harvard School of Business happy.

The shows did nothing to dissuade anyone from such notions. Although Frampton took a vacation at last this summer, his fans continue to adore him, though he is hardly liable to incite them to anything more daring than further album purchases. Befuddled, most media insiders offer only wisecracks, none of them illuminating. But then, in a rare moment of near eloquence, Frampton explains himself more than adequately:

> It don't matter, it don't matter
> I gotta home, I gotta eat
>
> *Rolling Stone*, 1976

Sly and the Family Stone

After more than a decade, the image remains indelible. Sly and the Family Stone are onstage, slamming out their music in all their leather, plumed velvet and satin finery. Sly himself is at the piano, fist pounding the air, shouting "I want to take you . . . HIGHER!" The audience responds with an affirmation of his command. The music explodes; the sweeping rhythms of voice and band pull the energy together. It's not quite soul, not quite rock and roll, but an epiphanous ritual that operates on its own terms. Nobody's thinking, everybody's grooving: pure exhilaration or seminal fascism in action, depending on where you sit. Maybe a line from Jimi Hendrix describes it best. "Is this love, baby, or is it, uh . . . con-*fu*-sion?"

For a while, anyway, Sly Stone was one of the greatest musical adventurers rock has ever known. Almost single-handedly he effected a revolution in soul music, one whose consequences reverberate everywhere today. With his band, Sly ended the domination of the sweet soul sound practiced by the Stax, Motown and Muscle Shoals rhythm sections. Eighteen months after "Dance to the Music," his first hit in 1968, everyone was following his lead. And the bulk of today's disco and funk rock simply works off variations of Sly and the Family Stone's innovations. No one has gone past them.

What Sly had done was so simple that it might have occurred to almost any black kid living in the late sixties in San Francisco. The antinomian spirit of R&B—recklessness personified—was grafted onto the close-knit, deliberately paced rock-band experience; the musical wildness of the rock band then was wedded to the utter discipline of the soul group. And the Family Stone's sound was totally integrated, not just musically, but sexually and racially—here was a band in which men and women, black and white, had not one fixed role but many fluid ones. The women played, the men sang; the blacks freaked out, the whites got funky; everyone did something unexpected, and that was the only thing the listener could expect. The result might have been only the heap of contradictions the description suggests, had Sly's talent not been equally unpredictable. As it was, the band lived up to the proud boast of its first album title: *A Whole New Thing*.

Before him, soul records had been conceived as vocal vehicles; even the often brilliant playing of a group like Booker T. and the MGs was merely supportive. Rock bands changed that: in San Francisco music, the vocals were often an afterthought. "Dance to the Music" pulverized those polarities by joining them not calmly but brutally: the voice and the music didn't achieve equality, they fought it out for space, right on the disc. The exhortation of the title may have been the whole message to many who bought it. But others listened more closely, and what they heard spelled the doom of American R&B's formal stasis.

The impresario of this barely contained cacophony was one Sylvester Stewart, born in Texas, bred a tough street fighter in Vallejo, a factory town on the wrong side of San Francisco Bay. A music theory course in high school inspired him, and he hooked up with local DJ Tom Donahue, then running Autumn Records. For Autumn, Sly produced some of the first Bay Area rock and roll records: local, regional and finally national hits for bands like the Mojo Men, the Vejtables and the Beau Brummels. When the acid rock gang itself moved in, Sly moved out—he tried to cut Grace Slick and the Great Society and wound up with one song in two hundred-odd takes.

He went to work for one of the area's black radio stations. As usual Sly did things differently, interrupting the flow of Stax and Motown singles with Beatles and Dylan tracks, fidgeting with commercials, raising the call-in dedication to a minor art form. In his off-hours, he had a band working in bars—the nucleus of Sly and the Family Stone. It ultimately included his brother Freddie, Jerry Martini, Jerry's cousin, Greg Errico, Sly's sister, Rose, Cynthia Robinson and Larry Graham.

The pop scene was at a turning point. Both soul and rock were trapped —the former by its own conventions, the latter by its increasing solemnity as it pursued High Art. Sensing a gap, Sly moved to fill it with his characteristic mixture of calculation, conviction and dumb luck. He made his music with the assurance of a man whose vision requires a new mode of expression. In the songs that followed "Dance to the Music," he toyed with everything from free-form doo-wop ("Hot Fun in the Summertime") to the stylized chanting ("Sing a Simple Song," "Stand!") that would be adopted by funk groups.

But Sly was also a philosopher, preaching a message of total reconciliation that lived up to the big sound. "Everyday People," "Everybody Is a Star," "Life," "I Want to Take You Higher" and "You Can Make It If You Try"—most of them hits—expressed as well as anything the sentiments of the Haight and the hopes of the ghetto. For a time, it seemed, Sly's approach could heal all wounds; offer black kids a model for something other than slick, Copacabana-level success; give whites a fairly wholesome black star; produce for both a meeting ground where they could work out their mistrust.

In the best songs, Sly promised to work it out for them. "Everyday People" contributed mightily to the hip lexicon—"different strokes for different folks" was Sly's whole ideology—but it was also a taunt and a proclamation. Nobody who heard that record could disbelieve Sly's power; he might actually turn a triumph of integration once again.

But even in a time when a good share of the rock population was flaky enough to believe in chemical salvation, Sly's utopianism couldn't triumph. The first symptom of trouble was his own increasing eccentricity. Then Sly started to blow gigs; half the thrill of buying a ticket became the anticipation of whether he would really show. Usually he did, but he missed enough dates—generally without any announcement until after the seats of an arena were filled—to earn a reputation for irresponsibility.

At Woodstock, only eighteen months from the beginning, the dark underside of his vision began to catch up. "Higher" became less a slogan of collective triumph than a means for ravishing the crowd. Otis Redding had died a year and a half earlier, and the Woodstock generation was looking for a new black hope, someone who could make race a safe issue.

With Jimi Hendrix already showing signs of resisting the role, Sly was the prime candidate.

In January 1970, Sly released the sardonic single "Thank You Falettinme Be Mice Elf Again." It was slinky, hip dance music, and no one thought much of it—the weird spelling was to be expected from such a spaced-out maverick. "I Want to Take You Higher," recycled as a single in May, was an afterthought, hardly an event. The gigs continued to be blown, while rumors of drug problems and threats from black political organizations floated around. Sly toured, canceled, recorded, failed to release. Meanwhile, no new music. It looked like the middle stage of a downward spiral. A Whole New Thing had simply petered out.

The spirit of that Thing was now dominant, however. Sly's influence had been completely absorbed into both black and white pop style, and it now coursed through the mainstream of soul. At Motown, the Jackson Five and the Temptations carried his banner; in Philadelphia, the Gamble-Huff organization was churning out Sly-derived funk pop; in Chicago, Curtis Mayfield, that sweetest of old soul singers, had made his move in the Family Stone's direction. Sly himself may have been in exile from the charts, but in the Top Hundred, his music reigned.

In November 1971, he finally released a new album, just in time for Christmas. It was less than a merry affair, however. The title was *There's a Riot Goin' On*, and the title song was precisely timed at no minutes and no seconds. That was just a clue.

The next hint lay in the revulsion felt by many listeners—particularly, it may safely be said, by white listeners. Where was the joyous, life-affirming black hero? This music stumbled, faltered, its rhythms hobbled like a heroin roller coaster, its entire tune was an affront to the spirit of the boogie. Sly had always built his songs from bits and pieces, unexpected scraps, parts zipping in (often half unformed) to *make* a song. But this sounded like the scrap heap; the connections were left unmade.

After you listened awhile, it got scary. "Feel so good / Feel so good / Don't wanna move" was what passed for exuberance on this record. It was the aural equivalent of William Burroughs' *Naked Lunch* (". . . when everyone sees what is on the end of every fork"). Those who didn't stop listening grew fascinated by the resultant chills and despair; even those who didn't want to know, though, couldn't shut them out. *Riot* had not one but three hit singles—"Family Affair," "(You Caught Me) Smilin' " and "Runnin' Away." The idea was beginning to form that maybe *There's a Riot Goin' On* was Sly's way of telling us something.

But as open as it was supposed to be, white rock society wasn't prepared for such a harsh, direct look at black experience. That audience was hardly prepared to deal with a black hero who decided to work completely on his own terms. And even if he had to create those terms from scratch, that's what Sly was doing. In effect he took the power of his stardom and shook it in every gray face. "Family Affair," the album's biggest hit, was pure bile. That three-day mud festival in Woodstock wasn't enough to make Sly forget who he had been back in Vallejo, or who he still was, without a name. In the days of Nixon's White House, Cambodian excursions and ODs all around, there wasn't much question where he discovered the blood referred to on "Family Affair," either. Greil Marcus got it right when he referred to *Riot* as "Muzak with its finger on the trigger."

Riot was perfectly timed. Maybe it ignited one of the greatest explosions of pop, or maybe it served simply as a sign that one was about to occur. In any event, the airwaves were soon filled with tough black testimony, unbending, seeking its own audience and not caring so much about the damage done to integrationist (in music biz terms, crossover) sensibilities. The Temptations scored their own experience with "Papa Was a Rolling Stone." Curtis Mayfield turned in *Superfly*, a cheap movie soundtrack that came to life on radio as one of the most searing antidrug diatribes ever written. War proclaimed that "The World Is a Ghetto" and warned against "Slippin' Into Darkness." Stevie Wonder excoriated "Superstition," caught the full misery of "Living for the City." Marvin Gaye simply asked "What's Going On?" The O'Jays railed against "Back Stabbers." There was no avoiding this music or what it had to say; every one of those songs was right there on the radio, a good many of them hitting Top Ten. You couldn't get in the car and run away from it, because the songs kept blasting through the static.

These songs had everything to do with America as it was at a time when an election was being stolen. They reflected an almost unspoken acknowledgment of a long list of sins, from the murder of Fred Hampton and thousands of Vietnamese and black GIs to crime in the streets and the everyday robbery at the grocery store, from the simple loss of friendship to the lack of any kind of emotional or moral center for most people's lives. It was the world of the sixties dream turned inside out. Sly's utopia had revealed its other face: hell. As if in proof, *Riot* ended with a reprise of "Thank You Falettinme Be Mice Elf Again." Only this time he called it, "Thank You for Talkin' to Me Africa."

The tempo now slowed to a heartbeat. Nothing but bass and drums for

the first minute, with some occasional jagged interjections from the guitar.
Then those awful freeze-frame lyrics:

> Lookin' at the devil
> Grinnin' at his gun
> Fingers start shakin'
> I begin to run
> Bullets start chasin'
> I begin to stop
> We begin to wrestle
> I was on the top

Now Sly pulled the trigger. It was torture, but torture that had been lived
out, not just fantasized.

Meanwhile, Sly had become one of the richest rock stars—perhaps the
richest black one. His contract with Epic Records provided more than
$500,000 for each album, an astronomical fee for the time. He lived in
plush Hollywood comfort—neither drugs, fast cars, women nor fancy
clothes were beyond his resources. To blow a gig, he had only to seize a
whim. Nevertheless, this is what it came down to: "We begin to wrestle / I
was on the top." No one—not even Sly—knew for how long.

Making that kind of music in the studio was one thing. Acting it out
onstage was another. In his live show, little of the *Riot* material turned
up; maybe it was too difficult for performance, but after *Riot*'s exorcism,
who could believe "Life" or "Higher" standing by themselves? And the
scars showed. The idealistic band disintegrated. Members drifted in and
out; the music faltered and fell. On his 1973 LP, *Fresh*, Sly performed the
ultimate cop-out, epitomized by his final brilliant statement: "Que Sera,
Sera" (whatever will be, will be). The music was still good, in its way
probably better than *Riot*, but it was over. "Que Sera" was a great move,
but it was also a marvelously concealed surrender. A year later, it took Sly's
onstage wedding to sell out Madison Square Garden.

By 1975, even the records had stopped coming. Sly was down and out
—who knew where? Black pop, transmuted via Europe into the big beat
dance music of disco, still hadn't gone any farther than where Sly had
taken it, but where had it taken Sly?

According to a 1976 *Jet* magazine article, he went broke; according to
rumors, Sly lived in a mansion without a telephone or much in the refriger-
ator, his money and his talent squandered. No one turned up to suggest
that such gossip was inaccurate in anything but degree.

The Rolling Stone Illustrated History of Rock and Roll, 1980

When this piece first appeared, as a chapter in the revised edition of Jim Miller's authoritative compilation of historical essays, it had an optimistic ending. Sly had just made an album for Warner Bros., Back on the Right Track, *which had enough energy—barely—to encourage my hopes of renewed musical commitment.*

It didn't work out that way. Since then, Sly has made a few records with George Clinton's troupe, surely one of the ensembles most influenced by his original ideas. And he has spiraled deeper and deeper into trouble with drugs and the law. The last I heard, he was faced with a serious likelihood of doing time on a dope charge, somewhere in the South, in 1984. That was as much as I cared to hear in the way of detail. Far better to recollect that one of the principal musical surprises of 1983 was Joan Jett's version of "Everyday People," the song Sly once told me was his favorite. (It's certainly mine.) Jett's version got played almost exclusively on black-oriented radio stations, of course, which only goes to show how much backsliding a society can do in a decade.

Bruce Springsteen's
Nebraska

American rock seemed almost completely divorced from the country's political climate when Nebraska *was released in 1982. Of course, as Orwell pointed out, even apolitical culture reflects its political bias, but the trend in 1982 was to synthpop, which meant not just music created for synthesizers but songs constructed with an emphasis upon emptiness, planned to be as devoid of social weight and emotional content as possible. Like all trends, synthpop was made to fade, but just as typically, it was symptomatic of the world outside itself. And its rise was especially dangerous because it came at a moment when rock's original black and working-class constituencies were under the most severe attacks they had faced in fifty years.*

Nebraska *flew so firmly in the face of studied shallowness and official callousness—albeit quite spontaneously, since Springsteen had planned to do no such thing—that its release seemed even more daring than it was. Given the traditional tension between critical credibility and mass appeal, the album was showered with hosannas exceptional even for American rock's most serious and celebrated mainstream star.*

Be that as it may be, Nebraska was clearly not an unmitigated success, and the lack of critical nay-saying posed its own set of problems. More than most people who analyze culture for a living, I'm mistrustful of what's right up my alley. I would far rather have rock and roll that spoke clearly and forcefully to its base audience of youth, blacks and working people than one which perfectly filled the needs of even an anti-establishment intelligentsia. And culture that presents itself as good for me has always stirred an unavoidable gag reflex.

For all of these reasons, it struck me as a good thing that Nebraska sold only about half as many copies as its predecessor, The River (800,000 to 2 million). That was enough to convince the industry that the record was a modest success, and yet it didn't make it so much of a smash that it could lead the artist or his critical coterie to believe that the experiment had plumbed a thirst for singer/songwriter folk music in the pop audience. That doesn't mean that I agree with those fans—some of them quite serious ones—who found the essential pessimism of Nebraska a betrayal of rock and roll and Springsteen's role in it. But it does mean that I'm damn glad that his next album didn't show that Bruce had become an eager eccentric after the fashion of Neil Young. Springsteen's ability to assert his right and need to make some personal, idiosyncratic statements is something to celebrate, especially since it coincides with an especially traumatic time in our country's political system. But that achievement would mean much less if in the process Springsteen lost his balance and fell, not from a state of grace neither he nor any other pop star has ever known anyway, but out of touch with the very people who lent his work meaning in the first place.

When he switched on his new four-track, Tascam cassette recorder in a bedroom of his rented Holmdel, New Jersey, home last January 3, Bruce Springsteen wasn't trying to make an album, just demos of a batch of songs written since his marathon 1980–81 tour. Springsteen was shortly due to begin rehearsals with the E Street Band before recording the followup to his first No. 1 album, *The River*.

The band would learn the songs from the solo demo tapes.

So Springsteen didn't need to worry that the straight-backed wooden chair in which he sat creaked as he swayed and sang. He wasn't concerned that a couple of songs repeated lines almost word for word; the lyrics were always the last item finished, anyway. Most of all, he relaxed as he played. With only roadie Mike Batlan, sitting in as engineer, for an audience, Springsteen let some of his extraordinary self-consciousness slip away. He didn't simply toss off the songs, though. Each number was an assured, measured performance. But the performances weren't calculated or studied. Like an artist sketching, Springsteen used the simplest implements: acoustic guitar, harmonica and occasionally, a muted electric guitar, without a reverb or fuzztone. Springsteen then put the Tascam through its paces, adding echo, a bit of synthesizer, doubling his voice in a few spots, dubbing in backing vocals in others.

Over the next few days, listening to the resulting cassette, Springsteen became more and more fascinated, not only by the songs but by his performances, too. The songs were as much of a piece as any album he had released, and the singing and playing, for all their starkness, flowed freely and elegantly, creating a mood that was intimate and uninhibited. There was something else, too, an eerie mystery that suggested the cassette had a life and will of its own. In a word, the tape sounded spooky.

Springsteen went into rehearsals and then the recording sessions, determined not to lose this quality. But such unworldly moments aren't simply repeated on command. Though the E Street Band made very good versions of some of the songs, none satisfied Bruce. The other songs he'd written were turning out fabulously, but the cassette resisted.

Through the spring, Springsteen fought with those songs. For technical reasons, the cassette would be difficult to master as an album, but he was being pulled toward doing the songs solo, nevertheless. Desperate, he even tried recording them over again, on his own but in the Power Station. Eventually, he and producer Chuck Plotkin simply determined that they would sweat out whatever it took to master the original cassette. Over the course of a couple of months, both Springsteen and Plotkin lost a lot of sleep and frazzled their nerves, but in a way, that just made the process seem more akin to the famous struggles that had resulted before the release of Springsteen's other albums. At any rate, by early August they'd won, with a master disc that kept the sound of the cassette and steadied the stylus in the grooves. Called it *Nebraska*.

That's one story to tell about the album. There's another version of the events leading up to *Nebraska* that also begs recounting, however.

In October 1980, when *The River* was released and his last tour began, Bruce Springsteen played to an enormous cult audience. This audience believed intensely in the transformative powers of a Springsteen performance. As a result, through his previous tours, a kind of compact was created between Bruce and his listeners. He would give them epic sagas of rock and roll grandeur, replete with power and glory, joy and despair, endless struggle and instant party. They would grant him complete attentiveness and a virtually insatiable desire for more, pushing not greedily so much as reflexively, keeping the faith the songs expressed, surfing the waves of the music. "The amount of freedom that I get from the crowd is really a lot," said Springsteen after a month on the road. He was especially fond of what he referred to as "the big silence," the contemplative stillness that greeted his quieter, more reflective pieces.

A month later, with "Hungry Heart" about to become his first Top Ten single, Springsteen faced a far different audience, no less enthusiastic but a great deal more casual about attending his shows. This was fitting and necessary; the ritualized cultism by itself was a dead end for an artist with Springsteen's broad ambition. And when it came to rocking out, the new audiences were amazing, quickly caught up in the rapturous E Street environment.

Nevertheless, the newer and larger audience diluted the depth of the rapport, which was especially noticeable in the restlessness with which Springsteen's slower, quieter songs were greeted. Caught in the exhilaration of the situation, nobody was complaining, though a few observers grew wary of whether even Springsteen could control his massive new audience.

In the spring of 1981, Springsteen and the E Street Band began their first full-scale European tour. Bruce was greeted as a rock and roll emissary whose mission was nothing less than the dissemination of the American dream, and he was given all the respect and devotion that went along with it.

Early in each evening's show, Springsteen would request that the audience maintain silence during the softer passages of the show. The result was as stunning as anything I've ever seen. When Springsteen offered a spoken introduction, sang a ballad or the nightly version of "This Land Is Your Land," the crowd became dead still. But this silence had a special quality—it was vibrant, electric and intense, broken, if at all, only by the soft murmur of friends who spoke English offering quick translations for others nearby. On especially good nights, I felt I could *hear* people listening. Their deep concentration hung tangibly in the air, and when Springsteen roared back into a rocker like "Badlands," the mood broke like a superb wave. Bruce rode it that way.

Meanwhile, back in the States, Springsteen's audience grew even younger and less sensitive to any kind of interchange with the star. It became more and more evident that Springsteen's listeners were beginning to hem him in, as every superstar's audience has hemmed him or her in. Reviewers mentioned this, wondering about how Springsteen would cope; long-time fans grew disgruntled as the newcomers stomped and clapped through "Independence Day" and "Point Blank," ostensibly in tribute but really asserting their impatience to get on with the rocking.

I don't know if this decreasing sense of rapport frustrated Bruce; it would be amazing if it hadn't disturbed him somehow. In any case, it seems certain that if he'd released another hard-rock record as the sequel to *The River*, that newer, more casual audience might have buried any possibility of regaining the special relationship his best concerts created. Those shows were genuinely two-way affairs, as all great rock shows must be; the new audiences weren't passive—they were demanding entertainment in the slow passages—but they weren't willing to work for their pleasure, either.

At the very least, *Nebraska* will tax the attention of such listeners. While I doubt that this had much to do with why Bruce Springsteen made this album, reclaiming his rapport with his listeners is one of *Nebraska*'s most important functions.

There's yet another reason to tell this tale. In some of *Nebraska*'s best songs—"Used Cars," "Highway Patrolman," "Mansion on the Hill"— Springsteen recaptures the hushed intimacy of those European concerts. Indeed, from time to time, these songs seem to have blossomed from the echoes of those vibrant silences.

Ten years ago, when Bruce Springsteen made his first album, Columbia Records and his manager/producer, Mike Appel, tried to force him into a mold: Springsteen was to be the "new Dylan," the apotheosis of the singer/songwriter. A largely acoustic solo set was what Appel and Columbia's John Hammond wanted and expected. So it's tempting to say that with the largely acoustic solo *Nebraska*, Bruce finally has his "Dylan" album.

But this isn't singer/songwriter music, any more than it is rock and roll. Nor is it folk music, despite the acoustic instrumentation. The chords and melodies from which Springsteen builds his songs are pop and rock rudiments. It's the coloration and phrasing that have changed. In the way his

guitar playing sometimes suggests a mandolin or his vocals recall Jimmie
Rodgers' yodeling or the cadences of white gospel singers, Springsteen,
rock's greatest synthesist of traditions, hints at an ability to incorporate,
for the first time in his music, genres older than rock and roll or rhythm
and blues. All of his resources, however, remain rooted in specifically
American styles: this provides an undeniable link to Dylan's best work, but
that doesn't make *Nebraska* neo-Dylan, unless you'd say that of *Willie and
the Poor Boys,* too.

Dylan's influence can be heard here, especially in the extended, sighing
"all" that links the last line of "Used Cars" to Dylan's first great song,
"Song to Woody." That's fitting, for if Dylan is the father of such a
musical approach, its grandfathers are Woody Guthrie and Hank Williams. Nor does it take an expert to trace this lineage to *Nebraska.* But
rooting about for antecedents gets you only so far, for more than anything
Nebraska is Bruce Springsteen himself, speaking more directly and more
personally than ever before.

Once you're past the shock of hearing Springsteen play and sing with
such stark assurance, *Nebraska* clearly works familiar territory. It has the
cars, the highways, the guilt and quest for redemption, and most importantly, many of the characters from Springsteen's other work. Joe Roberts,
the protagonist of "Highway Patrolman," is a more mature relation of the
men in "Racing in the Street," "The River" and "Born to Run." The
nameless narrator of "Atlantic City" might be reliving "Meeting Across
the River," and the anonymous wild man of "State Trooper" and "Open
All Night" is virtually indistinguishable from the hopeless romantics of
"Stolen Car" and "Ramrod." And who is Mary Lou but the girl whose
dress waves early in "Thunder Road"? Isn't the dreamer of "My Father's
House" the man whose other nightmares are recounted in "Darkness on
the Edge of Town" and "Wreck on the Highway"?

But there's someone missing from the cast, or rather, someone who is
almost unrecognizable here: the exuberantly hopeful singer of "Badlands"
and "The Promised Land," "Hungry Heart" and "Thunder Road." If that
man is here, his presence is stunted and twisted, stripped of the desperate
joy that is fundamental to his earlier incarnations.

This measures the degree to which Springsteen's world has changed.
Springsteen's first two rock and roll albums opened with proclamations of
vitality: "It ain't no sin to be glad you're alive" ("Badlands"); "This is a
town full of losers, I'm pullin' outta here to win" ("Thunder Road"). In
two of the first four songs on *Nebraska,* men virtually beg to be executed.
And in this album's most heartbreaking moment, the protagonist of "Used
Cars," a decent kid embittered by poverty, sings of a town full of losers

in which no one has even the hope of pulling away: "My dad sweats the same job from mornin' to morn / Me, I walk home on the same dirty streets where I was born."

In this world, someone like the highway patrolman Joe Roberts, the most beautifully drawn character Springsteen has ever created, may obey his most decent instincts and still find that he has betrayed himself. In this world, there are "debts no honest man could pay"—owed not by one man, but by many men. There is not just the scarcity of work found in *The River;* "they closed down the auto plant in Mahwah," and it stays shut. Bosses run wild over workers, and while one class hides behind "gates of hardened steel," the other works the night shift for punishment. In this land, it's no wonder that men can become as twisted as those in "Johnny 99," "Atlantic City" and most of all, "Nebraska."

The tragedy is that this world is recognizable; it is the land we now live in, the society being created by Reaganomics and neoconservatism. *Nebraska* is the first album by an American performer to come to terms with this political and emotional climate, in which mass murderer Charlie Starkweather's "meanness in the world" is unleashed and made a central tenet of the way human beings are expected to deal with one another.

In this climate, people go mad—not only crazy, but vicious. Nothing remains to check their casual cruelty, and even someone like Joe Roberts, a stolid center of gravity, can't keep his world from falling apart. In the face of this mean reality, hope, faith, the possibility of redemption—the very engines that have always propelled Springsteen's music—seem nothing less than absurd. In "Atlantic City," the singer toys with the idea of reincarnation as a signal that he'll soon be able to test its truth; in "Reason to Believe," the album's final song, the idea of a life after death is seen as no more ridiculous than the idea that people will treat one another with decency in this one.

In his European shows, Springsteen would sometimes sing an Elvis Presley song. He chose "Follow That Dream," writing a new verse that expressed his faith in an American possibility Elvis personified:

> Now every man has the right to live
> The right to a chance to give what he has to give
> The right to fight for the things he believes
> For the things that come to him in dreams

In many ways, Springsteen's life and career can be seen as an acting out of those lines, an unswerving attempt to put that faith into action.

In *Nebraska*'s final two songs, "My Father's House" and "Reason to Believe," Springsteen finally confronts the possibility that his faith will never be effective, that his idealism is in fact a view of the world turned upside down. "My Father's House," a song that moves with the ancient cadences of myth, is as fully realized as any song Springsteen has ever written. But its dream of reconciliation between father and son is ultimately hollow, and while this dream (which incorporates psychological, political and religious symbols) continues to beckon, at the end Springsteen just acknowledges that "our sins lie unatoned," something that not only has never occurred in Springsteen's other work but isn't even conceivable in most of it.

Cast so far from grace, the very fact that men continue to rise from their beds comes to seem wondrous and bizarre. "Reason to Believe," on which the album closes, is far from the upbeat, optimistic ending a superficial reading might suggest. Indeed, its title is a macabre joke, since the song is really a series of situations in which faith is all but impossible—situations in which believing may finally be inconsequential. And while Springsteen brings himself to accept that men (including he himself, he hints) do believe, he is unable to fathom *why*.

The quandary in which this leaves Springsteen isn't strictly personal. *Nebraska* is an album that speaks to a broad section of his audience not only through its images of unemployment and economic despair but also through the vehicle of radical doubt itself. However accidentally constructed, its parts are integrated in such an invigorating and complex way that it has the ability of important works to seize an entire historical moment. If all Bruce Springsteen had done in this album was "grow up" enough to question the remainder of his innocence, that would be an achievement, since most artists never get that far. But in asking such questions, he forces them upon his listeners, too.

There's no way of knowing how many will hear what *Nebraska* has to say. One of the functions of the political climate now being created is to sap people of their energy to respond, and since Springsteen is also wrestling with the preconceptions of his audience and, inevitably, the death-grip conservatism of the marketplace, the odds aren't exactly stacked in his favor. The tragedy is that too many—fans, DJs, critics—may not recall how to respond, may already have surrendered to the erosion of possibility and hope that *Nebraska* so eloquently depicts.

But grim as it is, *Nebraska* suggests to me a kind of hope. If in our dark, heartless land there is room for work this personal and challenging, then the battles are still being fought. And while that may be an insufficient response, it is one hell of a significant start.

Yet *Nebraska* continues to seem spooky, not only because it is invested with musical magic but also because these songs are inhabited by the ghost of a time when we knew very well how to respond. The most imposing question is whether the spirit represented by those ghosts can be made manifest once more. Toward that end, too, *Nebraska* is a start.

Record, 1982

3

Beyond the Fringe

Introduction

The music and musicians in these pieces are linked by their relationship to the cornucopia of American popular music. In one way or another, all of them have been overlooked, if not as celebrities, then as artists. That is, even such famous singers and players as Elvis Presley and Muddy Waters have only rarely had the true dimensions of their achievements described.

To outsiders, the music business, like any other form of show business, must seem pleasant, glamorous and infinitely rewarding on every material and psychological level. Compared to most jobs, it is often exactly that. But not always. James Jamerson, for instance, went to the grave resentful that his beautiful, groundbreaking playing had never given him even a few moments of glory. And Jamerson wasn't wrong —or alone.

American popular music has generally been culturally despised. It is only in the past half century that its achievements, having been finally and properly preserved in recordings, have been recognized for their creative merit. A few players and composers (Armstrong, Ellington and Basie, most prominently) have now been acknowledged, but the bulk of the artists creating in the American folk-based pop tradition remain unsung. And this is as true of Elvis Presley the singer as of James Jamerson. That Elvis was not just a star—that his music was not only exciting but significant—is a fact that will eventually be recognized. But like James Jamerson, those who are already aware can become exasperated waiting for the rest of the world to catch up.

From that exasperation, this chapter has been constructed. Because the historical development of American pop is also unrecognized, this is the single chapter in *Fortunate Son* in which the pieces are not arranged in the order in which they were written. Instead, the organization reflects the relative emergence of each performer and style into the pop mix. Because James Jamerson remains unsung even now, he remains last, though by no means least significant.

Muddy Waters, 1915–1983:
Let's Say He Was a Gentleman

Muddy Waters was my favorite of all the bluesmen who were perform-
ing as my musical taste developed. But more than that, he ranks
alongside Robert Johnson as the most singular and complete practi-
tioners of the bluesman's art. Among the American musicians of the
twentieth century, Muddy stands with such founding fathers as Louis
Armstrong, Bill Monroe, Elvis Presley, Reverend Thomas Dorsey,
Jimmie Rodgers, Charlie Parker and not too damn many more.
Muddy's use of wild roadhouse music to create statements character-
ized by the most complete and bottomless dignity personifies the best
use to which American music has been put. He remains for me one
of the benchmarks against which all else is measured.

It's all but impossible to concisely summarize Muddy Waters' achievements, much less get a handle on mourning him. If Muddy were merely
the first of the great Chicago bluesmen (which he was), he would be an
important figure in American music. That he was also the last great Delta
bluesman begins to give you a sense of dimensions. But he was so much
more: a fine songwriter, magnificent singer, marvelous bottleneck guitarist,
unparalleled bandleader, astute talent scout, generous and inspiring father
figure. In short, he had such clarity of vision, sheer talent and unshakable
self-possession that he galvanized everything around him. As an influential
master musician in postwar America, he ranks with Hank Williams, Elvis
Presley and Miles Davis.

It's a mammoth task just to list the greatest of Muddy's songs: "Louisi-
ana Blues," "I'm Ready," "I'm Your Hoochie Coochie Man," "I Just
Wanna Make Love to You," "Standin' Around Crying," "Rolling Stone,"
"Long Distance Call," "Rolling and Tumbling," "I Can't Be Satisfied,"
"Mannish Boy," "Got My Moho Working," "Baby Please Don't Go," "I
Feel Like Going Home," "She's All Right," "Sad Letter." Certainly any
list of classic postwar blues songs and performances would include more
than a few of these.

The list of those musicians to whom Muddy gave a start is also volumi-
nous, starting with Little Walter and Otis Spann, his two greatest disci-

ples, and continuing with Jimmie Rodgers, Big Walter Horton, Junior Wells, Buddy Guy, Fred Below, James Cotton, Francis Clay, Big Crawford, Elgar Edmonds, Pinetop Perkins, Sammy Lawhorn and continuing almost endlessly. Muddy wasn't above engaging in cutting contests, but he was also the single most generous musician in memory, offering his sidemen encouragement in their solo ambitions and bringing unknowns more attention than anyone else's endorsement could have offered. Ask Otis Rush—or for that matter Chuck Berry, who was brought to Chess Records by Muddy.

Discovering Berry was hardly the end of Muddy's impact on rock and roll. The Rolling Stones took their name, and their early sound, from his music. Surely Muddy was one of the things on Bob Dylan's mind when he made an album whose titled alluded to Highway 61, the major thoroughfare of the Mississippi Delta where Chicago blues gestated, and entitled its first and greatest track, "Like a Rolling Stone." The overpowering blues style developed by Eric Clapton, first in the Bluesbreakers, then with Cream, derived directly from the huge sound of Muddy's great fifties band—and in that sense all blues-rock and heavy metal music is descended from Muddy's ideas. Johnny Winter paid Muddy the finest homage by producing four solid albums with him in the last years of his life. The Band offered another kind of tribute in *The Last Waltz*, and typically, Muddy stole the show with his "Mannish Boy." Fleetwood Mac, the Paul Butterfield Blues Band and Jimi Hendrix all owed something to Muddy's music —and to Muddy's music specifically, not just to a generalized idea of the blues.

But none of these lists captures what the life and death of Muddy Waters really means. I'm not sure it can be defined, only described. Muddy's mere presence lent events weight and meaning. You can hear this in even his most raucous blues—"I'm Ready," for instance—where instead of spewing out the notes, each phrase and syllable and inflection and beat and chord are considered and then precisely placed. The calculated effect doesn't eliminate excitement. Instead, it creates it by establishing a specific tension between the logic of the song and what Muddy might do with it.

Creating this music required a kind of consciousness and control that's the definition of artistry. Uniquely among bluesmen, Muddy Waters was able to establish this tension to a greater and more complex degree with his band than without it. For most singers, the band has been a necessary obstacle to personal expression; but Muddy was able (from time to time but more frequently than the uninitiated will imagine) to create bands that furthered not only his personal sense of how the music ought to run but also that of the other musicians. Little Walter's personality is as fully established as Muddy's in many of these records, and later on, so is Otis Spann's. An even better indication of Muddy's sensitivity to the requirements of other players is that he was the bandleader behind both Walter's masterpiece, "Juke," and Sonny Boy Williamson's "Don't Start Me Talking."

The poles of Chicago blues were Muddy and Howlin' Wolf, the one a great and sympathetic collaborator, the other one of the most outrageous individualists in cultural history. Their styles represented different responses to the brutally racist environment in which they were reared. Understanding that because he was black, he would never have the full respect that his talent and intelligence deserved, Howlin' Wolf, the persona created by Chester Burnett, simply pissed on the very concepts of politeness and restraint. One never had the sense that there was anything Wolf wouldn't do—or, for that matter, that there was any way to get him to do anything except what he chose, however perverse his choices might be.

Muddy, on the other hand, took the cruel truths of black American life and used them to create a personality defined by a sense of limits and boundaries. There was a point beyond which he couldn't be pushed; there were *many* things Muddy would not do, which is one reason his performances were always less flamboyant than Wolf's. Like his music, Waters' identity was founded upon his creation of a world in which *he* imposed order, a world which he structured around his own needs and perceptions.

All of this is summed up in what Waters told James Rooney in the book *Bossmen.* "You don't have to have a white face to be a gentleman and up to date with what you're doing," Muddy said. "You can be black, brown or any color, but you've got to carry yourself in a way that people know that you're it. They might say I can't play or can't sing, but damn it, they'll say I was a gentleman."

His American ancestors were slaves, and after slavery, serfs—Mississippi sharecroppers, bound to the lush Delta flatlands where McKinley Morganfield was born to Bertha and Ollie Morganfield, on April 4, 1915, in Rolling Fork, Mississippi. Muddy, as he was dubbed very early for the shadowiest of reasons, moved to Clarksdale in 1918, to live with his grandmother after his mother died. There he grew up on Stovall's Plantation, drove a tractor, milked cows ("all that jive") and heard every blues performer that came to town. He particularly loved Son House, a farmer/performer from Robinsonville whom he saw often, and Robert Johnson, whom he knew only from records.

It is the hallmark of both Son House and Robert Johnson's styles that they are able to describe without blinking the most gruesome indignities

("Stones in My Passway," for instance). There is an emotional center in their work that is undeniably the product of life in one of the most racist areas in the world. To survive—especially to survive as free-floating performers, rootless and with bad reputations—required an inner centeredness that Muddy must have picked up as his ticket out of misery.

None of which implies passivity. It was in fact arrogance—the refusal to know his place—which led Muddy to a confrontation with Mr. Fulton, the Stovall overseer, in May 1943. (He said he and Fulton had "a fight," though whether this was an argument or whether Muddy punched the white man is unclear.) Muddy said goodbye to his grandmother that evening, grabbed his guitar, whatever little money he had and caught the train at Greenville. "The next morning I was in Chicago," he told me almost forty years later, still with a sense of relief.

In 1942, Muddy had made some recordings for the Library of Congress as a pure Delta bluesman, accompanied only by his own acoustic guitar. In Chicago, he kept on playing, mostly at rent parties and in bars, until 1948, when he made his first recording for Leonard Chess, "I Feel Like Going Home." It was an immediate hit in Chicago and allowed Muddy to give up his day jobs and work as a local star. It wasn't until 1951 and "Rollin' Stone" that he managed to establish much reputation outside of Chicago, though. By that time he was already working with Little Walter, Jimmie Rodgers and electric guitars, and the shape of blues and R&B had been permanently altered by this band.

The rise of rock and roll nearly destroyed the popularity of the blues, at least outside of Chicago. It wasn't until musicians like Brian Jones and Keith Richards began pointing their white listeners toward the other Chicago blues giants that Muddy again had much audience outside his home ground. Thereafter, he played most of his gigs at colleges and rock concerts. His very last appearance was at an Eric Clapton show in June 1983, where he did "Blow Wind Blow."

Through it all, Muddy didn't change much. His incredible array of vocal effects, his ability to mimic many of these on the guitar, his wonderful sense of timing remained at least partially intact throughout the seventies and even into the eighties. His last album, King Bee, contains a version of the Slim Harpo tune that gives the album its title, and Muddy sounds like he owns the song.

Mike Rowe's book, Chicago Breakdown, contains photos of Muddy as a young man which suggest how extraordinarily fine looking he was: bronze-brown skin, high Indian cheekbones, almost Oriental eyes, a dapper dresser. In later years he grew heavy but never less than handsome. The last time I saw him perform, that massive head looked so elegant it struck me that he ought to be the fifth face on Mount Rushmore. But the music Muddy Waters leaves behind him is a greater monument by far, and less subject to erosion as well.

Record, 1983

The Secret Life of Elvis Presley

After editing The Rolling Stone Record Guide, *I found myself frequently asked who I considered the most underrated performer in the book. Upon reflection, I was able to answer honestly that Elvis Presley was probably the most underrated singer of all.*

Elvis suffered from celebrity in many ways, and not the least of these was in his inability to be clearly seen as the innovative and startlingly original vocalist that he was. Furthermore, his step into the unrelenting maw of Hollywood hackdom cut short his creative growth just at a moment when his abilities seemed to be peaking. The obvious greatness of the sides he cut with Sam Phillips at Sun Records stems from a combination of sheer talent and ambition (on the part of everyone involved). But by the time Presley had some sense of what he really wanted to do, he was surrounded by impossible quantities of fluff and filler. And anyway, by then the audience best prepared to appreciate him had had its attention diverted. So he wandered in a wilderness of his own device.

> *"I was thinking," said Walter Mitty. "Does it ever occur to you that I am sometimes thinking?" She looked at him. "I'm going to take your temperature when I get you home," she said.*

The critical and journalistic commentary since Elvis Presley's death has been so determinedly solemn that one might think that what had ended was the life of an intellectual singer/songwriter. In fact Elvis Presley's life was not just tinged but saturated with the absurd. As much as anything else, the absurd was what exalted him.

Elvis is often portrayed, with justifiable awe, as the quintessential American, and our mass agog makes it easy to forget that the quality of the ridiculous was fundamental to his destiny. Elvis was indeed fiction come to life. Like Huckleberry Finn's or Ishmael's, his exploits often took on the aspect of the hilariously bizarre. But for me he remains most like James Thurber's immortal-despite-himself Walter Mitty, the everyday schlep who lives as gloriously in his fantasies as any hero of ancient or modern mythology.

Presley's thirty-odd films are the most notorious examples of the outrageous cast to his life. Only a person for whom reality remained extraordinarily mundane could possibly have stomached making these epics of impoverished imagination. Elvis Incarnate would have been fantasy come to life for most men, but in his films this is insufficient, or perhaps most aptly, it's seen as simply another surreal aspect of his image: once you've incarnated Paul Bunyan, Babe the Blue Ox (not to mention *Blue Hawaii*) is far less of a challenge. How unfortunate that Elvis never sang "When You Wish Upon a Star." He may have been the only American hero who really understood it. (Listen to him sing the children's song "Confidence" on *Clambake*.) And so Presley bore the supposed stigmata of these trashy films as matter-of-factly as Queequeg wears his tattoos. At the least, they kept things interesting—if not for him, for those of us willing to pay attention.

Elvis on record is another matter. The standard story says that he was truly great in his early, pre-Army recordings and again briefly in the late sixties when he made his remarkable comeback on television and returned to live stage performances in Las Vegas. In the middle lay a vast wasteland of pure schlock, garbage to which everyone sensible pays no mind.

But as with the theory that rock and roll died (or nearly did) during the period between Elvis' incarceration in the Army and the emergence of the Beatles, this interpretation is based mostly upon the withering away of the rock audience. As Berry Gordy and Phil Spector could tell you, lots of great rock was produced in the period between 1958 and 1962. And as the kind of genuinely hard-core Presley fan who is rarely heard in print knows, Elvis made some very interesting music in the years of his eclipse.

In all the pages of serious Presley lore, however, there's no complete catalogue of his work. All Presley criticism is at its best highly selective, bad-mouthing the soundtrack-era recordings (1961–67) without ever detailing their flaws, presumably because the specifics of his failure were so obvious they require no elaboration.

When Elvis died last summer, I was moved to tears, perhaps only because I am no great fan of the Inevitable. But even in my grief, I was canny enough to take up RCA on its offer to send over Presley's complete LP catalogue. It seemed fitting penance to listen, grieving, to the entire array, dread soundtracks and all, at least once through the whole batch of it, thereby atoning for the years in which the Master was allowed to wander in the wilderness, succored only (so it was said) by warm, soft blondes and cold, hard cash.

I later conceived a plan of reviewing the entire Presley discography, identifying the secret treasures. But like any great rocker or true hero, Presley delivers not only precisely what's expected of him but something more—every time. What I discovered was that it makes little sense to try to amplify the excellent commentary on the Sun records in Greil Marcus' *Mystery Train*, or to try to better Peter Guralnick's essay on the sixties Resurrection or even to assay another review of the early singles ("Heartbreak Hotel," "Jailhouse Rock," et al.).

The Presley who means the most to me these days is the Elvis we missed or spurned. And I'm prepared to argue that, if *Spinout* is hardly as great as the Sun sessions, it comes close to matching what followed the 1968 TV special, which temporarily brought the hard-rock flock back into the fold. *Spinout* was released in 1966, a full two years before his alleged comeback, though it contains "U.S. Male," one of the two singles (the other was "Guitar Man") that kicked off his "revival."

Spinout also features "Tomorrow Is a Long Time," Presley's only recording of a Dylan song. The version is a great one, with a cowboy pace and a beautiful acoustic guitar accompaniment. It is preceded by a much hotter song, "I'll Be Back," a loose, swaggering big-band blues arrangement, and is followed by "Down in the Alley," a dirty blues shout. Both are grittier by far than anything recorded in 1966 by such critical darlings as the Kinks and Hollies—far more tough-minded than such twaddle as "Waterloo Sunset" and "Bus Stop." (Far less sentimental than "Tomorrow Is a Long Time," for that matter.) Latter-day rockabillies like Billy Swann and Gary Stewart could be proud of either.

You don't need to make the case for Presley's middle period solely on the basis of *Spinout*, which isn't even his best soundtrack LP; it ranks about equally with *Speedway* and *Girls! Girls! Girls!* and doesn't compare with Elvis's least discussed pre-Army LP, *King Creole*. Nor do any of these justify such mindless trash as *It Happened at the World's Fair* or even the misguided attempts at recording New Orleans music on *Frankie and*

Johnny. But it does seem unlikely that we will ever fully appreciate Presley's music until such albums are given serious consideration.

Just as Presley's talent as an actor could never have been really tested, not even by a director as skillful as Don Siegel, because his scripts were so godawful, so Elvis' talents as a vocalist were hardly ever challenged in the early sixties because his material was so mediocre. This amounts to an indictment of the bankrupt American show-tune industry, and especially of Presley's song-publishing liaison, Hill and Range.

The pop songwriters had been the first to sneer at Elvis as a corny hillbilly or "white trash," a form of cultural condescension not far from the threatened bleats of "white nigger" emanating from Nashville about the same time. But given a chance to come up with material for the greatest white American musical talent of the post–World War II era— a man who could sing every kind of material and desperately wanted to do so—the best Tin Pan Alley could deliver was "Rock-a-Hula Baby" and "Song of the Shrimp." Part of the reason was the reluctance of Hill and Range to deal fairly with songwriters; they wanted to keep the lion's share (and more) of profits for themselves, and established pop writers weren't about to deal with them. But the established writers, by sneering, also steered away any sense of craftsmanship among their peers when it came to working with Presley.

When Elvis got the chance to work with songwriters of distinction— which almost always meant writers with background in R&B, most notably Jerry Leiber and Mike Stoller, Doc Pomus and Mort Shuman and Otis Blackwell—he not only outdid himself but everybody else around. Whenever the show-tune hacks gave him half a chance, as on "Let Yourself Go" on *Speedway*, he turned in a tour de force. But most of the time the material was on the order of "No Room to Rhumba in a Sports Car" and Elvis conducted himself accordingly.

The poverty of the Presley soundtracks reveals not only the banality of the American show-tune genre at this period (it had simply spent itself), but the contempt most of the particular writers who worked with Elvis held for themselves and their work. Only when Elvis was freed from their clutches—when he returned to Memphis for *From Elvis in Memphis* in 1968—did he reclaim his promise. And he did so immediately, partly by recording the songs of such excellent new pop writers as Kenneth Gamble and Leon Huff and even Burt Bacharach.

Presley fans, of course, know very well that some of his best singles were recorded after his release from the Army—especially three Pomus-Shuman numbers, "Viva Las Vegas," "Little Sister" and "Marie's Her Name (His Latest Flame)." The point is that this portion of his work is at least as deserving of critical exegesis as that which preceded and followed it. It would be a shame to bury this music, just as it would be a shame to pretend that after his brief popular resurgence in 1968–71, Elvis released only mediocre live albums with the exception of the ballyhooed 1972 hit, "Burning Love." In fact, like the soundtracks, his midseventies studio albums include some tremendously moving and metaphorically "important" tracks. (This discussion also skips right by his gospel albums, which deserve an essay to themselves. All are excellent, not only as Elvis discs but also as white gospel vocals.)

I'm thinking particularly of three studio albums—*Elvis Country* (1971), *Promised Land* and *Elvis Today* (both 1975). The latter ranks almost with *From Elvis in Memphis*; all are certainly more fulfilling than the brief heat generated by "Burning Love." *Elvis Country*, for instance, includes a mesmerizing version of "Snowbird," the Anne Murray hit, and good ones of Willie Nelson's "Funny How Time Slips Away" and Jerry Lee Lewis' "Whole Lotta Shakin' Goin' On." *Promised Land* features the title cut, which is Chuck Berry's version of the Presley legend, and Elvis sings the song as if to affirm that perception. *Elvis Today* contains ten formidable tracks, the most impressive of which is "I Can Help," in which Elvis interpolates his greatest statement of self-deprecation: "Have a laugh on me / I can help."

Even one of the live albums contains a Presley masterpiece, though it's probably really just a studio track with audience overdubs. "Bridge Over Troubled Water," from the soundtrack to Presley's concert film, *That's the Way It Is*, ought to be subtitled "From a Whisper to a Scream," for after a tender recitation of the verse and bridge, Elvis enters the final chorus as if sanctified—it's a performance that's as illuminating as even Aretha Franklin's masterful interpretation of the song.

If "Bridge" is one long crescendo of transcendence, "Hurt" (a 1976 hit included on *From Elvis Presley Boulevard, Memphis, Tennessee*) is the scream of pain and rage unbounded. It begins with Elvis sounding as if his passion could swallow the world and ends as it began. In the middle, he croons a message more tender than anything since the original "Are You Lonesome Tonight" in 1960. Here Elvis isn't pleading or promising; he's just delivering everything all at once, flat out, ripping guts out with the song. If there is a musical equivalent of self-immolation, "Hurt" is a funeral pyre. And the spare piano, bass and drums couldn't possibly make a noise so big without the genius of Presley's voice.

Well, "Hurt" is only a symbol of what we have lost. There are those, I guess, who will continue to think this grand Elvis merely a figment of the collective imagination of the obsessives. There are those that think that all that has been written so far is overweening in its praise. It may very well be that Elvis fans are all so many Mittys, creating an alter ego braver, lustier, and greater than ourselves. But the truth is that no one will ever know whether that's true simply by listening to the established canon of Presley recordings. The truth is somewhere out there in the apocrypha, crying to be heard. But for everyone who knows that Elvis was a legend with a middle, as well as a beginning and an end, the plain fact is that he's never been captured, that he's barely been outlined. Our resolution ought to be simply to do better by him.

Boston Phoenix, 1978

Rock and Roll's
Latin Tinge

An ironically timed piece of criticism, since within a few months after it appeared, Latin music made its most forceful reentry into the Anglo pop mainstream since the advent of rock and roll (thanks to Julio Iglesias and Menudo), and began to develop a critical following, thanks largely to Ruben Blades' marvelous 1984 LP, Buscando America. *Even more than Ruben Guevara, Blades stands a chance of defining a sensibility that makes sense both in terms of Latin culture and as a piece with rock and roll. How important this is on the other side of that line, I can't accurately estimate, but the implications for rockers are both unsettling and thrilling. And it isn't surprising that it's Blades, a Panamanian by birth, living in New York and performing music whose stylistic homeland is Puerto Rico, who has come closest to activating such a synthesis. Such migratory synthesis is the essence of how American pop is created.*

For the past couple of years, I've had a running argument with one of my colleagues about Latin influences in rock and roll. We've been rehashing this issue for so long that I believe both of us have memorized our basic exchange. Usually the debate has gone like this:

"Now we know that rock wasn't developed from the fusion of only black blues and white country music," he'll say. "There was also a lot of gospel in there and some Tin Pan Alley pop and the kind of rural, mountain-folk music Nashville hadn't gotten its hands on yet. Maybe even some light opera if you asked Elvis and Dion."

"And Latin music," I add insistently.

"No, no," says he.

"Ritchie Valens . . ."

"You can't make a case based on one performer who died before he graduated from junior high school."

"Leiber and Stoller used that habanera style—"

"*Baiao*—"

"Whatever it was called—that weird rhythm from the Drifters' records."

"Okay. You can have Santana, too, if you want. But that's about it. Latin's not *major.*"

At which point, I have always lost the argument through ignorance. Of all the ways to lose a disagreement, which I don't like to do in the first place, that's the most annoying—and it has been especially so in this case, when my silence suggested that neither of us quite knew what he was talking about.

But in the past couple of years, more precise Latin patterns have appeared in rock. After reading John Storm Roberts' *The Latin Tinge*, and after hearing a spate of new and reissued recordings, I've been able to make the following "Latin-influenced" list: Bo Diddley's beat (derived from the mambo); Professor Longhair's piano rhythms, which extend to New Orleans pianists from Fats Domino to Allen Toussaint; Chuck Willis' "C.C. Rider" and Ray Charles' "What'd I Say" (both grounded in the rumba beat); "96 Tears," by ? and the Mysterians, a band of Chicano migrant workers; "Land of 1,000 Dances," both because Chris Kenner was a Longhair disciple and because Cannibal and the Headhunters, who did the best version of the song, were Chicanos from East LA; surf music, whose entire guitar style—the raison d'être of the form—can be said to derive from "Malagueña" and similar Mexican-American standards; the Premiers' "Farmer John," an impeccable frat-rocker written and performed by another East LA band; such doo-wop groups as the Teenagers and Harptones, all of which had key Latin members; the Sir Douglas Quintet and the rest of the Tex-Mex bands; the boogaloo (based on the Latin *bugalu,* which was popularized in 1966 by Joe Cuba's instrumental version of "Bang Bang"); War's low-rider rock and its trickle-down effect on Stevie Wonder's midseventies records; the slick psychedelicized salsa of Earth,

Wind and Fire during their "Serpentine Fire" period; and finally the disco movement, which continues to adapt Caribbean rhythmic accents and arrangements (taking few, if any, from the English-speaking islands).

And that *is* major, so much so that it's worth getting perturbed all over again at how poorly the Latin forces in rock have been acknowledged, much less examined in detail. Latin music isn't just a part of the rock mixture—it's a fundamental ingredient in it. Yet there isn't a single critical study of rock that provides so much as a full-fledged essay on the subject.

For that matter, far too little has been written (at least in English) about how rock and R&B have helped reshape Latin musical styles. Even *The Latin Tinge*—which has so many interesting things to say about Bo Diddley and New Orleans and the penetration of Latin rhythmic accents in popular music both before and after Elvis, and which even makes intriguing points about Latin influences in contemporary country—hardly mentions the fertile, influential rock scene of the East Los Angeles barrio. That's ironic, because from a rock and roll perspective, East LA's the most accessible area of Latin-rock interchange. The development of surf music, garage rock, frat rock and blue-eyed soul is hardly comprehensible without some knowledge of Cannibal and the Headhunters, the Premiers, the Blendells, Thee Midniters, Ronnie and the Pomona Casuals and the other groups that developed in East LA during the late fifties and throughout the sixties.

Over the past few months, this scene has been rediscovered by the record industry, partly because some of the most interesting groups in the LA post-punk scene are from the barrio. (This makes sense, beyond any stereotype of "Latin roots," because punk was developed—musically, at least—out of the kind of garage rock and frat rock in which earlier generations of barrio bands specialized.) Last spring A&M released *Internal Exile* by Los Illegals, an East LA quintet whose metallic, punkish rock was only occasionally distinguished by garage ethnicity (a verse or two in Spanish, a bit of cheesy organ) but several of whose songs seethed with anger over the abuses and humiliations suffered by Chicanos at the hands of the Anglo immigration authorities. At the very least, despite Mick Ronson's overly professional production veneer, you could tell that Los Illegals were quite different from the general run of West Coast post-punk brats.

Last fall Slash released a seven-song mini-album, . . . *and a time to dance*, by Los Lobos. Produced by the ultimate contraprofessional, T-Bone Burnett, this quartet's EP is apolitical in its lyrics (with the broad exception of "Anselma"), but it uses such Mexican instruments as guitarrón and bajo to create some of the most urgent, evocative music anyone made in 1983. The songs here are about half originals, and though the only familiar cover is Valens' "Come On, Let's Go," Los Lobos build from the half-remembered and the semi-familiar far more effortlessly than do their labelmates, the Blasters. There are echoes here that reach past rock into the raunchy late forties R&B of Roy Brown and Wynonie Harris, into areas of Mexican music where no rock critic has ever trod. Best of all, Los Lobos feature a combat between the accordion of David Hidalgo and the riffling, shuffling drumming of Louie Perez that animates the Mexican material and gives a pungency and thrill to the original numbers, no matter how derivative. Hidalgo and Perez write loose, funny songs that are tributes to romance, to tradition, to Los Lobos' own sense of fun and dignity, without ever getting the wires crossed. Most of the cuts, in fact, circle territory not unfamiliar to mainstream rock fans—someone's always demanding that Los Lobos hang up their rock and roll shoes, and Los Lobos are forever refusing. Long may they continue to do so—and next time at full LP length.

Los Lobos are hardly the only point of interest in East Los Angeles' current music scene, however. As part of the initial release of its Zyanya subsidiary—which will be devoted exclusively to Latino rock and its antecedents and near relations—Rhino Records has released *Los Angelinos: The East Side Renaissance*, a twelve-song, ten-band anthology. *Los Angelinos* presents a group of bands that break away from the molds established by multinational rock and its new-wave bohemian branches. All the other recent regional collections I know, whether from London, Boston, Akron, Athens, Ann Arbor or LA itself, chronicle scenes without a distinctly local style, only variations on international approaches. Although the models may range from Boss Bruce to the B-52's, that's not an especially eclectic grouping. Almost never does one hear music that flows from track to track with *Los Angelinos'* unusual sense of tradition, culture and community.

The music on the record ranges from the hard-core punk of the Brat (an Anglophile-looking quartet) to the *rancheras* of Califas (an octet featuring traditional Mexican music). There is a helping of predictable new-wave internationalism from the Plugz and Odd Squad as well as the Brat, but the best groups here play idiosyncratic rock that comes from within the fifties to seventies pop spectrum but with distinct regional flavor: Felix and the Katz give a Latin twist to the ska horn stylings of UB40 and Madness; Thee Royal Gents spin torrid funk and sultry ballads with Chicano accents; Mestizos indulge in a bathetic Latin ballad but redeem it with an atypical, zingy, Isley-like guitar break. Juxtaposed with these, the new-wave material—particularly the Brat's "The Wolf" and "High School"—seems a more coherent reaction to the rationally expressed passions of the other styles: it grows straight out of that East LA garage-band tradition and can be seen as a response (as was the earlier variety) to the formulas and clichés of the more typical music of that community.

Yet the best track here is the most internationalized concoction of all: "c/s" by Con Safos. A scabrous, ranting funky history of Anglo abuses of Chicanos in LA, it resembles the scalding chants and blustering funk of Fela and Afrika 70, the kings of Nigerian pop. Telling the story of the Zoot Suit riots of the forties and the rebellious, proud young Chicanos of today's streets, "c/s" is anthem, exorcism, call to arms; nevertheless, it concludes: "Viva Los Angeles! Viva mi tierra! Long live LA!"

The album ends with Los Perros singing "El Corrido to End Barrio Warfare," the only number in Spanish and one of the few that sounds traditional in the sense that that term is usually used in reference to Latin music. But except as an explication of ideology, "El Corrido" can't stand up to "c/s." Los Perros sing *about* cruising "in our classic cars of yesteryear." But Ruben Guevara—*Los Angelinos'* compiler, the composer of "c/s" and the vocalist for Con Safos—has lived it more effectively, not only now but for a couple of decades. Guevara is the linchpin of Zyanya's albums, its direct link with East LA history. The four cuts he produced on *Los Angelinos* are its least homogenized and most durable—the ballads and funk of Thee Royal Gents as much so as the more rootsy sounds of Con Safos, Los Perros and Califas. Guevara also did the semi-psychedelic, quasi-Aztec lettering on the LP cover and contributed to the other inaugural releases. In its way, like the Mothers of Invention's *Ruben and the Jets, Los Angelinos* is a loving tribute to an aspect of a culture that Ruben Guevara knows and loves both wisely and well.

That the East LA rock scene has tradition and history is a point emphasized by the other Zyanya albums, *The History of Latino Rock, Volume One, 1956–1965* and *Best of Thee Midniters.* Both contain some extraordinary music, though neither is the ideal barrio sampler. That honor still falls to Rampart Records' double album, *East Side Revue*, which surveys the scene well past *History's* cutoff date, into the awkward dawning of acid consciousness. Anyone who digs *History*—which to my mind ought to include anyone who digs funky garage punk or punky soul—will want to have *East Side Revue,* though a second volume of *History* could change my opinion.

Volume One at least surveys many of the high points. The crucible from which came the rest is "La Bamba," the most Mexican of Ritchie Valens' hits. It's followed by Chan Romero's original of "Hippy Hippy Shake" (saner and less exciting than the Swinging Blue Jeans' British Invasion version, I'm afraid), the Blendells' near crossover "La La La," of 1964, the

Premiers' genuine crossover of the same year, "Farmer John," Cannibal's "Land of 1,000 Dances," and the funky but sleek "I Wanna Do the Jerk" by Ronnie and the Pomona Casuals (an integrated—black, white, Latin —septet). The rest of the material relies on ballads more than my battle-scarred and Motown-pampered ears would prefer, but then who am I to argue with Ruben Guevara?

No such problems attend *The Best of Thee Midniters*. Although once again some of the slow tunes suggest that the Association must have spent their time listening to corny Latino doo-wop, connoisseurs of sixties punk will consider the mere inclusion of "Empty Heart" proof of the band's killer instinct. The mixture of soul and British Invasion styles is certainly period, but compared to other alleged classics of the era, this one is genuinely high octane. The set also includes the group's 1969 single (one of its last), "Chicano Power"—hardly more than a chant over a funky little riff, but a distant cousin to "c/s" nevertheless. I wouldn't be surprised to learn that Guevara had drawn upon it for inspiration.

Such ties indicate that East LA is a rock scene with a rationale. But how long can it hold together? Can the bands find an adequate response to the increasingly vindictive anti-Latin political climate of Anglo California? Are the remaining regional and ethnic traits that make this music so vital and unusual only aberrations caused by a disparity in language and culture that is quickly being Osterized out of existence? Anyone who hears Los Lobos will know that the answers aren't all in place yet. For as long as it has participants as inventive, determined and historically conscious as David Hidalgo and Ruben Guevara, the East Los Angeles rock world will command respect as well as attention.

Boston Phoenix, 1984

Phil Spector:
The Paranoia of Romance

Phil Spector made records with lives of their own—bustling, claustro-phobic, raging urban lives for the most part. He proclaimed himself America's first teenage millionaire, which meant choosing the term "teenager" as a symbol of pride at a time when it had hardly ever been used except as a mild epithet. And he revolutionized the way in which records were made—one might even go further and say, as a result of his incessant self-promotion, he changed the way in which records were heard. Certainly he helped determine the terms on which rock criticism was written. Spector took rock as seriously as any musician in history, and that the result could be as deceptively simple as "Today I Met the Boy I'm Gonna Marry" is the essence of what rock writing must describe.

Which means that Phil Spector, above anyone else of his period in the American music business, understood rock and roll perfectly, however poorly he may have understood his own work.

Phil Spector was the key personality on almost every record that bore his name as producer, as a listen to the diverse singles on *Phil Spector's Greatest Hits,* the recent Warner Brothers compilation, demonstrates. Several of these tracks rank with the best rock ever: "Da Doo Ron Ron," "Be My Baby," "You've Lost That Lovin' Feelin'," "Black Pearl." And there's much more evidence on six albums the English Spector label reissued last year. Spector also made some junk—the Teddy Bears' "To Know Him Is to Love Him" and the Paris Sisters' execrable "I Love How You Love Me"—but generally, Spector's records are the equal of anyone's.

The characteristics of Spector's sounds are well-known: the Wall of Sound with its fixation on brilliant percussion, oddball instrumental fetishes (the eternal glockenspiel) and the totality of noise. But the Spector sound hasn't been as influential as the Spector sensibility. It is the spirit of his records, as much or more than their specifics, that have drawn Brian Wilson, John Lennon and Bruce Springsteen to his cult.

In myth, that spirit is romantic. The perfect Teen Dream, as critic Nik Cohn would have it: boy and girl meet in transcendental glory and remodel the universe to suit their mohair fancy. Perfect Devotion: "If they don't like him that way / They won't like me after today." And Perfect Agony when it's soon over, for only puppy love can be so true.

Which is just the point. However often his music pretends to find love joyous, doom is always the norm for Spector, happiness the aberration. Romance is momentary, with a life span somewhere between two and a half and three and a half minutes, in case you wonder why he never made a great LP.

The real Spector spirit is rampant paranoia, not ascendant romance. It's explicit in some of his songs—"You've Lost That Lovin' Feelin' " is an ode to anxiety—but it bubbles up unexpectedly in even his most exuberant hit, "Da Doo Ron Ron," where the ominous line of baritone saxophones buried in the mix tells the real story: in the last verse, lead vocalist Darlene Love admits she hasn't yet got her boy, and we're left to wonder if she ever will. Indeed, Spector's exhilaration is most often reserved for life's prospects: "Today I Met the Boy I'm *Gonna* Marry." Even in "Be My Baby," you know he won't be for long. (The great exception is Love's "A Fine Fine Boy.")

The advantage of *Greatest Hits* over the English series—almost its only one—is that it collects four of the Righteous Brothers' hits, which are the purest paranoia this side of Roy Orbison's "Running Scared." (If Spector had made that record, Orbison's girl would have walked away without him and the song would have faded out on a single pistol shot.) In "Just Once in My Life," Bill Medley is ready to give his soul for *just one thing* to go right, and Bobby Hatfield's contribution is a series of screams right out of Bedlam. In their "Hung on You," the singer is afraid to break off an affair because he knows it will only start up again—which is like refusing to get out of bed because you'll only become tired later on. It's entirely fitting that Spector produced John Lennon when Lennon (not to mention Yoko Ono) was at his wackiest.

You could argue, I guess, that Spector was merely sending up our adolescent naiveté, goofing on everyone's hope for the Perfect Date. Maybe that's true, but look at his interpretation of his own career. In 1966, Spector released Ike and Tina Turner's "River Deep Mountain High," after slaving over it for months. It flopped. In a fit of pique, Spector, in what may be his most notorious act of all, folded Philles Records and retired to a Bel Air mansion. "River Deep" was his masterpiece, Spector claimed, and only a conspiracy among the nation's radio programmers had prevented its success. Partly because George Harrison seconded his opinion (the record *was* a hit in the U.K.) and partly because Top-Forty programmers are always good scapegoats, no one has ever questioned Spector's judgment. The reason *felt* right, just as it felt right to say that his records were concerned with romantic innocence.

But listen to "River Deep" and you'll hear a jumble, not a hit. The song is mediocre, the lyric absurd; the production is more bombastic than millennial, and in Tina Turner, a harsh, adult blues singer, Spector encountered the most inappropriate object of his production style. "River Deep" flopped because *it wasn't all that good.* Spector was simply looking for an excuse—not an excuse to quit, but an excuse to admit defeat. What hampers paranoia more than success?

This is a fairly depressing view of the events of such an important career, but it makes me appreciate Phil Spector all the more. Artists ought to live lives consonant with their work, and Spector has done so in every way. Compared to throwing away a million-dollar career because you've misjudged your masterpiece (try "Lovin' Feelin' "), Spector's recent nagging suspicion that he was robbed of credit as the producer of every Beatles record actually seems reasonable. After all, why shouldn't it? Hunter Thompson said it best: "There is no paranoia. Only people who are uninformed."

Boston Phoenix, 1977

Let Us Now Praise
Lynyrd Skynyrd

Lenny Bruce pointed out that no one in American life dares possess a Southern accent. To have one is to be instantly discredited, and the stories of actors, disc jockeys and politicians doing their best to minimize or obliterate their native speech patterns are unfortunately legion. The most bizarre result of this was the dialogue in Elvis Presley's films, especially those ostensibly set in the South. Imagine one slowly drawling Mississippi voice amongst all those clipped, quick Yankee ones and you can begin to gauge his humiliation.

But there are those who refuse to surrender their style. It usually costs 'em: it cost Elvis, it cost Lyndon Johnson (which was Bruce's point) and it cost Lynyrd Skynyrd, as good a band as America produced after Woodstock whose redneck allegiances have kept them from being taken as seriously as many more half-baked but superficially serious competitors.

Of course it wasn't just their accents and stubborn Rebel pride that hurt Skynyrd. It was also the brash vulgarity of the kind of music they played, the stormy three-guitar sound that admitted no glimpse of what might superficially be seen as "discipline" or "restraint," plus stage deportment that just about defined male belligerence.

Yet Ronnie Van Zant and his cohorts were not only a great-sounding rock band. They were a truly smart one, too. What follows

*is a homage to them, and collaterally, I think, to all the other smart
but uncouth folks that the world ignores and sneers at.*

Although it was recorded primarily between 1970 and 1972, this album
isn't just a relic for Lynyrd Skynyrd fans. One of the best albums the band
ever made, *Skynyrd's First and . . . Last* ranks either a notch below
(undeveloped material) or one above (some of the most riveting playing
the group ever did) its first two albums, *Pronounced Leh-nerd Skin-nerd*
and *Second Helping*. A triumphant but ironic final chapter, it measures
the extent of the tragedy of the group's demise.

Historically speaking, the LP is hardly revelatory. Skynyrd's English
roots show more clearly than on any of its other albums ("Wino" is a copy
from Jack Bruce's pop songs for Cream), but that's mostly because Ronnie
Van Zant hadn't yet mastered the Southern idiom that was to become the
focus of the group's most familiar songs. But the density of the guitars/
drums/vocals interplay and the raw edge of intensity that dominates everything here are simply Van Zant and Company at their peak—which is
about as good as American rock got in the seventies.

As guitarist Gary Rossington has claimed, *Skynyrd's First and . . . Last*
contains some of the band's finest material, much of it revealingly personal.
If Van Zant seems less determinedly Southern than he later would, he
appears even more quintessentially American. (Perhaps he didn't need to
assert his Southernness so strongly until he was confronted regularly with
the world outside it.) While the naiveté of some of the band's political
songs ("Lend a Helpin' Hand," "Things Goin' On") would normally date
them, they serve here as examples of the forthright expression of American
working-class populism.

The very plainspokenness that was Skynyrd's glory, however, was also
what kept them from critical acclaim: they always seemed too vulgar, not
nearly arty enough. Mostly, the group's music is about simple pleasures and
grim but everyday problems. But if the songs are realistic, that reality has
been shaped with a romantic vision. In the main, Ronnie Van Zant's
writing has more in common with the films of Clint Eastwood than with
any rock and roll of its era. It's easy to picture Ronnie Van Zant as the
vengeful apparition of *High Plains Drifter* or the mean but moral Josey
Wales.

In fact, the record's best song, "Was I Right or Wrong," is a fantasy
similar to those pictures. Had it been released earlier, it might have become one of Skynyrd's anthems. The narrative is classic. Against his
parents' wishes, a young rocker sets out to seek his fortune. His dreams

come true, but when he returns home to his folks (the people he most wanted to convince of his abilities), he learns they're dead. The stark mythos of this song makes it hard to believe that the song is only a fantasy. But Van Zant didn't even have a record contract when he wrote and recorded it.

Much more than "That Smell" or even "Sweet Home Alabama," "Was I Right Or Wrong" offers the perfect epitaph for Ronnie Van Zant and his band:

> When I went home, to show they was wrong
> All that I found was two tombstones
> Somebody tell me, *please*
> Was I right or wrong . . .

This is great music, not only for those who have loved this band but for everyone who's ever endured a painful, inarticulate parental relationship. In it, Van Zant finally becomes a character out of American mythology: Huck Finn finding his father dead in the middle of a mighty river. It's exactly the sort of thing for which Lynyrd Skynyrd deserves to be remembered.

Rolling Stone, 1978

What Becomes of the Broken-Hearted?

I grew up worshiping Motown rhythms without ever having a clue— or even giving much thought—to the identities of the men who made the music move beneath the sumptuous vocal and instrumental textures. Motown's desperate signature was its beat, so much so that the idea that there were mere men—technicians, even—behind it never dawned. It wasn't until later, when I met a few people who did occasional sessions, that the litany of names was presented.

But once you've been clued in, the nuances of the players backstage at Motown become as personalized as anything available on rec-

ord. (Similarly with the great Al Jackson, the drummer at Stax.)

Knowing what few fragments we do about James Jamerson and his cohorts and their work, their story nevertheless remains indelible. This is possibly especially true in my case, because the notion of men doing a fine job in complete obscurity, without recognition or just compensation, is a major part of the circumstances that my rock and roll rebellion was all about. To find the same story repeated here, in the very citadel of what liberated me, is scary, not just ironic.

> I walk in shadows, searching for light
> Cold and alone, no comfort in sight
> Hoping and praying for someone who'll care
> Always moving and going nowhere

Writing about *The Motown Story,* the label's official anthology of its hits, Greil Marcus simply commented, "The history of James Jamerson's bass playing, on 58 hits," and left it at that.

The remark is audacious but apt. Today, listening to my own sampler, a decade-old hits package which has 64 hits and no narrative blather, James Jamerson's bass playing is a precise, popping, fluid and fundamental cornerstone of what makes me want to dance and celebrate. It's the engine that drives me skipping 'cross the carpet, and as it does, James Jamerson becomes as vivid a part of the Motown story as Smokey Robinson, Marvin Gaye, Holland-Dozier-Holland, Stevie Wonder, even Berry Gordy himself.

Yet I know next to nothing about Jamerson, except what I've read in the tiny obituaries that appeared in the wake of his death, of heart failure induced by alcoholism, in a Los Angeles nursing home on August 2. And those obituaries don't even agree on his age: one gave it as forty-five, the other as forty-seven. In the end, Marcus' encomium is not only Jamerson's greatest review, it's one of his most extensive. There is no James Jamerson entry in *Rock Record,* and while that book is ludicrously skimpy on black artists in general, *The Illustrated Encyclopedia of Black Music* is content to merely recite his name among Motown sessionmen. He gets two or three lines in *The Rolling Stone Illustrated History of Rock & Roll,* but nothing at all in Charlie Gillett's *The Sound of the City.* And so forth.

In fact, were it not for Nelson George of *Billboard,* who tracked Jamerson down for an extensive interview last winter, James Jamerson might easily have gone to the grave as shrouded in speculation as Robert Johnson. That's genuinely tragic, because as George discovered, Jamerson wasn't only willing but quite eager to tell his tale. And as anyone who reads that interview will quickly see, Jamerson was as insightful commenting upon Motown's musical development as he was in his comments behind Levi Stubbs' vocal in "Bernadette."

Had we lost James Jamerson altogether, never knowing his own perspective on his contribution to the Motown legend, the result would be more than tragic: it would be an outrage. As it stands, the reason he's not better known as the founding father of all electric bass lines in modern pop has to do with the veil of secrecy Berry Gordy, Jr., and the Motown organization tried to draw around their activities in general. There are a variety of complex reasons for Gordy's skittishness. Certainly, too much scrutiny could have led the Motown organization to be pillaged of its talent. (In a racist society, not even the most masterful black capitalist of them all could be safe.) But equally, James Jamerson's name remained unknown because, had he become as famous as the MGs' Duck Dunn or the Family Stone's Larry Graham, he could have commanded wages equal to what Marvin Gaye called his "genius." So Jamerson, along with his rhythm section partners, drummers Benny Benjamin, Uriel Jones and Richard "Pistol" Allen, and the Motown bassists who followed him, notably Carol Kaye and Bob Babbit, remained a mystery.

Yet based upon what we do know, Jamerson deserves as much credit as any instrumentalist for changing the way rock sounds. Not just Motown but all of the pop hits that have followed that label's success were shaped by his unique style, which (as Marshall Crenshaw pointed out in his *Rolling Stone* obituary) was the first to show producers the advantages of using electric bass. Previously, either a string bass or simply the bottom strings of a guitar had been favored. The limber, melodic and percussive effects Jamerson achieved on records as diverse as "Where Did Our Love Go" and "My Girl" set a new standard, establishing patterns upon which everyone who followed, from Paul McCartney to Michael Henderson, simply added embellishments.

The Motown producers must have been almost immediately aware of what Jamerson could add, which is one reason why so many Motown hits begin with a couple of bonging bass chords—"My Girl" is the classic example. At other times the song simply took its shape from the bass line or became exciting just at the moment when Jamerson made his entrance: "Ain't No Mountain High Enough," for instance, would have been lost without him. Even now the voice in our heads that says "Motown!" when we hear something like Hall and Oates' "Family Man" is usually responding to what's going on in the bass.

On *The Motown Story*, Jamerson makes his appearances only in the music—he's never interviewed. Similarly, the recent *Motown Twenty-fifth Anniversary Special*, wonderful as it was, gave no credit whatsoever to James Jamerson, or to Benny Benjamin, Earl Van Dyke, Pistol Allen, Jack Ashford or any of the other great players who were a sine qua non of the label's success. Yet as much as great jazz and blues sidemen, these musicians were brilliant artists who may have followed the orders of a production mill but also made significant contributions in their own right.

James Jamerson died certain his work would never be honored. In the greatest sense, that's probably a correct assumption, especially since what he did was truly work, with little glamour attached to it. Yet being forgotten need not be his fate. The next time a Four Tops or Temptations hit crosses your path (may it be soon), stop a minute and listen deep. Reach out. He'll be there.

Record, 1983

4

Don't Let Me Down

Introduction

B ecause I entered rock and roll's world thinking of the music as a means of salvation (and therefore the players and marketers of the stuff as next to saintly), my initial response to every failure and letdown was extremely bitter. By the time I wrote the pieces collected in this chapter, I had learned to live with a measure of merely going through the motions, even a smidgen of exploitation, and to appreciate the irony. Nevertheless, that original sense of mission never left me, and I have perhaps reacted (or overreacted) more harshly to popular music trendies and phonies and parasites than any other critic. In a certain sense, this all stems from watching the Rolling Stones hack around America for a summer; the meaninglessness of that experience, chronicled in the first piece collected here, changed the foundations of what I was writing, because it made it absolutely clear that musicians as well as promoters and fans could stand on either side of the line dividing pop-culture perdition from salvation. To all young men this revelation must come, I suppose, but I was fortunate enough to have venom and space to talk about it.

I Call and Call and Call on Mick

I joined the staff of Rolling Stone *in mid-1975, just as the Rolling Stones were embarking on their first American tour in three years. Jann Wenner, who'd hired me essentially to edit his record review section, apparently thought he was dispensing a great boon when the first task he gave me was to travel with the Stones for a full-scale cover story. (Jann's original choices for Stones tour coverage that summer, Joan Didion and John Gregory Dunne, had backed out.)*

Rolling Stone covers a Stones tour with the same sensibility that the daily press brings to a presidential campaign, which means minutely detailed coverage without ever touching on the larger issues. Not that the process of coverage has anything to do with democracy: the style of reporting is that associated with campaigns, but the content is expected to resemble a Tory commentary on coronation.

Consequently, sending me on this junket was asking for multiple kinds of trouble. The Rolling Stones were never my favorite rock band, and certainly, after Brian Jones died, they were important to me primarily for their few great hit singles ("Tumbling Dice," "Honky Tonk Women," "Happy"), not as icons of rock's essence. In fact, in my snobbish, Motown-bred way, I'd always found Mick Jagger a wimpy dancer. And since, for Jann, Jagger's wobbling about the stage is the epitome not just of the Stones but of rock itself, there was bound to be trouble.

The first rule of such stories is get the interview, and this I could not do. In retrospect, knowing more about Wenner and Jagger's relationship (they were business partners in the early seventies in an ill-starred attempt to create a British edition of Stone), I was obviously unaware of one of the most important elements in the dynamic of press coverage of the tour. It also didn't help that Jagger had taken Annie Leibovitz as his tour photographer, away from her Rolling Stone staff job. But it helped even less that the Stones 1975 tour was the one on which they discovered that they needed to do little more than go through the motions, and let hype take care of the rest. I was unutterably bored after the second or third show that I saw—and there were about a dozen to go.

That's not surprising, since the Stones' show was never intended to be seen so often, at such close range. Most patrons experience the group but once every two or three years. And the frenzy to get tickets, always in short supply, the hassles of getting in, the sheer spectacle of the Event tends to overwhelm any negative details. So I wasn't supposed to mention that the sound system was poorly balanced, the show was paced to give an aging Jagger frequent chances to catch his breath, and the material was both hackneyed (this was the only Stones tour of the seventies and eighties in which they didn't have a new LP to promote) and unimaginatively arranged.

No one has ever asked Jagger a series of hostile questions like that, and I suppose no one ever will. That was my intention and, as poorly concealed as my attitude was, I'm certain that his entourage knew it and kept me away from him. This doesn't reduce the sheer unprofessionalism of the experience, nor its decadent overtones, nor the fact that the press continues to roll over for the Stones whenever they hit the stage. Most especially, it doesn't excuse Mick Jagger making noises designed to get a young reporter fired for fuck-ups that were perpetrated by Jagger's own staff.

In this sense, this story, jumbled and written between the lines as it is, may be a singularly instructive case in point. It certainly changed my perception of big-time rock and roll forever. That tour was about hierarchy, courtiers, privilege and patronage. There was not a single thing glamorous about its excesses and abuses of common courtesy, its waste of talent and manpower, the way that it dealt the consumer/ listener out of the picture altogether. Seeing myself more as an idealized fan than as an objective authority, I naturally couldn't warm to such a situation, in which my only function was to fork over the cash and/or the praise. And so I wrote the closest thing to a hatchet job that Rolling Stone *was willing to print on the subject. If it seems mild, consider that the next time the group was panned in those pages—by Paul Nelson and me in 1978—Jann Wenner wrote a rebuttal!*

The Rolling Stones holed up at the Beverly Wilshire Hotel for their week in Los Angeles. I arrived on July 8 about twelve hours after the band, in the middle of the worst smog I've ever encountered. The result was a sore throat and a headache that lasted three weeks.

Like everything in Los Angeles that doesn't look like a tamale stand, the Beverly Wilshire has a hacienda feel. The old wing is the model of large-scale pseudo-Spanish architecture, with iron grillwork, red and green lights and clinging vines. The new wing looks like a stack of computer-designed taco huts.

On Tuesday afternoon the Wilshire was pretty sedate. The crew members were staying at the Continental Riot House on Sunset Strip. The band was even less visible than usual. The wives—Bianca Jagger, Chrissy Wood and Shirley Watts—had arrived with the group; Astrid Lindstrom hadn't been far from Bill Wyman since the tour began. Only Anita Pallenberg, Keith Richards' girlfriend, was missing. But Richards wasn't staying at the Wilshire anyway. He was up in some cañon or other, at the home of Freddie Sessler. Charlie Watts was particularly happy that his wife and daughter arrived. He spent the first two weeks of the tour popping in and out of the tour office in each city, asking for string or a box or postage stamps for his daily package home.

I was there on business—to gauge the mood of the tour, to find some semblance of gestalt among the personalities, statistics, memoranda and occasional music. In the meantime, I got to see if I could still dance— around politics, protocol and personal problems. It was not a great way to spend my summer vacation.

Bob "Mr. Goodbar" Bender, the 260-pound blond security guard, is possibly more enamored of his own body than anyone this side of Mick Jagger. Bender sat and sunned himself for ninety minutes every morning at the pool, currying his muscles as carefully as Keith Richards tuned his guitar, soaking the sun into them by day, then lifting weights in the training room at the Fabulous Forum before each evening's show.

Bender was browning placidly one morning when Lisa Robinson, one of the tour's two traveling press reps, called him over to her chaise longue. Robinson was among the tour's most eccentric characters. In New York, where she lives, she churns out three fan magazines and several gossip columns each month. She exudes an aura of hysteria that accompanies all that she does.

The normally stolid Bender was feeling almost loquacious that morning. He'd been a football player at Syracuse, he recalled, transferring to Kent State just in time for the shootings. There he'd met Bob Poweski, a wrestler, and Jim Stepp, a good-hit, no-field outfielder. When Stepp formed Sunshine Security to handle crowds at midwestern rock concerts, Bender and Poweski signed up. All three worked the Stones tour.

"I'm not used to being shouted at, much less pushed around. For a week or so there, I thought I might have to punch Peter Rudge out," Bender said, describing his introduction to the Stones' whip-tongued tour manager, "but then he got straightened out and knocked it off."

Bender had a decidedly unstraight experience when makeup man Pierre Laroche, who did Jagger's face each night, wiggled past on his way to poolside a few moments later, an event sure to unnerve any midwestern beefcake jock. Robinson then recounted odd tales of Laroche's boyfriends. "So last night, he calls me down to his room to look at this 'absolutely dee-vine boy I peeked up at ze show.' And he's lying there in this leather outfit with his cock hanging out and Pierre's snapping Polaroids."

Bender was aghast. "Uhh," he grunted, "can't you call 'em something besides his boyfriends? I don't want to *know* about this stuff."

"Well, what do you want me to call 'em?" snapped Robinson. "His *tricks?* Anyway, leave 'im alone. What are *you* worried about?"

Poolside follies aside, this was the most low-key Rolling Stones tour imaginable. In 1969, they reappeared out of nowhere, determined to live up to a reputation which, in their absence from the stage and the road, had become legendary. In 1972, they had a show designed to demolish the lingering resentments of Altamont. But this time they were simply touring to do what a rock band does: playing all summer at the biggest arenas and stadiums they could conscionably rent.

In fact, the biggest difference between this tour and their others was economic. The group used no limousines, for instance; they went to the halls in station wagons and panel trucks. Wild parties were out. Richards, Wood and Jagger stayed up all night, playing guitars and tapes, but the guests on the other floors of the hotels didn't know it, or at least the management received few complaints. Instead, the curse of the hotels was the fans, who lined up in dozens at driveways, stayed up all night in the lobbies, praying for a peek. In New York, Central Park South was lined forty deep through the night.

It was odd. Everything about the tour of the Americas (TOTA) was planned—indeed, overplanned—by the Rolling Stones' minions except for the public address system. That was subcontracted, though not to good advantage.

The tour seemed like a goddamned summer cruise. What was at stake was what mattered to the businessmen—and that had been settled on May 1, a month before the first gig, when 85 percent of the seats were sold within hours of the announcement of their availability.

The LA dates, like the New York ones, were the most lucrative because the Stones—under the moniker of Sunday Promotions—were promoting those shows themselves. The five shows were immediate sellouts and grossed roughly $1.25 million, of which the Stones took about 80 percent; the rest went for food and rent.

But all this was too easy. The Stones needed a challenge. The cool New York response to their mediocre performances seemed to provide it. They had to make up in Hollywood what they'd lost on Broadway . . . or maybe not.

I'd been tracking the Stones since Jagger granted me a pretour interview at La Guardia Airport. "Why are you touring?" I'd asked him then.

"It's my job, my vocation," he replied. "No musician is beyond that . . . until he gets too old. There's a certain magic in repetition . . . but that's a deep subject."

In Los Angeles, almost a whole tour later, the question was different: Did repetition still make magic—or had it become simple tedium?

. . .

The TOTA party spoke of Keith Richards with awe. While in Los Angeles, he didn't sleep for a solid week. Yet there, his playing was the best of the tour.

"I 'aven't slept in me fucking room since we got 'ere," said Jim Callaghan, the Stones' security chief, whose assignment was to bodyguard Keith between shows. "Last night we went to the gig, then to the party, then to another place and 'e's still up, 'e's still bouncin' and 'e's still got 'is 'ead togevver. And this ain't for a couple of days, this is through the fuckin' tour. 'E's brilliant, Keef Richards."

Peter Rudge had his own vision of Richards: "Keith is the only rock and roll gypsy in the world. He defies analysis onstage. There's something about Keith Richards that's what rock and roll is all about. It's the guy who goes with his friends, does what he wants—he plays great some nights, he plays lousy some nights. And the nights he plays lousy are the nights the Stones play badly. I mean, he is *the* Rolling Stone. There's no one else."

The crowd that packed the Inglewood Forum, a ten-minute drive from Los Angeles International, looked typical of this year's Rolling Stones concertgoer. The mob was young—by design, as tickets were put on sale in midday to give young fans a couple of hours' advantage over working adults—well scrubbed, if drugged and psyched for another rock concert.

I eavesdropped on a fifteen-year-old girl who remained impassive until she was told that Billy Preston was playing keyboards. "These guys must be pretty far out if they can get *him* to play with them," she said. (Of course, old Stones hands found Preston's dance-beat jive an extreme intrusion on the band's sensibility.)

The LA concert was filled with exotica. "They sent me ahead from Dallas on Saturday," stage manager Brian Croft told me. "We had to begin on Monday and we didn't have a concept. On Sunday night I called Mick and said, 'Let's go Oriental.' He said, 'Great.' Then we decided to have Chicano musicians and I had to go out and hire about $100,000 worth of them."

Opening night wasn't exactly jampacked with celebrities. Just George Harrison, Ringo Starr, Neil Young, Neil Diamond and Sarah Dylan were there to prove that rock and roll peerage wasn't entirely out of town. Keith Moon wandered around unmolested.

The big news was the movie stars. Barbra Streisand had been slated to appear. She never made it, perhaps because when she inquired, through her office, about security arrangements, Rudge had snapped, "How would a dozen hairdressers in bikinis suit you?" (And this memo on the morning of opening night: "Absolutely no cars backstage except the band's—no matter how many hairdressers you know." It's apparently a high point of

Hollywood prestige for stars attending such events to be able to park, not just in a VIP area, but within the arena itself.)

Bianca Jagger came through with a few celebs. Her ticket allotment was used for Sue Mengers, the agent, who came with two of her clients, Liza Minnelli and Lorna Luft, Judy Garland's daughters. Whether the Stones thought much of this was hard to tell. Rudge: "In 1972, Truman Capote got more press than Charlie or Bill, and that angered us a bit." (Capote had covered the tour for *Rolling Stone*; he wrote nothing, and the story was only dragged out of him through a pair of marathon interviews, published in the magazine. The first of these debriefings was conducted by Andy Warhol; the second and more productive by Jann S. Wenner himself.)

Opening night at the Forum was a flat show, not bad in the tour's context, though some who were seeing the 1975 production for the first time were shocked that it wasn't better. The galvanizing moment, visible only to those who knew where and when to look, came at the end of "Jumpin' Jack Flash." Jagger grabbed one of the four water buckets that he used to cool himself down and spray the front rows of the crowd; he turned to stage left, looking past Richards and Wyman, and spotted his wife standing with Liza Minnelli. He bounced over and dumped the bucket on them. "He's been trying to get her the whole tour," one of the female members of the touring party said, "and he couldn't have picked a better moment."

After the show, the Wilshire was lined with hangers-on. A beefy, T-shirted security man checked everyone; only registered guests with room keys and their invited guests made it past him. Warren Beatty was even stopped from getting in the elevator to go to his rooftop apartment.

Chuch Magee, the roadie Ron Wood brought with him from the Faces, was disgruntled by all the ado. "Look," he told me, "they're all afraid to go out of their fucking hotel rooms." Maybe it was British Invasion time lag—or maybe they were right, the hordes really would still have torn them limb from toenail. Magee had bought a camper and driven it from New York to the Coast and back, sightseeing and camping out at the arena sites.

Jagger was mostly staying out of sight. He was burned by the slick Hollywood press agent Allan Carr, who held a huge bash "in Mick's honor" on Tuesday night. Jagger had said no deal, but Carr left the star's name on his printed invitations and six hundred showed up. The evening's highlight, according to those present, was a performance near a pool filled with floating swans by the Cycle Sluts and certain other members of LA's bisexual demimonde.

Bianca Jagger was widely regarded as a pain in the ass by the tour party;

I suspected their attitude reflected the mood at the top, especially after I was told that conducting an interview with her would hurt my chances of obtaining an audience with Mick. Bianca was regarded as especially meddlesome in Washington, where she and Warhol attempted to drag Mick to the White House. She did arrive at the concert with Jack Ford in tow. ("Well," Rudge said later, "we had some visa problems, so we had some business to take care of in Washington.") On Tuesday night in Los Angeles, Mick, Bianca, managerial assistant Mary Beth Medley and press agent Paul Wasserman were up until 3:00 A.M. discussing Bianca's ticket allotment for the LA dates. She was supposed to get fifteen pair, same as in New York.

On Saturday night, Medley and Bianca had their big bout. Bianca wandered into the hotel room office where Medley was sorting out the final fifty tickets; requests from George Harrison, Neil Young and Sarah Dylan werre still unfilled. Bianca snatched up half of the remaining ducats and walked away. "Hey," Medley shouted, "you can't have those. They're taken."

Bianca turned, said, "Too bad, isn't it," in haughty tones and left.

Barbra Streisand never did meet the Stones. She showed for the midnight-to-6:00 A.M. party thrown by Atlantic Records on the tennis courts in Diana Ross' Beverly Hills backyard, but when told that she couldn't bring in her six-person entourage (although she was welcome herself), Streisand left. "We had too many goddamned hairdressers at the party already," an Atlantic Records exec laughed madly.

The Stones were scheduled to play Tuesday and Wednesday shows in San Francisco. I flew up on Monday afternoon with Jim Stepp, the security man, taking stock of my notes for the long-promised interview with Jagger at the Mark Hopkins. Stepp had his theories about in-hall security, but he'd quickly adjusted to the fact that there isn't much anyone can do about the audience, once it takes an idea into its head. Which is what Rolling Stones audiences are all about.

In St. Paul, Bob Bender had acid thrown in his face; the ex-football player threw his hand up just in time. "You can never tell when the weapons will come out," Lisa Robinson noted later. It wasn't a joke. That was the ultimate fruit of the droog image that the Rolling Stones had spun for themselves.

The Jagger interview could have come at any moment, so I spent Monday evening at the hotel. The group showed at 2:00 A.M. and went immediately to bed. Except for Jagger and Keith (who had delayed the plane); they both headed for the Orphanage, where they spent the early morning hours with Toots and the Maytals, the reggae pioneers with whom they'd become friendly while in Jamaica.

Rudge woke up Tuesday morning with fifty-four telephone messages. Four were from people he knew. I was corraled into answering the phones in the suite commandeered as an office. It was a far cry from LA, where Rudge had one afternoon been loose enough to run the hotel switchboard.

At the Cow Palace, I watched the crew set up and talked with Croft. "Look, there are any number of ways to go about a tour like this," he said. "One of them is simply to do what Ian Stewart always claimed we should do: put everything in the back of a van and haul the group around that way. You *always* have to remember it could be done that way.

"If there's one thing this tour has made clear to me, it's that I'm in this business for the esprit de corps. And that's just what's missing here."

The twelve-ton stagelight ring was unpacked at 6:00 A.M. and strung to the ceiling by 8:00 A.M. The crew was mostly one-time *Disney on Parade* riggers—acrobats and jugglers turned carpenters and handymen, led by a one-time human cannonball turned master electrician. When this crew found that some of the stage fittings were too high to be connected on foot, they went out and bought stilts.

The Tuesday show at the chilly Cow Palace was run of the mill, though it picked up when transportation master Allan Dunn charged to the front of the stage during "Happy." He bore a message for Jagger, written on a long piece of butcher paper. It read: "She's on the plane." [Bianca had taken the late flight back to New York.]

Afterwards, the Stones went to the Orphanage around 4:00 A.M., hanging out until about 10:00 A.M. Wednesday morning. That shot down my interview that day, but Rudge assured me that Jagger would talk before leaving town.

Wednesday's show was more inspired. Afterward, the crew and the group (except for Wyman, whose family was still in town, and Jagger, who wanted some sleep) went to the Trident in Sausalito, where Bill Graham had helped arrange a party (which the Stones paid for). In the middle of the entertainment, with Graham acting as host, Keith Richards and Ron Wood nearly bowled over a troupe of belly dancers as they got up to go to the Record Plant where they recorded all night. The party wasn't very wild; at its most extreme, it featured a few bug-eyed crewmen staring at the belly dancers' tits and at dawn, a shrimp-throwing food fight.

Never let it be said that Jagger's employees are disloyal. Even Croft, who seemed the most independent, said, "Mick's extremely sensitive to the crew. And I've seen him on the bad nights, counting off the numbers for the group, doing for them what they're supposed to be doing for him."

And when I told Rudge how Keith had dominated the opening moment with the introductory chords to "Honky Tonk Women," he responded, "Yeah, but remember it was Mick who decided to put that song first."

Jagger's stamina remains remarkable. Still, as Dunn said, "He's *really* tired after a show. He'll come back to the hotel and do a concentrated hour of recuperation and then he'll be all right."

Then why was the show so long? Was it to compete with the multihour extravaganzas of Led Zeppelin, Jethro Tull and the Allman Brothers? Maybe the goal of this tour was to prove that Jagger is not an old man at thirty-two, that he still has more staying power than anyone else on the rock and roll road.

"The thing is," Rudge said, "with other groups who do two hours, half of it is John Bonham's drum solo or whatever. Jagger never gets off that stage except for one number."

Maybe so, but the show's pace was obviously designed to spell him. A half-hour of hard-driving rock led straight into mid-tempo sludge like "Fingerprint File," a pointless but not purposeless exercise whose supposed function was to prove that Jagger could play guitar competently. It also gave him the chance to stop dancing for a few minutes, as did Billy Preston's solo spot, allegedly included because his manager insisted upon it—or, if you want to believe the press agents, because the group has "such incredible respect for his musical talent." In any event, its placement allowed Jagger to come back roaring for the last five numbers, all of them rockers.

The obvious person to answer such speculations was Jagger. He was the focus of the tour, the man who (with aid from Watts) designed the stage, the logo, the size and scope of it all, who fostered the rigmarole and encouraged the jostling for position. But Jagger continued to duck me.

In Los Angeles, Rudge had assured me that Jagger and I would speak in San Francisco. In San Francisco, he told me for two days that he was about to discuss the interview with Jagger. But when I woke up on the final morning of the Stones' stay in the Bay Area, I heard that Jagger had decided to drive up the coast toward Seattle, the next stop on the tour. I called Rudge; he confirmed the story. Now I didn't feel so bad about the rubber snake I'd put into his bed the night before.

Since Rudge continued to be so evasive, I contacted Wasserman, the official press liaison, who assured me that he'd let me know about getting together with Mick a few more days down the line, in Detroit.

The Thursday before the Sunday and Monday shows in Detroit, Wasserman's secretary telephoned. "Paul asked me to tell you that Mick is aware of the situation in Detroit," she said. Presuming that was the go-ahead, I booked a flight to Detroit, where I arrived at 11:00 A.M. Sunday morning. The entire staff was still asleep; their flight from Bloomington, Indiana, hadn't arrived until 4:30 A.M.

In the afternoon, Wasserman and I spoke once more. "I'll be speaking to Mick shortly," he assured me.

"Haven't you already talked to him about this?" I asked, stunned.

"Well, yes, but in Chicago," he confessed.

At the hall, backstage, I again questioned Wasserman. "He's not here yet," I was told. After all, he couldn't very well annoy Mick in his makeup room. The third time I asked, Wasserman simply grew testy; apparently, he didn't want to be bothered while squiring Knight Newspapers gossip columnist Shirley Eder around.

At 12:30 Wasserman and I rendezvoused back at the hotel. He was, he assured me again, going up ("with Peter") to speak to Mick immediately. At 2:00 A.M., he came to my room. "Mick's gone out," he said. "Ollie Brown's mother is having a party and he and Annie [Leibovitz] are going over there for a couple of hours. But he says he'll be right back and you can do the interview then."

Over the next two hours, Wasserman wandered in and out of my room to talk about Detroit. He said the town needed a press agent. I refrained from suggesting that he should stay there for the rest of his life, out of respect for my old home. At 3:00 A.M., Rudge called to assure me that Mick said everything was taken care of. Wasserman nonchalantly informed me around this time that he was going home to LA for a few days, and as he had a 10:00 A.M. flight, he had to be in bed by 4:30.

At 4:15, Wasserman phoned my room for the last time. He was curt. "It's nearly four-thirty and Mick's not back yet. That's it for tonight. Speak to Peter in the morning and I'll talk to you later."

At noon I phoned Rudge, waking him up. "Don't worry, Dave," he said pleasantly, "I'll take care of it." Well, you're leaving after the show for Atlanta, right? "Look, don't *worry*, Mick knows about it, it's all taken care of."

At 3:00 P.M. I wandered down to see Lisa Robinson, the only reasonably efficient person on the staff when it came to arranging interviews. She suggested I speak to Allan Dunn, who was getting Mick up forty-five minutes later, at 4:30 P.M. I wandered back to Robinson's room after a cordial chat with Dunn. "Sometimes Mick wakes up at four-thirty and he's ready to go," she said, "and sometimes he just stays in bed until it's time to go."

Five o'clock came and then six. At 6:45, having heard nothing, being able to reach no one and knowing that Jagger had already said he'd not make himself late in getting to the hall (where he was due at eight) in order to do an interview, I packed my bag and headed for the elevator. There I met Rudge.

"Where ya goin', Dave?" he inquired pleasantly.

"Home," I said. He grew flustered and sent Robinson downstairs after me. Lisa assured me Mick was in the shower and would see me backstage. After seven years of interviewing, and particularly after so many weeks on this story, I knew this assured absolutely nothing. I caught the 8:30 plane back to La Guardia.

Now, all of this might not be worth recounting if not for what happened later. After all, Jagger at one point found himself too busy to visit Howlin' Wolf's home when the Stones played Chicago. And surely Jagger owes more to Wolf than to you or me.

And, I was thinking, maybe it wasn't Mick's fault. After all, maybe Wasserman and Rudge hadn't told him about the interview when they said they had arranged it. Maybe it was they who were screwing around with the largest rock publication in America, not Mick.

But on the night after I got home, I found out that Mick Jagger had called a *Rolling Stone* editor at home to complain that I'd left Detroit too early. This seemed like a genuinely chickenshit exercise of power.

Two days later, Jagger called me at *Rolling Stone*'s New York office. Our conversation was brief. "Well," Jagger said in his best drawl, "I was thinking maybe we could do the interview on the telephone." Telephone interviews, I've discovered, are second only to backstage interviews in their rate of failure. I said so. And besides, I was beginning to think maybe I was wrong about whose responsibility what had happened was. Would Jagger cover the asses of his press agents and manager so thoroughly? Or would he extend himself only to protect his own image?

The rest of the conversation was brief. I said thanks, a little coldly. Mick said, "See you around." I'd like to think he sounded a bit disappointed, but then, if he was, it was only because he'd encountered a situation where he couldn't have it all his way. Maybe someday we will see each other again. But not too soon. Like everyone else, I have some sleep to catch up on. After all, I'm not Keith Richards.

Christopher "Bunny" Sykes, one of the tour's three "official" photographers, arrived from Milwaukee on the second week of the tour as an insider/outsider with, as he put it, "no political or business connection in the music business." (Sykes was a collateral member of the British aristocracy with some tony connections to both Jagger and Ahmet Ertegun. He joined the tour in order to work on a book with Annie Leibovitz.

"I arrived in Montauk [where the Stones rehearsed before beginning the tour]," he told me, "straight from London and New York, in mortal terror. I didn't know anyone. Very nervous, chewing up my fingernails and all that. I thought maybe nobody expected me. I went up to my room to sleep, woke up about six o'clock, went down the hall, and there was this enormous man standing by the lift.

"I walked up to him rather nervously and said, 'Are you something to do with the Rolling Stones?' He turned like some immoral twerp had slipped up the fire escape and I said, 'Well, uh, I'm, uh, s'posed to be with 'em too.' He obviously didn't believe me at all, so he grabbed my arm and snarled, 'Well, ya can't see 'em now!' and pushed me into the lift. Without the badge you couldn't explain to him."

The badge Sykes lacked was an orange laminated rectangle with a clip on the back. On the front was the photo of the person to whom it belonged; generally this was of the person's face, but in the case of the stewardesses on the chartered plane, the breasts were shown. Losing it supposedly meant a $500 fine.

"At the first concert I went to, in Milwaukee, I didn't have a badge," Sykes continued. "So wherever I went, I was thrown out. And I just sort of quietly said okay and kept in the background until I got my badge."

At any rate, Sykes finally got his credentials, and with it, he was able to integrate himself into the crew. "All one's sort of illusions about what things would be like on a rock and roll tour are immediately destroyed when you realize that it's just hard work," said this insider/outsider. "I cannot imagine anything more dreadful than going on tour just for fun. With nothing to do you'd go mad."

Rolling Stone, 1975

Do You Wanna Dance?

This review was one of the opening shots in the anti-disco backlash, an issue on which I generally found myself on the other side. The basic objections raised here still strike me as relevant ones, though they are

certainly the plaint of an outsider, not a member of the disco subculture itself. At the time, disco seemed to me (and many other observers)
little more than the latest development in black popular music, another link in the chain from blues and gospel to rhythm and blues and
soul. In that light, it was difficult to criticize, at least immediately,
since any white fan of black music must be sensitive to the generally
accurate charge that such fans are always one convolution behind the
trend: worshiping Muddy Waters when Motown is happening, and
Motown after Sly Stone and his heirs have taken the field. (One of
the first rock books I ever read actually attacked Holland-Dozier-
Holland's Supremes records for making Motown too slick! As if
Smokey Robinson were a rustic.)

In a way 1976 was the most propitious moment to write such a
piece, for even though the disco movement would not reach its popular
peak until 1978, the dance craze was reaching a creative apex at just
that moment. In fact, what was happening was that the soul-based
production style of Gamble and Huff, described here, was becoming
outmoded. As it was replaced by the European production methods
pioneered by Giorgio Moroder, disco made a distinct break with the
soul tradition, becoming less a manifestation of North American
blacks than a transnational commodity. (Which doesn't mean its
greatest practitioner, Donna Summer, isn't a fine recording artist—
just that she operates outside of the soul spectrum.)

The really regrettable aspect of this piece lies in the use to which
much of the rhetoric was later put by such Neanderthals as the midwestern disc jockey Steve Dahl, and other organizers of "anti-disco
crusades" and the like. (Dahl was responsible for the anti-disco record
burning at Comiskey Park in Chicago in 1978, which turned into a
riot.)

The anti-disco movement was essentially a revolt by rock's newer,
middle-class constituency against the very people who founded it:
blacks and working-class whites. In rejecting the new dance music, the
anti-disco faction was asserting skin privilege and snobbish preroga-
tive, and its bias was amply demonstrated when it fell wholeheartedly
in love with the same kind of sounds when they were recycled in the
early eighties by such white British performers as David Bowie and
Thomas Dolby. The questions asked here aren't that self-serving, even
though (as Vince Aletti charged in a Village Voice reply a couple of
weeks later) they certainly don't tell the full story.

The return of Archie Bell and the Drells sounds familiar in more ways than one. "Hi everybody! This is Archie Bell and these are the Drells, from Houston, Texas, and we're here to let *you* know that we ain't got no time to lose. So we want *every*body to get up and boogie and do a brand-new groove!"

That introduction could as easily have been transcribed from the Drells' Atlantic recordings of the late sixties as from this one. But in 1969, Archie Bell was little more than the jive dancing fool; he acquired a full-fledged personality because no one else was promoting the rhetoric of the dance floor. Maybe this makes him the father of disco.

But in 1976, father or not, Archie Bell is no longer an original: like any number of talented artists (Ben E. King and Joe Simon come to mind), he's become nothing more than a cog in the disco machine. *Dance Your Troubles Away* is a nearly perfect Philadelphia International formula record. It's executed with neither flaws nor feeling.

"Let's Groove," "The Soul City Walk" and "Let's Go Disco" are fine dance songs, but they aren't anything more than that. Certainly, there's nothing on this album to compare with "(There's Gonna Be a) Showdown," the street-life celebration that sparked the 1969 Atlantic album Philadelphia International's Gamble and Huff produced for the Drells. Five of the seven tracks are locked into a mechanical disco beat that won't quit even when you wish it would.

On a pair of ballads, the Drells sound like nothing so much as a third-rate Harold Melvin and the Blue Notes. The one song with a chance to break out, "I Won't Leave You Honey, Never," produced by the estimable Bunny Sigler, is dragged out to nine minutes, at least five more than it needs. Such filler is more glaring on slow numbers than on fast, obviously dance-fixated songs. Long cuts are better for dancing—they must be, because they're awful to listen to.

In fact, the length of Gamble-Huff organization songs probably has more to do with the company's failure to produce a talented staff of arrangers, writers and producers than with the necessity for lengthy dance cuts. Besides Gamble and Huff themselves, only Sigler has a consistently interesting body of work to show. The absence of Thom Bell is particularly striking in this respect.

This dearth of talent at Philadelphia International, coupled with the company's inability to build a real star personality (even the Blue Notes' Theodore Pendergrass is a studio tool), is what keeps them from assuming the mantle of Motown and Stax creatively, as they have already done commercially.

What makes the creative failure of Gamble and Huff really appalling is that their late sixties work with Jerry Butler and Archie Bell and the Drells showed an exciting aptitude for making classic vocal and rhythm records. While those records, particularly the Drells', also contained the seeds of the disco groove, they were far more meaningful. Butler's "Only the Strong Survive" and "Moody Woman," among others, rank with the very best rock records ever made, emotionally as well as technically. But Gamble and Huff's current limited philosophy is summed up by Archie Bell and the Drells on a song called "I Could Dance All Night": "See those kids on the *Bandstand* show / Dancing seems to be all they know." That's probably an accurate description of the disco market. But what about the rest of us?

Rolling Stone, 1976

Little Deuce Coup:
The Beach Boys' Pat Sounds

As I've previously confessed, the Beach Boys were among my original rock obsessions. However, as time wore on and the Beach Boys' music diminished not only in importance but (to me) in quality, while at the same time a claque of critical boosters grew up around the image of Brian Wilson, I've probably wound up writing more against the group than in its favor.

This certainly stems from the controversy surrounding Pet Sounds, *now accepted as a classic on a par with Sgt. Pepper's but allegedly without honor in its own land. As I point out in the article,* Pet Sounds *wasn't a commercial flop, but it did signal that the group was losing contact with its listeners (a charge that could not be leveled against the Beatles during the same period).*

It strikes me now that two important musical developments were at work. In the first place, Pet Sounds *was not made for the teenage record player—it was made for high fidelity stereo equipment, which was beyond the reach of the majority of its listeners in 1966. This technical gap, between the mechanics of record playing and the actual penetration of sophisticated listening devices into the marketplace, had a lot to with the way certain cults formed after the rock audience splintered at the end of that decade. I know from experience at least that the subtleties of something like* After Bathing at Baxter's *(overrated as those subtleties are) can't be appreciated on a $69.00 Sears Silvertone stereo system with self-contained speakers. I know because that was the system I used for even my first year of record reviewing. Peter Asher wouldn't approve.*

Given that splintering, it was almost inevitable that there would be a group or two who would wander far to the right of the American political spectrum, and (at least if you buy the thinking here) it's not especially surprising that the most notable right-wingers in rock, come the mideighties, are the Beach Boys. (They campaigned for George Bush in the 1980 presidential primaries, and posed in back-slapping posture with Ronald and Nancy Reagan in 1983, after being attacked by ultra-rightist Secretary of the Interior James Watt.) True, most of this movement rightward, which includes (according to his letter in their defense to the Washington Post *during the Watt flap) a personal relationship with G. Gordon Liddy, can be ascribed to Mike Love, the group's leader since Brian's incapacitation. Mike Love has a fondness for the authoritarian, which shows in his being the last pop star of consequence still following Sexy Sadie, the Maharishi Mahesh Yogi with his middlebrow yoga techniques. (Transcendental Meditation seems even more than most Western adaptations of Eastern disciplines to use inwardness as an excuse to callousness toward the lot of those who have less than the Seeker.) How far is it from ignoring Chuck Berry's copyrights to buying the logic of Ed Meese that there are no truly hungry—i.e., starving—people in America? Perhaps the Beach Boys in their salad days have created supply-side rock.*

But they haven't done it alone. "Little Deuce Coup" is quite wrong in its assessment of what might prove the undoing of California rock. Most of the performers mentioned herein are still prospering, and in the few cases where that's not true, the reasons are mostly down to self-destruction: the breakup of the Eagles, and Don Henley's bust for drugs and contributing to the delinquency of a minor, are the basis of the larger story, the inability of the group members (as individuals) to find a significant audience, for instance. [Even that changed in '85, when Henley made a couple of big hits.] Scaggs and Ronstadt seemed to have blanded themselves right off the map, though Ronstadt scored an exceedingly temporary comeback in 1983 with an album of show-

*biz standards arranged and conducted by Nelson Riddle. But Ron-
stadt also confirmed the supply-side tendencies of this group of rockers
when she ignored all sorts of advice and went willfully to South
Africa's bogus black homeland, Bophuthatswana, to perform at the
Sun City gambling resort. This earned her international sanctions,
there being a UN-sponsored boycott against appearing in South
Africa.*

*Ronstadt remained adamant that she had done the right thing,
supported strongly by her manager, Peter Asher, himself no doubt
determined to do what he could to support the final pathetic embers
of his homeland's Empire. The most fitting punishment for those who
believe that Exxon should rule the world is probably to live in it after
they do. However, the rest of us may be forgiven for trying to avoid
having this particular punishment fit the crime.*

Hard as it is to believe, there was a time when there was no California rock.
The Hollywood labels recorded rock artists, of course, all through the
fifties, but the black artists were from elsewhere (Little Richard on Specialty and Fats Domino on Imperial, both recorded in New Orleans), and
even the best white ones—Capitol's Gene Vincent, a Virginian, and
Imperial's Ricky Nelson, a Hollywood homeboy—just aped Elvis Presley,
albeit with sometimes remarkable artistic and commercial success. Still,
one could not isolate a peculiarly Californian rock and R&B style, as one
could in Memphis, New Orleans, Chicago, Detroit, Texas or even New
York City. Even preeminent Los Angeles bandleader Johnny Otis re-
cruited his talent and found his styles elsewhere in the Southwest.

All that changed in 1962, when the Beach Boys were born. With the
Beach Boys and the subsequent explosion of vocal-oriented surf groups,
American rock and roll changed drastically. It's true that for several years
Dick Clark had been sprucing up Italian street kids from Philadelphia,
turning Fabian and Frankie Avalon into supper-club Dions. But Brian
Wilson and his brothers (and cousin and neighbor) gave rock its first white
middle-class attraction with *authenticity*.

With "Surfin' U.S.A.," the group's first national hit, guitarist Carl
Wilson immediately established himself as a great Chuck Berry guitarist,
mastering that deceptively difficult skill with a fluidity possessed by no one
else save Keith Richards and its originator. Brian Wilson also played
imaginatively melodic bass lines from the beginning, and the drumming
—probably by the great sessionman Hal Blaine—had tremendous drive.

None of this was anything like the treacle proffered by the Philly slugs.

What the Beach Boys did share with the teen idols was singing. Mike Love's lead vocals on their first hits ("Surfin' Safari"/"409" and "Surfin' U.S.A."/"Shut Down") are as nasal and puerile as Fabian's. Worse, Love phrased like a pop singer—his diction never faltered and his reading of every Wilson lyric is transparent. It's not an accident that when Brian decided to record something emotionally complex or ambiguous, such as "Don't Worry, Baby" or "In My Room," he took the lead part himself. The harmonies were also not derived from the rock tradition: compare the vocal backing on "Shut Down," which is derived from white harmony groups like the Four Freshmen, to the rock'n'harmonies of the Beatles on "You Really Got a Hold On Me," which is straight doo-wop rhythm and blues. (Once again, it took the Beach Boys until "Don't Worry, Baby" in 1964 to introduce a doo-wop element—and then only in the buried bass voice figure.)

To put it simply, the Beach Boys had deracinated rock, and while this surely wasn't the first attempt to do the trick, it was the first time anybody had made it work. In fifties rock, all the white singers eventually confronted race. In some ways, the extent to which a performer faced the black elements of his style measured his greatness: at least, the greatest white rock and rollers—Presley, Buddy Holly, Jerry Lee Lewis, Charlie Rich—made the conflict most explicit. (Holly even did a version of Berry's "Brown-Eyed Handsome Man," which is nothing less than an early hymn to black pride.) In contrast, the Beach Boys simply ignored racial issues, even when they were pressing: their willingness to acknowledge the Four Freshmen as the source of their harmony while denying songwriting credit to Chuck Berry, from whose "Sweet Little Sixteen" their "Surfin' U.S.A." was blatantly plagiarized, may have been accidental, but it was symptomatic. Berry had to sue for his due; the miracle is that he never claimed authorship of "Fun Fun Fun" as well, since that song owes most of its impetus to his "Bye Bye Johnny."

Singers of the fifties—not just Southern ones, but also New York doo-wop whites like Dion and the Belmonts—were much more aware of blacks, because all shared an urban working-class background. Geographically and emotionally, blacks were never far away. The Beach Boys were the first to develop a rock style that was both truly rock and truly suburban middle-class. The Wilson brothers' father and would-be Svengali, Murray, didn't work in a factory; he owned one, albeit a small one. So the cars (whether pink Cadillacs or V8 Fords) that seemed miraculous to Presley and Berry were matters of fact to Brian Wilson, and that's how his songs treated them. The cars, like the surfboards, the California girls and the leisure to enjoy them, were taken for granted, not hard-won tokens of success but simply products of and for conspicuous consumption.

The Beach Boys also introduced a system of musical values different from those suggested by previous rock. Brian Wilson may have been Phil Spector's brightest pupil, but where Spector was willing to sacrifice everything, even reason, for a single noise that felt right, Wilson wanted—demanded—precisely detailed noises. The difference is everything—it changes rock from a music of emotion to a music of technique—and it's what has made the Beach Boys the most influential American recording group. Their legacy is California rock.

The Eagles, Linda Ronstadt, Jackson Browne, Steve Miller, Fleetwood Mac and the singers who have followed in the wake of Boz Scaggs' sterilized *Silk Degrees* (Pablo Cruise, for instance) are the most dominant and successful in the current rock scene. Theirs is commonly and properly thought of as California rock, even though few of these performers are native Californians. Whether they've arrived from Texas (Scaggs, Miller, the Eagles' Don Henley), the Midwest (Eagles Joe Walsh and Glenn Frey), elsewhere in the Southwest (Ronstadt, Buckingham and Nicks) or England (Rod Stewart, the rest of Fleetwood Mac), all these performers have much more to do with one another than with whatever they left home. And what they share—an emphasis on clarity, vocal harmony, craftsmanship and the tendency to sacrifice feeling for technique—is plainly an inheritance from the Beach Boys.

An exception might be made for Browne, an extremely limited singer who has often made poorly crafted recordings. But Browne's psychological miniaturism would not have been possible in rock except for Brian Wilson's self-searching sixties ballads (of which "Don't Worry, Baby" and "In My Room" are again the grandest examples). Still, Browne, like Joni Mitchell and to a lesser extent Neil Young and Warren Zevon, owes as much to the folk movement as he does to rock tradition. Indeed, Browne, Mitchell, Zevon and Young have much more in common with the East Coast's socially conscious bohemianism—which historically has attempted to stand outside of and transcend the class structure—than with even the dropout variant of California rock, which was dragged in by the earliest San Francisco bands. Appropriately enough, the most successful San Francisco band, Jefferson Starship, apes Fleetwood Mac on its latest album, while other veteran and insurgent San Franciscans, including Miller, Scaggs, Pablo Cruise and even Journey, have found their way to the top of the charts by applying Southern California embellishments to their

'Frisco roots. (In every other sense, the influence of the whole Haight-Ashbury sound on late seventies popular music is virtually imperceptible.)

Obviously, this is a restrictive and revisionist reading of the Beach Boys' influence, and of the importance of California rock, as well. I'm not saying that the Byrds' angle on country music hasn't affected the Eagles or Ronstadt, or that Shaun Cassidy doesn't display the Beach Boys' vocal style more blatantly than any of the artists I've listed, or even that Wilson's influence as a songwriter hasn't influenced everyone from Pete Townshend and Paul McCartney to John Fogerty and Billy Joel. These facts are interesting, and some of them are significant, but they don't tell us nearly as much about what has happened to rock and its audience as a result of the Beach Boys' success.

David Leaf's *The Beach Boys and the California Myth* (Today Press, $6.95) is a remarkable rock biography. It exposes a greater part of the sordid intrafamilial conflicts that have shaped the Beach Boys' career, and provides an almost unsightly glimpse of Brian Wilson as a borderline psychotic. It was shocking enough to read some years ago in *Rolling Stone* that Brian, the all-American composer, had so disliked his father that he once shat on a plate and served it to him for dinner. But it's another thing to discover that Murray Wilson was a tyrant given to child abuse who had the most intense love/hate relationship not only with Brian but with Carl and Dennis, too. This paternal relationship took such a bizarre turn in Brian's case, according to Leaf, that he lammed to New York rather than attend the old man's funeral. This makes Brian's strongest expression of filial outrage, "I'm Bugged at My Old Man," seem even more feeble and pathetic, while at the same time heightening the irony of such teen idylls as "Fun Fun Fun" and "Kiss Me, Baby."

Similarly, Leaf's between-the-lines hint that Brian has long been infatuated with his wife's sister, Diane Rovell, makes "My Diane," Brian's only solo contribution to the recently released *The M.I.U. Album*, not poignant but creepily fascinating—the cry of a very sick man for some sort of contact with reality. Compared to this, Leaf's failure to deliver on the issue of Dennis Wilson's exact relationship to Charles Manson and family is minor. And God knows there's plenty of detail I haven't cited: Murray Wilson tormenting Brian; Brian's high school "best friend" pissing on him in a locker-room shower; Brian and his friends tormenting Murray; plus more than anyone else has ever revealed about the machinations of the Wilson family to keep Brian psychologically afloat and productive. Leaf's book is fascinating reading for Beach Boys' fans and rock fans generally, but it's also grim, a picture of madness and betrayal that undercuts all the Transcendental Meditation soft soap as well as the clean-cut image that the band had in its early days.

Leaf does less well in his commentary on the Beach Boys' music, principally because he has little to add to the general thesis presented by Jim Miller in *The Rolling Stone Illustrated History of Rock and Roll* (and by Paul Williams in various *Crawdaddy!* articles of the sixties). Essentially, this orthodox argument asserts that the Beach Boys made greater music after their fall from popularity than they had while the surfing and hot-rod anthems and occasional ballads and love songs kept them in the Top Ten. The specific texts on which the case is based are *Pet Sounds,* the Beach Boys' 1967 "concept" album, which was also their first commercial failure; "Good Vibrations," the orchestral hit single from 1968; and the complex of songs that was to have constituted the album provisionally entitled *Smile. Smile*'s songs were never released in coherent form, and parts of the music were allegedly destroyed by Brian Wilson and his collaborators; those songs that have appeared are apparently so distorted by the other Beach Boys' fears of their lack of commercial appeal (says Leaf) that their original majesty is frequently lost. The album's storied centerpiece, "Surf's Up," was released (on a 1970 LP of the same name) and Leaf feels it lives up to all the claims made for it.

As Greil Marcus has also pointed out, an artistic reputation based so fundamentally on unheard music is at best a chimera, at worst a fraud. It is possible to lament the loss of Wilson's work, and to argue that it would have been his best, but it is not possible to ascertain its quality, much less to use it as a standard against which his other accomplishments should be measured (or for that matter, his failures forgiven). What strikes me as self-evident is that none of the *Smile* songs that have appeared are as compelling as earlier Wilson hits such as "Don't Worry, Baby," the 45 version of "Help Me, Rhonda," "California Girls" or even "Wendy." And certainly few have the kind of pop chamber-music beauty of the Beatles' baroque period. Brian Wilson's genius was his ability to encapsulate a certain kind of white, adolescent, mostly male American experience, to fantasize and mythicize it, and he reached his peak in the period beginning with the two-sided hit single, "I Get Around"/"Don't Worry, Baby," and sustained it in the next three albums, *All Summer Long, Summer Days (And Summer Nights)* and *The Beach Boys Today.* After which the music began to disintegrate under the combined weight of Brian's neurosis and his pretensions. By this theory, *Pet Sounds* (a very good album which happened to make *Billboard*'s Top Ten at the height of the British

Invasion) represents the initial unraveling of Brian Wilson, the moment when you could see him start to lose his touch, not the blossoming of his grandiose vision.

But there is, at least ostensibly, another subject in David Leaf's book: the California Myth. Leaf doesn't devote much space to this subject, except to describe songwriter Jimmy Webb's plowing a field in the Midwest as an adolescent and hearing "Surf City," whereupon he decided to go to California, and to reiterate the usual blather about the enshrinement of youth and "fun."

The idea of youth is easy enough to understand, though in the context of California (as in the case of rock and roll) its boundaries may be attitudinal as often as chronological. But fun—what's that? Certainly not everything that's pleasure or enjoyable, because that might include, for instance, reading books. Remember the girl in "Fun Fun Fun" who sneaks away in her father's hot car on the pretext of going to the library?

For the Beach Boys and California rock, fun has always meant certain kinds of consumption: whether surfing or sports cars in the early Beach Boys songs or complaisant sex and drugs for more recent articulations of the dream. It also implies a certain exhilaration, as in "Shut Down," or its dark underside, expressed vividly in songs from Jan and Dean's "Deadman's Curve" to the Eagles' "Life in the Fast Lane" and "Hotel California," and rejection of all sorts of authority, beginning with the parental. In this sense, Joe Walsh's recent "Life's Been Good," for all its irony, lives very much in the world created by Brian Wilson and his descendants.

Though this perspective may seem expansive, in fact it's restrictive. Anyone could "Rock Around with Ollie Vee," along with Buddy Holly, since the only indispensable resources were the guts and vision to get out there and bop. But not just anyone can go out and surf (the point of the first verse of "Surfin' U.S.A." is that everybody *doesn't* have an ocean, or the leisure to use it), and not everyone can drive a sports car without hot-wiring it. It isn't just blacks who disappear from the rock and roll world of the Beach Boys, then. It's also everyone without a comparatively great deal of wealth and leisure.

This is a new attitude in rock and roll. When Little Richard sang "Fool about my money / Don't try to save," he wasn't speaking from the point of view of someone for whom that was an affordable option. Whether he knew it or not, Little Richard was challenging the preconceptions of his middle-class listeners by brazenly asserting his right to blow all his dough. (Greil Marcus has mentioned being shocked by Richard's cavalier attitude toward cash when he first encountered it, and a propensity *not* to save is one of the distinguishing characteristics of the American working class in general.) The Beach Boys moved American rock and roll beyond this sort of challenge, because they were much more part of a separate, isolated subculture. Pink Cadillacs? Well, really, the color might be a little gauche, a Cadillac a little stodgy.

In America (an important distinction, since English rock is governed by a far different perception of class distinction) the middle class has covertly ruled rock and roll ever since the Beach Boys. (Before them, remember, Bob Dylan had faked a working-class background for credibility, denying midwestern middle-class roots not so far from the Beach Boys' own, even if Dylan's were more ethnic.) As a consequence, the overt "artistic" ambitions of the music became greater, more elementally bourgeois. One of the reasons that Brian Wilson's most contrived and inflated works seem the best to his most adoring critics is that they fit a more conventional set of artistic standards, almost classical ones (at least by middlebrow reckoning). During the sixties the only American rock musicians able to consistently express working-class values on a mass level were Creedence Clearwater Revival's John Fogerty, Sylvester Stewart of Sly and the Family Stone, and Jimi Hendrix, and Hendrix had to be certified cool in Britain first. Only at the very tag end of the period did this trend start to reverse itself, and then only ambiguously: For every Bob Seger or Bruce Springsteen who finds critical acclaim for the authenticity of his expression, there is a Ronnie Van Zant who's overlooked or trashed.

In light of the above, perhaps the most revealing California rock currently being made is Linda Ronstadt's, even though it's far from the best. Ronstadt has a remarkable voice, or at least one with enough power and range to make it worth remarking upon, and her producer/manager, Peter Asher, has perfected the art of recording basic tracks for this kind of music. Still, there's no way that Ronstadt's records have the punch of the Eagles', the diversity of Fleetwood Mac's or the emotional authority of Jackson Browne's.

On the other hand, her oldies covers—the Buddy Holly and Smokey Robinson songs, the old Chuck Berry and Elvis Presley hits that she reworks—amount to a revisionist history of rock and roll, especially on her new album, *Living in the U.S.A.*

Ronstadt manages, for instance, to delete all irony from Berry's "Back in the U.S.A.," her current hit. This isn't especially difficult, since Berry's original was founded in a well of sincerity. On the other hand, for Berry, his sincerity *was* ironic, since he could never be sure that the joint "where hamburgers sizzle on an open griddle night and day" would serve a black man like himself. For Ronstadt (who, according to her recent *Rolling Stone* interview, believes that Standard Oil should run the country), "Back in the U.S.A." is simply the facts.

Her "Ooo Baby Baby," the song Smokey Robinson once called "my national anthem," commits another cardinal error, as described by Berry in "Rock & Roll Music": it loses the beauty of the melody until it sounds just like a symphony. Ronstadt is so concerned with singing the song "right," in terms of time and pitch, that she sacrifices any hope of reaching the depth of feeling that made so unforgettable the version that Robinson sang so casually.

Ronstadt and Asher would, it seems, defend *Living in the U.S.A.* on two grounds: one, that it is silly to criticize proper technique, and second, that rock is supposed to be entertainment, and any other qualities are acquired haphazardly and unconsciously. The first attitude is possibly the proper one—I'd rather hear good chops than bad, if that's all that's at stake. But the second idea provides the link between the California rockers of today and the Beach Boys. For entertainment is the ultimate middlebrow, middle-class accolade to mediocre art. In some ways, in fact, it's accurate to say that rock and roll came to us with the intention of destroying entertainment. Surely no one has ever claimed that Frankie Laine or Vaughn Monroe or Johnny Ray or any other pre-Presley pop singer was not entertaining.

What Presley was that these others weren't is simple: he was moving, in both the literal senses (he made people want to dance and he all but forced them to feel what he was trying to communicate). He was moving in a more metaphoric sense, as well: Elvis inspired others to take action or to realize that there was action to take. It is in this sense that much of the current California crop ceases to have reference to rock and roll at all. There isn't any sense of choice implied in most of this music. Without any sense of racial clash, without any invigorating involvement with or challenge from its audience, today's California stars for the most part lead us back to their beginnings, to the kind of Hollywood "fun" and "entertainment" to which rock was originally an antithesis. In this kind of rock, one neither dies nor gets old but simply cruises the fast lane, making an occasional stop at Hotel California, there to be immersed in a hot tub of self-pity. In which case, we can fairly say that we have experienced the true curse of eternal youth: eternal petulance.

This is why the California attitude—which is by now not restricted to California musicians, by any means, though it is still typified by them—

feels most threatened by the punks. If rock should somehow cease to be entertainment and become something Other once again, the jig is up for the likes of Ronstadt—and for the likes of the Beach Boys, too.

I am reminded of poor Terry Toad, the hapless loser of *American Graffiti*. In one of the film's final scenes, he utters the true epitaph of California rock. Terry rises from his knees, where he has been puking his guts out in a parking lot, and looks around him, quaking. "Do you want to go home?" someone asks.

"Oh, no," he replies. "I'm having too much fun."

Boston Phoenix, 1978

The Weight

The attitudes expressed in this column run so drastically counter to the orthodox opinions of rock critics of my generation that they have spiced—perhaps ruined—more after-dinner conversations among my colleagues than almost any others I can think of. For me, however, the idea that the Band were a mere hobbyhorse for the talents of Robbie Robertson is preposterous. Not only does it rely upon a view of the group that stops after it has made only two or three albums—that is, runs contrary to the facts—but it also sets up the very terms and conditions that rock critics propose to alter in the first place. The difference between a teenage sex idol like Shaun Cassidy and a post-adolescent intellectual idol like Robbie Robertson is a matter of taste, not even degree. Neither is especially satisfying, if you bother to look closely at who's pulling the strings.

It's not hard to understand the release of *Anthology*, the second repackaging of Band material in two years. The group made only eight albums (one an oldies collection, another a live rehash) and has pretty much stopped recording; but Capitol needed a new set for the Christmas trade. The group is involved only because this way it can ensure a little quality control.

But *Anthology* has another purpose. Like Neil Young's *Decade*, it's meant to sanctify an artist's sense of self-importance. So was Martin Scorsese's film of the final Band concert, *The Last Waltz*; as in the movie, where Robbie Robertson demonstrated that he is one of the few people capable of making Bob Dylan seem humble, the effect of this conservatively chosen, elegantly (if inconsequentially) annotated presentation is to raise more questions than it answers.

There's no denying that much of the rock here is as powerful and imaginative as any ever made: "The Night They Drove Old Dixie Down," "Chest Fever," "The Weight" and "This Wheel's on Fire." But the rest of the Band's work has enjoyed a critical free ride for most of this decade. The group acquired its myth as a result of historical association (as the Hawks, they backed rockabilly demi-legend Ronnie Hawkins as well as the electrified Bob Dylan). But only the Band's first two albums, *Music from Big Pink* and *The Band*, lived up to the legend, and *Anthology* is as noteworthy for what it excludes as for what it contains. While the Band's first three albums are given two sides of this set, the final five are crammed into the second pair. Not that that isn't a fair appraisal of the Band's accomplishment. For instance, there are just two selections from *Cahoots*, the band's fourth and worst record—there aren't any others that deserve inclusion. And even "Life Is a Carnival" and "When I Paint My Masterpiece" are transparently inferior to the songs on *Stage Fright*, much less *The Band*.

A great deal has been claimed for the Band, not only by Robertson, Scorsese and the *Anthology*'s annotator, Robert Palmer, but also by such estimable critics as Jon Landau and Greil Marcus. Landau went so far as to stake the case for rock auteurism on *Cahoots*; Marcus devotes more space and passion to the Band in his book, *Mystery Train*, than to anyone save Elvis Presley. Most of the praise rises and falls with Robertson, the perfect object of the pop intellectual's star-struck gaze. He is a fastidious musician, presumably streetwise, since he began playing with Hawkins at fifteen, and he has a certified Outsider's vision of America. But listening to the Band's history is tantamount to tracking the deterioration of these qualities: Robertson's fastidiousness quickly became conservatism. How long can you mourn shattered tradition, anyway? His street wisdom quickly decayed into hucksterism; the interviews in *The Last Waltz*, where Robertson interrupts Rick Danko and Richard Manuel at almost every turn, are gross self-promotion, indulged with aplomb if little subtlety. And as for the Outsider—turning to *The Last Waltz* again, we see the Outsider as a blustering Aristocrat, an impression reinforced by the Robertson quotes in Palmer's liner notes.

Robertson's position as a pop aristocrat is anomalous. He has never had a hit single—unless you count Joan Baez's mummified version of "The Night They Drove Old Dixie Down"—and the Band's albums at best went gold, never platinum. Unlike rock's other great cult intellectuals— Young, say, or Peter Townshend—Robertson has never had a commercial success to go with his reviews: There's no *Tommy* or *Harvest* on his résumé. He makes up for the lack of public response with withering arrogance. And withering is the word. From *The Band* to *Northern Lights/Southern Cross*, only Robertson's songs appeared on Band albums, and no one has ever claimed this was because Rick Danko and Richard Manuel weren't writing. (Both made substantial contributions to *Music from Big Pink*.) If the Band was supposed to mean anything, it was as a collective effort. And in any case, Robertson has been the group's true leader mostly on the page (that is, in the press and on lead sheets). The heart of rock is in its beats, and the Band's is supplied by drummer Levon Helm—the oldest member, the only American (the rest are Canadian), the leader after they left the Hawks (he quit when they hooked up with Dylan, rather than play second fiddle to an upstart folksinger), the group's greatest singer. Helm is the only person in the Band to whom Robbie Robertson defers, as he does even in the interviews in *The Last Waltz*.

When the Band speaks best, most clearly, it almost always uses Levon Helm's voice. In "The Weight," Rick Danko sings just one verse and Levon takes *that* away from him with a yowled "Yeah!" that's among the three or four greatest interjections in the history of rock (a.k.a. the history of musical interjection). It is Helm's voice, dripping with southern-bred bitterness, that makes "The Night They Drove Old Dixie Down" genuinely tragic. It could be argued that in Helm, Robertson found his perfect vehicle. But maybe it was Helm who found in the more glib and articulate Robertson a marvelous mouthpiece: Who whispered the secrets of the American Dream in Robertson's young ear as he drifted through the Ozark wilderness? Who pointed him toward that wilderness in the first place? Levon Helm. And if all this is true, whose vision is this that we're hearing?

Because it fails to deliver on its assertions, *Anthology* doesn't matter much. But buried within is the story of what happened to the idealists of the sixties, those who were devoted to collectivism and tried to make it work. And how that ideal was discarded, maybe betrayed.

Boston Phoenix, 1978

Nixing the Knack

I have a reputation that must be upheld for no-holds-barred nastiness when something violates my sensibility sufficiently. No less an authority than Rona Barrett once averred that one of my reviews made Paul Williams cry; I am also the guy who offered shards of a shattered Devo LP to all comers. And so on.

This review was nasty and called for. It gives you an idea of how mean it can get. I have arguably learned a bit more self-control in ensuing years, though Lord knows how—much less why, considering the provocation, which hasn't slackened.

Of course there's no way to win with a record like this one. Like the Eddie Haskell type kid down the block, who was always spotless and mannerly but remained an innate creep (remember *Leave It to Beaver?*), there's no way to convince Mom—or the fans—that it's all a fraud. Who'd believe you?

There was once a pernicious rumor to the effect that Alice Cooper was Eddie Haskell. What Alice ever did to deserve that is beyond me—he was a pretty nice guy. On the other hand, the Knack's rhythm guitar mouthpiece, Doug Fieger, is the incarnation of the Haskell stereotype: in every photo of him I've ever seen, he's either smirking or about to, and his singing is just an aural smirk. It's not that Fieger or the Knack are closet bullies exactly—there's nothing that forceful about them—but there's a sense they'd like to have things both ways. Doug Fieger claims in his rare interviews that he's little more than a "craftsman," then turns around and utters philosophical pronouncements that reveal his profound ignorance of rock and roll history and make him sound like a poor man's Pete Townshend. Where does this terminally (I hope) cute joker get off?

Don't ask. The most salient characteristic of both Knack albums is their repulsive misogyny. Sexism pervades every song these guys have written, so much so that looking at that fresh, innocent young woman's face on the cover of . . . *but the Little Girls Understand* is enough to make you nauseous. I'm not talking about the usual heavy-metal, my-cock-is-harder-than-yours posturing either. In Fieger's lyrics, women are literally commodities whose chief purpose is to be brutalized. The kid in "Baby Talks Dirty" is a foul-mouthed windup doll, and in "Mr. Handleman," the tame calypso that's the new LP's catchiest number, the protagonist is pimping for his wife—a situation the group views with dispassion, if not outright approbation.

The music can't redeem the lyrics—not only because such dehumanization is irredeemable but also because the music is lame. Indeed, the Knack are the most nefarious kind of hacks. They're terribly competent and efficient; they have a seemingly inexhaustible storehouse of clichés, drawn from everybody from Buddy Holly and the Beatles—check out "Tell Me You're Mine" and "(Havin' a) Rave Up" here—to early Fleetwood Mac ("End of the Game") and the Lettermen ("How Can Love Hurt So Much"). In a way, Fieger and Company manipulate their stockpile of banalities with as much finesse as any band since Foreigner—though that's a little unfair to Foreigner, who at least grind out their radio fodder with verve.

But the Knack have a much greater achievement: making hard-rock clichés sound completely gutless. Which comes as no surprise, since Fieger's original Detroit group, Sky, was mewling Crosby, Stills, Nash and Young harmonies in Detroit at the same time that the MC5 were inventing the punk-rock genre that the Knack now dilutes and exploits.

To be entirely fair, I must admit that the Knack does have a message. All of Fieger's lyrics finally boil down to one sentiment: You gotta fuck me, honey. (When he's feeling ambitious, he'll write something like "Can't Put a Price on Love," which translates as: Fuck me for free, babe.) How pleasant it'd be to lock this clown in a closet with a tape loop of Marianne Faithfull's "Why D'Ya Do It." Because, at their most wimpoid, Fieger's puling vocals suggest that for him the ultimate agony would be to imagine that somewhere in the world there exists a woman who might find him sexually unattractive. Compared to Doug Fieger, that is, Rod Stewart is a paragon of sexual humility.

It can be argued that my analysis takes such a featherweight band far too seriously. But faced with an Eddie Haskell, there are only two choices: ignore him (which is what the homeboys used to do with Sky) or call his bluff and kick his ass. Take your pick. Me, I'm a man of action.

Rolling Stone, 1980

Bob Seger's "Wind" Is Mostly Hot Air/As the Crow Flies

"Don't back down" is one of the greatest songs the Beach Boys ever sang, but it's a useless critical precept, especially in terms of a medium as young and volatile as rock and roll. Whether writing under deadline pressure or not, there's no way that every immediate summary of a record or show will be correct. And of course, sometimes work that originally appeared major (or slight) is subsequently revealed (by refraction against later works by the same performer or history or both) to be slight (or major). If your reactions tend to be expressed as strongly as mine, this means that humble pie becomes, if not a specialty of the house, at least an unsurprising condiment.

These examples don't quite make the case. In the first place, I wasn't wrong about either of the records in question: Against the Wind *really* is that bad, The Distance *just* that good. In fact there are only three lines in all of the former review that I regret. The crack about Coca-Cola, because it's too smart-ass; the claim that there are no lines worth quoting in the ballads (the lines from "Against the Wind" in which Seger haltingly expresses his indecisiveness—"Well, those drifter's days are past me now / I've so much more to think about / Deadlines and commitments / What to leave in / What to leave out"—aren't just memorable but haunting) and of course the final kiss-off. Even so, it's only the third for which I apologized, because it's only the third that struck me as requiring an apology. Seger had made an empty windbag of a record, and it didn't live up to his previous standards, much less his potential, but that record can now be seen almost as a housecleaning before moving on toward what he's really capable of doing.

In fairness to myself, I must say that I can't think of another instance where a performer has made a record as hollow and disconnected from his earlier music as Against the Wind *and* followed it with anything comparable to The Distance, in quality and commitment. (At best, performers have reacted against their own commercial bloatedness by taking a sharp turn away from rock and the mass audience—e.g., Neil Young with the cycle of albums that began with Time Fades Away, *Bruce Springsteen with* Nebraska). The Distance

didn't sell nearly so well as Against the Wind, *but (having abandoned the AOR rocker/Top Forty ballad schematic) it still managed
to hold a rung in the Top Ten for several weeks, which is not at all
an insignificant achievement.*

*So I wrote my apology, which was due, after all. And went to see
Seger that summer expecting the good but not overwhelming show I
got. (The irony of his having achieved success through persistent
touring is that Bob has always been a far better songwriter and singer
than bandleader.) The performance I saw in 1983 had the same kind
of highlights and dull bits that have characterized all of Seger's shows
since I began seeing him in 1966: ferocious rockers that were overex-
tended with predictable soloing, beautiful ballads that were fuzzed out
by the sound system, vagaries of pacing that simply roller-coastered the
emotional level of the show. It was the kind of show that old-timers
might split a song or two early, in order to beat the rush in the parking
lot.*

*Which is just what I was going to do when the opening chords of
his final song caught my ear and sent me rushing back to my seat.
Seger stepped to the microphone and belted out one of the finest
versions I have ever heard of a song that everyone holding this book
will understand is extremely dear to my heart: John Fogerty's "Fortunate Son."*

It is an extreme mistake ever to underestimate this man.

Listeners who first discovered Bob Seger with *Night Moves* and *Stranger
in Town* clearly find his new album an even more palatable product, since
it leaped into the Top Ten with frightening rapidity. So I guess those
of us who remember Seger, the all-American rock and roller, just have
to take our lumps. But not necessarily in silence. At the risk of incur-
ring a barrage of hate mail from his West Coast cronies and backup
vocalists, I'd like to say that this is not only the worst record Bob
Seger has made but an absolutely cowardly one as well. *Against the
Wind* betrays all those years that Seger worked in the midwestern wilderness, trying to find a national audience for his odd blend of heavy
rock and pop smarts. He had to fight hard to prove there was still a
place in rock and roll for a guy like him, and with "Night Moves,"
he won.

This is the LP that makes that victory meaningless. *Against the Wind*
is all retreat. And the reason that its ascension to the pop-chart strato-

sphere is scary is that it got there so effortlessly—there was no tension, in the music or anywhere else, to make people think twice. Seger spent the past year crafting failure-proof songs that are utterly listenable and quite empty of content. His commercial tactics, I suppose, were a triumph. But as music, *Against the Wind* is heartless and mediocre—a lot worse than something like Billy Joel's *Glass Houses* (which is bad enough) because at least Joel is trying to expand his identity, is risking something. All that Seger risks here is his credibility, and that accidentally.

Still, Bob Seger always sings fantastically well, and if what you need is a carefully constructed album of gravelly crooning with a half-hearted snarl thrown in once in a while for effect, you've come to the right place. That's all you're getting from *Against the Wind*. At his best, Seger's been able to write songs (from "Ramblin' Gamblin' Man" to "Feel Like a Number") that are the very voice of the kid down the block. Now he doesn't sound like he's ever met such people: all the street life on the current record is seen from an outsider's perspective, and it feels the same way, like it's being faked. Even the hardest rockers—"Horizontal Bop," "Betty Lou's Gettin' Out Tonight"—are hollow. Sure, they're vignettes of ordinary life, as before, but this time the most any of Seger's characters can imagine is a long drunk or a quick lay. I keep expecting to hear him sing, "Have a Coke and a smile."

The fault can't be laid on the Silver Bullet Band. For one thing, Seger's work with the Muscle Shoals Rhythm Section is as uninspired as anything the hometown boys are playing. For another, *Against the Wind* has almost nothing of Seger's blustering, hard-driving concert sound, so talking about the rockers here distorts the issue. Fast tunes saved *Stranger in Town* from its excessive bathos, but this time the rock and roll cuts feel perfunctory, simply tossed in to separate the overinflated ballad "statements" (none of which contains a line sufficiently memorable to quote) from the flat country rockers, which have all the emotional depth of the latest batch of J. D. Souther ditties.

There's a feeling of rootlessness to *Against the Wind*, but it's not the same hungry rootlessness that Seger captured so brilliantly in "Turn the Page," his classic about life on the road. Now, in some strange way, he seems removed from his own instincts. The eerie manner in which the production lifts the singer's voice above the band, leaving it floating there so that the two never quite make contact, is a perfect example of the problem, and a perfect metaphor for it. It's such characteristics that make *Against the Wind* such a slap in the face. Bob Seger's roots were what once sustained him, and for him to turn his back on them in order to join the slick pop-star bandwagon is a genuine cop-out, a denial that his early years meant anything. Seger's always had the voice to be a superstar, but if all he wanted was the chance to sing pretty, why did he struggle for so long to find success with it?

Mostly, *Against the Wind* deals in stereotypes, particularly female ones. There's more than a hint of the Eagles' malicious misogyny and preppie snobbery in these numbers—not just "Fire Lake," to which the insufferable Glenn Frey, Don Henley and Timothy B. Schmit contribute precise backing vocals, but in almost all the rest as well. Just as the rockers continually sell the "kids" cynically short, the love songs are all about women—devil, angel or beloved "babe"—who exist only as commodities, to be worshiped when they're supportive ("Good for Me"), belittled when they try to assert themselves ("Her Strut") or chastised when they can't be controlled ("Against the Wind," "You'll Accompany Me"). There's no feeling for *people* in these compositions, which is not only a sharp reversal of form for Seger (whose lyrics have always been strongest in characterization), but a complete acquiescence to the Eagles' pop philosophy: a gram of cool is worth a pound of conviction. This is a splendid platform for nostalgia and self-pity, well-represented by the country rocker "Fire Lake" and the lugubriously poetic "No Man's Land," but in every other way it's worthless.

"Who wants to take that long-shot gamble?" asks Bob Seger in "Fire Lake." And his answer, despite superficial nods at rebelliousness, comes back clearly: *not me.* You could listen to this LP forever and never hear the singer picking up any sort of challenge. It makes me sad and it makes me angry (another emotion that's disappeared here, though it's often fueled Seger's finest songs). Maybe rock and roll never forgets, but the best thing anybody who ever had any hope for Bob Seger can do is try not to remember *Against the Wind* and pray for something better next time. I wouldn't hold my breath.

Rolling Stone, 1980

In 1980, I concluded my review of Bob Seger's *Against the Wind* by saying: "Maybe rock and roll never forgets, but the best thing anybody who ever had any hope for Bob Seger can do is try not to remember *Against the Wind* and pray for something better next time. I wouldn't hold my breath." It is now time for me to exhale, take another deep gulp and prepare for a public bite of crow. *The Distance*, Bob Seger's first new album in almost three years, is the best rock and roll record I have heard since *The River*, and more importantly, it's Seger's most committed, cohesive and exciting album ever.

What's most amazing about *The Distance* is its ambition. This is Seger's first focused set of songs—the first time he's attempted a song cycle in the fashion of Jackson Browne and Bruce Springsteen. Seger is a better singer and a more creative melodist than either Browne or Springsteen, but he's never had their shamelessness or their intense reach.

In "Against the Wind" itself, Seger moaned of having to decide "What to leave in / What to leave out," the plaint of the compulsively self-restrictive. And the schematic programming of his other albums (Top Forty ballads balanced by AOR rockers, "serious" versus fun, sex versus romance) is perhaps their worst limitation. The major achievement of *The Distance* is that it synthesizes these pop contradictions, with the result that the best songs are a kind of dialogue between two sides of an argument Seger has been having with himself.

The Distance begins and ends with love songs, "Even Now" and "Little Victories," which are really anthems of perseverance—they use personal relationships as metaphors for a vision of the world and the way that it works and what it takes (and costs) to cope with such a place and time. When Seger sings the key lines of "Little Victories"—"Every time you keep control when you're cut off at the knees / Every time you take a punch and still stand at ease"—he is obviously singing to every broken worker back home in Michigan as much as to fellow brokenhearted lovers. And this is true whether or not the subtext was planned, because the best music here is explicitly and defiantly about what has happened to Seger and his constituency in the past few years. (This is one of the things that makes it such an amazing improvement over *Against the Wind*, which seemed completely abstracted from such lives.)

This political context is easiest to see in the album's hardest-rocking song, "Makin' Thunderbirds," which is an unemployed auto worker's paean to the way his life (and those cars!) used to be. For those three minutes, the singer is as "young and proud" as ever, even though the last verse reckons with the deterioration of both product and pride. But in the very next song, "Boomtown Blues," he's coping with the Depression: moved South, found a job and begun a life robbed of whatever dignity, meaning and sense of connection it might ever have had. As an exposure of the false promise of industry's southern strategy, "Boomtown Blues" is the most radical and incisive song Seger has ever written. And he keeps the mood going with "Shame on the Moon," a Rodney Crowell song that illumines the new terms on which people deal with each other in the time of Reagan's New Federalism: "Some men go crazy / Some men go slow /

Some men go just where they want / Some men never go." This is the world in which Seger's characters try to maintain their "little victories," whether they're returning shattered to a place that's barely changed ("Comin' Home") or leaving a shattered home for a life that has to be better, though it never quite is (the anthemic "Roll Me Away").

In its portrayal of alienation and isolation and their consequences, personal and political, *The Distance* is most akin to *Nebraska* among recent rock albums. Seger's vision is less bleak than Springsteen's, and I suspect that makes it more realistic: people less often go crazy and commit murder in times like these than they simply stumble homeward, seeking what's no longer there, or wander aimlessly, trying to locate what they've falsely been promised. What *Nebraska* and *The Distance* share is a sense that times are more terrible than most men and women can bear and that every time anyone maintains human dignity in face of the terror, something of consequence has been achieved. It's their denial of nihilism that makes such albums most valuable.

So Seger's triumph stands not in isolation, but acquires greater meaning when linked with *Nebraska*, Billy Joel's *The Nylon Curtain* and even something like Don Henley's *I Can't Stand Still*. All of these are dealing with the real issues in people's lives right now, the sense of injustice and hopelessness that overwhelms so many rock listeners. I think it's fascinating that with the recent release of albums by Springsteen, Joel, Tom Petty and Seger, it is Petty's album, which is the only one that proceeds as though nothing has changed, which has met the most resistance. (It took nine weeks for Petty's *Long After Dark* to reach *Billboard*'s Top Ten; the others made it in two to three weeks.) So much for the apolitical apathy of the mainstream rock audience.

But it's also essential to remember that the music which is speaking most directly to the needs and concerns of Americans is not coming from trendy British bands or voguish new wavers, but from the center of rock. Most superstars are indeed immobilized by their success (that is both the overt and covert theme of *Against the Wind*). But the great ones find a way to struggle through and speak the truth again. And that is why *The Distance* is a record that moves me to the core and makes me want to apologize to Bob Seger.

Consider it rendered.

Record, 1983

Excerpts from *The New Rolling Stone Record Guide*

Whether or not a talent for invective is a prerequisite of criticism, I seem to be blessed—or cursed—with the gift. The following selection incorporates a proportion of such one-liners as could be adapted from The New Rolling Stone Record Guide, along with some more discursive (though hardly friendlier) commentary on major peeves and nemeses.

Kate Bush: English thrush who created a storm in certain critical quarters beginning in the late seventies. Not exactly new wave, not exactly art rock. Sort of like the consequences of mating Patti Smith with a Hoover vacuum cleaner.

Cher: Although she was the lead voice on one of rock's supreme trash classics, Sonny and Cher's "I Got You Babe," Cher has neither the spark of intelligence required of the competent interpretive singer nor sufficient vitality and expressiveness ("Gypsies, Tramps and Thieves" notwithstanding) to serve as a full-blown producer's ingenue. She remains that oddest of artistic breeds, the TV celebrity, famous for *being* rather than doing. She's perfect for the role, which requires the degree of narcissism revealed by listing her album titles: *Cher; Cher; Cher's Greatest Hits; Cherished; Cher; Cher Sings the Hits*.

Devo: Devo updates the smart-ass smarminess of Frank Zappa for contemporary preppies, which is probably what Robert Christgau meant when he called the group "Meat Loaf for college kids." But Devo does not possess an instrumentalist of Zappa's caliber, and the result is an ideological mediocrity in which only the most obvious targets are ever poked and prodded. This corresponds to the band's music, which manipulates the minimalist and abstract ideas associated with new wave into a series of complete clichés. The exception is "Whip It," which manipulates black street clichés, both musical and lyrical, ably enough to have become a hit.

Devo's most odious quality is its quasi-libertarian rhetoric, which is used

as a basis for elitist put-downs of everything "normal" (including its audience, but excluding the group itself). The puerility of most of its ideas,
founded in an unearned contempt for mass culture, makes it impossible
to take the quasi-totalitarian flavor of such album titles as *Duty Now for
the Future*, *Freedom of Choice*, and *New Traditionalists* seriously even as
satire. If there's anything frightening about Devo's social vision, it's that
so many fans are willing to scoop up this kind of nonsense in order to feel
smugly superior.

Especially to be missed are the band's cover versions of rock classics like
"Secret Agent Man" and "Satisfaction," which are not only badly performed but also ill conceived.

The Doors: While comparing the Doors to any of rock's greatest artists
—from Chuck Berry and Buddy Holly to Creedence Clearwater Revival
and the Clash—is clearly absurd, Jim Morrison was an important, if banal,
erotic politician, adolescent eye-opener and a genuinely dangerous teen
idol. In this way, and despite their obnoxious cult, the Doors take their
place in pop history as the progenitors of a wave of teenybopper anti-icons
ranging from Alice Cooper to Kiss.

The group's dabblings with Brechtian commentary, Artaudian reality
inversions and sub-Laingian psychology are perfectly appropriate expressions for an age dominated by *serious* adolescence. It should then go
without saying that the Doors' best album (notwithstanding the aberration
of *Morrison Hotel*) is its schematic first one, which enlists Kurt Weill in
pursuit of a hit single, stumbles across a tumescently pubescent classic in
"Light My Fire" and concludes with the ultimate confusion of dementia
praecox and profundity ("The End").

For the rest (again, with the exception of *Morrison Hotel*, a fairly
effective method of dealing with the specter of real American rock that
the Band and Creedence had re-created), the Doors were a singles act,
more alluring (maybe) and more shrewdly marketed than Tommy James
and the Shondells and the Guess Who, but not necessarily better. In fact,
arguably not as good, since the band possessed a drummer too laid-back
to ever really kick out the jams, an organist who sounded like he'd been
laid off from a cocktail lounge and a singer whose notion of the best way
to express passion was belching and grunting. Guitarist Robby Krieger
actually managed to get off some fairly listenable lines, but then he also
wrote the band's only really human song, "Running Blue," a tribute to
Otis Redding that's puppy-dog cute in its clumsiness and lack of anything
approaching genuine soulfulness. If Elektra Records ever has the courage

to create a package that is nothing but singles—including "Five to One," but forgetting that "The End" ever existed except as a mistaken plunge into pomposity—the Doors might yet look like a modestly successful act. As it stands, we are left with the spectacle of *Absolutely Live*, long ago eclipsed by Iggy Pop (among others) on nights when he wasn't even half trying. It hardly matters that Morrison originated the concept; others have done more with it, not that there was all that much to it in the first place.

Is this the most overrated group in rock history? Only a truly terminal case of arrested adolescence can hold out against such a judgment for very long.

Leif Garrett: Okay, so Shaun Cassidy's versions of the Beach Boys aren't as bad as they seem. But that doesn't excuse *cloning* him.

The Grateful Dead: The Grateful Dead epitomized hippie rock and roll, and unless you're a hippie yourself, this is one assertedly major oeuvre that's virtually worthless except for documentary purposes. The Dead's long modal jamming may be mesmerizing in concert (though even there, it's questionable), but they're simply self-indulgent and boring on disc. The band's attempts at pop, rock and country are rendered effortlessly irritating and stodgy by the lack of a crisp rhythm section and/or a single competent vocalist.

The Dead are worshiped for their image as hip patriarchs, which means that as long as Jerry Garcia has that acid twinkle in his eye, he'll never have to worry about his pedestrian chops. There simply isn't very much about this group that's impressive, except the devotion of its fans to a mythology created in Haight-Ashbury and now sustained in junior high schools across the U.S.A. And the group's patchouli-oil philosophy, which does nothing more than reinforce solipsism and self-indulgence in its listeners, except when it's nurturing its Hell's Angels fan club, is exactly the sort of stuff that gave peace 'n' love a bad name.

Kayak: Are the four "concept" LPs by these mid-seventies European art rockers so lame because the Dutch quintet doesn't understand its own English lyrics? Or is it just that pompous clowns like these had complete contempt for anyone who'd listen to this type of pop, which they were making only because the "serious music" they preferred wouldn't make them rich?

. . .

Nicolette Larson: A protégée of Linda Ronstadt's and a featured backing singer with Neil Young, Larson epitomizes the worst of LA seventies pop rock. So laid-back, it's a wonder she can stand up. Rock isn't dead, but anyone who remembers Little Eva may wish it were after hearing these.

Omega: For everyone who'd like to grow up to be a synthesizer.

Donny and Marie Osmond: The only people I've ever heard who deserved Andy Williams. Sometimes I wish they'd learn to ski and meet his ex-wife.

Pipedream: Not in your wildest fantasies.

Roger Powell: Why is it that the love of a boy for his automobile, his dog, even his guitar seems so warm and pleasant, while the love of a boy for his synthesizer seems so heartless and calculating? Probably because a lot less pretentious twaddle has resulted from the other infatuations.

Lou Reed: Reed is the perfect rock critic's darling: limited, abrasive, a bad case of stunted musical development meeting profoundly self-pitying lyrical professions of self-loathing and nihilism. On occasion, Reed has shown some real ability, primarily as a manipulator of rock traditions of singing and lyric writing (and primarily as a member of the Velvet Underground), but his songs are repetitious, his addled production concepts make some of his best music virtually unlistenable and his attempts to work in extended forms have been uniformly disastrous. This includes the oft-heralded song cycle *Berlin*, which achieves a certain decadent splendor more because producer Bob Ezrin provided Reed with the first competence at the controls he's ever had than because the material hung together well. It goes trebly for *Metal Machine Music*, an album of abrasive electronic noise that is both an artistic and commercial hustle: Reed's experimentalism is definitely sub-Cage in that the intended effect is nothing more than cheap shock and perhaps critical credibility for being willing to indulge in such monumental nihilism. It hardly matters whether Reed intended *Metal Machine Music* as an elaborate joke on the public and his record company or whether he actually thought that he was making an important electronic work. The joke is no more witty or original than the electronic composing.

In the end, the essential album of Reed's career is *Rock'n'Roll Diary*, which by juxtaposing his later work with his early days in the Velvet Underground, makes it clear what a sad case of arrested development Reed really is. However great his influence on punk (and it was enormous), Reed remains barely a minor artist.

Linda Ronstadt: As the most important interpretative singer of the singer/songwriter age, Linda Ronstadt is an anomaly. The irony of her success is compounded by the fact that, while she has a remarkable voice, Ronstadt is an utterly horrid interpreter of contemporary rock and soul material, frequently missing the essence of a song and almost never cutting below the surface of one. If the measure of an interpreter's skill is the ability to give listeners a fresh perspective on some grand old chestnut or insight into the work of a budding composer, Ronstadt must be judged at best a competent craftsman and at worst an empty-headed, soulless dispenser of music as sheer commodity.

Ronstadt's soprano voice is so rare in its purity of pitch and tone that she can actually override and obscure such issues. However, her technical ability has not always been able to save her from scrutiny, and in the beginning, may have been a liability. Neither Ronstadt nor any of her early producers had any idea what to do with that gorgeous voice.

Manager Peter Asher, who stepped in to produce *Heart Like a Wheel* (1974) and remained as her regular Svengali, organized an efficient band and arrangement process around the singer. Ronstadt's voice was finally pitted against worthy material and she was pushed to convey some of the spirit as well as the outline of the songs. The result was her first hits, "You're No Good" and "When Will I Be Loved," and an early introduction to Anna McGarrigle, the composer of the title track.

Ronstadt fulfilled a similar role for California singer/songwriters in the mid-seventies that Judy Collins had done for East Coast–based writer/performers in the late sixties. Indeed, it can be argued that Ronstadt's most important artistic contribution has been giving exposure to such new talent as McGarrigle, Karla Bonoff and Warren Zevon. In all three cases, though, while the writers possess barely a fragment of Ronstadt's vocal ability, their original versions of the songs are as good as or better than hers.

Asher's attempt to create a production formula exacerbated the problem, despite some admirable aspects. Asher's sound was state of the art, and it produced a steady stream of hits throughout the late seventies. But a fundamental part of Asher's formula was to have Ronstadt record "oldies"—material by writers such as Buddy Holly and Smokey Robinson. For anyone who loves the originals of "That'll Be the Day," "Ooo Baby Baby," "Blue Bayou," "Back in the U.S.A." or "Hurt So Bad," Ronstadt's heartless renditions are a travesty verging on sacrilege. She has robbed the soul from some of the greatest songs in the rock pantheon, rendered them as arch and leaden as the embalmed show tunes of a previous generation. (She broke out the formaldehyde for her show-tune set in 1983, an unaccountable hit which proved that a lack of emotionality was as great a liability in this field as in rock.)

Nor have Ronstadt's attempts to record contemporary composers outside of Hollywood fared much better. Her "reinterpretation" of Elvis Costello's "Alison" is opaque and impersonal—its most important innovation is a gender switch, but the added insight is negligible. And her awkward, strident remake of the Rolling Stones' "Tumbling Dice" is worse.

In the end, Ronstadt belongs to an era when technical precision and sheer quantity of talent was considered more significant than interpretative ability. Her Broadway debut in a giddy Gilbert and Sullivan operetta, *The Pirates of Penzance*, amounted to typecasting.

Rudy: LP title: *Just Take My Body*. Comment: Only if it's better than your music.

Silk: More disco cosmopolitanism. Back to the land is beginning to seem more attractive.

Toto: Conglomeration of LA session musicians made a hit out of a debut album that was all chops and no brains. The group has now sustained this approach through several more albums full of formula pop songs, singing that wouldn't go over in a Holiday Inn cocktail lounge and ever slicker, more vacuous arrangements. How these men can play so well on other artists' records and with such desultory results here is a mystery. Toto grows more popular every day, but then, cockroaches are supposed to outlast the human race, too.

Tycoon: Dynamics left over from flop film scores; vocals wrenched from hoarse throats; rhythms recycled from large machinery; lyrics dedicated to the propagation of sexism and other idiotic stereotypes. A name that says it all. This is the record industry's idea of progressive. Which is to say that compared to Tycoon, Journey is the Rolling Stones and Rush has transcended Jimi Hendrix.

· · ·

The Village People: Late seventies disco group (all male) raised gay visual stereotypes to an art form: an Indian, a leather freak, etc. Everything but a sissy, which would not have worked because their big hit was "Macho Man," a dumb but inspired dance chant. It was followed by "YMCA," which was more frank and just as dumb, if equally danceable. Kiss for grownups.

5

Mixed Media

Introduction

By the late sixties, the term rock and roll was beginning to designate a sensibility as much as a sound (or at least, it was doing that in the precincts in which I sojourned). The commentary gathered in this chapter, however, speaks of books and movies and radio that is directly tied to rock and roll. In a way, that's unfortunate, for the unique lessons rock has to teach—especially about cultural pretensions and the artificiality of many artistic categories—are never more useful than when they're applied to works that superficially have almost nothing to do with pop music, might even consider its vulgarity and lack of self-control antithetical. (Thus, John Wayne inspired Buddy Holly and it was good for both of them, though who knows what Wayne thought of this link—if indeed he was ever aware of it.)

A couple of these pieces struggle with the idea that rock and roll really does exist in a world of its own. Struggling not so much to break out of that world as to translate the experience of dwelling within it is not only part of the motivation for writing about rock—it's one of the reasons why the best of these books, films and movies express themselves as they do. This might, I hope, also be true to some degree of the reviews.

Crazy 'Bout the La La

*This piece was written when I was barely twenty years old. Like
anything that lingers from that period of one's life, there are aspects
of it that remain embarrassing.*

*It's fascinating to me that there was a time when two serious and
well-known rock critics thought that the healthiest and most hopeful
form of music in the world was heavy metal. Today heavy metal is
everybody's whipping boy for its slothful tempi, unabashed sexism,
covert authoritarianism, flirtation with sexism and alleged appeal to
all that's worst and most Quaaluded about white male teenagers.*

*It's also true, however, that third-generation rock bands (the term
was Alice Cooper's, and it referred to the next stream of bands after
the Beatles/Stones/psychedelic bunches) deteriorated into the pile of
muck partly because serious rock critics stopped paying attention to
them. This left no one to call them to account, and once the DJs made
their peace with the genre, what you had was all rock's worst tendencies unleashed to grow as wild as radioactive crabgrass. And the reason
that rock critics abandoned heavy metal wasn't that the music was so
awful—much of it was, but on a percentage basis, not that much more
than was awful in, say, singer/songwriter music. But even the most
horrid singer/songwriter operated at a level of verbal sophistication far
greater than the run-of-the-mill heavy metal group. And even the most
pathetically self-pitying singer/songwriter had a reasonably articulate,
well-bred audience, while every heavy metal band was playing for
low-life teens at their worst. Which is another way of describing
exactly the same system of snobbery which "Crazy 'Bout the La La"
castigates among DJs during heavy metal's youth.*

*This piece is included in this chapter because it is mostly about
radio. It points out two important things about that deservedly maligned medium: its inability to change rapidly (its resistance to any and
all changes, even those from which it will soon prosper mightily) and
its contempt for its own audience.*

*The particular people I was writing about didn't think it was all that
funny, which made life momentarily difficult, since one of them lived
in the same house. Got to pay your dues, though.*

Lester Bangs and I have both been listening to Black Sabbath a lot—actually, I sort of leave it up to him to put it on, since I OD'd on *Master of Reality* before his return from Sweet Home San Diego, and sometimes things need a rest. (For instance, I don't care to *ever* hear "Sympathy for the Devil" again.)

Then our local paper, the *Fifth Estate*, called to ask if I would write a piece on Grand Funk's second homecoming, since I've been known to shoot off my mouth both frequently and publicly on the subject of the Ferocious Flintlings and their rejection by all and sundry in the vaunted Alternative Media—a relatively monolithic syndrome, considering its pretensions. (I said okay. Of course.)

This got me thinking that just about every third-generation band suffers from the same blackout. Pick a heavy metal rock group, and even choosing at random, you'll note that there has never been a feature article written on them by a fan. All the other stuff is sort of like Al Aronowitz telling his old *New York Post* readers about the Beatles back in the days of yore. Even though Alice Cooper and the Stooges and the MC5 are constantly written about—and in the most adventurous, avant-garde and yea, even revolutionary parts of the country, their records may get played once or twice a week—it doesn't matter. Alice, Iggy and the Five are all second-generation rockers who just stumbled on to third-generation rock and liked it. I mean, they're absolutely heavy metal personalities but the culture from which they sprang was obviously aluminum saucepan. Whereas Sir Lord Baltimore's brats undoubtedly teethed upon Alice's exposed nipple and Iggy's dog collar and Fred Smith's myth-making—as opposed to Bob Dylan's or Chuck Berry's, for example . . .

The reasons the Media don't like third-generation bands are confusing. For instance, there's the problem of why writers have changed their minds about the situation and DJs haven't, thereby making it look like linear media is more mobile than electronic, which we all know shouldn't be true.

But you listen to these people and why they don't like all these bands or any particular one of them (Grand Funk being a synonym, in some senses, for all of them) and you just get confused.

For instance, one disc jockey tells me how aesthetically terrible the heavy metalers are, but I accidentally (since I never listen to FM radio on purpose) hear his show and he plays Frank Zappa telling terrible jokes—and I mean aesthetically OFFENSIVE ones—so what could he know?

Another disc jockular says that they're all politically offensive, because their success is founded on hype and they're controlled by evil capitalists, sucking the life force right out of the tender young loins of brethren and peers. True enough. But I got trapped into listening to his show and he played the Rolling Stones, whose label is owned by the Kinney Corporation, the largest media conglomerate in the nation, and the Beatles, whose label is owned by EMI—"the greatest [meaning "biggest"] recording organization in the world," as it says on every LP cover—and Bob Dylan, who records for CBS, which is not exactly my idea of a small business. If Grand Funk, Black Sabbath, SLB and the rest aren't any better, can they be any worse?

A third DJ claims that "Grand Funk and all those people" make kids take reds, the rationale being that since so much of the heavy metal audience takes those horrible downer pills (and they are horrible) then they must be making them do it. Which is an interesting point: I wonder why the Beatles weren't tried for Charlie Manson's Helter Skelter? And did you notice Bob Dylan's line about "I started out on burgundy and soon hit the harder stuff"? Didja? Why, let's get a grand jury and investigate this mongrel jew who is corrupting . . . Call Harry Anslinger, will you?

Finally, yet another disc jockey tells me that he has been able to get "the Grand Funk audience" to listen without actually playing their records. At that point, I finally figured out what the deal is. *They're scared.* Because they don't understand. And the reason they don't understand—oh, this revelation is all the lights on the Great Pinball Machine in the Sky going off at once and you get 5,678 free games and a double chocolate ice cream cone too—is *because they're too fucking old.*

Generation gap? Nah, just a spirit gap. It ain't so much because old Father Chronology's got 'em as it is that they're so old they can't grow up and do what's obvious with enough spirit in their dust to breathe daily.

Of course, it's awful to think of it, but what's gonna happen to these old farts? When the kids are still out on their own limb with Captain Beefheart blattin' in one ear and the Sabbath in t'other and not thinking either particularly far out but merely the core music of their lives, why what are we goina do with these old DJs and such, as they raise their horrified hands to their chests and fall in contorted despair, railing against the viperous youth and their NOISE, what's gonna happen?

They'll probably have a HEART ATTACK and FALL RIGHT OVER.

AND THEN WE'LL DRIVE 'EM TO THE HOSPITAL AND WHEN THEY WAKE UP AND FIND OUT THAT WE'RE USING THE SANCTIFIED SOUNDS OF PAUL McCARTNEY FOR ELEVATOR MUZAK—AND THAT GEORGE HARRISON HAS BEEN

BANISHED TO A COLONY *TENDED* BY LEPERS—WELL,
WHAT'RE THEY GONNA DO THEN?
Mutate or die.

Creem, 1970

Paperback Writer

*This review had tangible consequences: Mark Shipper's book, first
printed and sold privately by mail order, was soon afterward picked
up by Bantam. It remains as funny now as it was then—at least I can
still find bits that make me laugh. This may mean that* Paperback
Writer *is the ONLY truly successful Beatles book, since the most the
rest can inspire is a grimace.*

Am I jinxed or what? Only two issues ago in this space, I was bemoaning
the absence of any decent rock fiction. No sooner did that issue hit the
newsstands than Mark Shipper's novel, *Paperback Writer*, arrived in the
mail. This book is more than decent—sometimes it's indecent, but more
often it's terrific. Certainly, it's original, which gives it an immediate edge
on the competition.

Mark Shipper is a rock columnist of rather vicious proportions. "Pipe-
line," the column he writes for the LA-based *Phonograph Record*, makes
American Grandstand look like a forum for optimists. It's the acidity of
Shipper's outlook which makes *Paperback Writer* (subtitled "A New History of the Beatles") such a riot.

Another book about the Beatles is just what we needed, right? As
Shipper points out—in a fashion only he would use—nearly every secretary, footman and chauffeur the Beatles ever employed has written a book
about the experience of working for the world's most famous pop musicians. But Shipper has had the nerve to go them all one better—*he made
the whole thing up.*

That's right. From their first album, *We're Gonna Change the Face of Pop Music Forever*, to their last, *Get Back*, released in 1979 on Columbia, Shipper presents an exhaustive chronicle and commentary on what should have happened but didn't. He leaves enough facts untampered to make the story plausible, but he stretches everything else into sublime absurdity. *A Hard Day's Night* is a flop, mostly because it all takes place inside the London public library where Ringo hunts through the stacks in search of identity. *Sgt. Pepper* is about . . . pepper. Yoko Ono falls in love with the blues, and John Lennon's primal problems are solved by Sonny Bono (thus the Plastic Bono Band). George Harrison is guru blind from the beginning. He writes a song called "Disco Jesus" for *Get Back* ("You oughta see him do the Hustle on that funky cross"), and as a condition of signing with CBS requires that all his old solo albums be bought up and destroyed. Linda McCartney threatens Paul by taking a gig with Steely Dan, her "favorite group in the whole world." Ringo, meanwhile, enjoys many hits —almost all of them by others, in a joke that is eventually numbing. Brian Epstein is a plumber.

The key to the book is its conception of the Beatles reunion as a complete catastrophe. Not only does *Get Back* bomb—people trade it in for roach clips or Farrah Fawcett posters—but their U.S. tour is such a disaster that they're finally second-billed to Peter Frampton at Dodger Stadium and nearly hooted off the stage until they swing into their old hits.

Which means that *Paperback Writer*, written from deep inside a rock and roll head, not only solves the problem of rock fiction but also tells the real story behind the Beatles reunion. As they struggle to write the comeback hits, Lennon recalls what gave him his impetus as an artist in the grand old days: "It's that feeling of satisfaction from knowing that someday you were just going to *dump* on everyone who'd been dumping on you." And at the end, when their new work is rejected in favor of what they now consider the trivial old hits, Shipper has Lennon put it all in perspective: "They never really did want *us* to come back, Ringo. We were just symbols of the things they *did* want back—their youth, their innocence . . . That's all we meant to them."

In a way, though, the Beatles that Shipper invented are such a pack of slapstick stumblebums that *Paperback Writer* might be the only defense we have against the creeping scourge of revived Beatlemania. I mean, first the live albums—so they *could* have played their late music live!—and now this. Shipper isn't disillusioned; he seems never to have had any illusions to begin with. But I suspect many of his readers will be not only disabused of some pet fantasies but even threatened. Which is a healthy thing, if only it gets people thinking about something more interesting, like where Ron Wood and Keith Richards get all those scarves. (I happen to *know* they're not Mick's hand-me-downs.)

Shipper isn't a great writer, and some of his jokes are as immature as the Beatles reunion drive itself. But *Paperback Writer* is a book every potential Beatlemaniac of the seventies ought to have, if only because an ounce of prevention is worth a pound of cure. After all, if they get back together and what results is no more significant than *33 ⅓* or *Walls and Bridges*, not only are John, Paul, George and Ringo gonna feel stupid, so are we.

Rolling Stone, 1977

Schlock Around the Rock

In general, this remains an accurate assessment of what was going on during the 1978 cycle of music films, although its conclusion suffers somewhat from overoptimism: it was written just before the great slump that gave the major record labels an excuse to begin putting the creative clamps back on.

What I failed to predict or anticipate was the boom in music video, which in a way is part of my overoptimism. Video was a major force throughout the seventies in England and Europe, and it was one of the forces that ensured that pop music in those nations remained devoted to slick surfaces and cute faces, often obscuring other values. (Abba, the bubble-brained Swedish quartet that was for several years the largest selling group in Europe, is a grand case in point.) Bad as most of what's written about here may be, little of it is so devotedly harmless as what bludgeons its way across the cable wire on a 24-hour basis through MTV. But we'll come to that anon.

There's a fundamental problem with trying to get a fix on the current wave of rock-oriented movies. They share too little to give them an adequate center, much less the distinction of a genre. There isn't even a truly universal musical style here: disco, hard rock, folk rock, fifties rockabilly, English pop and Broadway with a beat are all represented. Nor is there any agreement on what function popular music ought to play. On one hand, music becomes a backdrop for more kinetic business: the dancing in *Saturday Night Fever* and *Thank God It's Friday*; the slapstick comedy in *I Wanna Hold Your Hand*; the romantic melodrama of *American Hot Wax*, *FM* and *The Buddy Holly Story*. On the other, rock is an icon to be celebrated (*The Last Waltz*, *Hot Wax*, *The Punk Rock Movie*) or nostalgically trivialized (*Grease*, *I Wanna Hold Your Hand*). There's not one movie among this batch that takes advantage of the special social perspective rock has to offer—only a couple act as if they really know it exists—and far too few even bother with the exceptional technical facilities rock has helped provide. The best-sounding film of the past year remains *Close Encounters of the Third Kind*, although *The Last Waltz* admittedly gives it a run for its money.

That isn't to say that these films don't have anything to offer. *The Last Waltz* and *The Punk Rock Movie* provide interesting glimpses of two of rock's more apposite scenes, although I don't think either of them tells us what its creators intended. *American Hot Wax*, the Alan Freed biography, and *The Buddy Holly Story* both have worthwhile subjects—Freed and Holly were two of the most important figures of rock's early days—although both trifle too much with history for my taste.

At the very least, those four movies, like *Saturday Night Fever* and *I Wanna Hold Your Hand*, catch some shadow of the energy at the core of rock. None of them is as fraudulent as *Grease* or *Thank God It's Friday* (or reportedly *FM*, which closed so fast I missed it altogether). *T.G.I.F.*, as it's alternately billed, is a production collaboration between two of the least savory companies in the rock business, Motown and Casablanca, which makes its sleazy treatment of the disco scene predictable, if not excusable. (The redeeming feature is the soundtrack LP, although even there, quality takes a big dip after Donna Summer and the Commodores.)

Grease is probably the one film here worthy of everyone's contempt. As if a bunch of middle-aged actors with Brooklyn accents portraying California high school kids wasn't offensive enough, the ending of the picture is a total bamboozle. The drag race at Thunder Road is simply botched, and when John Travolta and Olivia Newton-John ride off into the heavens after a graduation-day ceremony apparently modeled after one of producer Alan Carr's glitzier parties, you're justified in wondering why the hell he hasn't spent the last two hours playing chicken rather than sitting still for such piffle.

The music is horrible, with the exception of 'Liv and John's hit single,

"You're the One That I Want," which is also the only number that bears any relationship to the rock of the period *Grease* claims to represent. The Broadway establishment hated rock and roll for robbing Tin Pan Alley and the show-tune composers of their hegemony in the pop marketplace, but Barry Gibb's theme tune owes much more to Rodgers and Hart than to Elvis Presley or Chuck Berry, something pointed up by the inclusion of some real rock oldies in the malt-shop scenes. If this is the *West Side Story* of the Quaalude age, I'm still a Jet all the way.

But of course *Grease* can't be *West Side Story*—*Saturday Night Fever* already is. *Grease* and *Saturday Night* have a few things in common—Travolta, producer Robert Stigwood, the Bee Gees—all of which are displayed to the advantage of *Saturday Night*. In *Grease*, director Randal Kleiser's wide open spaces give Travolta just enough space to hang himself. Travolta is the most locked-up actor going—he makes Robert De Niro seem lucid—but that's perfect for John Badham's dingy *Saturday Night* look. If Kleiser and Carr had gotten their mitts on the *Saturday Night* script, it would have taken place in Studio 54, the natural home of the dilettante. But Brooklyn's Odyssey, where the movie takes place, is as far away from all that as the Fillmore was from Woodstock. It's a place where commitment counts—as it always does in the best pop music.

This isn't a minor issue. *Saturday Night Fever* offers the illusion of admitting the moviegoer to a semi-secret society. Even a club-footed dancer (like me) leaves feeling informed about an alien scene, which is a neat bit of trickery: Nik Cohn, who wrote the story on which *Saturday Night Fever* is based, spent a decade writing variations on the theme of the Perfect Teenager with the Perfect Pose seizing or instigating the Perfect Moment.

Travolta's gotten almost all of the attention, but his real co-star isn't Karen Lynn Gorney (so vacant she's a Johnny Rotten dream date). It's the film's soundtrack album. Travolta doesn't sing in *Saturday Night*, but the film's going to be outgrossed by the record, which has sold around 20 million copies (a $200 million gross). The reason the *Saturday Night Fever* soundtrack is so successful is obvious enough. Like the *Woodstock* soundtrack, a massive hit in its day, it's a perfect catalogue of the hottest performers in its particular idiom: the Bee Gees, KC and the Sunshine Band and the Trammps. In one discrete package, a kid can buy the ideal sampler and certify himself as hip, too. The *FM* soundtrack is also a Top Ten album; had executive producer Irving Azoff, one of the kingpins of California soft rock in his alternate incarnation as manager of the Eagles and the like, been less parochial in packaging it, *FM* might have been as huge as the *Saturday Night* set, which is regarded in the record business with the awe the film industry reserves for *Jaws* and *Star Wars*.

That's probably the bottom-line reason for the rock-film boom. Sound-track albums don't sell well as a rule, but when they do, they're enormously profitable. *FM*, a two-disc set, could more than conceivably sell a million units, for a gross of $8 to $10 million, and the profits ought to be substantial enough to help amortize the film's nosedive. (*Saturday Night Fever* sold a million copies *before* the film came out, which means it has prospered as more than a Travolta tag-along.)

The catch, maybe, is that this only works when you've got something that holds the soundtrack together conceptually—John Williams' theme songs for *Star Wars* and *Close Encounters* were pop hits, but his syrupy, rather old-fashioned LP interpretations weren't the versions that made the charts. Often what holds the successful soundtracks together is a story line with some youth or rock base. And even then, who knows? Why would a kid buy the Bee Gees singing *Sgt. Pepper's* when he can still get the original (inevitably superior) by the Beatles?

Well, maybe because no one really cares much about the Beatles anymore. Broadway's *Beatlemania* has done well in New York and Los Angeles, but the original cast album stiffed. And *I Wanna Hold Your Hand*, the only rock movie that has a sense of history and a sense of humor, has been unable to find an audience. This is disappointing not only because filmmakers Robert Zemeckis and Bob Gale are smart enough to treat the original wave of Beatlemania without contempt—though they may trivialize it, they don't hate it—but because *I Wanna Hold Your Hand* is the only rock movie that understands anything about the central role the audience plays in rock and roll. Nancy Allen's erotic daydream in the Beatles' hotel suite not only is a first-rate bit of sexual comedy but is true to the spirit of those times. And while her rejection of marriage (and the conventions that go with it) at the end is corny, it's also right: lives really did change permanently that weekend. Not that anyone remembers anymore. When people go to see the puppet-Beatles on Broadway, they aren't celebrating their own history, though they may think so. What they're really doing is worshiping their own awareness of the Beatles as superstar aristocrats. The difference is everything, and it says a great deal about what has happened to rock, how much vision and emotion it has lost in the past fifteen years.

Martin Scorsese's *The Last Waltz*, a documentary about the final appearance of the Band in San Francisco on Thanksgiving Day 1976, has even more to say on this subject, although Scorsese seems to think he's praising what his film effectively condemns. The Beatles' 1964 performances had to be great in order to equal the response to them; this was the original compact of rock and roll with its audience, which is part of what made it different from the rest of show biz. But by 1976 the situation had flip-flopped. Scorsese can now shoot a concert with only the most elliptical and occasional references to the crowd, because the audience plays virtually no part in the proceedings. All those celebrities aren't playing for their fans, they're posing for one another. The kids just get in the way.

The praise for *The Last Waltz* has come mostly from film critics, who like its visual style and its departure from the conventional patterns of shooting rock concert footage, established by *Woodstock* and *Monterey Pop* and *Gimme Shelter*. Rock critics have been more stingy with their encomiums (with the exception of such die-hard Band buffs as Greil Marcus and Robert Palmer), possibly because they know that at the heart of *The Last Waltz* lies a fraud—or two or three.

The first and most important of these little white lies is that the Last Waltz concert was a momentous event. It was not. At the time it got some coverage—mostly because Bob Dylan showed up, which is always supposed to be some kind of event—but the general sense of it was that the show was a bit boring, far too long, confused, a prime example of the Band taking its stature as an institution far too seriously. (There is allegedly no greater sin in rock.)

Unquestionably the Band is one of rock's institutions. They began playing together about 1960, backing a relatively obscure rockabilly singer, Ronnie Hawkins, in Canada (all the members but one are Canadian), and in 1965 began touring with Bob Dylan, in his first electrified shows, which *are* among the most important events in rock history. Their participation in Dylan's Woodstock-made *Basement Tapes* and their first two albums, *Music from Big Pink* (1968) and *The Band* (1970), helped change the sound of the music, playing a major role in stamping out the space drivel of West Coast pop (à la Grateful Dead) and returning rock to a more focused, song-oriented form. But to claim—as Robbie Robertson does, over and over again in Scorsese's rather sycophantish interview footage— that the Band had to stop performing because they spent "sixteen years on the road" is absurd. The Band toured very little, and for a lengthy period (from *Cahoots* in 1971 to *Northern Lights/Southern Cross* in 1975) simply played and recorded various versions of the same oldies and songs from its first three albums. That's not the height of creative pressure.

In fact, the Band had been one of the most creative forces in rock for a few years and then, typically, petered out. When it decided to split up, nobody was terribly surprised; sixteen years is a long time for any group of people to stay together, and, at least in the beginning, the Band had also to contend with a variety of songwriting and performing visions: Robbie Robertson's, Rick Danko's, Richard Manuel's, Garth Hudson's, Levon Helm's. Indeed, there was such a complexity of vision that Jon Landau, in reviewing *Cahoots* (their most mediocre album of original material), was willing to risk terming the Band auteurs as a group.

Thinking about rock musicians as auteurs has been a guaranteed way to get into trouble ever since. For one thing, no single role (singer, writer, instrumentalist, producer) dominates in rock as consistently as the director does in movie-making. For another, rock auteurism tends to be rather half-baked—so far, at least, there simply isn't a unified way of thinking about the music critically. But Scorsese seems to buy Landau's argument, as well as his judgment about who the most important figure in the group might be: Robbie Robertson, who functions as chief composer, guitarist and mouthpiece—and the producer of *The Last Waltz*. (Landau's assessment agrees with the orthodox critical position on the Band. I've always felt that Levon Helm, drummer, singer, and the man who held the group together between Hawkins and Dylan, properly holds that place.)

In any event, Robertson is shot lovingly by Scorsese as the most devotional object in a film that's about devotional objects. Robertson has been described in several reviews as having the aura of stardom, but my hunch is that this has a great deal more to do with the way Scorsese shot him, making the dissipation written all over his face seem symbolic of the ravages of the apocryphal time on the road, than with any innate quality. Robertson's everywhere, though: introducing the various celebrities as they come onstage, dominating the interviews so severely that he rarely lets anyone (except Helm) finish a sentence. To me, this made him obnoxious —the Band has always pushed community as the most transcendent value in its music—but maybe I'm just old-fashioned.

There remains a burning question about what ought to be the central subject of a documentary about rock: the music. It's far from great. The Band has played almost all of these songs—except the new "Last Waltz Theme" and "Mystery Train," which is rescued by Paul Butterfield's guest harp—better elsewhere. It helps that the quality of the sound is so excellent, but it's hard for me to imagine how great the Who would have sounded in *Woodstock* if they'd had the advantage of Dolby. The grand musical moments of *The Last Waltz* belong to others: to Bob Dylan, who knows how to take over a stage; to Muddy Waters, who looks like a national monument, singing "Mannish Boy" with all the dignity of a hundred years of blues tradition; to Van Morrison, so Irish he might as well be a leprechaun; to Neil Young, the one performer who really did treat the night as a big deal and with his one song turns in a performance from deep in the heart. Not that Dylan isn't better in the concert footage from *Renaldo and Clara*—the only bearable moments in that memorable act of self-immolation comes when he's playing—or that there's anything here that touches Jimi Hendrix or Otis Redding in *Monterey Pop*.

Yet, even feeling so skeptical and even hostile to much of what the film shows, I can't help admiring it. The best thing about Scorsese's style is that it can't hide the truth, which is mostly about deterioration. For rock and roll, this is a gathering of real old-timers (and the oldest of them all, Muddy Waters, comes close to stealing the show). Instead of trying to open them up, Scorsese shuts them down, makes a real conclusion out of the Band's fake one. It's a perfect setting for Scorsese, who makes the opening shots of the drive up to Winterland an ironic commentary on the glitter we're about to experience, as well as on the post-midnight street life of his other films. As a chronicle of a certain group of once important musical figures, *The Last Waltz* is a weird triumph: those dark spaces are perfect for a gang of aesthetic bankrupts trying to hide from a world in which there's no future for them.

"No future for you" was the rallying cry of the Sex Pistols, who were burning up stages and getting tossed off radio, TV and record labels at just the moment that the Band was celebrating the demise of the sixties scene in *The Last Waltz*. *The Punk Rock Movie*, shot in 8 millimeter (and blown up to 16 millimeter), with tinnier sound than any transistor radio, is a chronicle of the English punk rock scene that's as exhaustive and exhausting in its own way as Scorsese's treatment of sixties American rock. There's little of the sensationalism of the network TV treatment of punk: Even the scenes of drug shooting and the bit where the kid slashes his abdominal epidermis with a razor blade seem like integral parts of the environment, not just an outsider's exploitation of it. *The Punk Rock Movie* is an insider's film. Scorsese had to cut a shot from *The Last Waltz* because of a large gob of cocaine hanging from a certain artist's nose, but if something like that had happened in *The Punk Rock Movie*, it might have been used as the title sequence.

Punk was an attempt to redefine rock, make it a community once more, and as such, this scene is explicitly a reaction to the kind of rock portrayed by Scorsese. To the punks (and I don't see much evidence they were wrong), Dylan and the Band came to inhabit a world that was anti-rock: safe, conventional, boring, without personal conscience, much less collective value. So they went all the way in the other direction. One reason some of the people in this movie wear safety pins through their cheeks is because a pop icon like Joni Mitchell would be as horrified as their mothers by the sight.

Restoring rock's original values was a noble dream, and it produced some fine if amateurish music—the sequences featuring the Sex Pistols and the Clash have an informative importance for rock fans who've never seen them that transcends the squalidness of the scene and the raggedness of the camera work. There is no way to escape the technical limitations of a film shot in 8 millimeter, but that's part of the film's authenticity. The punks said to hell with rock's passion for technique as the first axiom of their reaction.

Disgust might be a logical response to some of the action in *The Punk Rock Movie*, but at least the shooting up and razor blades are up front. Some of the characters in *The Last Waltz* have equally destructive personal habits (who do you think put that cocaine up the guy's nose, the DEA?), but they'll never admit to them. What punk found out in its brief ride as a media craze was that honesty alone isn't sufficient to sustain public interest. That's also true of *The Punk Rock Movie*, but I'm glad Don Letts made it—even if what he intended to be a celebration has become something more like an autopsy. It provides a document we can turn to in twenty years, when *The Johnny Rotten Story* appears.

Too bad somebody couldn't do the same for Alan Freed and Buddy Holly, whose lives are considerably distorted by *American Hot Wax* and *The Buddy Holly Story*. Oddly, both of these films have a great deal of fidelity to the spirit of rock and roll in the fifties—they know where the lines were drawn, and *Holly* even knows why—but almost no interest in getting the details or even the facts of their subjects' lives straight. *American Hot Wax* tries to make Freed too heroic, whitewashing his involvement in payola, which could not have been quite that casual: it isn't an accident that he was given co-author credit for Chuck Berry's first hit, "Maybellene," a record he plugged heavily. On the other hand, it isn't true, as Pauline Kael and others have charged, that the film makes Freed too much of a father figure. Arnold Passman's *The Dee Jays* notes that, on Freed's final television show (he was kicked off the air when the payola scandal began), a young girl cried just that: "They've taken away our father." His specialty was doo-wop harmony records, the slowest, smoochiest, most sentimental rock of all.

Hot Wax, which has a nice smoky look that's seedy without becoming creepy, is nonetheless a much more authentic youth film than director Floyd Mutrux's *Aloha, Bobby and Rose*, a picture whose topic is similar adolescent discontent. And as long as it sticks with Freed (very well played by Tim McIntire) and the records he spun so well, it's as affecting as any fictional look at rock since *King Creole*. When Freed plays the Drifters' "There Goes My Baby," and the sound spins out over the theater, it doesn't matter that hardly anyone knows what a revolutionary song that was (the first rhythm and blues hit to use strings). All that counts is that the sound is right. And though I'm no big fan of the fictionalized concert sequences, the kid in the Chesterfields who imitates Frankie Lymon lingers in the memory. And that weird guy in the alley, banging out "Good Golly Miss Molly" on a trash-can lid, is the ghost of the music: if he'd shown up in a few more of these pictures, they'd be better off.

There's one scene in *American Hot Wax* which does illuminate what Freed meant to people, and what rock and roll does, and perhaps provides a link between some of the best of the new rock movies. A young kid— he looks very much like the kid whose father insists he have a haircut in *I Wanna Hold Your Hand*—comes to Freed on Buddy Holly's birthday, beseeching the disc jockey to play his hero's records. Instead Freed puts the boy on the air and lets him tell the story of what Holly meant to him and what the plane crash in which Holly died did to him. As he does, Freed and this fan exchange a look that's worth the price of admission . . . and it's even better when Freed segues into "Rave On," one of Holly's best records. There's a bond there, between the music and the DJ and the kid, that just can't be false. I don't know anyone who listened to Freed regularly who doesn't retain something of that moment when they talk about the picture. And that's what enabled the music to survive the witch hunts— which is what the payola scandal finally was—that loom in the background of *American Hot Wax* like Godzilla. If Mutrux had come up with a really believable villain (and he could have had one by sticking closer to the facts), this would have been one hell of a picture.

Which leaves us with *The Buddy Holly Story*, about which I'm very torn. Certainly Gary Busey pulls off the title role with great aplomb—he not only looks the part, sometimes he sounds it, which isn't as easy, for Holly was one of the three or four most distinctive musicians that early rock and roll produced. Busey can't sing Buddy's ballads with much style, but in the opening sequence, when the band jumps into "Rock Around with Ollie Vee," you can't help but believe him. (The soundtrack album doesn't work, though, probably because there's nothing to do but compare it with the originals, inevitably invidiously.)

But Busey fights a losing battle. The script distorts Holly's life all out of shape. He did not have a major conflict with his parents about his career. (His mother helped him write "Maybe Baby.") He did not begin recording his hits in New York, but in New Mexico. It was no accident that earned him his record deal, or the Crickets their name. His courtship with Maria Elena Santiago was not exceedingly arduous, it was exceedingly brief: they met at William Morris, where she worked as a secretary, went to P.J.

Clarke's for lunch and Buddy proposed. That fast. And most of all, Holly, the Big Bopper and Ritchie Valens did not charter a private plane in Clear Lake, Iowa, because of a bus breakdown but because they were eager to get to the tour's next stop, Fargo, North Dakota, in order to get their laundry done and pick up some mail. Maybe this is one of those cases where the truth is too strange to be believed, or too dramatic to be rendered, but it's also too well-known, at least to rock fans, to be ignored.

What *The Buddy Holly Story* finally becomes is *The Glenn Miller Story* updated. And why not? Holly was a pop star who wore glasses, and he died in a plane crash. This is what Hollywood has always done to rock stars— Elvis Presley had to suffer it in the flesh, poor boy—and there's no reason to suppose it's liable to stop now.

These distortions have another basis, I think. Quite clearly, the producers had help from Maria Elena Santiago Holly (she's remarried, but still a sort of professional widow) and none at all from his parents or his real record producer, Norman Petty (who is written out of the story altogether) or his band members (guitarist Sonny Curtis has written a song attacking the film). Essentially, the problem is that director Steve Rash, producer Fred Bauer and screenwriter Robert Gittler couldn't resist turning it into a mushy love story, a sort of fifties *Goodbye Girl* in which the departure of the male is permanent.

But the film doesn't lose its nerve until the very end, when stuff starts happening that's unbelievable. If the final scenes weren't so false (Holly appears with a lamé orchestra that wouldn't be out of place in *Grease* and bears no resemblance to the small group he actually did his final gig with; the Crickets show up at the Holly apartment on the night of his death to see about getting back together), I'd forgive everything else—because in its best moments, this story also has a fair understanding of what rock has been all about these past twenty years and particularly of what it has meant to be a rock artist.

For me, the best scenes in the movie are those that show Holly fighting to control his music, battling the pressure to hurry up and get the session over so he can be turned into more product or to change his songs into something more mild. A good deal of Holly's lasting significance is that he was the first rock performer to be involved in every step of record making: he wrote them, he sang them, he played on them, he helped produce them. This wasn't easy—there was always someone to tell him he should do things as they had "always" been done—but that he got away with it measures what makes rock and roll such an exceptional medium.

One of the reasons that there's never been a movie with more than an inkling of what the rock business is about is the complete difference in artistic perspective between the two industries. In no other communications area—not publishing, not broadcasting, certainly not film—can the artist presume that he will have almost complete control over his work without interference from the corporation. It is inconceivable today for a record company to exercise any form of "final cut" on even a semi-successful rock performer's work.

This was not always true: Holly had to fight for the license to break rules. But today record companies understand that they don't know how to make music as well as musicians do; their interference is minimal. It will be interesting to see if the emergence of rock businessmen like Robert Stigwood as film producers will have a similar effect on movies. Regardless of that, however, Holly's contribution to help attain basic artistic freedom for the rock and roll performer (if he recorded with orchestras, that was an experiment he wanted to try, not something he was forced to endure) is as important a part of his legacy as his songs. One reason these rock movies are so unsatisfying is that none of them quite appreciates how liberating that difference is.

The Buddy Holly Story comes close. Its final good scene, before the last fifteen minutes fall apart, has Holly in his New York apartment, resisting the pressure to tour (with apparent prescience), writing and arranging obsessively. It's Christmastime. There's a knock on the door and two boys enter. "Mr. Holly," asks the elder one, "my little brother broke my guitar. Can you fix it for me?"

He'll do more than that. He will teach them the E chord and a song he wrote with it. For the only time in the movie, Busey sings alone, with just the guitar, no other accompaniment. The song he sings is one of Buddy's strangest and most moving, "Well All Right." The opening verse, though, says to me what the movie would like to say:

> Well all right so I'm being foolish
> Well all right let the people know
> About the dreams and wishes you wish
> In the night when the lights are low
> Well all right, well all right
> We will live and love with all our might

And those things are ones that no rock movie has ever caught: the moments when you don't care anymore about propriety and caution, but just have to let it out, live life to its hilt and not give a damn about consequences. Not that these things are absent from movies. They are there, in *Mean Streets*, *Rebel Without a Cause*, *Red River* and many, many more. Not so strangely, Buddy Holly knew this twenty years ago, when he wrote his greatest song, "That'll Be the Day," which took its title from John Wayne's favorite expression in *The Searchers*. Somehow, though, I doubt that any of these movies will inspire anything so magnificent.

Film Comment, 1978

Blue Collar

This is certainly the most inspired I've ever become while watching a movie that I didn't even especially like. But both the setting and the characterizations—particularly those of Richard Pryor and Yaphet Khotto—set me back in the most basic meaning of that term. The extent of that moment of revelation, in which my past collapsed into the present and suggested a future direction for my work, is obvious from the volume that you hold in your hands.

There's a special order of terror involved in being held at gunpoint. You can remain oblivious to it while trying to get though the situation, but once it's over, the realization of what one wrong move could have cost sinks in. It's not something you'll forget overnight—if you ever do.

For me, growing up around Detroit was a little bit like that. I know something about being held up, which happened to me a couple of times in my misspent youth, and something more about the quality of life in Detroit and its environs, from which I escaped five years ago with more of my hide and psyche intact than I had any right to expect. It's a community of tank towns and bedrooms, all of which owe their existence to the auto industry, which runs the place in covert alliance with the labor unions, who keep the populace in check. It's a place where for working-class kids (even the relatively affluent ones of the sixties) the threat of a life on the assembly line is always real, the price you pay for fucking up your future. I got out. But I'll always know that one wrong step back there and my fate could have been forty hours per week of somebody else's nuts and bolts.

Of course my family never related to itself as working class. Nobody does. My father worked sixteen-hour days for the railroad, when the company wanted him; when it didn't, he waited for the phone to ring. By the time he got enough seniority to work steadily, we had a house in the suburbs, a color TV and two cars. He occasionally had enough time to enjoy them. And that made us middle class.

As Bo Diddley once said to Eric Burdon, that's the biggest load of rubbish I ever heard in my life. I have always been told that America is a classless society, which is something I resent more than any of the other lies moronic schoolteachers tried to shove down my throat. As Robert Christgau put it, class in America is simply the system that dares not speak its name. In a recent *Washington Monthly* article, Thomas Massey said it more clearly: "the differences can be defined in terms of income . . . culture . . . education and occupation and prestige. But the single clearest class difference, the sum of all the other parts, is the feeling of *control.*"

When you look into the barrel of a gun, you're not in control and you know it. When you grow up in a community where everyone has stupid, boring work, or none at all, you're not in control, but there are factors that serve to disguise it. For me, the best thing about moving to the suburbs was finding out that everyone didn't live that way. It's no coincidence that I got kicked in the ass by rock and roll at that time.

All of this came back to me when I saw Paul Schrader's *Blue Collar*, a movie that tries to depict the lives of three factory workers in Detroit. *Blue Collar* doesn't work—it gets too much wrong and it takes too much for granted—but it's the only piece of non-rock culture I've seen in years that tells anything close to the truth about the first half of my life.

For the past year, I've been trying to write something about rock and roll and its relationship to a class-based America. The problem is that there are so few sources to which one can turn to relieve the confusion. Class is rarely discussed outside the ultra-sectarian left, and the subject isn't often asked about by interviewers. That may be why rock critics often have so much trouble seeing that it is class that provides the missing link they seek among performers as superficially diverse as Patti Smith, Bob Seger, Bruce Springsteen, Graham Parker, Elvis Costello and Johnny Rotten. Nevertheless, an awareness of class runs through rock songs: the Coasters' "What About Us," Bob Seger's "Beautiful Loser," Bruce Springsteen's "Night," the Animals' versions of "It's My Life" and "I'm Mad Again," and most of all, John Fogerty's awesome "Fortunate Son."

What got to me about *Blue Collar* wasn't the silly story or the poorly developed characters, but the theme song that runs over the opening credits. It's an updated version of Bo Diddley's "I'm a Man," sung by Captain Beefheart. The lyrics are new, but this version is probably more significant for what Beefheart doesn't sing: the title itself. In an environment whose aural motif is the incessant banging of metal against metal at deafening volume, "I'm a man / Spell m-a-n" could never be the boast that Bo Diddley made it. This bludgeoning backbeat doesn't have that resilient sense of after-hours freedom and good humor anyway. It's a lockstep that makes maintaining a sense of humanity all but impossible. And when I heard it, it was like looking down at that gun again, knowing this time that it was only a message from home.

Rolling Stone, 1978

The Lonesome Death of Florence Thompson

When I began working on Fortunate Son, *I knew there were two unlikely subjects that I wanted to talk about: Dorothea Lange's photography and the music of the Stanley Brothers, or at least their greatest song, "Rank Strangers." So in a sense, the juxtapositions in this article were foreordained, but it wasn't until Thompson died that it struck me how clearly they fit together.*

Sometimes, I wonder whether future critics and historians will look back upon the eighties and wonder why so much agonized, desperate art was created in these times. (Presuming there are still historians and critics—that is, presuming there is still civilization rather than atomic rubble.) But even for those of us who've tried to develop some sense of hope and joy, the sight of so many newly destitute—homeless, shivering, hungry, driven mad by callousness—created an extremely depressing emotional climate. This piece is my gesture at describing the period.

Its sixth paragraph also contains the strongest, or at least the most direct, statement I've ever written about the roots of rock, and the value of them, and the purpose of the whole exercise of writing about it.

Florence Thompson was thirty-two years old in 1936, a widowed mother of six children, living in a migrant farmworkers' camp in San Luis Obispo County, California. The Thompsons lived in a shabby lean-to, not even a tent, from which they ventured to pick peas for wages that added up to less than starvation. They were so poor that they'd sold the tires off their car for food. When the photographer Dorothea Lange, on assignment for the Farm Security Administration, came into the camp, Florence Thompson was feeding her children vegetables that had frozen in the fields and a few birds that the kids had killed themselves.

"I do not remember how I explained my presence or my camera to her," Lange later wrote, "but I do remember she asked me no questions . . . There she sat in that lean-to tent with her children huddled around her and seemed to know that my pictures might help her, and so she helped me. There was a sort of equality about it."

The photo that Lange made of Florence Thompson's haunted face, wearing a cloak of weariness and worry that offered no more protection from the camera lens than from the elements, staring with dignity while cuddling children who averted their faces, was entitled "Migrant Mother." Sometimes referred to as "The Madonna of the Depression," it became one of the most powerful and painful symbolic images of its era.

As the epitome of Dorothea Lange's penetrating, humane style, "Migrant Mother" was by far her most famous photo. Yet it tells us nothing like the "truth" of Florence Thompson's life. In the other shots from the series Lange took that night, we see the environment in which it was taken: the pure squalor and filth of the camp, the full shabbiness of the lean-to tent, the utter lack of anything as tidy and green as the camp depicted in John Ford's *The Grapes of Wrath*. (The pictures are reproduced in *Photographs of a Lifetime* [Aperture, 1982], with a loving essay on Lange and her work by Robert Coles.)

That doesn't mean Lange's camera lied. She saw (or used) what was needed to make plain the dignity of the ravaged, not the fact of their misery. It's only today, when the reroutings of American streets and highways have made the poor and their pain invisible to us that the mere facts of the matter have become crucial. The real point is that we know almost nothing about how Florence Thompson felt that evening, or in the months and years afterwards when her face became famous.

We don't really expect to know, which is shameful. I've always felt that one of the secret strengths of rock and roll was that it provided a voice and a face for the forgotten and disenfranchised. In a way, Florence Thompson's serves for all the others. At least in its beginnings, rock was one of the few ways that poor people, country people, black people and

Southerners had of making themselves visible in a country whose media increasingly depict it as solely urban, affluent, white and northern. Rock's threat to spill the beans about such fictions is one reason why it remains so dangerous today in the minds of James Watt, Albert Goldman and their ilk.

Yet you can stare for long into the face of Florence Thompson without encountering a suggestion of the abandon and recklessness that rock expresses. And that doesn't mean that there is no music that tells her story. Although it often seems to think itself British, rock grew from a tradition of American music which had something special to say for "Migrant Mothers" and their kin: bluegrass, gospel music, all sorts of blues. And in these days of renewed Depression, I have found—often to my surprise— that these forms speak as eloquently as rock. As history unravels, this becomes more the case.

So when the news of Florence Thompson's death in early September 1983 came to me, I immediately turned to the music of the Stanley Brothers, to my mind the finest bluegrass singers, and to their greatest song, "Rank Strangers," which seemed to say everything necessary about a life such as Thompson's—about its consequences and the consequences the rest of us pay for not paying more attention. "Rank Strangers" is about the scariest song I know, more chilling than the blues of "Voodoo Chile" or the cold-blooded "Nebraska" or even Dylan's "Percy's Song." It shares with those stark numbers a sense of doom that is not so much immediate as eternal—constant not as a possibility but as a promise.

The Stanleys' songs are filled with death and imprisonment, like the Scotch-Irish ballads from which they derive. But "Rank Strangers" takes what's scary about such tunes into a new dimension, closer to *Invasion of the Body Snatchers* than "Matty Groves." Carter Stanley sings in accents so stately that it's hard to believe the song and performance were created after World War II. But the concept—desolation more complete than that surrounding the Thompsons' labor camp—is as contemporary as Belsen, Nagasaki or Palestinian refugee camps.

> I wandered again to my home in the mountains
> Where in youth's early dawn, I was happy and free
> I looked for my friends, but I never could find 'em
> I found they were all rank strangers to me

Florence Thompson may not have known those lines, but she surely would have understood each syllable of that song. Until just before her death, she lived not in luxury but in a trailer park. So does America honor genius and beauty.

Record, 1983

The Electrifying Mojo

Since this column was written, I've heard Mojo wreak radio magic on a much more regular basis, using everything from a hand-out, prerecorded Michael Jackson interview to brilliant segues of tracks as various as Stevie Nicks, the Gang of Four and Afrika Bambaataa and Soulsonic Force. By now there exists in Detroit a sort of Mojo fan club, the Midnight Funk Association, which has more than 60,000 members. Most of them are lucky enough to hear him every night, as I am not, but I try to get friends to send out airchecks every so often. It helps me stay in touch, not only with the best in radio and the best in music but also with the reasons why it's worth bothering.

Slip those cassettes in a portable cassette deck, stick it under your pillow and sweet dreams are guaranteed. At its best, pop radio offers the truest sort of confirmation that our best ideas and instincts are not operating in a vacuum. And Mojo is that best more often than anyone else around at this moment.

I listen to the radio mostly in the summertime, when I'm not home much. The rest of the year I hear radio in snatches, in shops and offices and taxis. But unless I'm in an automobile, I don't pay much attention. Until summer, when it's back behind the wheel, with one hand always on the dial.

At first this return always seems blessed. A few records, compressed as heavily as they are, make more sense over the air than they do on the turntable or tape deck. Even suffering from Loverboy to Kajagoogoo, while punching buttons looking for something decent, has its virtues. The sufferer feels connected to fellow listeners in an immediate way that only broadcasting can provide.

Soon enough the bloom wears off. As a mere tourist in radioland, I seem to become frustrated more easily than most, disagreeing with the taste of the programmers, the deadness of the jocks. As a visitor, rather than a resident, the hypocrisy of the system—format—is too easily evident. I get restless and start tossing the tape deck in the passenger seat and once again feel like hot-rodding, freed from the tyranny of punchcard DJs with their somber tones and self-important blather.

Twas not always thus, despite what the liars who run the airwaves try to say. Anyone over thirty can remember a time in this country when disc jockeys had true personalities, when a major fraction of life centered on them and the records they played, when the radio was a web connecting every rocker in town. And the fact that you have to be over thirty to have firsthand experience of this kind of radio isn't a symptom of what an old fogy I am—it measures how you've been cheated all your life.

Those disc jockeys weren't on the FM dial. They played hit singles— sometimes they *made* hits—and they did not speak as though they were about to proclaim a funeral or cut a solemn fart. They screamed, shouted and harangued, thumped and pounded, were one with the beat. In Detroit, Martha Jean the Queen offered up the number just after 5:00 P.M. each afternoon; in Philly, Jerry Blavat shrieked yon teens into smooth cruising speed; in Nashville, John R. and Hoss Allen preached on into the night, trying to sell you every record they played (and most were worth buying); in Tulsa, Scooter Seagraves and Jim Peters were the best sort of teachers, coupling reverence for the past to infectious enthusiasm for the present. And whether you were driving aimlessly or hiding in bed with the covers over your head, you were in *touch*.

With the arrival of Boss Radio in the midsixties, the personalities began to die out: they could no longer pick their own records; they were discouraged from speaking too much or doing any of the other things that made them stand out as human beings, rather than clocks and weather vanes or hip voice mannequins. When FM arrived, it was apparently decided that shouting was not cool and as the scene transformed from Little Richard to Crosby, Stills, Nash and Young, the DJs also began to slow down and croon. I got bored, bought a bunch of records and hid out among them. Most fans weren't that lucky. And as the solemnity grew, the community withered and was fragmented. That gave the liars room to maneuver, hardening their formats and spreading their fictions: that white people didn't want to hear black performers; that blacks didn't want to hear white ones; that separate but equal is an acceptable doctrine; that radio existed as a medium of entertainment and profit alone, not at all as a force in the world. Beaten and bored, the audience acquiesced. Those who knew better sometimes complained bitterly, but it served no particular purpose. Now the liars have moved into television too.

Every once in a while something happens to make us see the lies for what they are. A few months ago I began hearing about a disc jockey on WJLB-FM in Detroit. He was called the Electrifying Mojo, and though WJLB is an "urban contemporary" station, he played J. Geils and the Rollin' Stones (as he puts it) right alongside Prince and the Whispers. Mojo picked his own music, they told me, and he picked it for beat and movement. And he was a *success*. In a market where a rating of 4 ARBitron points would be impressive, Mojo's rating in the spring ARB book was *17.9.*

My friend Frank Joyce recently interviewed Mojo for WBCN in Boston. He was kind enough to send me a tape of their conversation, and it is probably the most impressive statement on radio and its potential power I have heard in my lifetime. "Personally, I think radio has not lost the power to be a mental/theatrical agent—it's just abandoned that particular power," Mojo said. And he makes it very clear that he means to reclaim that power: "I get people asking me, 'Why do you play white music?' Then I get people asking me, 'Why do you play black music?' But there's nothing wrong with people being curious. Nothing wrong with being curious at all. Because radio is serious to me. And I want people. . . . When you look at my numbers, what you see is a combination of people." Of course the combination Mojo describes is what the liars can't afford, because their power, as manipulators of demographics and other methods of fragmentation, is based upon dividing, separating and segregating, not combining, integrating, bringing us together.

Mojo's show is beyond format, even though there are segments that appear like clockwork. As a result there are nights he is not very good. But then I have tapes of Alan Freed on nights when *he* wasn't very good, either. The point is that the show comes from somewhere. As he told Joyce, "I put a lotta work into livin'. My show is probably a classic statement about my lifestyle, what I believe in, how I feel about things, what I think, what I've experienced, what I've seen on the news, schools I've spoken at, kids I've seen, the bagmen and bagwomen I've seen walking down the streets at four o'clock in the morning with nowhere to go. It's a combination of all those things."

That in a nutshell is the definition of great broadcasting. The Electrifying Mojo can afford some bad nights because his show is as alive as he is. He can afford to break the rules because he is a human being, and all of those have their bad days. If I lived in Detroit again, there's no way I would sell all my LPs and tapes and singles. But I know whose voice would be the last I heard each night before switching off the light. And I know that when I rolled over and tried to sleep, that connection would be felt. And rest would come much easier, for certain.

Record, 1983

6

The Biz

Introduction

I t's not any lack of interest on my part that makes this one of the shortest parts of *Fortunate Son*. Indeed, I've always taken the attitude that in order to understand a popular art form in a society such as ours, one needed to understand also the thinking of the industry that marketed (and from time to time created) the artful product. That's so true that there is hardly a part of this book—or to put it more precisely, an article or review that I've ever written—that isn't suffused with some sense of how the rock business, the entertainment business or, for that matter, corporate capitalism in general might operate. Consequently, there are important discussions of the intersection of commodity and creativity—for instance, the role played by the artist's struggle to control his or her own work— in other sections of this book.

The pieces that *are* collected in this part have in common an attempt to work through issues, either as "news" or as an attempt to tackle what's taken for granted and show it in new light, explaining what's behind something as superficially gratuitous as the Grammy Awards program or as apparently benificent as the rise of all-music cable television. The adversarial tone increases as time goes on, which demonstrates both how naive I was when I started out and how dire things have been in the supposedly "recession-proof" entertainment field these past few years.

One consequence of having illusions turn to smoke was the decision in mid-1983 to start my own publication, *Rock & Roll Confidential*, a monthly, subscription-only newsletter that is free of advertising and analyzes both industry elements (which can mean anything from large record and radio companies to individual artists and even listeners) and the music itself with a politicized eye. The final item in this chapter is from RRC's third issue, published in July 1983. Look upon it as a comment upon the condition of the record business as of this book's publication.

The Profits Go
Up Up Up

You may be wondering why new records by Steve Martin, Billy Joel, Ted Nugent, Chicago, Santana and Boston now carry an $8.98 list price, one dollar higher than what Warner Bros. (in the first instance) and CBS (which markets the other five) used to receive. The answer has to do with the "economic adversities" suffered by those conglomerates in the past few months. In the third quarter of 1978, CBS Record Division sales rose 32 percent but "costs increased at a greater rate," according to the company's report. As a result, and given the additional burden of a TV network with ratings that the Sex Pistols wouldn't envy, the company's profits increased only 8 percent, to $48.5 million—for three months, that is. Warner Bros., which faces the same cost increases but doesn't have *WKRP in Cincinnati* to subsidize, suffered less: its profits rose from $15.6 million in last year's third quarter to $19.8 million last summer (July through September).

Or as Tom Modica, a record retailer from Portland, Oregon, told *Record World*, the music trade weekly: "Last time [when record prices jumped to $7.98 in November 1976], I thought there was going to be consumer resistance. I tried to anticipate that and I tried to get behind their position and they weren't there . . . At this point, I say if the companies believe that the market can bear the price, I'm going to go along with it."

What Modica knows is that companies that make $15 to $50 million *every three months* are not paupers. Nobody in the record business is talking about losing money as an excuse for price increases; nobody's talking about breaking even. For giant corporations like CBS and Warner Communications, success isn't measured by profit but by *growth* in profits. Profits of $100 million yearly are nice, but unless the profit increases by 10 percent or more each year, Wall Street is dissatisfied, the price of the company's stock falls and management heads may roll.

What do you care? Well, it's your money the companies toy with. Of course you won't pay the $8.98 list price for *Chicago MCLXVII* or whatever it's called—but then, you weren't going to pay $7.98 for it either. You will pay a dollar more than the discount price you have been paying, or you'll buy fewer records. If you do the former, you're entitled to resent it. But if you make the latter decision, you ought to understand that you're contributing to the shrinking variety of widely distributed recorded music.

Here's how that works. Any new artist must sell 50,000 to 100,000 copies of his initial LP in order to continue recording for a major record label—otherwise he'll be written off as a failure and discarded. If 100,000 people buy fewer records, whose records are they most likely to find expendable? Albums by established stars or those by interesting newcomers? In all probability, the records passed over will be the ones heard about but not yet heard; the ones with the interesting covers but unknown music; the ones heard on the radio but so infrequently that they remain unfamiliar. This is true whether or not the price of albums by new artists is raised (which it will be in the next few months, of course). And this is the height of corporate irresponsibility, for it amounts to a guarantee that no performer has more than one or two chances to make his or her first hit. Under this system, Bob Seger, Billy Joel and Ted Nugent would never have had a chance.

Rising costs are the scapegoat of these price increases, but no corporation could show increases in prices of vinyl and paper (records and jackets) that justify the jump from $5.98 to $8.98 in three years. Artists' costs have risen more—some performers are now paid nearly what they're worth—but record price rises won't solve that: artists get paid a percentage of the album's price, which means more for one that costs $8.98 than for one that's $7.98. And anyway, no one is talking "reasonable" profit anymore, unless there's someone out there prepared to argue that a profit of $20 million or so every quarter is insufficient incentive to be in business.

Record prices increase because the manufacturers have not yet found the price at which the market will rebel. If they can sell shoddy records for $8.98 without any complications, why offer well-made ones for less? For these prices, at least we ought to get virgin vinyl. But instead we keep getting screwed. Not that it isn't our own fault.

Rolling Stone, 1978

As it turned out, $8.98 was a price at which the market rebelled—for a time at least. Though the record companies don't like to talk about it, such price gouging was a major factor in the crash of 1978–79, and for the next few years their own greed had companies talking about thinner and thinner profits. Recovery began in part when prices were de-escalated, catalogue albums reissued at a list price of $5.98 and some new artists released at that level, too. Of course by the mideighties not only was $8.98 a standard list price for hit LPs, but the days of deep discounting were all but ended, too. Similarly, record company *surveys, in one of the few believable statistics they returned, found that one of the major causes of the slump was the decline in multiple purchases predicted in this column. The impact this had on the major labels' inability to develop significant new artists for the first few years of the eighties is only too obvious. Perhaps it's not home taping that is killing music so much as it is plain corporate greed.*

Learning the Game; Changing the Rules

In 1978 the creative freedom of which this piece speaks was genuine, and not only for superstars. But by mid-1979 the clamps began coming down again, as the recording industry flailed about in search of a scapegoat for its massive economic decline.

In the midseventies, not only established rock stars but beginners had a chance to make music their way, with an absolute minimum of corporate interference. Budgets were fairly flexible, and for stars hardly existed at all. (Of course recording budgets are ultimately paid for by the performers, not the record companies.) The record labels seemed to have finally learned that they knew a great deal less about creating music than the performers themselves, and had settled in to learn to effectively manufacture, market and promote sounds, rather than trying to dictate styles and approaches.

At the slightest hint of a decline the reins were tightened, and of course this only exacerbated the problems of overproduction, poor planning and hype that accounted for the parts of the slump that weren't accounted for by the fact that the country was beginning to slide into a major depression cycle. In my view, it's no coincidence that the years of the slump coincided with this rollback of creative slack —or that "recovery" was based upon the work of performers who could not have been predicted or created by the record labels' formulas. (Unless you think Boy George and Michael Jackson are the phantasms of bureaucrats.)

In any event, the historical process at work in rock does have some
continuing relationship to the one described here, although there is
more tension between the regulators and the artists than this over-
optimistic survey suggests.

Last fall, some friends threw an after-midnight party in a movie theater
to show some old rock footage. There was Presley on *Sullivan*, of course,
and nearly everybody else on *Shindig!*, *Hullabaloo*, *Ready Steady Go* and
Top of the Pops. But for me the evening's outstanding moment was its
first, a three-minute clip of Buddy Holly and the Crickets singing "Peggy
Sue" on *Sullivan*.

Until recently, Buddy Holly was thought not to have survived on film,
which is part of what had made him the most underrated of rock's found-
ers, at least in America. (England is a different story, as usual.) Then, a
year or so ago, someone in Europe turned up with this clip and it's a
revelation: Holly must have been not only one of early rock's best record
makers but one of its most riveting live performers, too. He shakes and
quivers through every second of "Peggy Sue" and he absolutely raves on
guitar. If CBS had any sense of cultural history, it would show this clip
next February 3, on the twentieth anniversary of Holly's famous plane
crash.

Since CBS is unreliable, however, we're left with *The Buddy Holly Story*,
which is (unlike most of the recent rock movies) a lot better than nothing.
Gary Busey pulls off the title role with great aplomb. He doesn't really
sound like Holly, but from the opening scene, when he risks being kicked
off the radio by switching from straight country to a tough "Rock Around
with Ollie Vee," he has you pulling for him. At least until the very end,
when he's saddled with an orchestra. (Busey's singing isn't nearly so convincing on the soundtrack LP, where there's no magic, only the inevitable
opportunity for comparison.)

The orchestra is typical of the problem with the *Holly* script, which just
can't leave well enough alone. On the night of his death, as in all his other
concerts, Holly played with a trio, not a big band. Similarly, he made his
first hits in New Mexico, not New York; his first Nashville session was not
a disaster; the courtship of his wife was not exceptionally arduous, but
exceedingly brief, lasting less than a day; he did not charter the plane in
which he died because of a bus breakdown, but because he wanted to get
to the next stop of the final tour in time to do his laundry and pick up
some mail; his parents weren't opposed to his music—his mother cowrote

"Maybe Baby," for God's sake. Those mistakes aren't necessary. John Goldrosen's *Buddy Holly: His Life and Music* is a solid, accurate biography.

Even though it follows only a vague outline of real life, *The Buddy Holly Story* strikes me as an important movie. Its best scenes show Holly struggling for control of his sound. Nearly everyone wanted him to water it down, make him sound more pop and stop rocking so hard. That's certainly true to life.

I believe that rock and roll is somehow separate from the rest of the entertainment business, and *The Buddy Holly Story* helps me understand why and how that came to pass. To put it most simply, today's rock musicians have more direct, personal control over their work than novelists, broadcasters, moviemakers or any other toilers in the popular arts.

This wasn't always true—there were those who wanted things to be done according to formula—and one of Buddy Holly's greatest contributions was his involvement with every step of the record-making process: songwriting, production, arranging and, as one of the pioneers of the overdub, engineering. When Busey, as Holly, storms out of a Nashville studio because the producer doesn't want him to record with drums, that isn't true to his life. But it is part of learning the game—and changing the rules.

In a way, it's this part of Holly's vision that is his greatest legacy. Today rock musicians are free to spend months in the studio, trying to craft perfect recordings without much corporate interference, in large part because of battles fought by such earlier musicians. Holly helped contribute to rock the notion that it was possible to do it all, no matter what anybody said. And while it's true that those who made *The Buddy Holly Story* probably had in mind *The Glenn Miller Story*, another tale of a bespectacled musician who died in an air wreck, that larger vision shines through. Although his influence spread to a host of utterly conventional singers (Bobby Vee, Peter and Gordon, Linda Ronstadt), what's worth remembering is that Buddy Holly refused to play the game, as even Elvis did.

At a time when every third-rate rock musician is heading to the Hollywood back lots, it's nice to remember that Buddy Holly also had exquisite taste in movies. His best song, "That'll Be the Day," takes its title from John Wayne's favorite expression in John Ford's sublime *The Searchers*. In that respect Buddy Holly may have as much to teach today's rock and roll movies as he does contemporary rock musicians—and listeners.

Rolling Stone, 1978

THE BIZ 179

Grammys: Gaffes and a Little Good News

This was a watershed year for the Grammys. The list of nominees was toothsome, for while some of what was best about 1978 was ignored (*Darkness on the Edge of Town*, Warren Zevon), others were finally honored: Jackson Browne's "Running on Empty"; the *Saturday Night Fever* soundtrack; Earth, Wind and Fire. There is also a solid body of craftsmanship up for awards: Billy Joel, the Commodores, Asleep at the Wheel. The Best New Artist nominees were the most adventurous group ever assembled at one of these notoriously conservative affairs: the Cars, who scored with the first American new wave LP to go platinum; Elvis Costello, the only UK new waver showing any signs of commercial vitality; Chris Rea, whose debut LP was unjustly ignored by critics; Toto, whose formulaic West Coast pop nonetheless presented a chance to give overdue credit to some of LA's finer sessionmen; and A Taste of Honey, whose "Boogie Oogie Oogie" was 1978's most charmingly mindless hit.

For rock fans, then, the twenty-first annual Grammy presentations, telecast on CBS February 15, 1979, ended about forty-five minutes after the two-hour show began. That was when A Taste of Honey won the Best New Artist award. I don't object to this because of the mindlessness of "Boogie Oogie Oogie," which is the central and legitimate source of its charm, nor because it conforms to disco formulas—at least it's more lively than Toto's distanced approximation of funk. But objectively speaking, A Taste of Honey is the least likely of all the nominees to build a career out of its hit. Like the rest of the Grammy presentations, it indicates primarily that the National Academy of Recording Arts and Sciences (NARAS), which votes for the awards, would know neither art nor science in the recording field were its collective membership to be severely bitten in the ass by one or the other. Or even both.

One might say the Grammys are justified by their consistency. The voters always prefer pop to rock, mass sales to artistry, convention to innovation, Australians to Englishmen (and, generally, Americans to either, which is just how "Just the Way You Are" beat out "Stayin' Alive" in both categories in which the Billy Joel and Bee Gees songs were pitted against each other). But it's an obnoxious consistency that the Grammys offer, because they fail—or refuse—to acknowledge music business realities at the same time that they're supposed to represent them.

This has sometimes been blamed on television, as if the Grammys served television well. Indeed, replacing Andy Williams as emcee (a musical necessity) smacks of network thinking, since his successor, John Denver, was chosen just as his career was on the downslope. If there was nothing as gauche as the American Music Awards tribute to Perry Como —hardly the premier saloon singer of his own generation and barely remembered now except as a TV show host—there was also nothing as moving as *Heroes of Rock'n'Roll* and *Elvis*, which both aired only a week before.

But the Grammys aren't just bad TV. The voting also diminishes the prestige of the record industry. Certainly everyone but NARAS must have been embarrassed by the "tribute to San Francisco," which was only a decade late and furthermore failed to mention the last two vital recording operations—Fantasy Records and Beserkley Records—still functioning there. The S.F. tribute had all the relevance and reality of an NCAA campus blurb at halftime.

Meanwhile, the voting remains mystifying at every level. Does anyone understand how Billy Joel's "Just the Way You Are" can be the Best Record of the Year and Joel not be selected as the best pop male vocalist? Just what was it about the song that made people vote for it?

There are genuine possibilities for improvement here. While it's obvious that the academy knows nothing and cares less about artistry, it is a travesty to allow performers as clumsy as A Taste of Honey to perform on the program. (A Taste of Honey looked so awkward I was convinced they were lip-synching; apparently not, but that gives an added dimension to the gaffe of having them win.) Rather than the stilted, lifeless performances of Barbara Mandrell, Kenny Rogers and Dottie West and Chuck Mangione, why not offer videotapes of Billy Joel, the Bee Gees and other nominees? If the tamest performers must be chosen as presenters, at least someone should make sure that Frankie Valli knows that Barbra Streisand's song isn't called "You Don't *Send* Me Flowers" and that the network announcer is informed of how to properly pronounce Tavares. Finally, rather than having Martin Mull make smarmy fun of the voting process, why not explain what an award like Producer of the Year signifies and why it might be a category of sufficient importance to televise?

That wouldn't rectify the injustice of giving the production Grammy to the Bee Gees, Karl Richardson and Albhy Galuten, who have only perpetuated a format devised by the Bee Gees' earlier producer, Arif Mardin. But it might instruct the public about how records are made and marketed. And given the right presenter, it might even be entertaining. After all, just because the record business offers pleasure 364 days a year, there's no

justification to bore us all to death, coast to coast, on the one that's left.
TV does that well enough without any assistance from the music world.

Rolling Stone, 1979

*A Taste of Honey never had another hit of consequence. Neither did
Chris Rea, and Elvis Costello has struggled, but both the Cars and
Toto have been massively successful since striking out on Grammy
night. The Grammy broadcast has yet to improve much, although
beginning in 1983, it did begin to use a few videotapes of performances.*

The Changing of
The Guard

*In the record industry, you can discover a trend a month and all of
them eagerly described as fundamentally altering the structure or
fundamental perception of something or other. However wise it may
be to ignore all of these and simply concentrate on inspired individuals, some are simply too obnoxious and/or fatuous to remain unremarked. And even though it seems stupid now to lump Talking Heads
with Elvis Costello, at that moment lots of insiders were doing it.*

*What was really happening, of course, unassessed by almost any-
one, was the decline and fall of FM album-rock radio, as it narrow-
casted itself to the point of obliteration. Since the power poppers were
notable mostly as makers of a hip track or two, it was time for the
reemergence of Top Forty radio (called today contemporary hit radio,
but the difference is almost purely nomenclatural). And with no one
save a few Anglo-oriented dinosaurs continuing to make interesting
or even playable non-single album cuts, album-rock broadcasting became so dully hermetic that it exposed the soft underbelly of the
music, which had also grown way too insular. And the reaction to that
has produced, in the mideighties, a smattering of genuinely interesting*

performers whose music specifically rejects those isolationist tenden-
cies, mingling all sorts of rhythms, textures and influences without
indulging in selfish eclecticism. I don't know if this is quite what Sam
Phillips had in mind, but I find it suits me fine, or at least a whole
lot better than anything else that has constituted a trend in the past
decade.

At the close of their Carnegie Hall concert last month, the Knack's Doug
Fieger issued a warning to the assembled audience and critics. Rock's old
guard bands were on the way out, he said, about to be replaced by younger,
bolder ones. To hammer home the point, the Knack then pounded out a
rendition of Bob Dylan's 1963 protest song, "The Times They Are A-
Changin'."

Aside from demonstrating that Fieger is a particularly clumsy opportun-
ist, that incident didn't prove much. But Fieger's attitude reflects the
feeling of many observers that a revolution occurred in pop music this year.
It was in 1979, after all, that we saw power pop (watered-down heir to punk
and new wave) achieve commercial success, not only with the Knack but
through records by the Cars, Cheap Trick, the Talking Heads, the Police,
Joe Jackson, Elvis Costello, Nick Lowe and Blondie. To certify the authenticity of this trend, record companies have spewed out a couple of dozen
bands playing in similar styles: the Beat, the Sports, the Records, 20/20,
the Yachts, the Inmates, the Members, Bram Tchaikovsky.

By sheer weight of numbers, power pop is now ruling FM radio, pushing
aside the soft rock that has dominated broadcasts and trade paper reports
for the bulk of this decade. For many, this resurgence of straight-ahead
rock seems to verify the original accusations of the seventies punks: rock's
superstars are washed up and tired, meek and conservative, spiritless and
decadent.

So how come the top three albums in the country this week are Led
Zeppelin's *In Through the Out Door*, the Eagles' *The Long Run* and
Fleetwood Mac's *Tusk*? Not a skinny tie in the bunch.

Perhaps the millennium is not yet at hand. Clearly, something is happening, though it may not be what Doug Fieger—himself a reformed soft
rocker—claims. Maybe all that new talent was simply filling a void, while
rock's reigning heavyweights were dawdling in the studio. Maybe we have
reached a transitional stage, wherein many of the celebrated hard rock acts
of recent years—Kiss, Aerosmith, Alice Cooper—are being outgrown by
their no-longer-teenage listeners.

Unquestionably, radio sounds more lively today than it has in years, thanks mostly to the power pop brigade. But this resurgence doesn't necessarily mean that popular taste has changed. In a year when Billy Joel and Paul Simon released no new music, white American pop was rendered commercially impotent. And while disco may be withering, it would be hard for anyone this side of a diehard new-wave ideologue to argue that rock disco (for example, Donna Summer's "Hot Stuff," the Doobie Brothers' "What a Fool Believes" or "Pop Muzik" by M) didn't provide some of 1979's most exciting moments. If the guard is changing, the government still stands—and the new music that's replacing the old may not be what wishful reporting would have it.

The question is really whether power pop's marketplace success makes any difference. A revolutionary band like the Clash, or even just a hard-driving, abrasive one like the Ramones, is only slightly more likely to be heard today than when the airwaves were dominated by Linda Ronstadt and James Taylor. In their way, the power poppers may make things *more* difficult for the hard-line punks like the Clash and Ramones, because they offer a safe middle ground for the unconvinced. And any link between the Sex Pistols, who rejected all previous rock stars as corrupt, and a prepackaged "phenomenon" like the Knack, who have based their entire career on as many superficial parallels with the early Beatles as possible, is tenuous at best.

The trouble with power pop is that it's nothing new. The Knack and Cheap Trick recycle old Beatles' riffs with the regularity with which Meat Loaf swipes licks from Bruce Springsteen, and of the other new bands mentioned here, only Elvis Costello and the Talking Heads have anything like a unique personal vision or musical style. The real kudos for the limited success of these bands properly belong to the music industry, which has become so adept at selling its product that it was even able to turn punk, an anti-product that explicitly despised the marketing machinery, into a profitable commodity.

If the business has become smarter, it's been immeasurably aided by an audience grown so complacent that it's unable to respond to any change unless a large number of diverse individuals (just what do the members of Blondie have in common with Joe Jackson?) are lumped together in an arbitrarily designated "trend." If power pop has done anything worthwhile, it has gotten the audience excited again—but only by putting new names in the same old niches.

So power pop seems to me not so much a changing of the guard and a resurgence of rock's aged spirit as the ultimate betrayal. The times are changing but not necessarily in the direction that we'd like to think. I am struck by something Sam Phillips, who produced Elvis Presley's first hits at Sun Records, told Peter Guralnick in the latter's new book, *Lost High-way*. "Listen," says Phillips, "they're talking about what you've got to have —well, what is the trend now? Well, *Jesus God*, now if there's anything we don't need, it's a trend."

For Phillips, and for me, the real rock millennium comes when an individual like Presley appears with a voice and a vision so clear and true that it demolishes trends. If we have heard such a voice in the past few years, it belonged not to any of today's chic Americans, but to an angry English kid, Johnny Rotten, whose rage was mostly ignored in this country. Today none of the power pop legions pay Rotten even lip service, though it's unlikely that any of them would even have a record contract without the Sex Pistols having set the stage.

Something else Sam Phillips told Guralnick sticks with me. "As we go longer and longer into the lack of individual expression, as we go along, if we get too far we're going to get away from some of the real basic things. All of us damn cats and people that appreciate not the fifties necessarily but that freedom are gonna forget about the feel. We gonna be in jail and not even know it." And in that case, the guard can change daily or even hourly and it won't make a whole lot of difference.

New York Daily News, 1979

The Only Rock
That Matters

Dan Daley never got the record contract that he deserves. So far his biggest moment of recognition has been playing at the 1983 convention of the Vietnam Veterans of America, to an audience that was undoubtedly more receptive and enthusiastic than any batch of record-label minions, but that hardly gives the young performer a clue about what to do next. (Work on songs about Central American intervention, so he can be ready for the next wave of vets?)

Daley's case is far from the most outrageous I've ever encountered, though. In 1978 I became aware of a Rhode Island band, Beaver Brown, which played the Atlantic Coast from Narragansett to New

Jersey. The group was—and is—an amazingly solid collection of mainstream rock players, plenty powerful and perfectly integrated. Their lead singer and songwriter, John Cafferty, has an unmistakable resemblance to Bruce Springsteen, however, and this caused the record industry to refuse even to consider signing them. I mean, everybody passed. In 1981, an independently released 45 of their song "Wild Summer Nights" sold 40,000 copies on the East Coast alone, with very little airplay. Still no record-label interest; still too many charges that Cafferty was a "Springsteen clone." (God, how come they never say that about the Foreigner clones? Those they gobble up.)

Finally, desperate, Cafferty agreed to lend his music, including some of his most preciously hoarded songs, to a film project, Eddie and the Cruisers. The film was godawful, and for Beaver Brown fans, there was something especially gruesome about seeing Cafferty's voice emerging from the throat of a clumsy actor. But the soundtrack album was released and it sold more than two million copies. And Cafferty and Beaver Brown now have a career—despite what's hip, and without a shred of assistance from the process laughably called "artist development."

In mid-September of 1984, Beaver Brown played the Bottom Line in New York City to an audience of the same A&R types who had sneered and split early three years before. Several of the songs they played were identical. No one left early this time, the group was greeted with veritable hosannas and the general atmosphere reeked of "Bruce who?" This is called front-running, but that doesn't mean it wasn't nice for some of us old-timers to watch the music industry have its face rubbed in the product of its own insufferable laziness and prejudices. Someday I suspect I'll hear Dan Daley sing "Still in Saigon" under similar circumstances and leave feeling just as joyously avenged.

Early in July, I saw Dan Daley play at the Bottom Line as the opening act for the estimable Marshall Crenshaw. Crenshaw's musical vision is so precisely focused that it immediately and unavoidably drew attention to the limitations of Daley's more scattered presentation. But in a way, this contrast between crafty stylization and awkward enthusiasm only made Daley's potential seem more impressive. At least he wasn't afraid to stand before a gaggle of big city hipsters and play heartland rock and roll.

Daley is blond and lanky and still wears T-shirts and jeans onstage, the last sort of rocker you'd expect to find in Greenwich Village these days.

(Crenshaw may be from Detroit, but his horn-rims provide an immediate stylistic connection to the new wave.) Daley's stage presence is grounded more in intensity of desire than charisma, and his band, which played fairly well, looked as if the members hadn't known one another long enough to feel polite in suggesting an appropriate mutual wardrobe. Their arrangements are rather elastic, heavy on guitars (which owe more to Gary Rossington than Robert Fripp), and Daley's songs tend to be terse proclamations of faith and stories of conventional rock and roll citizens (who are sometimes, but only sometimes, eccentrics by other standards), rather than parables of metaphysics, ethnology or ideology. That is, there's not much about Daley or his music that's hip, except that he happens to have written some very good music, including "Still in Saigon," the only great song about Vietnam so far, and one of the most powerful songs I've heard in the past few years.

When Charlie Daniels released his version of "Still in Saigon," a few months back—and came close to having a hit—one Cleveland disc jockey burst into tears over the air after playing it. When's the last time you heard of a DJ acting so human? But "Still in Saigon" is that kind of song; it wrenches humanity from unsuspected corners. If for Bruce Springsteen, the legacy of Vietnam is "like some dark street," in which the worst shadows lurk, "Still in Saigon" is the moment when the demons dwelling in those shadows spring to life, reminding each of us how little recovery we've made. "Still in Saigon" speaks not only for the Vietnam combat veterans about whom it was written, but for all of us who were torn apart by the war: the sense Bobby Muller of the Vietnam Veterans of America has in mind when he refers to an entire generation of Vietnam vets. "Nowhere to run to that I didn't feel that war," as the song says.

This comes across even more clearly in Dan Daley's own version. Daley never served in the military, but listening to him sing, you realize how immaterial that is. His demo is a simply shattering piece of music, and when he comes to the bridge—"Every summer when it rains / I smell the jungle, I hear the planes / Can't tell no one, I feel ashamed . . ."—the horror of what we visited upon ourselves (as well as the Vietnamese) in that conflict comes home with tearful power.

Daley's "Still in Saigon" remains only a demo, because no record label will make a commitment to recording him. As I hope I've made clear, Daley's music is ragged right now; it needs a great deal of development. But when record labels try to justify price increases and blank tape taxes, their argument is that they develop talent, and that this is expensive.

It's also a lie, and it's been a lie for some years. Once performers like Dan Daley worked out their artistic problems in the course of recording their first few singles and albums, with the aid of professional advice. No more. Today the performer develops him or herself without any industry assistance. And when that development is nearly complete, the labels step in to reap the fruits of the artist's labor, while singing their "talent development" song, implying that they are doing the artist or the audience or simply everybody a big favor.

Labels used to provide some guidance, and many of today's most significant careers are the result of patience, sticking with a performer through many false starts. This is the process that gave us Bob Seger, Bruce Springsteen, the J. Geils Band, Billy Joel—the cream of American rock and pop, some of its most profitable performers. Today all of these artists would either remain unsigned, because none of them fits a current trend, or be dropped from a major label artist roster when their first two albums failed to "produce." And these artists would also be coerced into signing shamefully exploitative deals—barely livable advances, scandalous publishing arrangements—which are in some cases worse than the "baby deals" they really did sign a decade ago, *which were shameful enough*. All for the mere chance to make a record and have it distributed with some semblance of effectiveness.

Dan Daley isn't alone; I could name a half-dozen other cases almost as outrageous. But when I think of the refusal to get such an important recording as Daley's own "Still in Saigon" onto vinyl, the urge to fling the moneychangers from the temple grows especially great. Because "Still in Saigon," with its broad-based musical ambitions and lyric concerns, is the kind of song that can put us back on the track of what made rock great in the first place—which was not simply hummability but commitment, passion, relevance, soul.

What goes on now in the record business is not only gutless but stupid. Well-bred cultural values weren't what made rock into a profit gusher— the biggest rock records in history were among the most deeply felt and involved stuff ever written. In the end, then, the only proper response to industry propaganda about the loss of profits is: "Why don't you record something somebody needs to hear?"

Record, 1982

I Don't Want
My MTV

On September 1, 1982, MTV, the cable channel that presents twenty-four-hour rock video, finally made its New York City debut. This is something for which MTV waged a long and apparently expensive media campaign, using TV ads in which rock stars, among them Pat Benatar, Mick Jagger and Pete Townshend, were suborned into urging viewers of other stations to phone their cable company to say "I want my MTV" in the same spoiled-brat voice with which baby boomers were once asked to whine for Maypo.

A New York outlet is crucial to the operations of such a channel for a number of reasons. Among the more salient, if less obvious, is that New York City is the home of the advertising industry. It is one thing to have to ferry reviewers to Fort Lee, New Jersey, to show them your programming in action. It's another thing to transport advertisers, as one can easily tell by the fact that, with the exception of relentlessly unsubtle MTV promotions and one spot for a typical oldies LP package, the several advertisers MTV claims to have are rarely visible to the naked eye (except on weekend specials).

For those not yet blessed with this most recent joint venture of the Warner Communications Corporation and the American Express Company, this is how MTV works: it shows promotional video clips of "contemporary music groups," wall to wall and back to back, rotated in roughly the same way as a typical FM radio station rotates current top tracks. From time to time the flow of tapes is interrupted, most often by whichever of the station's video jockeys happens to be pulling the current shift. (These VJs, incidentally, all look like they were hired by the casting director of *WKRP in Cincinnati*, though none of them has ever cracked a discernible joke in my presence.) Mostly the VJs spend their time extolling what MTV has just shown or is about to show, but from time to time they recite record-label press releases under the guise of "news," and about once an hour they present two-to-three-minute "interviews," which are placed in the same sort of rotation as the promo clips. These interviews operate from a principle established and articulated by Bob Dylan: "Nothing was delivered." Nothing is asked, either.

The auteur of MTV's format is a failed radio programmer, Robert

Pittman, who was bounced from his previous job, programming New York's WNBC-AM, when that station's ratings failed to surpass those of WABC, just as WABC was getting its ass whomped by WKTU. Advising Mr. Pittman are Kent Burkhart, of the firm which devised FM's noxious Superstars format, and Les Garland, another AM programmer with a dubious track record. In practice, MTV's format is as adventurous as the current FM radio formats, which means that new wavers such as Thomas Dolby, the Go-Go's, the Human League and the Clash get about one-third as much airtime as Queen, Benatar, Fleetwood Mac, Kansas and Heart. By contemporary standards, this is a genuine broadcasting alternative, though I must say that by my standards, Haircut 100 is not an antidote to heavy metal doldrums.

I was going to say that one never sees black people on MTV, but this is obviously untrue. One of the VJs, J. J. Jackson, is black, though he does his best not to let it show, and I have seen blacks in bit parts in two promos (George Thorogood's and Duran Duran's). No one I know has ever seen a black artist's promo clip on MTV and, give or take Jimi Hendrix, no one ever will. This is a matter of policy, applied without discrimination to Gary Bonds, Rick James and Stevie Wonder, Donna Summer, Grandmaster Flash and Shalamar, in the same way the policy is applied at typical FM radio stations. The wisdom of sparing MTV's viewers such exotic music will be immediately apparent to anyone asked to stomach even momentarily the videos of Le Roux and Landscape.

In addition to being racist, MTV's programming is by definition ahistorical: one is no more likely to see Bob Dylan than Dion, since neither made promo videos. And for one reason or another, MTV has been unwilling or unable to acquire the kind of rock movies that the USA Network has been running almost every weekend. For example, MTV viewers don't see *Mr. Rock and Roll*, featuring Chuck Berry and the Moonglows. Personally, I think that footage of Chuck Berry might help place Billy Squier in perspective, but then this is probably just another argument against it, from Mr. Pittman and Mr. Burkhart and Mr. Garland's point of view.

In truth, there's barely enough competently produced rock promo video to sustain twenty-four interesting *minutes* of television. Aside from a few J. Geils and Elvis Costello pieces and the odd documentary snippet (like Janis Joplin's tragically bombastic "Tell Mama"), what the eye is offered on MTV is a choice between hackneyed industrial filmmaking, somewhat less exciting than your average sports-car commercial, or stuff that looks to have been too pretentious for good grades in film school. The folks who make this junk apparently lack the simply ability to narrate a song's lyrics, though when they try, the results can be disastrous: check Pete Townshend's "Face Dances, Pt. 2," in which he *shaves*.

As it stands, MTV offers the worst of FM playlist rigidity without any of its advantages: no local involvement, no personality among its VJs, no news or sports or weather, just rock music in a hermetically sealed capsule. This may very well be the industry's future—*Billboard* reports that MTV exposure sells records—but if so, it's an irrelevant future. And because no art prospers for long in an environment that shuts out the rest of the world, neither the rock business nor MTV may have much future left, if the present course of either continues.

Record, 1982

Because this column struck so early in MTV's spread, before the press had a chance to become as inured to its inconsistencies and bigotry as it has to those of FM radio, it helped create almost a crusade against the channel's programming policies, which divided the rock world into opposing camps: laissez faire against socially concerned, I guess.

Many of the charges leveled here against MTV still stand. It is still programmed with a mentality composed of the most mediocre elements of AM and FM radio. The VJs are still an embarrassment, the interviews would still be appalling in even the most juvenile fan magazine, there's still no involvement in the world outside.

MTV has made some cosmetic changes: It now adds a few promos by black performers to its rotation each month, though with the exception of blockbusters such as Michael Jackson's or Donna Summer's, these are rarely exhibited, and almost never in prime time. The station does broadcast an even higher concentration of the so-called new music than it initially did, largely because it discovered it had the most industry impact by doing so. However, since most new music has reacted to the chance of public success by becoming completely powderpuff in both music and articulated sensibility, that's less of a big deal than MTV or new music partisans claim: "new product" is probably a more proper designation. And the station has begun to show "Closet Classics," a chance to show videos and film clips of pre-seventies vintage. (Almost all of these are by white performers, despite the fact that the story of the rock world for its first fifteen years was the story of integrated music.)

The quality of the promo videos shown has escalated dramatically, though much of the film is wasted in the service of lame music. It's worth noting, once again, that much of this improvement in quality can be traced directly to the adventurous clips created by Michael Jackson and his collaborators, videos which MTV had to be coerced into playing because Jackson is black. And it's also worth observing that as the technical quality of the videos has risen, largely as the result of working with directors whose experience is in advertising, so has the amount of casual sexual stereotyping and, worse, violence against women.

In early 1985, in other words, it's clear that MTV is a genuine power in the record business—it's all but unthinkable to have a significant rock hit without making a video clip today. But it is also true that unless and until its problems are solved, the future of MTV, and the record business that is ever more closely attached to it, remains as dubious as it did when "I Don't Want My MTV" was written. "Success" that burns this brightly can all too easily turn into supernova, flameout, a black hole. For MTV, that might be the ultimate irony.

Boomtown Blues

This is called taking the bull by the horns. Of course the public can't seem to recall that workers aren't to blame for the mess that the economy is in, but then it is as hard to discover any mention of the real culprits in the press as it is to find a paragraph that acknowledges that musicians and other toilers in the area of culture might have something in common with people who do manual labor. Rock & Roll Confidential is often more fun and not always quite so sassy, but this seems a good statement of principles on which to conclude a discussion of what the music industry really amounts to.

No sooner had the record business been blessed with a couple of multi-platinum hits than one began hearing hosannas of recovery while industry mouthpieces such as *The Hollywood Reporter*'s Dianne Bennett dragged out the ancient warnings of impending crisis due to competitive bidding for established rock acts. Both positions are false and dangerous. While it's true that a very few records have recently begun selling at the old multi-platinum levels (Michael Jackson and Men at Work chief among them), the record business has *not* regained overall prosperity. In general, the industry is still contracting, not growing. In the past few months, there has been some "growth," but the industry's progress has been achieved at the expense of new acts and small producers, just as the general economy has "recovered" on the backs of workers. And neither has reached pre-1978 levels of success, and neither has begun to compensate for the tremendous dislocations and losses of the past three to five years.

Perhaps more importantly, the idea that rock performers are overpaid is a myth. All but two or three of the industry's largest deals have made a net profit for the companies involved: even David Bowie's $10 to $17 million contract with EMI has been ensured profitability by the success of a single worldwide hit. In any event, the record companies simply write off bad deals against the excess profits made by exploiting young acts with low royalty rates. And don't forget, many acts whose advances leave them in the red in fact turn a profit for the record label, which needs to sell only about 50 percent as many records to make a profit as the act does to earn royalties.

As is the case with the economy as a whole, the problems faced by recording companies are structural in nature. They cut much deeper than supposed profligate investment in talent. Those problems include, most prominently, a lack of competent management, especially in crucial middle-level areas of A&R and promotion; the commitment on the part of the largest corporations (RCA, CBS, WEA, EMI, Polygram, MCA) to outmoded technology (the disc) when a new form (cassette tape) was in greater demand, which is the direct result of the huge corporate investment in LP pressing plants; the sort of wild overproduction that resulted in MCA selling off 400,000 copies of its final Elton John LP for under $1 per unit last winter; the corporate acquiescence in a corrupt and inefficient broadcasting system that squanders millions in the pursuit of graft and easier access to moguls of radio and cable TV. Not to mention the worst world depression in fifty years.

As Reagan and Volcker's economic policies fail and the Democrats are unable to develop anything resembling solutions, it will be essential to remember that the deficiencies of the U.S. (and world) economy are *not*

the product of "greedy" workers—in the record business or elsewhere—
but of the shortsightedness and callousness of the owners and managers
of American (and world) business itself.

Rock & Roll Confidential, 1983

The Incident

In late November 1979 the Who returned to America for another tour,
this time a month of dates that opened at the smallish Masonic Temple
in Detroit. They appeared at a variety of other venues, from the 80,000-
seat Silverdome in Pontiac to large hockey arenas and even a few other
3,000-to-5,000-seat theaters.

This tour was planned as a typical superstar tour of the late seventies.
In general, the Who played modern facilities with poor but serviceable
acoustics and elaborate security and ticket-taking precautions. In these
halls, the management was oriented to the sports world and resented the
intrusion of the long-haired young people, whose enthusiasm was often
misunderstood as rowdiness. Sometimes the adolescent belligerence of
rock fans was provoked into something nastier, just so that the staff could
have the pleasure of bullying the crowd. (It was much harder to harass the
bands, since the economic fate of the sports arenas and their employees
was determined by how many functions were held there, and rock was their
surest draw.)

The rock audience was not only shafted by the staff at the hall but also
by the ticket setup. Scalping and the siphoning off of the best seats in the
house for insiders was widespread, and in some halls, the practice of festival
seating, which ostensibly made all ticketholders equal, simply played into
the greediest inclinations of the fans themselves.

Festival seating is a general admission ticket policy in which there are
no chairs or benches placed on the floor in the front of the stage. Into this
empty space, listeners crowd on a first-come, first-served basis. Theoretically, festival seating equalizes the pressure for good seats, since those who
line up first have their pick of the place. But in fact festival seating is an
excuse to pack more people onto the arena floor—in some buildings, an

additional two thousand or more people can be jammed in if there are no chairs. And in the end, the practice merely transferred the inequities of ticket-buying, taking the advantage from those with the money to pay off scalpers (or with inside connections) and giving it to those with the leisure or patience to waste long hours queuing. Festival seating also ensured a mob scene, as early arrivals jostled for good position and latecomers tried to crash their way to better vantage points. (Promoters had an additional reason for preferring festival seating. It's easy to count the number of chairs on the floor and demand that, for a sold-out show, there be a ticket for each of them. But there's no way to accurately measure the number of bodies crammed into a space, and of course any inaccuracy in body count means a discrepancy in what the band gets paid. It didn't take an especially wily promoter to see how to turn that to advantage.)

For the Who's show at Riverfront Coliseum in Cincinnati on December 3, 1979, the crowd began lining up in the bitterly cold wind many hours before the scheduled 8:00 P.M. starting time. By 2:15 that afternoon, there was a crush of bodies around the single set of doors through which Riverfront's staff permitted patrons to pass. And by 6:15, thousands of people were lined up, shaking with cold, many pushing and slamming into those in front of them, jostling for position. The doors remained barred.

The crowd thrust at each other with unbelievable force, magnified by the numbers and lack of space. Those in the middle were in constant danger of being swept underfoot and trampled; those in front were pressed so hard that they feared the plate-glass doors—still shackled shut—would shatter.

The crowd was now growing steadily. A good share of the 18,000 patrons had arrived early, and still they were herded into the small plaza in front of that single rank of doors. Although there were warnings from the police outside, the Coliseum staff and the concert promoters, Electric Factory Concerts of Philadelphia, refused to open the doors before 7:00 P.M., even when the crowd started shoving furiously as the Who went through its sound check just after six o'clock.

When the doors were opened, the crowd rushed in, ignoring the pleas of those caught in its center who were thrust forward rapidly against their will. Some of the glass in the doorways shattered. In the wake of the stampede for the seats, many were injured. Eleven died: Walter Adams, Jr., age seventeen; Peter Bowes, eighteen; Connie Burns, twenty-one; Jacqueline Eckerle, fifteen; David J. Heck, nineteen; Teva Ladd, twenty-seven; Karen Morrison, fifteen; Stephan Preston, nineteen; Philip K. Snyder, twenty; Bryan Wagner, seventeen; and James Warmouth, twenty-one. Most were trampled; some suffocated. The dead included seven teens, four adults; seven men, four women—a representative demographic ratio of Who fans. It could have been anybody.

Inside, most of the crowd didn't know what had happened. Many of the early arrivals stepped over bodies but never knew it, so quickly were they swept along. Some of the fans had been badly frightened at being hemmed in, but even they weren't aware that anyone had been seriously injured, much less killed. Latecomers saw that there had been trouble, but had no idea how bad. The Who played their full show, unaware of the deaths. Manager Bill Curbishley informed them after the show, as was proper. If an announcement had been made from the stage about what had really happened—or if the Who had stopped the show—an even worse stampede could have ensued.

The Who was in shock. How great was their responsibility? Obviously, even the uninvolved could ponder that question for decades without reaching any certain answers. Still, the blame had to be parceled out and it was. Quite correctly, some of it went to the police, who had not forcefully exercised their authority once they'd spotted a potentially life-threatening problem. A good deal more went to the Coliseum staff and to the promoters, who had ignored not only past experiences at Riverfront and the police warnings but also their own senses as they let the situation grow more and more dangerous without altering their prearranged plans. (Since no one could reach the plaza where the crowd was formed without having shown a ticket at a lower level, there was little chance of gate-crashers being admitted—not that the need to protect the show against crashers was any excuse.) Too little blame was directed at the crowd itself, which had behaved selfishly, exhibiting a greed for entertainment that was the antithesis of the principled idealism of which Who fans often liked to boast.

The blame remaining belonged to the Who itself. Not because the Riverfront deaths happened but because the Who had finally become so divorced from their listeners that they had allowed themselves to participate in the greedy scheme of festival seating, one essential precondition for such a disaster.

That doesn't mean that the Who had behaved badly that night. Certainly, if the promoter or hall staff had asked the band or its representatives if the doors could be opened earlier, the band would have understood the situation and agreed. But the Who's understanding of their function as a group was imbued with the notion of a basic identification between themselves and the audience. They were especially shaken not just by the fact that something like this could happen at a rock gig, but by the fact that it had happened at *theirs*.

What had occurred at Riverfront Coliseum could have happened to almost any rock band. In itself, that's one measure of how drastically the Who had changed since 1963, when they had been at one with their crowd. But it has little to do with the Who's changes since Moon died. In a way, given the band's rowdy image, it's surprising that some haunting catastrophe hadn't occurred earlier.

The real difference between the old Who and the new one was in what happened after the incident. Cincinnati was a ten-day wonder in the press but soon forgotten, dredged up only in passing in press accounts of the band's career. The Who played out the rest of the tour and spent most of the spring and early summer of 1980 touring the United States. Since no one asked about "the incident," after a time it ceased to be a factor in their public image. Daltrey said that the band would do "anything we can do to stop it from ever happening again." But on succeeding tours the band took only minimal steps to protect its fans. The Who still played shows with festival seating. (Many other bands refused to.) In the interviews the band did in 1981 and 1982, Cincinnati was not a major issue. Often it didn't come up at all.

But the Cincinnati deaths seemed to send Pete Townshend into another spiral of depression, anxiety, alcoholism and worse. In a way he seemed to accept the eleven corpses as proof that the Who should not have continued without Keith Moon. And in another way he simply didn't want to think about it. Pete said as much to disc jockey Tom Bender in Detroit only a few days after the disaster: "I just want to work and be happy. We didn't know anything about the accident. But everything in my life tells me to stop—my two little girls, my brain, my body, everything tells me to stop. I'm not going to stop. I just don't *care*, really. I really don't *care* what happens anymore."

That didn't mean that Townshend didn't feel badly about those who died. He did. But Pete's comments indicate his acceptance that his time as a rock idealist was past. Townshend now wanted to become nothing more than a music professional. Roger Daltrey had won, all right. The Who were entertainers now, and except to the fanatic and the naive, that's all the new version of the band stood for.

Often enough, Townshend seemed to have to work extra hard in his new role, which certainly didn't come naturally to him. Of the Who, Pete alone would sometimes raise the specter of Cincinnati, even when an interviewer had not. Once again he grew gaunt and spooky.

Along with the concert promoter, the Coliseum and the city of Cincinnati, the Who were sued by the relatives of the dead, and even though the band was insured, the liabilities were extremely high. Inevitably, Townshend's penchant for making confusing and contradictory remarks (reflecting his own confusions and contradictions) got him into trouble. In the spring of 1980 a settlement was nearly reached between the band and the families. The group was willing to do something to indemnify the bereaved against their loss. The families were willing to be a bit understanding.

Then Townshend did an interview with Greil Marcus of *Rolling Stone*. Marcus is a rock critic of the old school and he pressed for Townshend's answers on what had happened and, more importantly, pushed Pete to spell out his emotions about the Riverfront deaths. Townshend poured it all out.

"The amazing thing, for us, was the fact that when we were told about what happened at that gig, that eleven kids had died, for a second our guard dropped. Just for a second. Then it was back up again.

"It was, 'Fuck it! We're not gonna let a *little thing* like this stop us.' That was the way we *had* to think. We had to reduce it, because if we'd actually *admitted* to ourselves the *true* significance of the event, the *true* tragedy of the event—not just in term of 'rock,' but the fact that it happened at one of our concerts—the tragedy to us, in particular, if we'd admitted that, we could not have gone on and worked. And we had a tour to do. We're a rock and roll band. You know, we *don't fuck around*, worrying about eleven people dying. We *care* about it, but there is a particular attitude I call the 'tour armor': When you go on the road, you throw up an armor around yourself, you almost go into a trance. I don't think you lose your humanity, but think: For ten, maybe fifteen years, the Who smashed up hotel rooms—why? Where's the pleasure in it? We actually quite relished general violence. I don't understand why it happened . . . It doesn't happen now, but it did happen, for a long time. I think that for me, tours were like a dream.

"Immediately after the Cincinnati gig, to protect ourselves partly from *legal* recriminations, we doubled, trebled and quadrupled external security at halls . . . But a lot of kids complained: Everywhere they'd look there was a cop. It spoiled their evening for them. They felt, 'Okay, it happened in Cincinnati, *but we don't need that . . .*' "

Pete's logic was unsatisfactory. (The fact the people liked festival seating was irrelevant to its causal relationship in Cincinnati or to the question of banning it.) His tirade tried to fend off the depth of the question by dealing with its most pungent superficialities. And Marcus called him on it, and Townshend responded by talking about how the Who had responded personally.

"The other side of it is worth mentioning," he said. "The fact that the Who don't just get their strength from wearing armor. We did go home and we did think about it and we talked about it with our families and our friends. I went home to about ten letters from the families of the kids who'd died: letters full of deep, deep affection and support and encouragement. It wasn't like these people were being recriminatory. The father of the girl who died who had two children was writing to say that it would hurt *him*, the family, the friends of the family and friends of the girl if they knew that because of what happened, because of her death, we changed our feelings about rock. They understood her feelings about the band and about the music—you know what I'm saying?

"I think only time will tell. If I could dare say it, I'd say that Cincinnati was a very, very positive event for the Who. I think it changed the way we feel about people. It's changed the way we feel about our audience . . . in terms of affection and also remembering constantly that they are human beings—and not just people in rows. And I hope the reverse: that people who come to see the band will know that we're human beings, too, and not this *myth* . . .

"I mean, I watched Roger Daltrey cry his eyes out after that show. I didn't, but he did. But now, whenever a fucking journalist—sorry—asks you about Cincinnati, they expect you to come up with a fucking theatrical tear in your eye! You know: 'Have you got anything to say about Cincinnati?' 'Oh we were *deeply* moved, terrible tragedy, the horror, loss of life.' *Arrrghh!* What do you do? We did all the things that we thought were right to do at the time: sent flowers to the fucking funerals. All . . . *wasted*. I think when people are dead they're dead."

That did it. Townshend's sarcasm sank him. The problem wasn't that he was wrong; the sanctimonious show business attitude that uses all tragedy as an excuse to exhibit dramatic emotion is a real issue in the response to and coverage of events like the deaths in Cincinnati. But Pete had suggested (whether or not he knew it) that his own remorse was less than sincere.

(Townshend said more recently that he found the entire *Rolling Stone* episode "unfortunate," because the quotations were "sensationally framed, without vocal inflections; it actually looks like I actually mean what I'm saying or at least, that I believe what I'm saying is worth saying. When I spoke to Greil Marcus, I was sarcastic and—I thought—self-detrimental about the group's bloody-minded determination to carry on after the tragedy. I was simply trying to illustrate how absurd show business thinking is. It didn't come off and hurt the feelings of the relatives." He clearly regrets the entire statement. However, it should be pointed out that all the italics in the quotes above were in the original article.)

After the *Rolling Stone* story appeared, the families stopped talking about a settlement; by mid-1983 the Who still hadn't been able to settle the case. Given the way that American justice grinds—so exceedingly slowly that it might well grind finer than that of the Lord—it may be many more years before the Cincinnati lawsuits are out of the courts.*

Greil Marcus defined the tragedy that remained. "What strikes me most about what happened in Cincinnati is that it seems, now, not to have happened at all," he told Townshend. "It has not become part of the rock and roll frame of reference, as Altamont instantly and permanently did. It seems to me that it was an event that should have signified that something new about the relationship between bands and their audiences, or about rock and roll as mass culture, was taking place. It ought to have forced people to reexamine a lot of assumptions, a lot of what they took for granted. That hasn't happened."

Nor would the new Who ever encourage it to happen. That was perhaps the biggest tragedy of all.

From Before I Get Old, 1983

*The lawsuits were settled out of court in 1983.

7

Marx and Lennon

Introduction

ock and politics are said by the doctrinaire on both sides to mix poorly, if at all, but I've never been able to afford to agree with that, mostly because my encounters with rock have led directly to political conclusions. After all, there is no human activity that has no political implications, and rock—given its origins in polarities of class, race and religion—may even exhibit this truth *more* clearly than most other phenomena.

Of course, the everyday distinction that old and new leftists like to make between cultural and "serious" matters was happily obliterated in Detroit by the confluence of the MC5, a great band, and a political community that was, at least in part, ready for 'em. This prevented me (and most of my acquaintances) from falling for the dire condescension of wackos like the Weathermen, though I don't think that artificial attempt to *force* a fusion of pop culture and politics could have succeeded in any environment. The connection is organic, unmistakable once you've cracked a couple of minor cultural codes and participated even briefly in a few of rock's rituals.

That doesn't mean rock isn't product or that that product isn't the fruit of industrial capitalism, one of the ugliest systems men have ever devised. But if one's purity leads to the conclusion that all products of that system must be spurned, you're left with nothing at all, since even the people who inhabit America (and most of the rest of the world) have been shaped by the same forces. In other words, you play the hand you're dealt using strategies as subversive as you care to imagine. If you do it right, you'll never need a weatherman again.

The MC5:
Back on Shakin' Street

*"Back on Shakin' Street" is the most heavily rewritten piece in
Fortunate Son, and one of the longest. The reason is fairly simple:
this is where I came in. The MC5 helped get me my first full-time job
in journalism, their incredible buzz-saw rock (echoes of which can be
heard in the New York Dolls, the Sex Pistols and every other band
that terms itself punk or hard core) illuminated the shadowy corners
of my adolescence, their fusion of rock and politics expressed my own
early, fumbling attempts to reconcile the two.*

*During my brief semesters at Wayne State University, teenage
Detroit was obsessed with the MC5, its homegrown rock and revolution band, and my mania knew few bounds: to see the Five two or
three nights a week was not unusual. And there was good reason for
such fanaticism. The MC5 remain every bit as good in my memory
as they are on the few surviving tapes of their performances. As I wrote
in 1983: "They were crude, their jazz-rock fantasies were never realized, their politics never progressed beyond new left naive, but they
were one of the three greatest rock bands I've ever seen and the true
sonic originators of punk . . . It all operates somewhere in a twilight
zone between Chuck Berry and Cuisinart; there is no greater noise."*

*Just as important as the MC5's music was its politics, and that's
true even though those politics were disastrous. Working with John
Sinclair and the so-called White Panther Party, in reality little more
than a quasi-fan club and front for Sinclair's mania for agit-pop
proselytism, the MC5 burst upon the scene backed only by a hard-core
Detroit cult and encountered a world that was mutually befuddling.
Magazines from* Rolling Stone *to* Newsweek *found them both comi-
cal and faintly disgusting, in lifestyle and rhetoric as much as music,
and radio took their measure by ignoring their records (outside of
Michigan) as effortlessly as it would ignore those of their descendants.*

*The White Panthers' political program was not much, half a projec-
tion of a personality cult based upon not just the Five but also Sinclair
—the self-styled "cigar-chomping psychedelic gangster" today most
famous for the song John Lennon wrote about his Kafkaesque ten-year*

sentence for pot possession—and half an aping of the Black Panthers' community do-goodism and macho muscle. There was also the infamous three-point plan for youth culture rebellion: "Rock and roll, dope and fucking in the streets." No one has ever offered more blatant ammo to old left snickerers and right-wing hysterics.

And yet so powerfully did the MC5's music unite its listeners that leaving those 1968 and 1969 shows, one literally felt that anything, even that implausible set of White Panther slogans, could come to pass. In that sense, the MC5, with their bacchanalian orgy of high energy sound, was a truer reflection of the positive spirit of the counterculture than the laid-back Apollonians of Haight-Ashbury ever could have been. And from the glimmerings of that confused babble, from the evidence of its hints of success, one could begin to construct an aesthetic and perhaps even a program that proposed how rock culture fit into society as something more significant than a diversion. You could say that the very idea is crazy, but not if you were a part of those shows—which weren't concerts or dances but something more spectacular and fulfilling.

Just as everything must contain the seeds of its opposite, so too with the MC5. The White Panthers degenerated into a mere pothead personality cult based upon Sinclair's beatniky egomania. The Five attempted to rationalize its sound, and crashed as hard as anyone ever has. All the members are living, true, but Wayne Kramer spent time at the federal narcotics prison at Lexington, Kentucky, and Fred Smith, the most talented of all, hasn't made a record or appeared onstage in several years. (Fred is now married to the poet-singer Patti Smith, and we are waiting . . . anticipating.)

This article was written at the moment of the Five's last album release. It also happened to be written at the moment when the whole story was about to fall apart. A combination of civil liberties lawsuits and radical chic lifted Sinclair's sentence a few months later, and soon after that, the Five fell apart. Many of the roots of these occurrences are dredged up within this article, which barely does justice to the splendor and power of their sound.

As for me, I do my best to keep current with rock and roll, haven't touched dope in ten years, have the weight of not only my own sex life but, I suppose, those of my teenage daughters on my mind. As best I can, I stay in touch with the musicians of my youth, but—irony of ironies—the only MC5 associate I see much is Jon Landau, who lives around the corner and is one of my best friends.

The rewriting here is meant to clarify and amplify, not to distort.
Parts are embarrassing to me even yet, and yet I think it is an adequate
summary of how this strange career felt as it reached its climax.

I

Their mamas all warned 'em not to come into town
But they got it in their blood, now they gotta get down
—"Shakin' Street"

Few rock and roll bands have been saddled with such import, right from
the beginning, as the MC5. The pressure was inevitable and fitting, because the Five approached the rock scene with guns drawn, armed to the
teeth. They were gonna take over, be the Baddest Boys in the bad boy
world of rock and roll, fuse politics with rock, dope (their religion) and
fucking in the streets and market all of it as a single neat package, precisely
labeled: The Revolution.

They possessed roots all the way back to the futile, doomed Children's
Crusaders of the thirteenth century; they were filled with righteous American zeal, religious fervor, a sense of purpose and of necessity. This was the
MC5, brothers and sisters, the hottest, highest energy crew of dudes to
come pouring out of the bad-assed Motor City into the American cultural
continuum since the days of the notorious Purple Gang. And what's more:
the MC5 meant business.

Or so it seemed.

And despite all the complications, the reception given their albums has
been good, in many places as phenomenal as they knew all along it would
be—as they were once confident that it *had* to be.

Their live performances were another question, though, especially in
those early days. The Five's sets tended more toward flash'n'frenzy than
anyone aside from the Who's, and the problem was that there were
numerous people in the dark days of the late sixties who just weren't ready
for shock rock.

So the Five always left one flank unguarded, where detractors could
sneak up and ask: "Well, yeah, I can see that that's something, that's
something there all right. But is it *music?*" An almost imperceptible sneer
accompanied a chortle of glee at your choked stare.

Because of course it was music (even though it might not have mattered
if it wasn't). More than that, it was rock and roll music, and rock and roll
music at its finest. Maybe it's that I cut my teeth on the MC5, or that

I am possessed by the peculiar Motor City aesthetic bias, but I'd go and see that brand of the MC5 even if the Rolling Stones were across the street. Nothing I've ever experienced has been nearly comparable, and it may be a long time coming before we have the collective spirit to do it again. So I cherish those memories; be forewarned or read no further. And that's as much caveat as you get.

The dream, for the MC5, was that of tough-assed downriver kids who came from factoryville to metropolis, became neobeatniks, prehippies and —in the end—the most avant-garde rock and roll group the world has ever known. That's the dream. For a while it looked as though the MC5 had made it real.

Their first album, *Kick Out the Jams*, *was* musically avant-garde, for it attempted to tap into both the unrealized energies that rock and roll had been suggesting were there all along and the Chicago/New York black music of Coltrane, the AACM bunch and Sun Ra (whose "Starship" closed the set). Those who were prepared for a total assault on the sensory culture to which they'd been accustomed were delighted with this dancing, tribal epiphany, while those who weren't ready were aghast, horrified as they never had been before by a mere rock group. The ready were immediately and completely swept up, the unready cast out equally quickly. Halfway didn't exist for the MC5. A Real Problem.

Since the Five were the one band that attempted to let its music carry an explicitly and implicitly political, even revolutionary, message (as they interpreted it), they were laid wide open for other, more cutting attacks. Not the least of them came from the Aquarian Brigade: you know, "Fuck, ma-un, hell wid polertiks, le's jest go out and have a GUD TAHM!" Yet in the end, equally damaging barbs were cast by hard-core politicos who couldn't understand a political musical group that didn't even know any Pete Seeger songs (which is what "Street Fighting Man" is, even if it does have "Jumpin' Jack Flash" as music).

Such criticisms were most heavily levied during the period when the band was allied with the White Panthers through their manager, John Sinclair, though some of the allegations have come from their leaving the Panthers, and even from that party itself.

But to anyone familiar with the first album, the Five's political premise would seem to be musical rather than rhetorical in the first place. They weren't talking revolution, they were making it (as far as they were concerned), and the only "political" song they cared to put on *Kick Out the Jams* was John Lee Hooker's "Motor City Is Burning." And if that makes a Marxist revolutionary, then both Hooker and Gordon Lightfoot can be hung on your bedroom wall next to Mao Tse-tung and Huey Newton.

Rather, the Five's politics were an outgrowth of their very unsophistica-
tion, their teenage frenzy and their musical approach, which encompassed
both. They carried these values and qualities into each successive battle
like a tattered flag, doing macho duels with the forces of Good Vibes and
Capital M Music as well as partisans of the Correct Line. That's what
turned people off, and that's what caused the Five to be accused of being
a crew of violently irresponsible scions of senseless bloodshed.

Anyway, those accusations were and are ridiculous. The biggest fear that
any of the Five's politically aware admirers in Detroit had was that they
weren't political *enough*, placing star status before politics. It was a confusing moment—and it's still confusing. Then again, where the MC5 are
concerned maybe it always will be.

II

The people on Shakin' Street, they find it so shockin'
But all of the kids just keep on rockin'

The intent of the MC5 was, of course, primarily musical. "Rock and
roll *is* the revolution" was about the heaviest political statement they ever
made, and that's not so heavy. The attempt to make *Kick Out the Jams*
seem like some sort of Maoist tract or an excursion into jazz rock is simply
ludicrous. That album has far more to do with the Who than with Sun
Ra, and it always did.

The captivating influence that the Five possessed was basically that of
naive white boys playing (discovering?) techno-rock, pushing electronics to
its ear-splitting limits. The idea was to see how close to the pain threshold
one could come and still survive. If that seems a familiar idea, it should.
"I Can't Explain," the Who's first single, was a hit in Detroit, and rock
theater was their idea in the first place.

The Who, along with the nasty Them and the powerful Rolling Stones,
provided the prototypes for the Five. Wayne Kramer and Fred Smith's
cosmo-wiggle stage act was directly derived from Peter Townshend's stage
moves, while Daltrey must have been the major influence in Rob Tyner's
mike-dangling stage-humping act. It was almost a surreal Who parody,
right down to Dennis Thompson, who kicked his set with the abandon and
energy of Moon, and the Entwistle-like Mike Davis, content to stand in
the shadows of his bass amp, amidst the carnage created by the others.
(One key moment for every Detroit rock group was the Who's appearance
at the Fifth Dimension club in Ann Arbor, the weekend prior to Monterey

Pop. In a club that held maybe six hundred, the Who were devastatingly loud, but more than anything, it was Roger Daltrey, scampering across tables and looking tough enough to take on the entire Rouge plant and win, who left a lasting impression.)

But the Five took things much, much further than the Who. "I Can't Explain" was a warning clear as Hiroshima that a new day was dawning in rock, and "Kick Out the Jams" was the rock equivalent of the Viet Cong. They even called it "guerrilla rock" in those days. It was subversive in a certain sense of the term, and surely, avant-garde and liberating too. And though the time is past for taking rock as revolution seriously, the time isn't past for seeking connections between the music and political and social questions.

There was another aspect of what the MC5 represented, however, for they did not represent Revolution merely as a matter of guns and butter. They planned, as the sixties children that they were, to revolutionize the spirit of their listeners as well. That is, their revolution was meant to have a dimension wherein they entered an ozone where the spitfire images projected with a glee that recalled William Burroughs at his most malicious were only the beginning of something *really* apocalyptic. Will it do to simply say that, given LSD and Tyner's science fiction mania, they set out to be both killer and cosmic?

III
The Blanket Statement
to the Folkosphere

We the MC5 know that there is altogether too much confusion on this planet, Terra, Sol 3 . . . CANCER OF THE MIND AND BODY OF THE SPECIES!!! . . . all leading to ultimate chaos and destruction. Never before have we seen a planet so AFRAID of the necessary and indicated alterations to resolve the gross imbalance that exists on the Planet as a whole . . . at every site of our energy blast we have witnessed . . . the colonial White Man's brutal degradation of the World that gave him life and breath. The sight was and is a stink to our nostrils . . .

WE SPEAK TO YOU AT THIS INSTANT!!! WE COME TO YOU WITH THE JOYOUS MESSAGE OF YOUR OWN CAPABILITIES WHICH ARE LIMITLESS AND WAITING FOR THE TOUCH OF YOUR ACTIONS!!! WE CALL UPON ALL FREE ANIMALS (YOU KNOW WHO YOU ARE) TO TAKE UP THE BANNER OF RIGHTEOUSNESS AND THE FLAMING SWORD OF REALITY AND SLASH ALL BONDS WITH THE

DEATH-WORSHIPPING SALAMANDER CULTURE OF THE MENOPAUSAL ROTTING CADAVERS OF AMERICA!!! WE, THE MC5, DEDICATE OUR BILLIONS OF MEGA-TONS OF ENERGY AND EVERY DROP OF OUR BLOOD TO SEE THAT THIS BLASPHEMY STOPS *NOW*!!! WE ARE PISSED . . . THE TIME IS RIGHT NOW!!! WE CALL FOR . . . CONSOLIDATION, A GATHERING OF OUR ENERGIES, A POLARIZATION OF THE COSMIC ENERGY THAT BURNS THROUGH US ALL!!! WE MUST SAVE THE PLANET AND OUR PEOPLE!! WE MUST REAL-IZE (MAKE REAL) OUR HUMAN POTENTIALITIES TO THE ULTIMATE!!! . . . THIS IS OUR PROGRAM. THIS IS OUR CRY . . . IT IS OUR LIFE!!! . . . WE SALUTE YOU! WE PRAISE YOU FOR YOUR STRENGTH! WE BLESS YOU!! WE STAND ON THE PINNA-CLE OF COMM, OUR FISTS RAISED IN THE CAUSE OF OUR PEOPLE, OUR PLANET AND THE BALANCE OF THE IM-MORTAL UNIVERSE . . . WE ARE WITH YOU!!! WE ARE YOU!!

—The MC5, April 9, 1969

Such manifestos bore the same relationship to "politics" as sociological science fiction like Isaac Asimov's *Foundation* trilogy and Frank Herbert's *Dune*. And in their stage shows, the MC5 carried out the parallel, which is one reason they were so attracted to Sun Ra's "Starship," that post-atomic Garveyite anthem that closes *Kick Out the Jams*, their first album.

Unfortunately, the Five never recorded the ultimate sci-fi rocker, "Black to Comm" (which Wayne Kramer used to introduce as "The Hydrogen Bomb"). "Black to Comm" was a totally exciting, communal, highly ritualized experience, designed to shake people up, excite and incite them. With Sinclair and the rest of Detroit's hip inner circle pulling horns, percussion and whistles out of nowhere, Tyner chanted and sang lyrics even more bizarre than those of "Starship." "Comm" opened with a five-minute guitar line from Fred Smith's monstrous, tinny Mosrite that was more than a mere solo: it was the original yawp of the Beginning. Like winding up a yo-yo, the Mosrite's whining electronic surge made the nerve center of the entire room taut, ready to go. And when the yo-yo made its plunge, the band came in like a herd of unknown beasts, thundering and storming as though they were the very Armageddon.

This energy release didn't have the gradual peaking and building of the Apollonian Grateful Dead. The Five were Dionysian high energy all the way, with not a second's letup, blasting and surging with a relentless, nervous energy, then total release, all at once in a flood tide that was both shattering and melodramatic. "Let your love comm down, let it comm on down, I said, Down down down, let it comm on down in the midnight hour. I said Get Down! Get Down! Get Down!" So sang Tyner, and the band, and as it built, the whole crowd, restoring the song's energy until it exploded once more, shattering the sound into a twenty-minute drift of various degrees of randomness and intensity, until "Black to Comm" ended as it began, with a screaming, soaring burst of feedback from the righteously charged guitars and amplifiers of the equally righteous MC5.

But what did it all *mean?*

The MC5 were consciously chosen by Sinclair and his cronies to be shaman for an entire community. Sinclair was a familiar of the beats, and he shared their penchant for dabblings in Orientalia, and especially, the trend that manifested itself as beatnik developed toward the mass bohemianism of hippie, in an attempt to "retribalize" society. Allen Ginsberg's famous line "Poet is priest" was a watchword with the Trans-Love Energies crowd.

In fact, Sinclair knew more about visionary poetry and artsy ideology than he did about Marxism, as borne out by his *Kick Out the Jams* liner notes, which boil all the White Panther Party's other statements into five hundred half-baked words, at least half of them slogans.

According to Sinclair, the MC5 were "a working model of the new paleo-cybernetic culture in action." And, he proclaimed, "we are a lonely desperate people pulled apart by the killer forces of capitalism and competition and we need the music to hold us together. Separation is doom. We are free men and we demand a free music, a free high energy source that will drive us wild into the streets of America yelling and screaming and tearing down everything that would keep people slaves." Does this sound like Tom Paine on acid? Robespierre in the atomic age? Well, anything but Marx and Lenin.

There was another aspect to Sinclair's writings and the role the White Panther group hoped to play. The slogans ("Everything is everything," "Separation is doom," "All power to the people," "There is no separation") have religious overtones; they are invocations, part of a liturgy in the making. In this sense, the various manifestos by Sinclair constitute exhortations from someone who self-consciously conceived of himself as a High Priest.

And in order to understand the MC5 and John Sinclair, you have to accept their metaphysics as more than a riff—or if you can only see it as a hype, then you have to believe that they were sincere, that they were hyping themselves, too. Certainly, the hype operated at a different level for those who just heard it compared to those who lived it, but there's really little question that everyone intimately involved with the MC5 truly believed that something extraordinary and perhaps momentous was transpiring at their shows. In a certain sense, they were right—their shows inspired frenzy and fervor, a desire to go out and proselytize among one's friends and neighbors about this cataclysmic, devastating, shocking experience.

At any rate, if the band members saw the whole White Panther shtick as a game, they played with such zeal and intensity that it was undeniable that they took the game seriously. Politics? Sure it's political, they might have said, but only at the highest political level. At the time that the first album was released, Sinclair and his group agreed with them, because that group was only nominally Marxist, still in the process of becoming something other than a loose group of abused hippies. But as the Five became more hard core in their rock and roll anti-professionalism, and as the White Panthers became more and more entrenched in their fantasy of Maoist Marxism, a split was inevitable.

The other night Rob Tyner and I spoke for a few minutes and agreed that were *Kick Out the Jams* released this year, it wouldn't meet half the resistance that it encountered in 1969. People are ready now for what the original MC5 had to offer.

But in 1969 the importance of rock and roll was determined by a hip elite in London, Los Angeles, San Francisco and New York. The MC5 released its first album just about midway between the festivals at Monterey and Woodstock, but they were neither part of the international community of pop musicians that surfaced at Monterey nor keyed into the "peace, love and music" philosophy of Woodstock. It was not until later that Sinclair could write ". . . a revolutionary consciousness . . . is finally the cosmic consciousness we used to talk about before it started to sound corny—and we have to realize that *it only started to sound corny because there were so many cynical creeps around us who were laughing at our naiveté and ripping us off for what we had created out of it at the same time.*"

Unfortunately, that was Sinclair's vision, not the band's. The MC5 might have seen themselves as playing a mystical or revolutionary role, but only as an adjunct to their principal position as rock and roll stars. They might have hoped to be rock stars at a higher, more conscious level than any before them had achieved, but nevertheless, it was rock stars they wanted to be. Sinclair's problem was that he became so close that he was virtually a part of the band, which led him to see them mainly as a device for furthering *his* ideas. Thus, his letter from his Jackson State Prison cell to Wayne Kramer: "You wanted to be bigger than the Beatles, while I only wanted you to be as big as Chairman Mao." (Neither ambition is marred by modesty, of course. Nor, given their limitations of musicianship and statesmanship, especially realistic.)

But then rock and roll can't define ideology, even if it can point out where that ideology might be leading us. (The Weatherpeople's use of Bob Dylan's *New Morning* is an example.) But to deliberately parade rock and roll stars as theoreticians of rebellions is pretty ridiculous, especially since rock stars is what most of them wish to remain. Do you really envision Paul Kantner and David Crosby as leaders of the future? Would you want them to be?

In a situation where a rock and roll group is tied to a political party—even a party as often chimerical as the White Panthers were—the band becomes the leader of some sort of cult, and that's precisely what the Five and the White Panthers tried to do. But this had to be a cult more dedicated and committed, more willing to follow wherever the group led, than the cults that Dylan, the Beatles and the Stones had unintentionally fostered.

One would either be fully committed to this cult or else be excommunicated from it altogether—from the cult's point of view, perhaps either a member of the cult or committed to its extermination. The MC5 had to be defined as the very best rock and roll band in the whole world or else as no good at all. Again, the problem of lacking a middle, a halfway point where the interested but unaffiliated could stand. When the MC5's message was manhandled and misunderstood by the press, they were finished politically, and that meant that their music wasn't heard as much as it should have been. That doomed the cult. Crunch.

The Five and the Panthers grew further and further apart as a result, which led each of them to many more public and private mistakes, as their definitions of what was happening, why and what priorities should be established diverged further and further. There was a complete lack of preparation when the Five moved into the national arena. The group's rhetoric seemed like just another rock star hype. In the few places where proper preparations had taken place, the result was success: the audiences loved the band and few political objections were raised. But where such planning didn't take place, the result was a disaster of public relations.

At home, everything was different, because the group had had five years to acclimate its audience, and swept a large part of its audience along with them, at least as far as political rhetoric was concerned. Yet the Panthers, under pressure from other breeds of radical cats, were becoming less and less oriented to pop music as a radicalizing device. Yet the MC5 had a certain amount of radical credibility, as the only group to play Lincoln Park during the 1968 Democratic Convention in Chicago. As a result, they were written up by Norman Mailer in *Miami and the Siege of Chicago* and beloved by certain Yippie elements, despite (or because of) the Yippies' low regard for rock bands as anything but cannon fodder. But playing Lincoln Park for hippie tourists gave the MC5 (and the White Panthers) no base in the Chicago community.

IV

Baby baby help, you really really must
I need a healthy outlet for my Teenage Lust
—"Teenage Lust," MC5

Since their politics had alienated them from the rock business, there was nobody left for the MC5 to relate to but their audience. And I don't think that the MC5 ever let an audience down, when they got a chance to play. Of course, after Bill Graham got beat up at their Fillmore East show, and there were a few minor busts associated with the group (half from Michigan police harassment, half from the group's own stupidity), jobs were few and far between. Especially jobs playing for young people.

And the young audience was what mattered to the Five in the first place, because that is *the* audience for hard rock and roll. Without a base outside Detroit, and with their stature at home threatened by their absences and an influx of good new bands, the Five's resources were stretched thin. Even Sinclair had to confess that "we tried to do too much at once."

The problem of time was complicated by Sinclair's repeated courtroom appearances. By midsummer 1969 he had been convicted in Oakland County and given thirty days. (He was out on appeal bond in half an hour, which was about twice as much time as it took the cops to cut off three years' growth of hair.) In the same trial, MC5 guitarist Fred Smith was acquitted; this did nothing to better the relationship between the band and the White Panthers.

Next, Sinclair was arrested for crossing the U.S./Canadian border without registering as a "narcotics violator"—which his parole officer had explicitly exempted him from doing. Finally, in July, Sinclair went on trial with his marijuana bust and was given his famous conviction of nine and a half to ten years for possession of two joints. Half of the time, in all fairness, was due to the fact that he managed "that rock and roll band."

(Though a good share of the other half must be attributed to Sinclair's own stupidity, since everyone in his neighborhood, including his own brother, knew that the undercover agent to whom he had given the two joints was a cop.)

In the meantime, the Five had moved to the country, living together in a new house which was separate from the bulk of Sinclair's Trans-Love/White Panther organization, where they had resided for the previous year. Sinclair was still managing the band, but from prison. Additionally, a new force had emerged. He was exactly what the musicianly, star-bound part of the MC5 most desired: Jon Landau, their new producer, Mr. Rationality. It was like Descartes visiting the Sphinx. The result of their coupling was as strange as any in rock history, as the cool *Rolling Stone* critic began to reshape one of the most anarchic forces in contemporary culture.

The plan was for the Five to be cleaned up, to make them "Better Musicians," now that they had left Elektra records, home of much psychedelic weirdness, for Atlantic, a birthplace of rhythm and blues. With Sinclair's influence dwindling and soon to disappear altogether, Landau quickly became the major outside influence on the Five. The album that the combination produced, *Back in the USA*, has his hand stamped on it as clearly as *Kick Out the Jams* was influenced by Sinclair.

The situation was not without parallel. The Five was only one of a number of bands that had grown up in the latter half of the sixties that related intensely to a specific hippie community: the Grateful Dead in San Francisco is only the most obvious example. As each of these groups moved out in the larger world and have come to terms (or failed to do so) with the record business, they've lost their grip on their community roots. The Dead, for instance, now have a larger audience in New York than they do in San Francisco. Others couldn't take the whiplash of perspective and, like Boston's Remains, broke up.

Of course it was no different with the MC5.

When it was first released, *Back in the USA* bewildered most Five fans. Some reacted bitterly, some with hostility to the spruced-up, more controlled sound. Others were just confused, as the band altered its identity, played the revolutionary material for laughs rather than seriously. Yet eighteen months later, the record hardly seems *that* bad: less flawed and less important than it struck one initially.

The Five had decided that they would reject what they were initially about—whether they did this consciously or not doesn't matter. Talking to *Creem*'s Deday LaRene in the fall of 1969, they said, "You see, there are a lot of bands calling themselves rock and roll bands, when actually what they're playing is mind music, not rock and roll at all . . . Our last album, unfortunately, there wasn't a lot of rock and roll on it. It was quote psychedelic unquote . . . We're now getting deep into a rock and roll theme . . . It's closer to it than we've ever been and we really like it because rock and roll feels good when you play it. You feel good and the people listening feel good, because they can dance to it. I doubt very strongly if you could dance to the first album. How could you dance to 'Starship'?"

Well, I'd seen hundreds of people do that, so it was no mystery to me at all. You just shook your thing in one direction or another. And if what the MC5 was doing was "psychedelic," it wasn't anything like the laid-back psychedelia of the San Francisco bands. But the Five were convinced —half by Landau, half by themselves—that what they'd been doing was improper or at least doomed to be ineffective. The band now began defining rock in a much more limited sense, and you could pick a lot of their phraseology out of Landau's writings, just as you could pick a lot of their previous terminology out of Sinclair's. And just as Sinclair's fascination with free jazz affected *Kick Out the Jams*, Landau's love for the hard rhythm and blues of Little Richard affected *Back in the USA*.

Tyner: "Landau came into the situation and defined a lot of the things that we ought to be aware of . . ."

"The thing is," Kramer added, "before Landau came out here, we were an amateur band." It was as though they were suffering from collective amnesia, as if they needed to deny that they'd ever made *Kick Out the Jams*. They were denying that album and that music with a vengeance.

"That first album . . . wasn't an album," Kramer said. "It was just what we played on our gig that night. If they would've recorded us on another night, they would have gotten an incredibly better response . . . We were intimidated by the equipment." All of that might be true, but it begs the question. *Kick Out the Jams* stands on its own merits as one of the great high-energy rock and roll records. The MC5 should have been the first to see that that was true.

The rejection of their roots went much deeper. It also encompassed a denial of the ethos from which that sound grew. Mike Davis: "Our tunes were structured super-free. Like in each tune, everybody'd just play what they wanted to play and there'd just be a very general idea of what the song was gonna be, and the musician would just take that idea and go. So consequently our tunes turned out to be great conglomerations of no solid things."

Removed from their community/audience, placed in a context where they were just a bunch of kids with some good ideas and a rather unique gimmick (rock'n'revolution was about as far as the Dee Anthony management/Premier Talent bookers could see it), the Five had to come to the Biz on *its* terms. They couldn't see any way to get the Biz to come to them, and the sad part of that is that they were probably correct. Even sadder is that they needed to settle for that kind of stardom at all. Not that that makes the MC5 sellouts, because they did what they honestly felt that the situation demanded. If anything, they made an honest mistake.

Landau put it this way: "I think that rock and roll in a lot of ways is bigger than that [politics]." Landau apparently didn't understand or agree that the MC5's politics were broader than rock and roll, because they encompassed the music and on a good night transcended both. *Kick Out the Jams* remains a good and important album because it attempts to do so much that matters, stretching the limits of the music both in terms of the way it sounds and is played and in terms of what the song's "message" might be able to contain. If the experiment wasn't a total success, it laid some very necessary groundwork and taught some equally important lessons for groups which were to follow.

Landau was really making two claims. The first was a musical judgment, and in terms of commerciality, the rationalization of sounds that eventually sells records, there's little point in arguing about it. As for whether the MC5's original sound stood on its own for pure excitement, only those who saw them can know the answer. I did, and for me, they were as exciting and as involving as any music ever made. I'm not alone in thinking so.

The other question concerns how much politics rock and roll can carry, and I haven't the answer to that one. But explicitly political content may tend to overburden a medium which is at its roots fairly (some would say extremely) simple and even simplistic. Rock and roll is never going to carry the burden of defining anyone's ideology, as I've already said, but it is always going to point out some things and heighten awareness of others, and—perhaps most importantly—there will be things contained in any great rock record that cause its listeners to think and act in a certain manner. To the extent that rock can do that, it's a viable and essential tool with which to wage cultural battles. If we're still into that.

But maybe that's the trick: The MC5's first single was "I Can Only Give You Everything" backed with "I Just Don't Know." The juxtaposition remains relevant.

Strangely, given Landau's position, *Back in the USA* is the MC5's most lyrically political work. Partly that's inevitable, given the songs that weren't included on *Kick Out the Jams*, which leaned heavily on the sci-fi side of the Five. Nevertheless, the entire second side of their second album, beginning with "High School" and ending with the rousing Chuck Berry–penned title track, is loaded with political lines. Of course the majority of these songs were written long before the group had ever encountered Landau, and, with one exception, the ones that were written after they joined forces ("High School," and "Tonight" on side one) are so self-conscious that they're embarrassing. But tunes like "American Ruse," "Human Being Lawnmower" and "Call Me Animal" use political rhetoric as broadly as Dylan's "Masters of War," and no less shamelessly. It's that lack of self-consciousness that makes them successful.

The second side of *Back in the USA* contains one lyrical masterpiece, Fred Smith's "Shakin' Street." It may be the finest tune that the Five has ever recorded, and its Dylanesque lyrics, stinging guitar line and laconic vocal are all definitively Fred Smith's.

The lyric is precisely the sort of fantasy that rock carries off most easily. "Shakin' Street" has the form and content of a song by Berry or Dylan, or Townshend, Jagger-Richards and Lennon among the British subjects. It tells a story: a guy travels from the Coast to a teenage paradise where "all the kids go," in order to cut loose from petty restrictions. The kids are tough (they'll "never give in") and knowing ("alla their lives they been livin' in sin"), and they dance and groove like mad—that's how it got its name.

"Shakin' Street," like any great rock song, defines the rock audience, as a group and as individuals; it delineates the weaknesses and strengths of its listeners. The music that carries these messages is absolutely beautiful, absolutely danceable, qualities that rise directly from Smith's voice and guitar, without any deliberate reference to the words. "Shakin' Street" hardly belongs on the same record with the rhetoric and shrillness of the Five's other songs. Smith gets more carnal enthusiasm into the *"Ha!"* just before the first chorus than the band captures in the rest of the LP.

Back in the USA isn't a successful album. The Five can't make the tightly structured music work; as pros, they're pointless. Even the band is dissatisfied with its work here. Told that *Back in the USA* was Lester Bangs' favorite of the group's records, Rob Tyner responded: "I even find that a little hard to understand." (Of course Bangs never saw the band that made *Kick Out the Jams*, an album he mercilessly mocked in a *Rolling Stone* review.) But for that one song, *Back in the USA* is everything the MC5 ever promised to do in the recording studio: it's a great rock and roll record. And with their third album, *High Time*, the MC5 indicate that they are headed in the very same direction.

V

High Time is back on Shakin' Street for most of its length, and that's right where the MC5 belong. Still, *High Time* resolves none of the problems that the MC5 and its audience face. It doesn't come to grips with the issues raised by the first two albums.

Maybe that's okay. If the MC5 have taught their fans anything, it's that rock and roll can no longer be leaned upon, that the job gets done by us or no one, and finally, that rockin' out is sometimes but only sometimes the best solution.

When the MC5 attempt a return to the sort of metaphysical, science fiction rock that could suggest some approaches to the broader issues raised by their work (in the same way that a novel by William Burroughs might), they fail miserably—this is the bane of the second side of *High Time*. Ironically, there are just two songs on that side that are successful: One is "Skunk," a scorching piece of jazz-rock funk that sputters occasionally but mostly manages to place the MC5 once more in the white rock avant-garde. The other is "Over and Over," a pointed slap at radicalism in the same spirit as the Who's "Won't Get Fooled Again." Ironically, "Over and Over" moves with much the same high energy as *Kick Out the Jams*, though Fred Smith propels the song with taut guitar lines that are more reminiscent of *Back in the USA*. (Tyner's pseudo-cosmic recitation comes close to undoing this balance.)

Side one flows much more effectively. It's the distillation of the MC5's approach to what Iggy Pop calls "the dull throbbing undertow," and represents their claim to be the best of what Alice Cooper calls "third-generation rock." The Five deserve to be the best third-generation band, because in so many ways they were the first. While Cream stretched some of the Yardbirds' horizons, the MC5 took the Yardbirds, Them, the Who, the Stones and wrapped it all up into a unique new package that did the job: bringing it all back home indeed. And in this way they used British rock to tangle with America as it had rarely been tangled with before. If they failed, the attempt is just about infinitely admirable, anyhow.

Listen to "Sister Anne," a remarkable reworking of Them's "Mystic Eyes," to Fred Smith's "Baby Won't Ya," which continues his exploration of terrain first mapped by Dylan and Berry, and to Wayne Kramer's wonderful Beatles' pastiche, "Miss X," which represents a whole new dimension for the Five.

In more ways than one, this is a Fred Smith album, fulfilling the promise of "Shakin' Street," although it lacks a vocal quite as distinctive as the one on that song.

Smith's two songs on side one, "Baby Won't Ya" and "Sister Anne," the story of a nymphomaniac nun, establish Smith as a brilliantly comic lyric writer, moving constantly between the poles of rock and roll: getting down, getting laid, getting high and getting on with it.

Finally, though, *High Time* is entirely rooted in solid rock and roll music, the crashing guitars of Smith and Kramer melding as they always should have, Dennis Thompson's drumming once more frenetic after the disciplined listlessness of *Back in the USA*. Tyner's vocals are also looser and mixed better. For pure music, *High Time* needs to bow to neither of the other albums.

In the end, the resolution of all the problems that the story of the MC5 symbolizes probably don't lie in rock and roll anyhow. They're a band with an inescapable history, but for right now, it's enough that they're one of the finest rock and roll bands alive. To return to the beginning: that's as it always should have been.

Creem, 1971

Some Time in
New York City

The connection between this review and "Back on Shakin' Street" is clear: Some Time in New York City *is even the album that contains John and Yoko's "Free John" song. The piece also connects naturally to the next group of pieces, insofar as it suggests not only an opposi-tional stance to the American status quo but much more skepticism about the radical left, especially "cultural" radicals, than my writing had earlier expressed.*

It's a long jump in time from this review to the comments inspired by Elvis Costello's Armed Forces *seven years later. Of course I wasn't idle in the interim. Nor was my writing unpolitical. But neither* Newsday *nor* Rolling Stone *was particularly conducive to working out the kind of politics I've always felt (even when I haven't been articulating them). For the most part, my politics in those years expressed themselves through commentary on the music business, as seen in section six.*

*The dilemma, of course, was anything but unusual for countercul-
ture radicals of the sixties caught up in the moral inflation of the
midseventies. And moral inflation defines precisely what happened as
the alternatives we'd attempted to create were demolished or self-
destructed or proved themselves illusory. Everyone had the right,
hipster answers then; the lines were no longer drawn, or at least not
drawn so clearly and it was possible to deny much of what had been
achieved, or to be talked into accepting the half-measures. The war
was over.*

*Not for long, of course. Today, as we're dragged nearer and nearer
the same kinds of quagmire (created this time in Central America),
as racism and sexism grow more and more vicious, as civil liberties are
further eroded, it's quite clear that that midseventies respite was expensive indeed. And so, as the last of the articles in this chapter makes
clear, new measures (quite resembling the old, though hopefully that's
because similar principles are applied with more maturity and intelligence) must be taken. This time there's no point in turning back, since
I for one simply can't bear the thought of watching yet another idiotic
war on the evening news.*

If you thought, as I did, that *Some Time in New York City* was going to
be a complete disaster, cheer up. It's not half bad. It may be 49.9 percent
bad, but not half.

Strangely enough, for once this political vaudeville acts sounds good.
Credit for this improvement in sound is probably due as much or more
to Elephant's Memory, producer Phil Spector and Lennon's intuition
than to design but nonetheless: *Some Time in New York City* sounds
good.

At any rate, the album isn't terrible. It's more than listenable. Some
parts of it—including one of Yoko's songs, a cosmic rocker called "We're
All Water," which just might be the very best thing here—are as good as
anything the Plastic Onos have ever done. Musically, it's perhaps an 80
percent success.

Problem is, the album isn't conceived in terms of music. It stands and
falls on its lyrical themes and the ways in which they're carried out. And
I'm afraid that it doesn't always treat them very well.

It isn't just a question of good politics vs. bad. The problem runs deeper.
Good songwriting is juxtaposed with bad, posturing with commitment,
real life with someone's inadequate fantasies.

That last is what it's really about. This may come as a surprise to John and Yoko, but "real" songwriters—from Dylan on—have rarely written about real events. They've sometimes written about events that you've heard of previously, but in general, "Penny Lane" still means more than "Hollis Brown."

The songs on *Some Time in New York City* aren't content to be "just songs." They try to be something more than that, and as a result they often deliver less than what a good song offers. They're forced and frequently pretentious; good songs are neither. They're literal, and the best songs— the genre classics, a few of which John Lennon has written—are mythic.

Lennon seems to have made a decision with the *Plastic Ono Band* LP. Richard Williams describes it perfectly in his book on Phil Spector, *Out of His Head:*

> The answer was total honesty. No longer could his music be "art"; his words must carry nothing but the most naked truth, the starkest expression of honesty. No more images, conscious or instinctive, could be allowed to get in the way of the message.

There's John and Yoko's real dilemma. They are idealists, in a world that certainly has little room for that brand of conviction. But they are also didactic and painstakingly boring, because they refuse to give us images. And frankly, as nice as either might be, when John and Yoko stopped offering reflections of other things, they started giving us images of themselves only. And they won't stand up. By their third album in this style, we're ready for a change.

Beyond that, there's a problem with trying to inform people about public events. If the events matter in and of themselves, the point is moot. Everyone already knows, and so the reportage is superfluous and even a little bit pompous. No matter what Yoko's theories are, each newspaper song drives home the awful truth once more: You can't communicate news to The World with ballads. They're just too slow.

Songs that try to be newspapers don't belong onstage. Like David Peel, they belong in the streets. They're no longer entertainment. And if Lennon really wants to write such songs, he'd be best advised to keep them there.

He doesn't, of course. If he did, he'd probably do something like Peter Green of Fleetwood Mac once did: disappear for a while and reappear incognito on the streets of Liverpool. But Lennon remains a public person.

That's to the good, since Lennon, when he's on, is the kind of person who belongs out in front. His dilemma is to find a way of transferring his political concerns into entertainment and, while that isn't easy to do, he seems to be avoiding the task altogether at the moment.

If what happened to John Sinclair and Angela Davis ain't fair—and it ain't—saying only that is nevertheless redundant. These quasi-political songs are just the sort of "political" acts that allow Lennon's audience to feel righteous without challenging our assumptions or testing our commitment. Telling Angela Davis that she's "one of the millions of political prisoners in the world" is doubly ridiculous. We know if we can hear, and so does she.

Maybe the supposition is that we don't know. That's false too. I don't have much use for voting songs, but that they're so preponderant this year is evidence enough that American rock and roll kids are already politicized in the minimum ways.

In a way, it's extremely funny that the cover of this album satirizes the *New York Times*. This record is anti-ecological, just more ideological clutter. And sometimes it's worse than that. "Luck of the Irish" is a beautiful melody, but it's also about the Irish the way "Old Black Joe" is about blacks, fostering stereotypes that are both false and (inadvertently but nonetheless) racist, in the same way that John's Yoko-hype is inverted sexism. In any event, the IRA don't need and probably don't want a pop star to shill for them. Having the luck of the Irish hasn't made the *Irish* wish they were English instead. It's made them prouder and more committed to being Irish.

Mouthing political statements—especially ones that aren't fully thought out—isn't the same as making political action. Here Yoko seems to have convinced John—or they've convinced each other—that it is form, not content, that matters. But it's only the integration of the two which makes greatness and brilliance and all the other things that Lennon could conceivably be.

John used to write songs that worked dialectically. It was exciting to listen to the contradictions of "Revolution" almost ripping it apart, and the same thing happened in a different way with "Power to the People." But the songs on *Some Time in New York City* have already flown; the new dialectic is a challenge between the words and the music and it's always the music that is negated, that must fight its way into the spotlight.

Yet even though many of the songs are hodgepodge, it's the music that most excites me about the album. "Sunday Bloody Sunday" cuts McCartney's "Give Ireland Back to the Irish" and it doesn't even matter much that "Backoff Boogaloo" is a better statement on the subject than either. "Luck of the Irish" does at least establish that Lennon cares about the

IRA, in much the same way that he cared about "Julia": that is, it's convincing musically, not lyrically. And with "We're All Water," Ono begins to figure out how to effectively apply her ideas to Western music.

It all says that Elephant's Memory is a killer band. And if you're wondering whether John Lennon still knows how to rock consistently, it's the *Elephant's Memory* album that proves the point. Lennon produced *Elephant's Memory*, and it is much thicker, denser, heavier than the Spector production on *Some Time*, which mostly sounds like vintage John and Phil with occasional overlays of T. Rex overproduced rhythms.

The Elephants were a "political" band long before they met John and Yoko. Their last album, *Take It to the Streets*, isn't laden with the sort of newspaper statements that *Some Time* has, but it does reflect a concern with the same issues. While "Sisters O Sisters" finally sounds like Spector playing a joke on Yoko—the gag is how much like a lame Darlene Love tune it sounds—Elephant's Memory are obviously in on all their album's laughs. Tex Gabriel's guitar playing is monstrously good on both records, and so is the sax playing of Stan Bronstein, whose powerful vocals sound literal on *Elephant's Memory*'s "Gypsy Wolf."

Elephant's Memory have made a good, tough rock and roll album, which is political but not self-righteous, conscious but not self-conscious. If anything, their problem is that they are always wide open. This works splendidly live, where they immediately sweep the crowd off its feet, but less so on record, where some respite is wanted. If you listen to *Elephant's Memory* and *Some Time in New York City* back to back, of course, you get it. Otherwise, you'd better be prepared for some high-intensity rocking for a half-hour or so.

Finally, Elephant's Memory have better politics than the Lennons, starting with the fact that the lyrics *aren't* printed on the Elephant Memory's album cover. Though I haven't yet figured them all out, with "Power Boogie" and "Liberation Special," they are more to my mind what the sound of revolution might be like. But then, so is *Beatles '65*.

Creem, 1972

Rock and Rhetoric

Just so you don't get the idea that my taste in political art runs to agitprop, consider these words of wisdom.

But it's also worth noting that Robinson remains the first openly gay rock singer—all the others, even Bowie and Boy George, hedge their bets. For that matter, there remains only one well-known out-of-the-closet rock critic, even though dozens of hits in recent years have had relatively explicit gay subtexts. (Of course there are rock stars who admit to "bisexuality," such as Elton John and David Bowie, and there are those, such as Little Richard, who "were" gay, as though one changed one's sexuality as styles altered.)

Robinson's career didn't founder because he was gay, but because he was unable to resolve exactly those issues of art and politics with which this review is concerned. He's more recently made some music for smaller record companies, but it has been dance music, the genre which is more commonly associated with the gay stereotype. One of the most important qualities of his first two albums, in retrospect, is that they challenged the image of what gays listen to. The specific task remains unfinished, and I wish Tom—or someone like him—would come along to complete it.

Tom Robinson, as most rock fans must know by now, not only fronts the most interestingly and fully political band to come out of Britain's new wave in recent months, but he is also the first openly gay rock singer. So *Power in the Darkness* would be an extremely significant double album even if it weren't as good as it is.

Robinson is probably going to throw a lot of straight listeners, even those who are aware that the group that wrote that jolly British hit "2-4-6-8 Motorway" also wrote a song called "Glad to Be Gay." Because he doesn't exploit any of the gay stereotypes rock audiences expect from Mick Jagger, Rod Stewart or David Bowie types, Robinson seems to unnerve some listeners. "He doesn't look [act] gay," I've heard people say, as if there were circumscribed roles homosexuals must play. Maybe the most important function of the Tom Robinson Band, for all its musical excellence, will be to break down that image.

The problem lies, as it too often does for leftist performers, with the

Tom Robinson Band's methodology. Perhaps the most instructive comparison is with the Clash. Because the Clash plays rock at its most raucous, the political themes can almost be ignored—but these themes are reinforced by music that's as bitter and angry as the lyrics. For the Clash, their sound itself is a fundamental part of politics.

But Robinson's group plays much more conservatively: even new wave haters might think them good musicians. Essentially, this band's music is the same combination of mainstream rock and roll and English music-hall tradition that the Kinks have developed (Ray Davies was Robinson's original mentor), but it's been years since the Kinks have shown the commitment of the Tom Robinson Band's "The Winter of '79," the social insight of "Grey Cortina" or the charm of "2-4-6-8 Motorway." And neither they nor any previous new wave group has been capable of anything as funky as Robinson's "Power in the Darkness."

The problem isn't that Tom Robinson can't live up to an artificial standard of punk purity. His music derives a great deal of its force from clarity, and that means the lyrics are up front where they can't be missed. Which might not matter, if all the lyrics were as artfully personal as those of "Glad to Be Gay" or as intricate as "The Winter of '79." But Robinson is also a preacher, and that stance is overwhelming in all the wrong ways on such sloganeering items as "Right on Sister" and "Better Decide Which Side You're On." This kind of strident proselytizing would be much better off obscured by feedback.

The Tom Robinson Band is literally too good to be wasted on such leftist broadsides, and Robinson's far too sophisticated both politically and musically to make a career of writing them. (Especially since they aren't the sort of thing that will help fulfill his ambitions for mass success anyway.) If the radical rhetoric is more aggravating than usual here, it's because the Tom Robinson Band's best songs deserve greater emotion. When they get it—when the Tom Robinson Band sings about the price one pays for being gay in London or the exhilaration of motor-vating on the highway—*Power in the Darkness* is the most convincing fusion of rock and roll and politics in years.

Rolling Stone, 1978

Arms and the Man
I Sing

Armed Forces, *Elvis Costello's third album, remains for me not only his best work but the most intelligent and compassionate record to come out of the entire new wave. I don't think that I realized until this piece was prepared for* Fortunate Son *how everything else in the genre has been measured against it in my mind. If he'd continued in the direction this music suggests, rather than heading off at various tangents and depleting his pop credibility, Costello might today be as big as he should be.*

Not that he hasn't made great records since: Imperial Bedroom, *his 1982 album, is a musical masterpiece, albeit an emotionally closeted one, and the best parts of his 1983 LP,* Punch the Clock, *preserve the richness of musical texture while sounding engaged with the world once more. In fact, "Shipbuilding" and "Pills and Soap" are among the mere handful of songs that have faced Britain's Thatcherite philosophy and seen it for the militaristic authoritarianism it is.*

In between, Costello retreated from the public, especially the American public. In part, this was because he'd reached gold record status in the U.S. (500,000 LPs sold) and, as a proper member of the punk generation, instinctively shunned full-scale stardom. But Costello's retreat had another cause. He wanted an ugly incident, in which he was baited by older American musicians into making racist remarks about Ray Charles, to disappear. Which it essentially has.

That it took so long to leave the scene is partly my fault, since I was the one who took him to task in Rolling Stone *in no uncertain terms. This has been portrayed as a silly, moralistic thing to have done, somehow placing the judgment of Costello's remarks on the same plane as the motives of the sixties has-beens who goaded Costello into those remarks. And their motives were putrid: a resentment of Costello based on his youth, his Englishness, his association with the new wave movement whose time had come and wiped theirs out.*

But to understand how Costello could have been put in the position of saying that Ray Charles was a "blind, ignorant nigger" is a long

way from excusing him for having said it. And it's a long way from
explaining why it took him so long to apologize for the remarks, or
why he hedged when he did.

I say this not as someone who hates Elvis Costello but as someone
who loved him. Armed Forces *contains music I love—and trust—*
as much as any I've ever heard. But in one drunken late-night instant,
Elvis Costello betrayed what that music stands for, and though the
rest of the world may forget it, I can't. It smells too much like what
I entered rock and roll to escape.

> *"Adolf Eichmann went to his grave*
> *with great dignity."*
> —Hannah Arendt

Elvis Costello's *Armed Forces* contronts such horrors of modern life full-
face. Arendt's *Eichmann in Jerusalem* was a "Report on the Banality of
Evil"; *Armed Forces* might as well be subtitled "A Statement on the
Complicity of Existence." Adolf Eichmann was spiritually dead long before the noose was knotted, and as far as Elvis Costello is concerned, he
has been this year's model ever since. In response, Costello seems determined to live or die by another sentence of Arendt's: "For politics is not
like the nursery; in politics, obedience and support are the same."

Elvis Costello (Declan McManus) has never given society his support,
except in the most general ways. He pays taxes, he makes profits for
multinational corporations (CBS in the United States, Warner Communications in the UK). But when I say that Costello confronts evil—for that
is what *Armed Forces* is about, facing up to evil as big as the world—I
mean to imply that he has changed tactics. Great rock and roll is about
tension and release, and one of the reasons *Armed Forces* is Costello's most
exciting album is that he has finally learned to balance these qualities. His
debut album, *My Aim Is True*, was all tension—Costello was furious, but
he never exploded—while *This Year's Model* was pure release: on most of
it, Costello was venting his spleen.

On *Armed Forces*, Costello is in far greater command. You can hear this
on the surface of his music, which is easily the most melodically seductive
he (or any new wave performer) has produced. "Oliver's Army" has a
transcendent piano melody—my wife calls it a cross between Bruce
Springsteen and Abba—that undercuts its despair. The rock and roll
attack of "(What's So Funny 'bout) Peace Love and Understanding"
dispels any hints of sentimentality.

Perhaps most important is the change in Costello's attitude. Never had simple point of view meant so much to a rock star as it did on Costello's first two records, which were attractive more for what what they stood for (and against) than for their intricacies. *Armed Forces* offers a more complex and detailed emotional and musical vision: the chip isn't off his shoulder—Elvis Costello remains quaveringly *alive*—but he's now capable not only of passion, which he's owned in spades from the start, but also of compassion. He doesn't condemn the pathetic creatures in "Party Girls" (as he surely would have with last year's model), nor does he waste pity on them. He reaches out, tries to fathom their dissipation before judging anything but their sorrow. The difference bespeaks a maturity born of love and understanding. As for peace . . . not yet.

But Costello has arrived at a truce with pop form. He's always been eclectic, mingling reggae rhythm and country accents with straightforward rock. But the very surface of *Armed Forces* announces that this is an aesthetic departure of major proportions. With the adept support of producer Nick Lowe and the constantly improving Attractions, Costello reaches out and discovers that not only can he do anything, but that he can do just about everything: classical piano figures, power-chorded guitar, Beach Boys harmonies, orchestral organ passages, reggae bass lines, Keith Moon style drumming, Beatlesque guitar/bass interludes. The cover tells the real story—an Elvis pensive, brooding, smoldering in shades and black leather, is not the Elvis who looked like Buddy Holly on *My Aim Is True.* This Elvis Costello might be the shade of Phil Spector—and the list above reads like a catalogue of Spectorian effect. *Armed Forces* stops short of complete homage (at least I haven't *noticed* a glockenspiel), but the resemblance is hardly unintentional. Not with Lowe at the helm.

Lowe and Costello are a fascinating pair, mostly because of what they don't share. Lowe is the most frivolous figure associated with the British new wave. He's a cultural ideologue, fascinated by trashy surfaces and comedic outrage within seemingly schmaltzy contexts ("Marie Provost"). But Lowe is also a cynic. You can like, or even love his music, but you'd be foolish ever to entirely trust him. There's something manipulative—not to say mechanical—about his work: It lacks a political basis not so much because Lowe is a pop reactionary but because he is a product of hippie culture and just doesn't give a damn. That's what his version of "Peace Love and Understanding" (written and recorded while he was a member of Brinsley Schwarz) is about. The singer is a man who's witnessed the Balkanization of the counterculture and simply refuses to look at that situation any longer.

Costello has been an endearing figure from the beginning, even at his most icily arrogant. That's because he looks so vulnerable—part of the secret of *Armed Forces* is that he lets himself sound vulnerable, too. The difference between "Alison" as recorded on *My Aim Is True* and "Alison" on the EP included in the first 200,000 pressings of *Armed Forces* isn't just the phrasing. It's also the difference in diction between a man who's fighting himself and a man who is trying to come to terms. On the former version, Costello is trying to convince Alison that their relationship will be her salvation; on the latter, he cajoles her out of simple *need*.

Part of what this indicates is that Costello has displaced his cynicism, which often bordered on contempt for both his fans and his admirers in the press. At times, being an Elvis Costello fan has felt like a perfect substitute for masochism. On *Armed Forces*, this problem is solved, often by simply grafting the warmth of Lowe's beloved pop formulas onto Costello's harder-edged sound. But the more meaningful solution is found in Costello's acceptance of his own perpetual dissatisfaction. He isn't blaming anyone else for his unhappiness, and the result is a truly great compromise: by knowing and respecting his limits, he blasts them into oblivion.

The apex of misanthropy Costello reached with *This Year's Model* couldn't be sustained anyway. But here, in "Oliver's Army," Costello catches a man on the verge of becoming a mercenary for no better reason than ennui, and far from condemning him, he empathizes. The result is a breakthrough, not just for Elvis Costello but for rock. When Costello sings, "There's no danger / It's a professional career," he's expressing an idea that seems beyond most leftists and glib, youth-culture militarists like Warren Zevon—soldiers (even those in repressive, reactionary armies) don't just kill but also die, and most often they die because they're deluded —a delusion that begins with the idea that they're either safe or guaranteed glory. Costello understands the emotional incentives in becoming a soldier and the social forces that create those incentives: Why not join the army if you'd really "rather be anywhere else but here"? What else is there except waiting around for retirement, like the poor sap in "Senior Service"? That really is a "death that's worse than fate."

What links the worker in "Senior Service," the recruit in "Oliver's Army," the dissolute hustlers in "Party Girls," the boys in (and victims of) the "Goon Squad," and all of Costello's other characters is a sense of revoked options. But not only choice has been denied them: what's lost is their humanity. Costello's personae are leading finished, inevitable lives, which are, finally, no lives at all. And Costello's realization that there's no way out is what I mean by the complicity of existence. The observer of the "Party Girls" is in no way superior to them. Even success only perpetuates the evil he hates the most. What are Costello's considerable forces armed against? The litany of places in "Oliver's Army" isn't casual. Unlike the Clash, Costello sees the enemy everywhere, even when he's alone.

Perhaps the clearest metaphor for all this is offered in "Two Little Hitlers," which is not so much about what society does to impinge upon our humanity as about what we do to each other: "Two little Hitlers who fight it out until / One little Hitler does the other one's will." The song is a reggae nursery rhyme, which suggests how universal the exploitation ultimately is. And the solution is a cliché: the triumph of the will ("I will return / I will not burn").

It's presumably inevitable that solutions to such problems emerge as cliché. This may be the truest measure of how banal evil has made us. But what of "Peace Love and Understanding," which like Springsteen's anthems to car culture, is not simple cliché but redeemed cliché, veracious cliché? When Elvis Costello sings this song he offers us no solace, not even catharsis. He offers to purge us, momentarily to unite us in our vulnerability. This is the peculiar task rock and roll sets for itself—it halfway makes me want to endorse the medical studies that claim it weakens the muscles. And in this context—especially in a rock and roll world where everyone, punk, disco dancer, rocker, bopper, finger-snapper, one and all, chips away at everyone else like so many little Hitlers of the soul—rock and roll stands glorious, free, liberating in its very inability to accomplish much or anything at all. It won't save you, but it might give you a clue about how to stay alive (really alive), which is the true challenge.

"Peace Love and Understanding" could never be, for Elvis Costello, the act of satiric resignation it might have been for a reformed hippie like Nick Lowe. Its platitudes are converted by Costello's singing into an act of war against everything that costs us our passion, our compassion and thus our lives. In the sense that it enlists the best parts of ourselves against the worst, *Armed Forces* is the only military force in the world worth saluting.

Boston Phoenix, 1979

Shut Down, Vol. 3

*For those of us who grew up with rock and roll as a radical and
radicalizing device, it is somewhat disorienting to find it keeping such
comfortable company with Republicanism and worse these days.
However, when the reactionaries turn out to be artistic nemeses as
well, one can wind up feeling as much confirmed as confused. So it
was when James Watt attacked the Beach Boys and everyone from
Nancy Reagan to G. Gordon Liddy leaped to the group's defense—
out of friendship with singer Mike Love.*

*The heartfelt thanks I received from several Beach Boys insiders
when this piece appeared was one of the delights of my career. If ever
an artistic entity's downfall could be traced to one bad apple, the
Beach Boys are it. I am skeptical of the Brian Wilson As True Genius
theory of rock, but there's no denying that Brian's absence and Love's
ascendance symbolized exactly why the areas of sixties rock that the
Beach Boys represented bear such mean and stunted fruit today.*

The recent controversy over Secretary of the Interior James Watt's banning of the Beach Boys from a July 4 celebration in Washington, D.C.,
reminded me that I've despised Mike Love since the spring of 1964, when
the Beach Boys released *Shut Down, Vol. 2*, which included the track,
" 'Cassius' Love vs. 'Sonny' Wilson," a milestone in the annals of LP filler.
This was a mock battle (verbal) between Love, the Beach Boys' terminally
nasal vocalist, and Brian Wilson, its great falsetto voice. Like any rational
fourteen-year-old, I concluded that anyone who cackled at such a lame set
of jokes was a complete jerk. (At least Brian sounded uncomfortable—
Brian *always* sounded uncomfortable.) Since then, Love has consistently
lived up to what I expect of a jerk, from endorsing the spiritual humbuggery of Sexy Sadie, the Indian nirvana merchant, to inviting Gordon Liddy
to dinner to reshaping the Beach Boys in his own image, which has made
them the artistic equivalent of a shabby used-car dealership.

At his recent spate of press conferences, Love has appeared with a new
look. He's shaved off his pseudo-patriarchal beard, which for several years
made him look like a retarded kahuna, and slimmed down. Wearing a golf
sweater and a baseball cap, Love now resembles Peter Allen after electro-
shock.

Love was always the kind of Eddie Haskell prototype who pushed around people like Randy Newman and Brian Wilson (not me!) in the high school lunchroom. So it makes sense that he's grown up to be the kind of hypocrite who plays charity benefits in aid of the mentally handicapped and then endorses the Reagan administration, which has so drastically cut funding for such souls that hundreds of the mentally disabled now live, homeless and destitute, on the streets of our cities. Maybe it's part of the Maharishi's plan to turn New York into Calcutta or some equally noble aim.

It was pathetic to see the photos of Love, an avowed supporter of the Reagan administration, which is pushing for the creation of MX and other *first-strike* nuclear missiles, with his arm around Carl Wilson, a great guitarist who was also a conscientious objector in the sixties. In the photos, Carl, the only Wilson brother present, looked like he had drawn the short straw as the family's representative. I hope that's the case.

Mike Love says that the Beach Boys' politics are "happiness, harmony, joy and celebration of love. Being young, growing up and falling in love. We just want to go on singing about good vibrations and having fun, fun, fun." Fine. I propose that as soon as Cap Weinberger makes us all glow in the dark, this should be the twenty-four-hour-a-day policy of the entire United States, which will then resemble Las Vegas, where Love's chief competitor as a Reagan administration entertainment lackey, Wayne Newton, is a casino owner.

Meanwhile, the most outrageous behavior in Washington was not James Watt's. Watt's stature as a smirking cultural demagogue has been apparent since he became secretary of the interior. What's interesting is the part of Watt's attack which has *not* been repudiated: the bit about hard-rock fans being the "wrong element," stoned on drugs and booze. (Wayne Newton fans, of course, are models of decorum. As *Washington Post* columnist Richard Cohen observed: "It is Wayne Newton, after all, who performs in saloons before drunks . . . dressed loudly, holding highballs, squeezing women they have rented for the occasion.") Not one of the Reagan administration's mealy-mouthed apologies to the band made amends for Watt's lies about rock fans, and neither did any of the opportunistic speeches made in Congress.

It's easy to see why. Rock fans are only citizens, for whom both major American political parties aren't shy about expressing utter contempt. But the Beach Boys are entertainers—that is, over the next eighteen months, they will belong to that holiest of all Washington interest groups: Fund Raisers. In 1980 the Beach Boys contributed their time (and your cash) to the noted transcendentalist George Bush. In 1984, perhaps they'll work for the spiritually enlightened Senator Robert Dole, who defended them in Congress. Or will the Beach Boys become Fourth of July regulars on the Capitol Mall as a trade-off for the support of the Reagan Administration, the most inhumane, anti-democratic government America has ever known?

In the end, there's not much difference between Mike Love, who finds endorsing the policies of a warmonger consistent with his meditative ideals, and James Watt, who talks about his love for the environment while defiling it. Both Love and Watt preach about American virtues while behaving as utter hypocrites, licking the boots of the powerful. (Where was the Beach Boys' defense of their fans?) I wouldn't buy a used car from either of them.

Record, 1983

8

The Punk Perplex

Introduction

WI prayed for it and yet it's too late for me to truly participate. I feel like an engineer," wrote Pete Townshend in the midst of Britain's 1976 punk uprising. He was not alone in his sentiments, for if Townshend and the Who were the musical grandfathers of punk rock, then *Creem* and the whole Motor City milieu of agitprop blitzkrieg bop were its spiritual godfathers. Yet punk and its various descendants left me feeling uneasy; I was not able to welcome the movement wholeheartedly, as almost all of my colleagues did.

Punk's rebellion was necessary as an antidote to what rock had become: a stuffy institution led by a Pecksniffian aristocracy of merchant-craftsmen in London and Los Angeles. Punk reasserted a version of the garage-rock aesthetic, which boils down to "Anybody can do this shit." This supposedly cut the legs from under the merchant-craftsmen, but that was true only because punk avoided the central contradiction of that philosophy: not everyone can do it equally well. And because it could not avoid this contradiction between egalitarian rhetoric and demotic reality, punk splintered.

Oddly, the remaining fragments reflected splits in many ways similar to those that affected sixties rock after its consensus had been ripped apart (though far less famously, since few of the original punk groups had lasted long enough to sell records or even get played on the conservative radio stations that reached the bulk of the pop audience). One prominent splinter featured elitist groups whose allegiance to what was left of the punk aesthetic was a fascination or obsession with certain primitivist styles. (There is only one really productive example of this style: the Talking Heads, who are in essence a dance band.) Another grew strictly cynical and asserted that as pop was all a matter of fashion, only the latest trend was of any consequence. This paid some bizarre homage to punk's deliberate disruption of history, but most of the pop it actually produced—with a few exceptions such as Culture Club—was made by cute and well-dressed British boys straining to sound soulful, and failing miserably. Finally, there was the splinter that refused to recognize the disintegration of punk and attempted to carry on as before: this became hard-core and its multitudinous subvariants of the mideighties. And while there were some excellent groups playing in this style also (notably the Minutemen and Husker Du), within a couple of years even they had to move on from two chords and a cloud of dust. Presumably starting the whole process of rebellion over again for an incrementally smaller segment of the listenership.

Those were punk's internal dilemmas. My problem, as an insider in the rock world who chose to stay outside the punk enclave, was that punk was so deeply insulated from the society it presumed to alter. Like other sectarian cults, punk partly foundered on the idea that the population wanted something in which most folks had no interest: challenging and abrasive popular music. As a result, punk fared much less well in the marketplace—both of records and ideas—than, for instance, the original soft-rock singer/songwriters, who had made the more workable, if not more sensible, case that people wanted challenging and soothing popular music (a set of contradictions that had sowed the seed of *its* own undoing).

Faced with this situation, I chose to keep my distance. In a way, that meant I missed the most exhilarating opportunity rock critics ever had, for punks were mostly acting out scenarios for which we'd been calling ever since the early issues of *Creem*: returning rock to its roots in rebellion and rudeness, without dispensing entirely with intellectual self-consciousness. On the other hand, even in its origins, punk bespoke a contempt for everyday people living everyday lives that I have never been able to share. Ultimately, punk in America was a student-led music with all the collegiate population's biases against growing up and participating in the mainstream of society. And while I loathe many things about the society in question, I've never wanted to stand absolutely outside it (partly because there were times when I feared being forced to do so).

Since another aspect of the punk premise was that all presently existing pop music not participating in the rebellion was equally corrupt (a premise I also didn't share), not to participate as a partisan in the punk movement could make you feel like a hack or a traitor. Even if you helped name the stuff.

From within this maze of contradiction and guilt-edged responsibility, I wrote these pieces.

Rudy Martinez
Returns

The arrival of punk rock—that last bastion of pop music noise and anger—is perhaps the central issue in white rock and roll and has been for the past decade. The issue, even boiled down, is incredibly complex, but in essence, punk poses two questions: first, it asks that we define (or redefine) music, and second, it asks that we define (or redefine) our relationship to that music. Furthermore, punk requires that these definitions operate on its own noisy and noisome terms. Punk meant to revolutionize rock and roll, strip it of its conventions and force it to re-create itself in some image other than that of Elvis Presley's bloated body floating down the highway in a pink Cadillac. All of the essays in this chapter are concerned with those definitions, redefinitions and the range of success and failure that the punk revolution created.

Punk's intention was to destroy rock history, and in many ways it succeeded. So thorough was its demolition of what had come before that, if you buy all of punk's rhetoric, memory itself becomes a mistaken atavism. However, punk has a history, as a phrase, as a sound and perhaps even as a concept.

The term "punk rock" first appeared in print (so far as I can discern) in the following column. But what it meant was much more complicated than simple homage to a rock critic's high school favorite. The idea of punk rock began with a group of writers at Creem *magazine, most prominently me, the late Lester Bangs and Greg Shaw (who today runs Bomp Records). Our point of view—which suffused each issue of* Creem *from roughly 1969 to 1973—was vulgar, belligerent, often less respectful to rock's major institutions than many thought proper, with the result that all of us—and especially me as the most militant of the bunch—were frequently given fish-eye glances and assaulted with the epithet: "You are such a punk." Culturally perverse from birth, I decided that this insult would be better construed as a compliment, especially given the alternative to such punkist behavior, which I figured was acting like a dignified asshole. (There are those who'd argue that in my middle age I have found the best or worst of both worlds. But never mind.)*

Creem's critics were also committed to the revisionist aesthetic and
alternative version of pop history that insisted that psychedelia wasn't
a triumph but a failure; that the glimmering singer/songwriter movement was a setback, not progress; that rock hadn't died 'twixt Presley
and Beatles; and so forth—in essence, this is the version of rock
history presented in Fortunate Son and now accepted by knowledge-
able critics.

All of these were still contentious propositions in 1970, however,
and in order to emphasize our delight in rock's essential barbarism
(and the worth of its vulgarism), we seized upon the amateurish but
energetic garage-band stylists of the midsixties as objects of devotion.
A classic compendium of such music is the Nuggets anthology album
compiled by Lenny Kaye (first issued by Elektra, it was later reissued
by Sire, but is now hard to find). Other landmarks of rock crit revision-
ism in this period included Lester Bangs' essays on the Stooges and
Captain Beefheart and his long fantasy-review of the collected oeuvre
of Count Five, a group that was in fact well known for only one song,
"Psychotic Reaction," the various issues of Shaw's Bomp fanzine and
my own writing about the Stooges and "96 Tears."

This was the context in which we made our hejira to Sherwood
Forest and rediscovered ? and the Mysterians, a band I really had seen
fairly often one or two summers in high school. (Michigan seems far
north for Mexicans only to those who aren't aware that it is primarily
migrant laborers who pick the state's crops.) The show was nearly as
terrific as the resulting column attempted to make it seem. Though
perhaps you had to be there—something which can be said about all
the greatest punk rock.

I couldn't imagine it happening, but there I was, swaggering and jiving
again like I did at Mount Holly back in '66. And there he was, swaggering
and jiving again like he did at Mount Holly back in '66.

Yes, friends, ? and the Mysterians have re-formed, and they're better'-
n'ever, if only because of the lack of competition.

A few weeks ago, Pete Cavanaugh of Flint's teen/rock station WTAC
informed Charlie Auringer and me that the revitalized Mysterians would
be appearing at his club, Sherwood Forest, located in the wilds of Davison,
Michigan, about fifty miles north of Detroit. Needless to say, it was
impossible to pass up such a landmark exposition of punk rock, even
after two nights running of Tina Turner. So we piled into Charlie's
'66 Mustang—the perfect car for the occasion, a lot like piling into

a '56 Chevy back in '61—and commenced the ninety-minute drive.

Now I don't want to insinuate that Aurginer's auto is a death trap, and it was probably only my phobia that caused it, but even sober, that was a harrowing hour and a half. For one thing, the Mustang's doors don't close too well, and for another, the car began to overheat as we approached Pontiac, my old hometown. Visions of emergency wards danced in my head.

We finally did arrive, though, and walking up to the club, we encountered a six-foot-two greaser, thin as a rail, smoking Lucky Strikes and spitting on the sidewalk. An honest-to-god throwback.

Sherwood's clientele is even more bizarre than such a time-warp incident suggests. It's a sort of limited version of the midsixties teen clubs in which my rock and roll fanaticism took root. The kids are now stoned and strung out instead of juiced, but the aura is similar enough: cruisin' for action, waitin' to become either old enough to drive or old enough to leave the American armpit where they reside.

Up on the stage, the strangest-looking band in the world. On drums, a hard-looking Chicano, bearded and stocky, crashing away at a furious pace which was determined less by the rhythms of the music, in many cases, as by the consumables flowing through his veins. On bass, a typically post-collegiate hippie type, who knew how to dance and play off the drummer and bob his head and sing harmony and generally got it on to everyone's delight. These two might even have been in the original Mysterians (according to Cavanaugh, they were).

The other two Mysterians were brand new, however. Chunks of baby fat still clung to their facial structure, so much so that the organist looked like Froggy from the *Spanky and Our Gang* serials. The guitar player, the band's prime musical deficiency because of his excessive love for the wah-wah pedal, is almost as heavy and possibly even younger. In fact, if either of these guys can buy alcohol without a scrupulous ID check, Michigan has changed more than any of us suspect.

No matter, though. Fronting the whole show is the main man himself. There's no question about it—? and the Mysterians indeed possess the original, the one and only Question Mark Himself.

He is today a heavily bearded (although shaven—maybe I mean Nixonesque?) Mexican, about twenty-five years old. Luxuriant jet-black hair, so wavy it's almost curly, falls to his shoulders and covers his forehead. His thin, near-emaciated chest is covered by an orange lace see-through blouse. Dangling still from a gold chain around his neck is the quixotic symbol of modern-day midwestern rock and roll:

?

His flamenco dancer's legs are sheathed in hip-hugger pants of cheap brown cloth, his boots are pointy-toed and possess two-inch stacked heels. The latter he uses to great effect, stomping defiantly through his set.

For ? is the greatest dancer in the history of rock and roll (provided we leave James Brown safely a soul man). True, Mick Jagger and Iggy Stooge can shake their asses competently, but were ? a woman, he could get a job at any go-go joint in the nation and win contests.

? stamps his feet in flamenco-like fury, writhes his limber loins in paroxysms of self-parody and moves each limb in a different direction, as if calling upon all the forces of the universe to propel his energy right into the viscera of the poor, uncomprehending souls who vegetate on this sad dance floor, where no one any longer twirls, spins or even boogies.

It goes on in this fashion, the band playing well, though hampered by the lack of PA power. Question Mark runs through such numbers as "If I Can't Have You Bitch—I'm Gonna Make You Like Me (But You're Not Gonna Bring Me Down)." Shades of '66. When's the last time you heard a singer insult his audience because he wasn't getting laid often enough? No, now it's odes to the woman who "gives me sweet, sweet head / As she kneels beside my bed." And I'll bet someone would've written those words in an actual song if I hadn't just used them up.

But the apex of the evening comes during that climactic moment of transition between "Trudi, Trudi, Eloise" (a vaudeville-psychedelic song that finds ? engaged in a fine satire of a flapper, which is also a satire of a rock and roll dancer, which is parody in the first place) and the instant when he stomps into the legend:

TOO MANY TEAR DROPS
FOR ONE HEART
TO BE CRYIN'!

This is it. Even before the first words are out of his mouth, the organ is pumping out its insanely repetitive and enthralling three-finger pattern and I find my ass shaking of its own volition. And suddenly I'm not alone. We are witnessing the first appearance in two years of the original bizarro rock band, the one that had the nerve and the imagination to do it before Iggy or Alice or any of the rest, the dude who was insulting audiences and being way too far out for almost any Keeper of the Cool as far back as 1966. Yes, Question Mark wasn't just back, but up to his old tricks.

At the end he gets down on his back and screams as his legs flail the air: "Ya Gonna Cry—96 Tears" over and over again. Then he rises up and puts it right in your face: "LEMME HEAR YA CRY NOW—ALL NIGHT LONG!"

Then he's dancing like a maniac again and suddenly executing a knee-drop and splits that James Brown might envy. He's the only one in punk rock who's still got 'em, and he's makin' a comeback. For the past two years he's lived on a bean farm in Clio and he's makin' a comeback. And he still can dance, he still can sing, real good at that, too.

Goddamn, what a holy moment!

Creem, 1970

Elements of Style

One of punk's least-heralded precursors was glitter rock, a move on the part of young bands of the early seventies to get away from the self-consciously unstylish, jeans and T-shirt images of post-psyche-delic pop stars. The glitter bands included the New York Dolls and the other groups that emerged from New York's Mercer Arts Center and other clubs during this period, and a whole horde of British pop bands, including David Bowie, then in his draggy phase, Mott the Hoople, whose androgynous hymn, "All the Young Dudes" (produced by Bowie), summarizes both glitter style and attitude, Marc Bolan and T. Rex and such teenybop singles makers as the Sweet. The music was driving, direct and glossily produced (many of the English hits by the team of Michael Chapman and Nicky Chinn, who went on to fashion similar-sounding hits with Blondie, Pat Benatar and others in the late seventies). The aim was outrage, a return to the sweet innocence of the British Invasion in terms of sound but with droogy, sexually ambivalent postures.

In the glitter movement, the idea of "teenage" was raised to fever pitch. When I did the reporting on this story, I was twenty-two or twenty-three years old, and yet I felt like a prudish old man. The reason—beyond the fact that I am pretty prudish—was that this was my first encounter with the post-baby boom generation, kids who were

growing up when the economy was contracting rather than expanding,
when the innocence of the sixties was curdling into seventies cynicism,
when dreams of peace and love were replaced by a fear of nuclear
holocaust about which it was completely uncool even to speak, "poli-
tics" having been discredited by the sixties. (Their thinking, not
mine.) The kids in Los Angeles were only an early, extreme manifesta-
tion of a nihilism that is today prevalent throughout the United States
and in much of Western Europe. Those kids were frightening to me
in 1974; they are still frightening today. And they were the cause, the
source and the downfall of the punk movement in the United States.

I've always been amazed that there has never been a fashion magazine for
the teenage trade, something that could exploit what passes for haute
couture in the junior high school set. I don't mean *Rolling Stone*'s incom-
prehensible Tom Wolfe piece on denim chic—the readers of *Rolling
Stone* needed to be informed about *that?*—but a pop *Vogue*, which could
let the suburban demimonde know when snakeskin boots are outré and
bare midriffs de rigueur, when too much mascara is a must and when the
natural look has run its course.

In Los Angeles, where rivalry for the sleaziest styles is most earnest,
there was once (in 1972 and 1973) a splendidly vainglorious attempt at
creating such a publication. It was called *Star* and it nearly realized the
ambition of every former boutique owner with a literary bent and a taste
for pedophilia. In the process, it pushed the truth of teen licentiousness
a little further into the open.

One issue of *Star* featured a "minute-to-minute Nose Job Diary," and
in its quizzes, there was always at least one mind-blower question and
answer. For example:

Q: You're at a drive-in movie with a Very Special Guy on your first
date with him and the movie is a real drag.
Correct Answer: Suggest that the two of you check out the view from
the backseat and then read *Star*'s movie review on the flick in case
your mom asks you what it was about.

Such pandering deserved further investigation, I thought, and so I
found myself in Los Angeles last spring walking among fourteen-year-olds
who could make a 42nd Street woman of the night blush.

I already knew that *Star* had drawn its inspiration, at least in part, from
the glitter crowd that frequented Rodney Bingenheimer's English Disco,

a sleazy bar on Sunset Strip that flaunted California's liquor laws with true impudence. Most of Rodney's clientele were not only under twenty-one but under sixteen. Many of his most interesting customers were only fourteen and had been groupies, for real, since they were eleven. Among them were the current girlfriend of a noted New York rock guitarist; a young woman featured in a movie that garnered an Academy Award nomination (and whose father would once have been considered a prime score by earlier groupies); a fourteen-year-old who reported having engaged in anal intercourse for more than four hours with an English pop star who's supposed to be gay; an authentic twelve-year-old who informed me that when her boyfriend asked which she had learned to do first, tie her shoes or give head, she replied, "I learned to tie my shoes when I was three. I didn't learn to give head until I was eleven."

This Toulouse-Lautrec setting has since been immortalized by that great and patrician figure of kitsch, Alan King, on one of his television specials, which are fortunately aired well after the more corruptible elements—not to say, the most innocent ones—of the television audience are safely abed. Theoretically. In fact, some of the girls King interviewed may not have been up to watch the show—presuming they'd stayed home that evening, which they probably didn't.

But King didn't really know what to do with these women, who *will not* dance with men—only each other—unless the male in question is first of all, English, and more importantly, in a glitter rock band. (A few exceptions might be made: for the New York Dolls, for instance. But not many.) *Star*, on the other hand, understood these prejudices perfectly. It interviewed the girls and photographed them, generally attempting to establish the bunch at Bingenheimer's as the prototype of the chic female teenager for however many hundred thousand readers its grocery-store distribution gave it.

The Look, as encapsulated in *Star*'s final issue: "She had on a black widow wide-brimmed hat over her kinky-blond natural. And a colorful Japanese-looking kimono with wide-open slit sleeves exposing a tiny sequined vest and black bikini panties with scarlet red garters holding up her black stockings. Too much for words. As for [her friend]—she wore a silver lamé hot pants suit revealing incredibly spidery long legs on six-inch silver wedgie platforms."

Too much for words? Hah! Those two are mild, just the center of the cyclone. Most of the girls I met at Rodney's wore their very best, most minuscule bikini bathing suits, with perhaps a feather boa to ward off the chill blowing in from the desert at night. Their conversation had the same sense of decorum Julie Christie displayed in *Shampoo*. Not even rock idols were safe. A personage as seemingly omnipotent as Mick Jagger could be shredded by a fifteen-year-old (in *Star*) with short cutting sentences: "He looks just like a bellboy, he's nothing great at all! Mick is just ugly; dope has just eaten him apart. He's just really deformed looking. He just got his hair cut and it looked ugly. [Bianca] sounded like a man. She is a real shrew. All she wants is Mick's money."

This is *tame*. Another of the Rodney's crowd is said to have shown up at the Jaggers' LA hotel room, and, being told by Bianca that she should go play in the traffic like a good little kid, responded: "Oh, I wish you'd been in Nicaragua when the earthquake hit."

When I was on the Strip, the acknowledged Queen of the Foxes (fox was *Star*'s term for its ideal of girlhood) was fifteen-year-old Sable Starr. She was tough and hard, a blond minx in the proper Fox tradition— chestless and assless—but intensely erotic anyway. Sable carried tangible innocence the way she must have carried a Barbie Doll not so long ago. But her face, dotted with unregal acne—God, doesn't all that makeup even cover the zits? I wondered—was so worn, she might as well have been thirty.

Sable defined the style of the Strip that year. She hadn't anything in common with her hippie predecessors, the ones who crammed the Whiskey for the Byrds and caused so much commotion in the streets that they inspired Buffalo Springfield's "For What It's Worth." It is not quite true that Sable would sneer at members of those groups, if she encountered them today, but she wouldn't be very interested in them, either. First of all, by her standards, they're old. And they're American.

The glitter girls think their style comes from England. But aside from a similar propensity for orthopedic platform shoes, kids in England just don't dress this way. The weather is too chilly to allow bathing suits and hot pants to proliferate, and fifteen-year-olds in England couldn't get out of the house in them, if it weren't. In fact the ultimate question may be how the California girls manage to sneak past their mothers, not to mention how in a city where public transportation is virtually nonexistent and they're too young to drive, they manage to get back to their homes in the Valley at 4:00 A.M. when the clubs close and the hanging out is finished. Or for that matter, how they avoid going home earlier. In London, where the tube stops at midnight and working-class girls have to rise early anyway, groupie-ism is for older women from the leisure classes. In LA, where leisure is among the most noticeable occupations of the working classes and everybody else, Sable and her friends might as well, so they do—an all-purpose justification.

What they think of as English chic is really American cheapo. To dress the way the English starfuckers really do is beyond the means of fifteen-year-olds anywhere. To grab a bathing suit, invent hot pants from tattered Levis, to buy some Frederick's of Hollywood net nylons, is within the means of (almost) anyone. Because clothes are bait, because the tackily outrageous is more obvious, the highest fashion on the Strip is that which would be crummiest anywhere else.

None of this has anything to do with androgyny or unisex, of course. The purpose of the Strip's fashion is to expose flesh, bare the midriff and the thigh, to emphasize the difference. Androgyny is T-shirts and jeans, and in that sense Cambridge is far more unisexual than Hollywood can ever be. So are the Allman Brothers. But not David Bowie or Lou Reed —who can imagine mistaking either of them for women? Even in drag, they're dudes.

There are reasons, of course, why there are only a few teenagers, concentrated in Southern California, who have really bought the glitter fad. Part of it is just that they're able to get away it—but another aspect is that England isn't just one but really two continents removed from Hollywood. The glitter girls have no idea, because their ambition and tradition don't encompass it, what things might be like even in Iggy Pop's flat, depressing, boring Midwest. If your father worked in the aerospace industry, the moon might seem more attainable than London or even New York. And of course, whatever anyone sold you as British would be the real thing.

Maybe Lou Reed was right: "The makeup thing is just a fad now, a style, like platform shoes. The notion that everyone's bisexual is a very popular line, but I think its validity is limited. I could say something like, if in any way my albums help people decide who they are, then I will feel I have accomplished something in my life. But I don't feel that way at all. You can't listen to a record and say, 'Oh, that really turned me on to gay life. I'm gonna be gay.' "

But of course if you're fifteen and not accustomed to thinking very deeply, you might not know that. I think my last encounter with Sable Starr was the most illuminating in this regard. It was at a Dolls recording session in Manhattan. I stared at her for five minutes, knowing I knew her but not able to place the face. Then suddenly I knew. That hard-faced girl from the Strip, come to evil New York, and living a supposedly decadent life with a glitter rock star, had somehow regained her innocence. She looked her age. I couldn't help wondering how many of the friends she'd left behind never would.

Creem, 1974

Hey, Rocky, What's a Punk?

This is almost unimaginably out of touch with the seventies punk mentality, but it strikes me that it's nevertheless valuable in demonstrating how late in the game (the piece was published in March 1977, which means it was written sometime in January or February) definitions and limits were still up for grabs. Only in England was punk a specific kind of music. In the States, the title still applied to just about anything that was an alternative to heavy metal, progressive and other corporatized forms of rock. Since the industry's "new wave" nomenclature hadn't yet been developed, punk could apply to anything on the circuit from the Sex Pistols to the Talking Heads to the Damned: that is, from complex reductionism to funky/arty to the purely crude.

It is also worth noting that the idea of punk is an American one —though the British scene of 1976–78 came to define the word in a new and more limited dimension, those punks built on an idea that was as American as soul music or rockabilly. (How could the British have developed garage rock, in a country where almost no one has garages?)

What's missing, then, is a sense of the scene defined at the poles by the Clash and the Sex Pistols—that is, a spectrum from intelligently hostile to inspired primitivism. Or something like that. The moral drawn at the end, however, feels prophetic, unless you believe that Sid Vicious' death (and all the others associated with punk and its descendants) was in some kind of Good Cause.

It's also interesting to conceive of this wrongheaded attitude as the product of working at monolithic Rolling Stone, *for whom the changing of the guard seemed more like a British fad than something long-lasting and profoundly different. In that sense, this interpretation of the punks—asserting that they fit in—was to the left of its context, even if it was to the right of events.*

As *Rolling Stone* has developed a nonrock readership, columnists from William Buckley to Russell Baker have been confused by some of the more arcane rock jargon. In a way, it's hard to understand why: rock never developed the double-talk complexity of Mezz Mezzrow's jazz argot. On the other hand, I can guess the problem: rock opera isn't opera (or even particularly operatic), jazz rock is often neither here nor there, and ARP 2600 probably doesn't have real specific connotations for most of the public.

Nineteen seventy-seven's pet phrase is punk. It has been used to describe almost everyone: Patti Smith, John Cale, the CBGB bands of Manhattan, the Beserkley Records artists in California, Bruce Springsteen, English demolitionists like the Sex Pistols, even Rod Stewart and Mick Jagger. (The latter, one supposes, are "punques.") A far cry from the young toughs pointed out to us on streetcorners in our tender years, those who originally bore (and earned) the epithet. But punk no longer describes style, much less music. It's become a marketing device, an excuse for decadence, often with a macho bent. Thus the dreaded Fonz—who at least would never have impaled his cheeks with safety pins—is currently the fashion among British "punk" audiences. They've gone rockabilly without knowing it.

Because of a certain churlish attitude and a deep-seated distate for elites and the effete, I have myself sometimes been described as a punk. This would be endlessly amusing to those hard guys back on the block. But however vicarious my experiences, the punk sensibility (as I define it) is at the heart of what I care about in American culture, not least of all in rock and roll.

For me, the punk sensibility in its original form offered something better and deeper than a way to walk and talk, or an excuse for petty crime and amateur nihilism. Punk in its fifties sense could never be merely music or merely fashion. The pose implied a set of standards, a code of behavior, founded on friendship, carried out as a matter of principle. This sensibility runs through American folklore from the mythic (if not actual) Billy the Kid to what once were known as antiheroes—Cagney and Bogart, later Dean and Brando. That sort of punkitude reached its greatest glory with Elvis Presley, who could bring teenage women to the edge of orgasm while dedicating songs to his mother. The punk code is simple, direct street philosophy: loyalty and self-respect are its highest values, the camaraderie between friends the only society it recognizes.

Not surprisingly, given that this version of punk is basically a cinematic tradition, the most recent and straightforward articulation of its code comes from Rocky Balboa, the Italian Stallion, in the movie *Rocky*:

"It ain't so bad, 'cause I was nothing before . . . But that don't bother me—I just wanna prove something. I ain't no bum . . . The only thing

I wanna do is go the distance, that's all . . . If I go them fifteen rounds an' that bell rings and I'm still standin', I'm gonna know then that I wasn't just another bum from the neighborhood."

Those are the sentiments of an artist, not a pug. The essence of punk is the struggle to make an honest stand, not even the honest stand itself. For Rock, as for John Lennon in *Plastic Ono Band* or Peter Townshend in "The Seeker" or Johnny Rotten on his "Holiday in the Sun," the response to being set up is to lash out. And perhaps inevitably, like the sad characters of Martin Scorsese's *Mean Streets* or Magic Rat in Springsteen's "Jungleland," the punk's ending is not even tragic. The destiny of the punk is to "wind up wounded, *not even* dead." Or like Quadrophenia's mod hero, Jimmy, to be stranded on a rock in search of a future that can't or won't replicate the past.

Almost everyone mentioned here would reject the name punk, partly because the term has pejorative connotations, partly because it seems like part of a marketing mechanism. I find the word honorable, but then, I'm one of those who initiated its use as a term of praise rather than derogation. But one must wonder about some of those who currently embrace the name. I enjoy (if that's the proper term) the Ramones' music and its deconstructive ambitions, but there's something gruesomely distasteful about an anthemic song called "I Wanna Sniff Some Glue." When Rocky steers a young girl home and lectures her about the dangers of acquiring a "reputation," his perspective may seem quaint or sexist. But at least he's acknowledging a value system—he's not just another numbed-out nihilist, and that's why we root for him.

I mourn the prostitution of true punks by performers for whom public vomiting is a rebellious act of stagecraft, but that's not what really disturbs me. It's the idea of the dilution of that concept as another symptom of rock's loss of moral force. That's not to say that the Ramones and the Sex Pistols are immoral—though they're definitely a little mixed up. But what these performers and their fans (not to mention their promoters) mistake for rebellion—the honest stand—is too often merely marketable outrage. Once I thought that it was at least theoretically possible that *Rocky's* ethics could really work.

A few years ago *Esquire* called me the last man in American who believed that rock could save the world. I responded that I was, instead, the last who believed that rock could destroy the world. But I never expected to see my prediction confirmed so soon.

Rolling Stone, 1977

Kick Out the Jams

A literally quixotic response to the Sex Pistols and the revival of the punk rock I'd dreamed. Written with studious tentativeness, from the bitter awareness that if I really loved this music as much as I proclaimed, this was probably the wrong publication to be writing for full time. In other words, it strikes me now that I would have written something much more passionate had I been writing for anything other than the Monolith. Part of the price you pay, I guess, but obviously, "God Save the Queen" is and was great as well as important. (Though I think one reason I hedged my bet was that I liked "Anarchy in the U.K." a lot better—still do.)

Keeping my distance from the New York punk scene, swiftly evolving into no-wave avant-gardism, is something unregrettable, even though it cost me considerable points with the avant-rock intelligentsia. My perception of rock's constituency, however, has always precluded much sympathy for elitism in any form, and particularly for snobbish music that doesn't even much want to be liked by the unwashed and unlettered. Then there's the fact that I never liked the way Richard Hell and Tom Verlaine sounded . . .

Certainly this latter-day punk rock did prove to be nihilistic, and at least in England and California, its associations with fascism have been tangible from time to time. And God knows, it was true that when "God Save the Queen" was released in the States, its function was precisely to titillate a couple of hundred thousand listeners—though to the extent that it led five or six years later to the increasingly fertile and exciting "hard-core" scene, that may not have been such a bad thing.

The last paragraph of this piece reworks the main anthems of the three groups discussed.

It contravenes logic, but there's little doubt in my mind that the most important record of the past year is the Sex Pistols' "God Save the Queen." This doesn't qualify it for immortality—significance is not always art—but it does beg closer scrutiny. And the funny thing is, as the group bounces back and forth from record label to record label, banned hither and yon and inciting both praise and damnation for its obnoxious qualities, the case of the Sex Pistols begins to seem more and more familiar.

To me, at least, it's no surprise that the punk-rock rage in the U.K. has brought about the re-release in that country of the MC5's three LPs (they remain unavailable in the land where they were stillborn) and the emergence of at least one good group, the Heartbreakers, from the ashes of the New York Dolls. For as new as they may seem, the Sex Pistols have direct ancestry in those American bands, also much maligned in their time.

Like the Sex Pistols, the MC5 and the Dolls suffered because of willful distortions in the press and the scorn of the radio establishment. And like the Dolls and the MC5, the Pistols are more than a little bit political (by which I do not mean Friends of the Whale). And all three share an aesthetic based on outrage.

Although their "political program"—rock and roll, dope and fucking in the streets—left a lot to be desired for everyone but white male adolescents, the MC5 had firm musical roots in the Who (listen to their "Come Together," a knockoff of "I Can See for Miles"), Them (their first single was Van Morrison's "I Can Only Give You Everything"), the Yardbirds and the Rolling Stones. And the Five's program at least pointed a way out of the morass of depression in which Iggy Pop and the current New York primitivist/minimalists are so fond of wallowing. (In America, only Patti Smith—who professed a warped political program of her own on *Radio Ethiopia*—acknowledges the Five's influence.)

Superficially, the Dolls were as different from the MC5 as could be imagined. The Five were said to be lean carnivores, Clint Eastwood on acid; the Dolls were allegedly decadent transvestites. Almost no one noticed that the Dolls' first album contained "Vietnamese Babies," a song overtly about the war, or that songs like "Human Being" and "Frankenstein" were the most political form of artistic sociology. Nor was the obvious musical influence of the MC5 much remarked, though the Dolls themselves, particularly guitarist Johnny Thunders, often proclaimed it.

I loved both bands, saw them firsthand—the Five dozens of times, the Dolls nearly as many—and lived among the strange community of protopunks, artists and intelligentsia they gathered. Onstage, those bands along with the Who shaped my idea of live rock and roll: highly visual, forced into focus with power supplied principally by guitars, vividly costumed, loud beyond belief.

When the Five disintegrated in a mess of bad debts and drugs—two of the members wound up in Lexington taking the cure—and the Dolls disbanded with similar problems, I virtually gave up on that standard.

CBGB, where the New York whatchamacallit groups play, lacked sufficient diversity of music and audience the few times I went. And I didn't
like the cool distance of the New York bands; if all it amounted to was
the celebration of one's own alienation, rather than fighting that alienation
off, then I figured outcast rock deserved to die.

But a couple of weeks ago I saw a Sex Pistols videotape and the spark
returned. The Pistols' leader/singer, Johnny Rotten, even acknowledges
the Dolls as an influence—they're almost the only people he admits liking
—and the Pistols' stage show owes an obvious, if less specific, debt to the
Five, as the content of "God Save the Queen" surely does. (Typically, little
of the work that the Pistols have inspired—with a couple of exceptions like
Chelsea's "Right to Work"—is worth a damn.)

It makes me a bit wistful. I won't drop everything and rush to England
—would I be welcome?—and the overtones of fascist groupings bother me
as much as similar trappings must have disturbed the Five's detractors, but
the essence of the thing is so nearly right that it makes me feel homesick.

I also don't really care whether "God Save the Queen" is ever released
in America; the few hundred thousand who hear it will only be titillated.
We have our own pompous royalty to rail against, and it would be a better
thing if someone picked up the cudgel on this side of the water. In any
event, "God Save the Queen" has served its purpose: the Sex Pistols are
stars; anything is possible.

Still, I cherish my copy of that record, because I thought the brutal
essence of rock—pure anger, a willingness to try anything and airplay be
damned—had gone out of the music. Whether it was stomped out by big
business or a generation too numb and blank to be worth talkin' to (much
less about), or whether it simply withered in the dust of my old friends
didn't matter much. Nor did this situation seem an altogether bad thing
—a lot of people with less gall make better music. Still, such bands as the
Five, the Dolls and the Pistols are dear to the rock and roll heart, because
they won't let us forget the core of the matter: rock and roll came not to
celebrate convention and apathy but to bury them.

That essence lives on in the Sex Pistols. If you hate them, perhaps that
proves it. And that is certainly what makes "God Save the Queen" so
important, above and beyond the fact that it's the only hard-rock hit in
recent years to possess an important lyric. To me at least, the success of
the Sex Pistols means that smug, somnolent disc jockeys, reluctant record
execs, outraged politicos and civilization in general can never prevail
against the lunatic fringe, or at least they can never stomp it out altogether.

Is it strange to find hype in a record whose transcendent moment is "No future, no future" chanted over and over again? Well, you know what they say: kick out the jams, motherfuckers. And if they ask you what it means, just tell 'em you gotta dream, 'cause you're a human being.

Rolling Stone, 1977

Punk Inc.

Peter Rudge, who manages the Rolling Stones' American tours and likes to speculate about rock and roll almost as much as I do, suggested recently that the Real Meaning and Significance of New Wave Rock might be that those groups have managed to ignore the problems presented by sophisticated studio technology. In fact, he suggested, crudity was at the core of their success and appeal.

Because new wave has had popular support only in Britain and Europe, Rudge's contention is hard to demonstrate or disprove. In America, the notion that passionate primitivism can move very many listeners has yet to make the charts. What we're about to discover, I have a hunch, is that American pop musical taste has become too sophisticated for its own good. Which may be beneficial for the new wave.

I would hardly complain if the Talking Heads or the Sex Pistols, the Ramones or Elvis Costello had hits. Some of them, I guess, certainly will, if only because too much capital is behind too many talented people simultaneously for all to fail. But I also think that even if new wave performers achieve gold records or whatever, it won't matter very much. If the Sex Pistols' *Never Mind the Bollocks* album goes platinum, it seems mostly likely to do so on the basis of novelty and notoriety, which are not the basis of long-term success.

But it also seems that large-scale success need not matter to the new wave, which after all sprang up in opposition to the established star-making machinery. If people are confused by a new wave which encompasses music as diverse as the Talking Heads and the Ramones, it's because what unifies new wave as a movement is its opposition to the inexorable processes of manufacturing hits, its rejection of the standard formulas for achieving fame. Indeed, the clearest statement that emerges from the matrix of the new wave is: "Does success matter? How much?"

Rock and roll—as opposed to "rock," which punk, the best aspect of the new wave, is *not*—is never the most popular music. In the sixties it wasn't only the Beatles who balanced pop and rock and roll styles and thus outsold the Rolling Stones. So did Simon and Garfunkel and, now and again, Barbra Streisand, who never made rock and roll at all. Rock is a matter of entertainment, but rock and roll is also anti-entertainment—or at least anti–show business—because it's designed to alienate as often as it attracts and accomplishes both alienation and attraction by means of each other. So it made me shudder to read in John Rockwell's *New York Times* review of *Never Mind the Bollocks* that "the Pistols may be tomorrow's mainstream." For a group like the Sex Pistols that would not be success, that would be the worst imaginable failure.

Because it reflects an attitude widely held by music business insiders, another sentence in Rockwell's review is even more disturbing. "Certainly, if this record dies ignominiously in the marketplace, it will set back the whole cause of technically unpolished, angry new rock."

This has it backward in my opinion. There's no way for the Sex Pistols album to die an ignominious death. Its very existence, if only as an affront to the various established power bases of rock, assures its honor. (Its aesthetic success is another matter—the Pistols were, it turns out, mostly a great singles band.) It's absurd to think that rejection by an increasingly desiccated radio establishment or an increasingly conservative audience means anything shameful. As long as the Pistols retain their principles, they'll remain successful in the only way that matters. If they aren't heard widely, it's everyone's loss.

It is not necessarily ironic that the emblem of Warner Brothers' recent release of Sire's new wave product was Bugs Bunny in a black leather jacket. The Ramones and the Talking Heads are not simply the new makers of Looney Toons for kicks and commerce; the biggest advantage the Ramones have had is not being taken seriously in the marketplace. Without pressure, they've developed into the best band in the American new wave and, with the exception of the Pistols (who have a big advantage in the charisma of Johnny Rotten), perhaps the best in the world. One hopes they will continue to develop *despite* the marketplace.

Punk began as a movement that understood the difference between Mick Jagger singing "Play with Fire," with its direct antagonism of English class structure, and Mick Jagger at society dinner parties. It is now said that when the Sex Pistols come to America, they'll begin by playing Madison Square Garden. Knowing what I do about the acoustics of that particular hockey barn, I wonder why. And also, what they can do to make their presentation different from the cash-in concerts of the superstars they purportedly despise. Presumably, the Sex Pistols are important in part because they understand the difference between getting one's kicks in Stepney and Knightsbridge, the Bowery and Midtown. This isn't to say that the new wave deserves nothing better than slum bars like CBGB's. But merely changing one's rhetoric, then playing out the tired show-biz formulas of champagne, limousines and arena performances, plays directly into the hands of those who would treat the Sex Pistols and the rest of new wave as nothing more than a novelty—this year's version of "Disco Duck."

Rolling Stone, 1973

Written from the depth of despair as punk's cynical innocence began to lose its charm and the "movement" edged ever more willingly toward business as usual. Never Mind the Bollocks did die on the charts, and the industry interpreted it on just the terms Rockwell predicted. It was not until the new rock abandoned its technical crudity and began to manipulate the sophisticated new computer/synthesizer technologies that it gained a commercial foothold in the U.S. Meantime, the apostles of punk rawness, with the exception of the Clash (not mentioned here), either ended in blood and pretension (the Pistols) or petered out into anger and spiteful reaction (Ramones).

Part of the point is that one ignores technology at one's peril. But an equally important concept to hold in mind here is that the portion of the new wave that succeeded—represented in this piece by Talking Heads, but epitomized by the Police—was polished, technically proficient, intellectualized: everything that punk stood against in theory. In part this just proves that old dictum "Melody beats the big beat every time." In the marketplace, that may never stop being true. But it also measures the extent to which the hostility to a manipulated mainstream expressed here was counterproductive. One of the greatest failures of the punk insurrection, and especially the punk-oriented critics and record business people, was abandoning that audience simply because it seemed too tough a nut to crack. The hardest core punk groups, such as the Clash, did break through to some sort of acceptance, if they remained committed to outreach (though by then they were dragging behind them a shroud, not a movement). Because too much of the rest of the punk movement turned its back on that audience, the door was opened for some of the most flimsy and exploitative performers of the rock era—Duran Duran and its ilk. It is not only ironic, but almost disgusting, that these performers should have ridden to fame on the basis of a vague association with the original punk/new wave impulse.

Rebel Rouser

One of the principal reasons I wound up founding my own publication, the newsletter Rock & Roll Confidential, *in 1983, was my disgust with the distanced, generally apolitical and cultish behavior of the rock press, an institution that more than once has mistaken its own anesthesia for aestheticism. The particular target of this column was not idly chosen, however. Malcolm McLaren, as the impetus behind the Sex Pistols, a string of London hipster clothing emporiums, erstwhile manager of the New York Dolls and dilettante mass articulator of situationist theory, possesses just about all the requisite qualities for villainy in my book.*

McLaren originally distinguished himself in my presence by causing the New York Dolls to perform some of their final shows in the United States in front of a large Chinese Communist flag, a gesture as symbolically appropriate as Eisenstein screening his films against one side of the Washington Monument. McLaren then fostered the birth of the Sex Pistols (if not punk rock as music, that is, punk rock as fashion), further distinguishing himself after they broke up by insisting that their music was essentially worthless. This bit of idiotic judgment confirmed most of my suspicions, though it didn't seem even to raise the hackles of the most fanatically punk-centered critics, which says a lot about the role and nature of self-loathing in that genre (and rock in general).

As for the more general thesis at stake here, let's take a look at what's happened in the period since this column was originally pub-

lished. McLaren went on to make much of his "discovery" of an allegedly "obscure" American square dance tune, "Buffalo Gals," and the press was sufficiently credulous about a tune most should have known from grade school folk dance exercises that his statement went unchallenged (except by me, naturally). "Buffalo Gals" was the first of a series of records made by McLaren using the music of black Americans and Africans. He keeps songwriting credit for the resulting mélange for himself and his (white, European) collaborators, of course. In at least a couple of instances he has been sued by musicians who claim that they, not he, originated the songs in question. Very few of his depredations have been commented upon by rock columnists, although the records themselves (and the video clips made in conjunction with them) are frequently and favorably reviewed.

Elvis Costello has recovered much of his credibility, partly through making some brilliant music but also by writing a couple of the most impeccably leftist songs ever composed by a rock composer, most importantly "Shipbuilding," an attack on Mrs. Thatcher's tawdry war for the Malvinas, and "Pills and Soap," an attack on Mrs. Thatcher's Neanderthal social policies that is rock's most scarifying look at the Holocaust since the Pistols' "Holiday in the Sun" (in which they vacationed at Belsen concentration camp).

Billy Joel now dates Christie Brinkley and imitates the Four Seasons.

The Gang of Four, committed feminists and socialists at the start of their career, threw out their drummer, crossed a union picket line to get to a gig in British Columbia, and last week broke up. I heard the news on MTV.

Bow Wow Wow's "Louis Quatorze" is the most exciting reworking of "Louie Louie" since Stories' "Brother Louie" (1973), which is pretty amazing, when you consider how fundamental to punk rock's rise that chunky beat was. But "Louis Quatorze" is thoroughly up-to-date, as you might expect from a record co-written by the radical rock theoretician and consumer fraud expert Malcolm McLaren and produced by Joan Jett svengali Kenny Laguna. Indeed, the old refrain crops up only in a couple of choruses, and rather than the modified reggae of primordial "Louie Louie," "Louis Quatorze" has "tribal" (i.e., pseudo-African) rhythms underpinning a hard-rock rhythm guitar and a vocal that is half chanted, half sung with genuine enthusiasm, not to say glee, by Annabella Lewin, Bow Wow Wow's teenaged front-person.

"Louis Quatorze," like all "Louie Louie" rewrites, has a plot. To synopsize: Annabella has a boyfriend, Louis Quatorze. Louis' idea of a nice surprise is to pop up at the front door with a gun in his hand and, sticking it in his beloved's back, act out a rape fantasy. Annabella squeals her studied delight at these events: "With his gun in my back / I start to undress / You just don't mess with Louis Quatorze / He's my partner in this crime / Of happiness / 'Cause I'm just fourteen." Louis himself has little to say except "Close your eyes and think of England."

There are many intriguing questions about this record. For instance, what is implied by the fact that Annabella is in real life just sixteen years old, brown-skinned and female, while her bosses, McLaren and Laguna, are fortyish, white and male? What's the difference between "Louis Quatorze" and the Rolling Stones' similar interracial rape fantasy, "Brown Sugar"? Where are the Au Pairs fan club and similar rock critic/feminists when fantasies of teenage rape are being joyously portrayed by radical rock theoreticians and consumer fraud experts?

Or more to the point, what would be the critical reaction to "Louis Quatorze" if it had been sung by David Lee Roth, Rod Stewart, Pat Benatar or Johnny Van Zant, rather than created by a new wave kingpin? Only then, having asked such a question, one might wonder where *Rolling Stone*, the *Village Voice*, the *New York* and *Los Angeles Times* and *New York Rocker*, amongst other bastions of intelligent and respectable criticism, have been on the matter of the content of this not entirely irrelevant recording.

The issue isn't that "Louis Quatorze" hasn't been condemned or that a flop single's bigotry is by itself especially threatening. The issue is that in the most prominent publications where rock is discussed, this song, which by my standards is at least crypto-racist and is certainly overtly sexist, has not been discussed politically at all.

"Louis Quatorze" is not an isolated example. When they can be taken seriously at all, discussions about rock have deteriorated to the extent that gestures speak louder than profitable behavior. For instance, when Malcolm McLaren made his speech at last July's New Music Seminar in New York, much attention was paid to his championing the cassette revolution. Apparently no one picked up on his racist remarks introducing the topic: "If you walk on the streets of New York, the one obvious thing is the guy with the ghetto blaster, that huge bazooka, walking down the street. He's always black; he's never white . . ." Still, one does not comment upon an important rock entrepreneur's quite conscious connection of blacks with primitive power, weaponry and phallic symbolism. It's not done. This is *Malcolm McLaren*, arguable auteur of the Sex Pistols, pioneer of situationist theory in rock, tribune of all that's semi-popular and subculturally tribal.

There's a pushover mentality at work here. It allows performers and producers to define the terms of all discussions of rock, even when the terms they stipulate are largely irrelevant to the facts. Thus Elvis Costello can assert that it is the press reaction to his remarks about Ray Charles which caused the commercial collapse of his U.S. career, thus neatly implying that the reaction to Costello's public remark that Charles, one of the greatest artists American popular music has produced, was "a blind, ignorant nigger" was somehow exaggerated. In fact the press quickly forgave and forgot. No interviewer has bothered to mention that Costello's career has gone downhill and is currently gasping for breath in America because his music lacks appeal to lily-white, anti-new wave AOR radio stations. Meanwhile, English rock weeklies blame the softheaded U.S. rock market for the ascendancy of Meat Loaf, even as his record rises to No. 1 there and stiffs on this side of the puddle.

This standard of discourse is not enforced only to the benefit of new wave performers, though because the press has more clout with new wave acts, it's largely biased in favor of such as McLaren and Costello. Yet matters have deteriorated to the point where Billy Joel, after his rabidly anti-political *Playboy* interview, can be praised for the "courage" of his song about Vietnam, "Goodnight Saigon," a piece of opportunistic, dead-hearted muck that piggybacks on the genuine guts of Dan Daley and Charlie Daniels' "Still in Saigon." But then, this sort of aversion of the eyes is axiomatic in a system in which sacred cows are protected—whether those cattle are holy because of their hipness or their profitability matters little. But maybe mattering as little as possible is the basic idea—sometimes I think Foreigner and Journey and the like might not be the only dinosaurs still afoot in rock. It seems insane to me to live in a world where the hairsplitting of Gang of Four is so radically admired, while fundamental issues which strike to the heart of the relationship between performer and listener (and critic) are ignored. Like the music industry and radio broadcasting, what the rock press is creating only looks like a monument from a distance. Up close, it's just another headstone.

Record, 1982

Anglophobia

The movement described in this section reached its commercial apogee in 1983, when a new crop of performers began to dominate the Top Ten: Boy George of Culture Club, Annie Lennox of Eurythmics and such bands as U2 and Big Country foretold a new cycle of pop stars, for whom British punk and Euro-American disco were as significant as soul music, Merseybeat and psychedelia had been for their predecessors. Whether these performers would be capable of restoring meaning to rock, as the punks had hoped to do, is another matter. Certainly in the sense that they were making mainstream pop music without too much ambition to do anything else, the answer is of course not. But U2 and the Eurythmics, of the groups cited above, have evidenced some desire to at least advance a critique of society with their hits.

But meaning returned to the Top Forty in 1984 in large measure as the result of a resurgence of records made by U.S. acts: Bruce Springsteen, Tina Turner, Cyndi Lauper, a host of rappers. British rock has never seemed more irrelevant.

This column was inspired by three events. The first was the release of the Pretenders' Learning to Crawl, *as good an album as anyone had made in the first half of the eighties, and one whose depths remained fairly unplumbed, despite mass sales acceptance and many reviews. The second was the appearance on the cover of* Newsweek *of a story celebrating rock's New British Invasion, just twenty years after the first. The third, and the one that was truly catalytic, was a letter written to* Record *by the Stray Cats, concerning statements made by Stuart Adamson of Big Country in a previous issue.*

Adamson had said, "Americans have never produced a thing worth calling art themselves. They've borrowed everything from Europe including punk rock." As this section will perhaps prove, that is amazingly far from the truth, yet in both U.S. and U.K. it is accepted as a fact.

"Well, who the hell does he think invented rock'n'roll, anyway," asked the Stray Cats. "Oh right, Angus McPresley. Sorry! Who invented the blues, and jazz, and country and western? . . . They've never had anyone to compare to Duke Ellington, George Gershwin, Robert Johnson, Elvis Presley or Hank Williams." Reading that letter was

thrilling to me, because it indicated that American musicians still did, in some cases, remember their ancestry, and were willing to fight to keep it. These comments are merely an amplification, borne out by events.

According to *Newsweek*, the pop press, TV and other pundits, rock is in the midst of a British invasion. Depending upon the accuracy and honesty of the pundit, it's either the second or fourth of the past twenty years, but in any event, the phenomenon is undeniable. At least it's undeniable as long as what's meant by "invasion" is that British acts are taking up a disproportionate share of the American charts.

If, however, the British invasion is supposed to indicate that what we're experiencing is part of a revolution in American pop music taste, there's just one appropriate response:

HOOEY!

For while invasions are launched for many reasons, they're successful only if they succeed in establishing something more than a beachhead—substantial and lasting changes in the hearts and minds of the population are also essential. By these lights, the British invasion of 1964–65 was highly successful, in the same sense as the Allied invasion of Normandy. But the punk incursion of 1976–78 was as great a debacle as the Bay of Pigs.

Not only did the punks, with the sole (and somewhat ambiguous.) exception of the Clash, fail to establish themselves or the alternative they represented in the U.S. (or in the long run, even in the U.K.), the terms of their failure opened the door for the success of musicians and promoters who are punk's radical antithesis. Consider: if the punk premise that rock has died of internal corruption is true, but if punk itself can't either purify the music scene or establish any sort of livable alternative, then what's left except hustle, exploitation and jive?

That's a central reason why the present British Invasion partakes of so much Spandau Ballet, ABC, and Human League, a new brand of shallow soft-rock MOR, and why it has been more successful in dragging the worst kinds of old fart art rockers (Yes, Genesis) back to the Top Ten than in establishing such groups as U2 or even Elvis Costello as major stars. If this British invasion has succeeded in the narrowest commercial sense, it's also one that has failed in the broadest artistic or even just cultural terms. Consider these statistics: In the February 25 *Billboard* chart, five of the Top Ten and ten of the Top Twenty albums are by British acts. But in order to arrive at these statistics, one has to include those old farts of the worst order as Yes and Genesis, as well as such partially English acts as John Lennon and Yoko Ono (recorded in America, with U.S. musicians), the Police (the Copeland connection), and the Pretenders ("How can I miss America when I am America?" quoth Chrissie Hynde).

There are five "new music" acts in the Top Twenty (Culture Club, Duran Duran, the Police, the Pretenders and the Eurhythmics). There are also five heavy metal groups (ZZ Top, Van Halen, Judas Priest, Motley Crue, Quiet Riot), although nobody is shouting about a heavy metal invasion or the death of techno-pop. And if you want to make a case against the heavy metal status of ZZ Top (or Van Halen), that's okay with me, as long as you don't mind my asking why calling Culture Club's recycled Smokey Robinson and country harmonica "new" isn't as inane as terming forty-four-year-old Phil Niekro a rookie because he's never pitched in the American League before. (And that doesn't mean I don't love Colour by Numbers, any more than I hate knuckleballs. As it happens, I love both, but the former much more than the latter.)

The British Invasion isn't an illusion, of course. There are more British hits in the States lately than there have been in the recent past. But all the talk of invasion is hype, by which I mean that writers as intelligent as Newsweek's Jim Miller wouldn't argue so strongly for the importance of a phenomenon that operates closer to the level of Herman's Hermits than the Kinks (let alone the Beatles or Stones) unless that characterization of what's happening lent credence to a more important set of values.

For the Anglophile, the importance of British rock stems from its trend-mongering and fashion-pandering, its celebration of the trivial and trivializing, and most of all, its emphasis upon the evanescence of not just success but meaning, too. That is, the Brits have developed a pop culture that knows its place and never insists upon equal rights with Serious Art. For snobs and conservatives, this is always reassuring. No one shouts about heavy metal, because its listeners—not its practitioners—are so uncouth they're beneath the pundits' gaze.

At present, rock writing is dominated by Anglophilia in this sense, which is one reason the American rock press comes more and more to resemble Britain's. And in England, the No. 1 rock publication is Smash Hits, which is nothing less than 16 without a visionary editor. Discussions of rock are thus reduced to pure market judgments: A record as brilliant as the Pretenders' Learning to Crawl is discussed almost entirely in terms of how many of its tracks have already been released as singles!

Albums like Learning to Crawl are judged by such nonsensical standards because dealing with their contents would constitute an immediate refutation of the basis for Anglophilia. For what the Pretenders, through Chrissie Hynde, are all about on this record is establishing a means of growing up and continuing to rock. *Learning to Crawl* is a refusal and a denial of the trivialization and trend-mongering the British invasion theorists believe is the essence of the matter. That is why this group and their album will be around long after the current British Invasion has become just another tempest in a tea bag.

Record, 1984

9

Ain't That a Groove

Introduction

This chapter is entirely devoted to soul music, its antecedent, rhythm and blues, and its most important descendant, disco. On grounds of passion, it ought to be much longer—of the 5,000 records that clutter my house, at least half fall into those categories. And it's a frustration to omit extended discussions of such favorites as Otis Redding, Wilson Pickett, Aretha Franklin, Donna Summer, Marvin Gaye, Curtis Mayfield and the Impressions, and Ray Charles. Not to mention dozens of lesser lights, from Barbara Acklin to O. V. Wright, and figures from such related genres as Delta and Chicago blues and gospel. Some of these artists and genres are discussed elsewhere in *Fortunate Son*; others are surveyed in my essays in *The New Rolling Stone Record Guide*.

Still, I can't help wishing there were more here, for two important reasons. One is professional: Rock criticism, staffed as it is by whites, has too often ignored great soul music while championing marginal rock. (A complaint also heard elsewhere in this chapter, but worth repeating.) This is so, I guess, because soul is about music and emotion. It often lacks pretension and overtly artistic ambition, though that's used to advantage. But it's harder to write about music and emotion—these pieces themselves often focus on issues just to the side of the music, trying to identify trends or pin down specific occurrences.

Second, soul music is for me the glue that holds contemporary music together, a refraction point that's the standard against which I most often measure what's new. Otis Redding's "Cigarettes and Coffee," the Miracles' "I'll Try Something New," James Brown's "Ain't That a Groove," Marvin Gaye's "I Heard It Through the Grapevine," Aretha's "Respect," the Righteous Brothers' "Just Once in My Life" and the Rascals' "People Got to Be Free" (the latter reminding us that soul artists are not always black) are the records that form my benchmarks of musical accomplishment and meaning. Meaning, of course, it's the glue that holds me together, when it's 4:00 A.M. and the wick is burning low.

Freddie's Dead and
Diana Ross Is Singing
the Blues

Since the critic's job is to analyze and assess, not predict, I've never felt all that badly about being such a lousy prognosticator. The conclusion of this piece is half prophetic and half nonsensical, but it's probably as close as I've ever come to gauging the way in which a trend would develop. Black pop did go through its period of LP-oriented indulgence; white audiences did shun the music.

What neither I or anybody else could predict on the basis of that incredible outpouring of great, committed music in 1972–73 was the rise of disco, a music in which the performer was generally invisible, a secondary consideration to the beat, and thus played into the hands of white racists (both those who hated the stuff, and used it to bait, and those who liked it, and used it to avoid a more direct confrontation). As it turned out, my colleague Vince Aletti was correct when he wrote to me after the critical hoopla over There's a Riot Goin' On *that what had made that record popular was its hip dance music, not its commentary.*

In the end that's less surprising than the fact that the records which revolutionized soul and insured black rhythm music's place in the pop mainstream came out of a context which was for the first time fully, proudly conscious of its blackness. It's possible to argue that the most influential soul hits of 1972 and 1973 were the proto-disco "Armed and Extremely Dangerous" and "Smarty Pants" by First Choice and the proto-funk "Troglodyte" by Jimmy Castor and "Funky Worm" by the Ohio Players.

But those records weren't as important by themselves as they were emerging from a militantly, determinedly black context that also produced Sly Stone's hit, the Temptations' "Papa Was a Rolling Stone," James Brown's "King Heroin" and "Down and Out in New York City," Gladys Knight's "Daddy Could Swear I Declare" and "Midnight Train to Georgia," the Curtis Mayfield numbers from Superfly, *the O'Jays "Back Stabbers" and "Love Train," Billy Paul's "Am I Black Enough for You," the Spinners' "Ghetto Child," Stories'*

"Brother Louie" (once again, the movement was not entirely segregated), War's "Slippin' Into Darkness" and "The World Is a Ghetto," or Stevie Wonder's "Superstition," "Higher Ground" and most monumentally, "Living for the City."

Not all of these songs were "progressive"—Bobby Womack's "Harry Hippie" was divisive and reactionary—and many of them used love metaphors that were only marginally "about" black life or issues. But merely speaking in a ghetto tongue was a breakthrough, and it is a long tradition that soul songwriters have written their most insightful and philosophical lines couched in the guise of romance. In this context, even Denise LaSalle's proto-feminist "Now Run and Tell That" must be counted—a better song and more earth-shaking than anything Helen Reddy ever did.

This was the context in which this piece was written for a long-gone British magazine. It was an inspiring time for me as a critic and as a listener.

Sometime last fall, John Percy Boyd, Mark Bethune and Michael Brown, a trio of black college students in Detroit, decided to put an end to that city's heroin trade. Bethune, the most politically radical of the three, gave his brother, a dope dealer, forty-eight hours to get out of town or be murdered. The brother left the next morning for the West Coast.

A few weeks later, Boyd, Bethune and Brown decided to escalate their activities. They had been breaking into shooting galleries and dope houses, destroying sets of works and the smack on hand, beating and threatening the dealers and fixers, using the cash they stole as a means of support. The next step was, maybe not so surprisingly, straight from the plot of *Shaft*. They decided to kidnap the wife and daughter of a well-known heroin supplier.

The plot immediately went awry. When Boyd, Bethune and Brown showed up the dealer himself was unexpectedly present. They saw his car in the drive and split. Tearing down the street, they were pulled over by members of Detroit's racist paramilitary squad, STRESS (Stop The Robberies—Enjoy Safe Streets).

A shoot-out resulted. Brown, Boyd and Bethune survived it. The two STRESS cops didn't. It was a dive from *Shaft* into *Superfly*.

The actions of this tragic/heroic trio had an inevitable conclusion. Ninety days later, Brown was in jail on multiple charges of murder (two other STRESS officers were killed, several more injured, in a series of clandestine battles). In late February, Bethune and Boyd were shot and killed in Atlanta.

The lives of Mark Bethune, John Percy Boyd and Michael Brown speak more eloquently than anything else about the tremendous impact that black movies and the music on their soundtracks are having on young black America. Even Motown, that most bourgeois of black institutions, is involved in its own fashion with a trio of blaxploitation (the trade term) films. And black movies have probably been more important musically than in any other way. "Shaft" was the supreme black hit of 1971, "Freddie's Dead" (from *Superfly*) the catchiest soul song of 1972. Marvin Gaye had a hit with "Trouble Man," from the motion picture of the same name (it flopped). Diana Ross didn't have a hit from the soundtrack of *Lady Sings the Blues*, but she has used her starring role to rejuvenate her career, raise her persona to a new level of mass acceptance. Even Taj Mahal, whose music is black but hardly soul, has made an appearance in and an excellent soundtrack record from *Sounder*.

Each of these movies embraces a black consciousness that was unacceptable to the soul music industry—with the exception of Nashville, the most conservative wing of the record business—even three years previously. This politically charged, socially conscious black music has erupted from a number of sources, each of them symbolized by events with devastating implications.

Motown kicked off the trend, with the 1970 Edwin Starr hit "War," significant both for its anti-Vietnam context and for the raw blackness of Starr's delivery. Compared to "War," Freda Payne's Holland-Dozier-Holland-produced "Bring the Boys Home" (a Top Twelve hit the next year) is subdued and prettified. And "Bring the Boys Home" is a great record. The news in both cases, however, was that the crossover-oriented, respectability-craving producers had decided that it was acceptable (or more likely, necessary) to come out against the war.

But it was with Sly Stone's *There's a Riot Goin' On*, released at Christmas 1971, that black political consciousness entered American pop. That consciousness had always been in Sly's music (just as it was expressed in a different way in Jimi Hendrix's music—check out "Machine Gun" from *Band of Gypsies*). But with the release of *Riot*, Sly brought these concerns into the center of his music, and as a result of that album's multimillion sales and multiple hit singles, pushed the issues forward for all black performers. With the coming to prominence of such music in America, that meant that angry, uncompromising black voices were a force in every automobile, if not home, in the land.

Greil Marcus called Sly's new music "Muzak with its finger on the trigger" and wrote: "Sly has taken the aesthetic of the group that sings like a band plays away from the context of celebration, which has seemed not only appropriate but necessary to it, and made it the means to a dramatization of events and moods that are bitter, mocking and scary. On a purely musical level, this is probably the greatest triumph of the new music, for nothing is more difficult than making the old form deliver new truths. The equality is still there: no one is a star."

Bitter, mocking and scary, indeed. Sly's breakthrough was felt all around but not with equal degrees of acceptance (despite the Top Ten singles). The white counterculture responded with all the racism that a decade of failed consciousness-raising hadn't stamped out. White kids may have danced to Sly's new music, but they weren't happy with it. They found it too . . . bitter, mocking, scary.

When bitterness erupts from black people, the white American liberal's attitude has always been the same: Sure, they have a right to be bitter—but not toward *me*. And never before has black music been so bitter, never so bitter or so brave as to deliberately mock and terrify (scare seems mild) white Americans. (In accidental ways, of course, much black culture has always mocked and scared whites, for reasons too numerous and perhaps obvious to detail here.) The complaints that ring in the ears of media critics—mostly white men, of course—epitomize the unconscious racism of the seventies. *Lady Sings the Blues* "distorts the life" of Billie Holiday; it was not the fault of those particular white men that she became an addict and ruined her career, her talent, her life. *Superfly* "glorifies drugs, decadence and violence"; never mind that it presents a remarkably imaginative response to a set of ugly social conditions imposed upon its protagonist, not sought out by him. Meanwhile, Fellini may glorify human abasement, Ken Russell distort more completely the life of Tchaikovsky, but they are celebrated as auteurs tinged with genius.

All black movies are trash, at least as far as conventional stereotyping is concerned. Even *Lady Sings the Blues*, with its big budget and costumed gloss, is as far from the art houses as *The Godfather*, farther probably. (*The Godfather* has Brando, *Lady* only Richard Pryor.) But there's something about black trash which is undeniably important and vital. What matters most is the music that's grown from these films. The two best examples—partly because they're so far apart—are Diana Ross's soundtrack album from *Lady Sings the Blues* and the one that Curtis Mayfield composed and performed for *Superfly.*

As a movie, *Lady* is better made and more important, though that isn't true of the music within the movie. The expert reaction (not mine) is that Diana Ross is a poor imitation of Billie Holiday, that she and Motown have turned Billie's life into an essay on the contemporary heroin problem and that the film, by doing this, has diminished the Holiday genius.

There's some truth to each of these charges, but they also miss the point. Certainly Diana Ross isn't Billie Holiday, but as a star, she's her equal. Could Billie Holiday have successfully conveyed the breathless naiveté of "Where Did Our Love Go?" What Holiday and Bessie Smith meant to music listeners of the twenties and thirties is surely just what Ross and Aretha Franklin mean to us now. Diana doesn't try to imitate Holiday (which any second-rate jazz singer could have done); she does Diana Ross versions of the Holiday hits. She doesn't try to do a movie that's *only* about Billie Holiday's life but tries to bring to our times the importance of Holiday's battles with dope and racist cultural values, systems jury-rigged against black performers ever cashing in on the jazz they created.

Lady Sings the Blues is another chapter in the Motown story, so it's big and bold and glamorous and not very much concerned with the details of Billie Holiday's life. To the extent that it refuses to be respectful, *Lady* is a rock and roll movie, more interested in the spirit of the subject than whether Artie Shaw and Harry James were the specific agents of Holiday's addiction. If Berry Gordy had Sly Stone's brass, he'd answer the cries of inaccuracy by asking what difference it made, as long as the villains were white.

What *Lady Sings the Blues* is really about is the relationship between heroin and racism—the ways in which racism makes addiction attractive, the ways in which it makes it necessary, the ways in which the structure of a racist society creates institutions that support the dealer while wreaking havoc with the junkie. Billie Holiday isn't important to Motown because she was the world's greatest jazz singer (Berry Gordy began his career as a jazz fan, but Motown has never recorded anything recognizable as jazz). She's important because her life and its sordid conclusion is an amalgam of everything that's wrong with the way that blacks are dealt with in America. Then and now. For all its faults, *Lady* sums up this history in the same way as the Temptations' "Papa Was a Rolling Stone." You can see (or hear) everything from Billie Holiday/Robert Johnson to Sly Stone/Berry Gordy in both or either.

If you thought that things were much improved for black people generally or for black artists particularly in midseventies America than in the gloomy days of the Depression, consider the case of Curtis Mayfield.

"Freddie's Dead" was the most mesmerizing tune of 1972, yet it didn't win a Grammy and it was not even nominated for an Academy Award. In fact the entire *Superfly* soundtrack was gerrymandered out of eligibility. There are no black people on the Academy Awards nominating committee. But at least in those precincts Mayfield may seem like too much of an upstart, since *Shaft* won last year. (Though to my ears, comparing *Shaft* to *Superfly* is like comparing "You're So Vain" to "My Generation.") The Grammy voters haven't that excuse: Mayfield has been making hits since the late fifties, as the leader of the Impressions and on his own. Was there something more influential honored in 1972? Certainly not Isaac Hayes' *Black Moses*, which won the male R&B vocal category. (We won't even consider that a black man—even today—could have had a shot at best pop vocal.)

Nevertheless, Curtis Mayfield's score for *Superfly* is the best example of the New Black Music in what may be looked back upon as the year of its ascendance. What competition Mayfield has, though! Stevie Wonder made two powerful albums, plus a crusher of a single in "Superstition"; Marvin Gaye's *What's Goin' On*, itself a landmark, stretched its popularity into the first half of the year before yielding to his self-descriptive *Trouble Man* near the end; the Temptations created their first really modern hit, the all-embracing "Papa Was a Rolling Stone"; Johnny Nash's synthetic reggae "I Can See Clearly Now"; Aretha's *Young, Gifted and Black* another kind of sensibility (less commercial) with a sense of roots that the Sly-derived strain for the most part lacks. Then there's Diana Ross, Mahal, the O'Jays, the Stylistics, the Detroit Emeralds, the Staple Singers and on and on, reverberating through all styles and shades of black music in a way that 1972's white rock could only envy.

What's we've got here is the forging of a new cycle in the black musical tradition, one that's as self-consciousness as white rock but that may be able to see itself with more perspective. Racism and heroin, bitter and scary—the themes have been sounded. But there's a final point to make.

The best popular culture continues to emerge from the conflict between aspiration and commercial success. If it's remarkable that Stevie Wonder and Marvin Gaye have overcome Motown's machine and found themselves artistically, it's also true that without the restrictions and tensions Motown forced upon them, they would not have been in a position to capitalize so completely on their license.

This need for structure and discipline is one reason so much good black music comes from movies—soundtracks are *supposed* to be unobtrusively evocative, so they demand to be fitted into commercial slots. But who has seen a movie of the last few years so thoroughly dominated by its score as *Superfly*? Or seen a great song rise from a picture as trashy as *Trouble Man*? For that matter, when's the last time anyone made a musical as vigorous and moving as *Lady Sings the Blues*? Motown went to Hollywood to learn the movie business, but it may end up teaching Hollywood how to revitalize its most treacly form, the musical.

Black music (black singers and musicians) can do a number of things at this juncture. Most likely, or most cynically, the music will splinter, its message becoming as garbled and uncommunicative as the majority of white rock after *Sgt. Pepper's* and *Blonde on Blonde*: forget about the immediacy and conciseness of singles in favor of bloated LPs, get involved with music at the expense of sound and song. The awful portent is Isaac Hayes. But we might get something like the new phenomenon we've hoped for out of it. Not the new Beatles, but perhaps a black Elvis, a development that could shake racism to its core.

In 1972 the political and musical vision of Sly Stone mated with the peculiar commercial needs of blaxploitation films and the result was an extraordinary richness. The problem for the white audience is to reconcile the vitality of that music and the bitterness of its theme—to find a point of action that isn't reactionary, to marry what they've seen to what they've heard. The paternalism of the blues collector, the exoticism of the soul fan no longer are suitable responses to black pop's maturity. While these songs indict racism more bitterly than ever before, they're also dominating white-oriented pop charts more than ever. It's an uneasy and exciting conjunction.

Let It Rock, 1973

A Dose of the Real Thing

Soul music is a manifestation of black culture, and the majority of its greatest practitioners have been black. However, it isn't a segregated situation. Whites have always had important roles in the music as writers, producers, record executives and from time to time even as

performers: think of Mitch Ryder, the Rascals, the Righteous Broth-
ers, Johnny Otis, Boy George.

However, as soul music in its classic form began to be swept aside
by newer styles, it was picked up by exploitationists, the contemporary
equivalents of blackface minstrels. The difference between John Belu-
shi yowling "Soul Man" as a patronizing parody of Sam and Dave,
and Al Jolson yowling "Mammy" as a patronizing parody of some
ex-slave whose name we don't know isn't wide enough to spit through.
The difference is that Jolson was sentimental and old-fashioned, while
Belushi was hip and up-to-date. Neither man meant to be racist, I'm
sure. Both men were. But not because they "plagiarized" black styles
—it was the manner in which they used those styles that condemns
them. That doesn't mean that Boy George could ever hope to be
Smokey Robinson's equal, only that they offer different degrees of the
same pleasure. The difference between Culture Club and the Blues
Brothers is as dramatic as the difference between an affectionate
glance and a condescending smirk.

Anyone who thinks that the great guitarists of the sixties were all British
deserves to be locked in a closet and forced to listen to a tape loop of Sam
and Dave's "Soul Man" for a while—not for punishment, but for education. On it, there's a guitar solo by Steve Cropper in which he manages
to imply just about everything worthwhile that Eric Clapton, Jeff Beck and
Pete Townshend had to say. Not technically, emotionally—and that's the
point. In one of the most exciting records of its era, Cropper's solo is clearly
the apex—and the lick he plays throughout the verses is just as hot.

The shrewdest thing the Blues Brothers have done is hire Cropper and
his former Booker T. and the MGs sidekick, bassist Duck Dunn. Cropper
plays the same lick and the same solo on the Brothers' hit version of "Soul
Man," and while Dunn must miss his partner, the late great drummer Al
Jackson, he still gives the rhythm bed whatever solidity it has. Without
those two players, John Belushi and Danny Aykroyd might just as well have
traded in their sharkskins for catsup-spattered togas.

In almost everything that's been written about the Blues Brothers, the
presence of Cropper and Dunn has been regarded as either quaint or
authenticating. That is, hiring members of the great Memphis session
band was either an affectation on the part of Belushi and Aykroyd—like
Johnny Winter performing with Muddy Waters or Maria Muldaur building a backup group around Benny Carter—or proof of the Blues Brothers'
unquestionable sincerity. No one has suggested that the only thing keeping

the Blues Brothers from slopping over into awesomely racist parody is the participation of these Stax masters, which—from the point of view of this crotchety old bastard—seems a lot closer to the truth.

But then, these days rock and roll is a funny game. You can hardly get up in the morning without stumbling over an anti-disco diatribe that heaps scorn upon the new dance music for pushing "classic" R&B and soul music off the charts. Which is curious because, with few exceptions, most of the writers and disc jockeys doing the complaining never bothered to write about soul or play R&B records when they were the dominant style of black popular music. When Motown was living up to its claims as the Sound of Young America, when Stax was the most exciting record company in the country, white record reviewers were discovering Chicago blues while FM radio stations were slipping the occasional track from *Otis Redding Live in Europe* in amongst the British "blues" bands and thinking they had the job done. That is, white rock was about ten years behind black trends, a typical situation.

Tens of thousands of words have been written about the artistry of second-level white rock bands like the Kinks and the Doors for every sentence devoted to such soul artists of the first order as Marvin Gaye, James Brown or . . . Sam and Dave, for that matter. (And to carry the point another step in that direction, the proportion is about the same for those blue-eyed soulsters, such as the Righteous Brothers and the Rascals, who rank at more or less the same level as the Kinks and the Doors.) This might just reflect what kind of overeducated white kid becomes a rock critic, but it sure don't say much for their taste.

The point was brought home dramatically a couple of weeks ago when Sam and Dave snuck into New York for a one-nighter at the Bottom Line. It was a Sunday night show, but no one even knew it was booked until Thursday. Still, since there wasn't another name act in town that weekend, I figured all the rockers would come out for their annual dose of the real thing.

Wrong. Keith Richards showed up and so did one other critic. There wasn't any buzz about celebrities at the earlier show, so I presume the late one was typically star studded. It's not like tickets weren't available—the house was maybe two-thirds full. That's not bad for a black act without a record company (and therefore with a bare minimum of advertising) playing a white club.

It's arguable that those who weren't there missed very little. The band wasn't exactly the Mar-Keys, and in soul show style, they "warmed up" the crowd for half an hour with listless Ohio Players style funk, loud, turgid and witless—*that* was reminiscent of the old days, though not in the way that George Thorogood or Southside Johnny intends. Sam and Dave sang only a half dozen songs when they did come onstage, and since the band knew about as much about playing R&B licks as Emerson, Lake and Palmer do, not even "Soul Man" stood much chance. It was pretty shabby considering the days when Sam and Dave were up there with James Brown, Jackie Wilson and Otis Redding. It was shabbier still when you consider that this was the best band that these pioneers, on whose back somebody else is riding in the bad old tradition of blackface minstrelsy, could afford.

But at the end of the set, the ever-reclusive Dave Prater made up for all the trivia and heartache. Sam Moore set up "When Something Is Wrong with My Baby," and though you missed Cropper's guitar and Isaac Hayes' beautiful piano, Prater took it over, singing the song like a man who's in desperate conversation with himself, over the state not only of his love life but of his very soul itself.

On the record of "When Something Is Wrong," the band challenges Dave; he has to shout to make himself heard over the horns. Sam endorses his sentiments with "sho' nuff" and "unh-*huh*!"

But at the Bottom Line, Dave just sang the song and no one could touch him. I'll tell you what: It was better than going to church. Sometime Belushi and Aykroyd ought to pay back their debt to Sam and Dave by letting them do it this way, just one time, on *Saturday Night Live.* Then the Blues Brothers should try to follow these men, and we'll see who's got the meat and who's just faking the motion.

Rolling Stone, 1979

Scoring Blind

Throughout the seventies, Stevie Wonder was the most prolific and inspiring artist black music produced. He mastered any number of forms—disco, reggae, funk, white rock. He pioneered the use of syn-

*thesizers, one-man production, drum machines and other techniques
and devices too diverse and arcane to list comfortably. He is perhaps
the most prolific great writer in pop. By 1976 he was so dominant that
Paul Simon, accepting a Grammy, made a point of thanking Wonder
"for not releasing an album this year."*

*As any great artist would, Wonder eventually went his own way,
operating against the grain of the market, while his production (at
least that portion of it released) dwindled through the early eighties.
A part of the reason might have been the lukewarm, sometimes hostile
response given* Journey Through the Secret Life of Plants, *the album
under discussion here. The project was founded in such a web of
naiveté and inexplicably convoluted ambition that it's small wonder
that its point was missed. But I'm a fan and inclined to be generous.
I can say, however, that listening to the album recently, I find it holds
up much better than other, more highly praised work from the same
time. The dilemma Stevie faced was getting people to listen. He didn't
succeed, and the failure (which was an extra-musical one) has colored
what little he's done since. As it happens, until 1984 that didn't quite
amount to a full album of new material, just the few new songs included in the 1982 anthology,* Stevie Wonder's Original Musiquar-
ium. *Stevie reappeared with another soundtrack, from* The Woman
in Red, *with the monstrous, if bathetic, hit "I Just Called to Say I
Love You." Whatever its limitations, though, Stevie Wonder remains
one of the two or three greatest popular musicians of our time.*

In the early sixties, every town had its weekend dance party on TV—a
chance to see local DJs whose voices were often the most intimately
associated with rock and roll, to catch a few new songs or dance steps,
maybe watch a lip-synched performance by whoever happened to be passing through town. In Detroit, there were an abundance of such programs.
The best was *Swingin' Time,* done by Robin Seymour of WKNR, but
there was also *Club 1270,* on the ABC-owned-and-operated WXYZ.
Watching it, I had two near-apocalyptic experiences: hearing Little Eva's
"Locomotion" for the first time, and for the first time, seeing Little Stevie
Wonder, the "Twelve-Year-Old Genius of Soul."

They led Stevie out from the wings, a fragile-looking kid whose chro-
matic harmonica (one of the big jobs with the levers) looked half as long
as his whole body. His wraparound shades and close-cropped hair only
called more attention to his head, which jerked in tight circles, back and

forth, at random—common enough among blind people, but who knew that then? Still, even that strange gaze and his shambling gait, like a colt about to break and run, gave a sense that he might count cadences the rest of us couldn't imagine.

They sat Little Stevie on a stool, and he began to sing to a prerecorded backing track—only his voice and harmonica were live. But he didn't sing. He exhorted us, preached and pleaded. "Everybody say yeah," he'd shout and everybody said "Yeah!" "Clap your hands just a little bit louder! Clap your *hands* just a little bit *louder!*" No point in arguing with that, either.

Seeing child stars was nothing extraordinary in those years. But Little Stevie was one pre-adolescent who always seemed in command—if not of his career, at least of the music he did sing. Sure, part of what was beguiling about him was that he was a freak, in the great tradition of blind musical genius, but that freakiness meant something only because his talent was quite literally awesome—as was his ambition. This was not so much a little blind black kid, then, as a purely musical being, by which I mean a lot more than just a kid who loved to play.

And that was scary, especially if *you* were twelve at the time, too. I was, and there's very little I recall from that time so clearly as that Saturday afternoon show: the very chair in which I sat remains an accessible memory every time I hear "Fingertips Pt. 2" or the other song Stevie sang that day, "Contract on Love." Mostly it stays with me because it was frightening. I'd heard lots of secularized gospel ecstasy before—the radio was full of it, from the Drifters on down—but this was something else. When he was a kid, Stevie Wonder had a way of strangling certain syllables, aspirating them. The result was a sound halfway between a grunt and a snort (it's the way he sings the word "sign" in "Contract on Love"). It made him sound as if he were about to explode, as if all the mucous chambers in his body would open and overflow—splat! That's how hard he pushed, trying (I suppose, now that I'm too mature to be so graphically fearful) to reach music he could imagine but not yet express.

This memory remains fresh after seventeen years mostly because Stevie has changed so little. He's grown a lot, but at heart he remains as innocent as that prepubescent on the screen, still willing to try anything, no matter how crude (or sophisticated) to make his point. Which makes his new album, *Journey Through the Secret Life of Plants* (Tamla) about the strangest pop music I've ever encountered. Wonder was perfect for this project, for he is such a mystical pantheist that he will take the concept to its outer limit—almost every one of his vocals here is sung from the point of view of the plants themselves: "You need us to live / But we don't

need you," he says in "Race Babbling," which is pretty self-effacing coming from a human.

Stevie has never used his voice as anything but another instrumental
option; likely as not, when he wants to sound personal, he plays the
harmonica—as he often does on *Plants*. This gives a lot of people the idea
that he's incoherent: words, especially lyrics, aren't much more than syllables for him. Like any blind person, he doesn't see things our way, and
lyrics need only make musical sense to satisfy him. After all, a line like "But
waiting are they the day they once let slip away" (from "Send One Your
Love") sure doesn't make any other kind of sense. But Wonder communi-
cates almost entirely through evocation of mood. A song like "Living for
the City," from *Innervisions*, would explain itself even without lyrics—
very rare in pop music.

This doesn't make the more quixotic portions of *Plants* any less naive.
In part, at least for myself and other white listeners, that's a racial and
cultural problem, the same kind of thing we confront each time a black
act introduces itself by mentioning its astrological signs. Wonder is first
and foremost a pantheist; but he's also an extremely self-conscious black
artist, which is why this album's major statement, "A Seed's a Star's a
Seed," first pops up as "Kesse Ye Lolo De Ye," which is the same message
translated into an African language, Baramba, and rearranged into a
modified high-life format.

But Wonder refuses to see himself as just a black American composer/
performer; his limitless ambition demands more. While it might alienate
George Clinton's militant funk army that anyone (much less a black artist
of the highest caliber) could conceive of such a thing, *The Secret Life of
Plants* is purposely nonfunky. Or so I suspect. Wonder has already established himself as a great pop and soul vocalist (his 1968 hit, "For Once
in My Life," is nothing less than Frank Sinatra with soul) and a major
instrumentalist as harmonica player, drummer and synthesizer master, not
to mention his formidable compositional skills. Over his last few albums,
he's consistently reached for more in each area, a trend that continues on
Plants, where he plays about 80 percent of the music himself—only the
guitars and backing vocals are farmed out with any regularity.

What else could he want? Well, it's always struck me that the most
significant public statement of Stevie's career passed virtually unnoticed:
his dedication of his 1974 Grammys to the late Duke Ellington. Which
is to say that Wonder would ultimately like to be regarded as a major
American composer, and is now beginning to reach out to the European
conservatory tradition—into which Ellington, almost alone among twen-
tieth-century American pop composers, can be fitted. Judged on that scale,

Journey Through the Secret Life of Plants is admittedly a fairly feeble effort —but it's probably as much as Ellington might have done when he was nearing thirty.

Still, the best songs here, or at least the most successful ones, are ballads, and ballads more committed to romanticism than anything any of Wonder's contemporaries (except, I suppose, Barry Manilow) is doing. Compared to Stevie, Teddy Pendergrass is just a stud—the bottom line is that Stevie Wonder's innocence and his intensity stem from a real conviction that love is the answer to most questions of consequence. And that's where his songs simply get too gooey for most listeners: about the time that the cloying "Black Orchid" pops up on side three.

Side three is also the meat of *Plants*, containing as it does not only "Black Orchid," contextually an ultimate affirmation of romanticism, but also the hit single "Send One Your Love," the Baramba/high-life "Kesse Ye Lolo De Ye" and the intriguingly ethereal "Come Back as a Flower," expressing what seems to be a sincere desire to be reincarnated amongst flora rather than fauna. (I know that's a preposterous premise for a song, but he makes it work, just as he makes all of his plant-perspective songs work.)

Among such company, the brief instrumental, "Ecclesiastes," is almost lost. But "Ecclesiastes" stands on its own, because it's the best movie music on the album, manipulating a siren-like vocal, death-march organ, menacing electric guitars and rumbling drums into the best approximation I've ever heard of Ennio Morricone's scores for Sergio Leone's spaghetti Westerns. And Morricone's soundtracks are the best of the past couple of decades—John Williams and John Barry get the ink, but it's this middle-aged Italian who's done the best work in his field, creating the only soundtrack recordings of our era that effectively stand on their own. It's no accident that "Ecclesiastes" sounds as if it could have been lifted whole from *Once Upon a Time in the West* or *The Good, the Bad and the Ugly*. Like any innocent young man, Stevie Wonder does his homework.

But that brings us to the final weird thing about *Plants*, which is that it's a soundtrack album at all. There are moments, particularly in the programmatic but elusive incidental instrumentals, when one longs to see the footage that inspired them. Because if it isn't great black pop and if it isn't funky, *Journey Through the Secret Life of Plants* is at least a far more fully realized score than overinflated garbage like Francis and Carmine Coppola's *Apocalypse Now*.

The trick is that Stevie Wonder has never seen—will never see—*The Secret Life of Plants*. That he accepted a scoring assignment at all ought to earn him high marks for audacity—it ought to inspire a measure of the same awe in which we hold the symphonies Beethoven wrote while he was deaf. Apparently Stevie based his impressionistic instrumentals on descriptions whispered into his ears over headphones, and upon the film's extensive narration. And that's an all but unfathomable way to work—as unfathomable in its way as blindness itself, or as the street scenes in "Living in the City" must be to people who've never entered the ghetto.

When *Innervisions,* which contains "Living in the City," was released in 1973, Wonder's press aides blindfolded a busload of media personages, put them on a bus and took them by a circuitous route to a recording studio for a listening session. The experience couldn't have lasted more than a couple of hours, but it made its point. I was there that day, and I spent the afternoon so befuddled that I never did realize that the sighted person leading me around was Stevie's friend Patti Smith, whom I'd known well for several years.

For Stevie Wonder, perhaps his blindness is a kind of gift—one he tried to share that afternoon. In some sense, he seems to believe that the sighted are disadvantaged, because they simply don't hear—can't *listen*—with his highly developed acuity. If a large part of what you do for a living is listen to music and then try to translate it into a visually oriented language such as English, an afternoon like the *Innervision* listening session isn't just frustrating and disorienting but also humbling and threatening.

This comment is appropriate to *Journey Through the Secret Life of Plants* because it's a record that, so far at least, has been treated cavalierly, as a weird aberration, "just" a soundtrack, a symptom of Stevie's self-indulgence. But for the blind, *all* music is soundtrack music—which is to say, that it all attempts to describe an unseen visual. It might very well be that presenting this record to us without the film in release is the perfect way to establish its context.

Surely this isn't the year's most successful album; its flaws leap out and grab you, almost obscuring its beauty. But *Journey Through the Secret Life of Plants* is just as surely among the year's most worthwhile musical experiences (which satisfies the criterion Stevie Wonder establishes in his liner notes). What I've had to say here may be more or less than the truth about it—frankly, I got lost somewhere in its vastness. Like a lot of Stevie's best music, it probably won't come clear for a couple of years anyhow, when the trends catch up to it.

Boston Phoenix, 1980

Where There's Smoke

A tribute to my first and most enduring favorite. And on the other hand, a review that captures the watershed when the gains of disco and funk were incorporated and the way was opened for further changes —rap, hip-hop, a kind of neoclassical soul epitomized by "Cruisin' " and Warm Thoughts—*that I have enjoyed far more than the rather mechanical and instrumentally oriented hits of the mid and late seventies. In the eighties, that is,* soul *singing has been restored to its preeminence, even if the underlying beats are very different. And that suits me just fine.*

First loves die hard, if they ever do. So I'll always remember the first moment I heard Smokey Robinson's voice come over the radio, on a Sunday night in 1963, singing "You Really Got a Hold On Me" and making me understand that statement as a simple truth. I'll also never forget the afternoon I heard his return last winter while I was driving down Sunset Boulevard in a Cadillac. For me, Smokey Robinson has always been the perfect singer, my ideal. And with "Cruisin'," he simply reasserted his right to preeminence.

But "Cruisin'," for all its glory, promised to be little more than a marvelous one-shot hit. *Where There's Smoke*, the album from which it sprang, was hardly less erratic than the rest of his solo work. Robinson never adapted well to the changing trends of pop and soul—which isn't surprising, since few singers of his generation have.

So it's not really odd that Smokey Robinson couldn't cope with the permutation of soul music into disco, even though his greatest songs were always about love and dancing and their interrelationship amid a maze of masks and poses. Robinson's tunes were for dancing close, and to him love was a matter of romance before sexuality. For the man who sang "I Gotta Dance to Keep from Crying," the hedonistic revelries of Donna Summer must have seemed virtually sacrilegious. And as a result, his finest pre-"Cruisin' " solo material ("Virgin Man" from *Pure Smokey*, the wondrously slinky *A Quiet Storm*) was strangely out of synch, while his one semisuccessful funk foray (side one of *Smokey's Family Robinson*) was interesting mostly as the best showcase guitarist Marv Tarplin ever had.

Warm Thoughts is up-to-date proof that "Cruisin' " was anything but a fluke. The new LP is a watershed, a genuine creative breakthrough for Smokey Robinson as producer, writer, lyricist and singer. For the first time, his music has been modernized without being compromised. He's a mature artist now.

Most strikingly, Robinson—whose upper register is understandably a lot less scintillating than it was in his younger days—has become a much more adept vocalist. He wraps himself around the beat here rather than riding atop it, and explores phrasings that were dormant or only implicit in his youthful music. At last he can be both knowing and believable and the masks of his earlier work can be discarded.

This is a tremendous and necessary step forward, because what was touchingly ingenuous at twenty and superficially provocative at thirty would clearly be fraudulent at forty. But it was a little easier for Robinson to make such a move than it might have been for most of his peers, since he's always drawn as much inspiration from pop stylists like Johnny Mathis and Frank Sinatra as from the standard litany of R&B and gospel shouters and crooners.

The only other male Motown singer capable of this sort of transformation is Stevie Wonder. So perhaps it's more than coincidence that one of the key compositions on *Warm Thoughts* is "Melody Man," co-written by Wonder and Robinson. "Melody Man" is a hymn not just to a woman (Robinson's specialty) but also to a muse (Wonder's forte). In the end, it's a collaborative statement of identity, speaking directly about what Stevie Wonder and Smokey Robinson share: an awesomely naive faith in the redemptive power of love and music.

Wonder's influence is apparent throughout *Warm Thoughts*, and his glossy sense of pop detail affects all the arrangements. So it isn't unusual that "Heavy on Pride (Light on Love)"—the finest dance music that Robinson's written in years, with its brilliant merger of traditional riffing Motown strings and a big-footed disco bass drum—sounds like something left off Wonder's *Songs in the Key of Life*. Indeed, the only number here that conforms to Robinson's patented sixties soul standards ("I Second That Emotion," "The Tracks of My Tears") is "Let Me Be the Clock," which is considerably more modern, even in its use of extended lyric metaphor. The rest of the tunes are models of sophisticated contemporary pop.

The best of them do something more. They reestablish Smokey Robinson as a great love-song philosopher, one who's somehow managed to come to grips with adulthood. Though he believes no less firmly in the transcendent power of love than he did when he wrote "I'll Try Something New" and "Ooo Baby Baby," Robinson isn't afraid to admit to newfound realities. In "Wine, Women and Song" (a dialogue with his wife, Claudette, herself a former Miracle) a pop star's wife and her paramour—ironically, a fan of the husband—confess their frustrations and dissatisfactions. In his past work, Robinson regarded love as either pure joy or crushing degradation, which is exactly what made all his poses and masks necessary. Now he has found a livable middle ground and he hews to it, not only in "Wine, Women and Song" (in which the wife goes back to her husband and the fan accepts that choice) but everywhere: "Never mind wasting time talking about who did who wrong," he sings in "Heavy on Pride."

Having come through an era in which most of the major musical trends rejected the possibility of successful human relationships (punk did so explicitly, disco implicitly), Smokey Robinson nevertheless reasserts his conviction that personal contact is not only possible but *essential.* If "Heavy on Pride" takes its bows toward purposeless lust, if "Wine, Women and Song" acknowledges that even the strongest romantics sometimes stray, *Warm Thoughts'* other compositions reaffirm the singer's essential faith in men and women. "Into Each Rain Some Life Must Fall," as great a vocal performance as Robinson has ever given, underscores this faith over and over again, and "Let Me Be the Clock" makes it a major priority: "Let it begin because / Every moment we're apart / Is some good feeling wasted."

It's not accidental that both tunes reach back so far—the one through paraphrases of soul classics, blues standards and nursery rhymes; the other as a musical evocation of the artist's early hits. Listening to Robinson sing, nearly twenty years after he first opened my heart, I think of what Jean Renoir wrote of Charles Chaplin: "Chaplin takes note of the egotism and absurdity of the world and, like the early Christians, he meekly accepts it. It is an acceptance that softens the public heart . . ."

Smokey Robinson has done something similar with his music, and it's more than sufficient. If he's written only songs about love and dancing, they aren't silly songs. When Bob Dylan said that Robinson was America's greatest living poet, he was not talking about rhyme schemes and meter —but he knew what he was talking about.

The first time I heard *Warm Thoughts*, I got a lump in my throat. The tenderness with which Smokey Robinson sings just seemed so damned necessary—and so utterly forgotten. Now, weeks later, it's two o'clock on a Friday night. Motown is twenty, I'm thirty, Smokey is forty. He's still singing, I'm still believing. This not only seems right, it feels inevitable. I don't know about you, but he's still a miracle to me.

Rolling Stone, 1980

Soul on Ice

Once again a failure of prognostication—at least to a degree since,
as already noted, the soul vocal style has returned, though in other
guises. However, "Soul on Ice" is mostly a cautionary tale, centered
on that anomaly, the white lover of black music. Though I hate
segregation as much as the next guy, the spectacle of what my friend
Tony Heilbut terms "white blues boys" celebrating the always-out-of-
date can be maddening.

I try to take my own advice and obviously don't always succeed. It
hurts somewhat that the black styles on which I cut my teeth were
almost finished by the time that I became a critic. And yet in five years'
time, it would not surprise me if the early eighties period that has
produced Afrika Bambaataa, Prince Grandmaster Flash and a myriad
of rap and hip-hop hits is also regarded as a kind of Golden Age of
black pop. But the point remains to dig it now, when it's happening,
rather than retrospectively.

The best way of discovering what music a person truly cherishes, I've
always thought, is to turn them loose between midnight and dawn. In the
daylight you can tolerate almost anything, and after dinner a certain
conviviality is a necessity. But in the midnight hours, when the lights go
down and the air grows hazy, the treasures come out. One turns in those
moments to what's most sustaining, if only as a hedge against heading for
bed.

For me, that's always meant soul music of the bleakest variety. I'm liable
to put on the Miracles' *From the Beginning* most any time, but when it
gets late enough for the lingerers to head home, when only the hard core
is hanging in alone, nothing satisfies quite as much as James Carr purring
"Pouring Water on a Drowning Man" or Clarence Carter's hilarious and
hair-raising "Making Love (At the Dark End of the Street)," the great Sam
Cooke ballads or Bobby Bland's forlornly splendid "Lead Me On." Lately,
the number for me has been an obscure song from Otis Redding's *Soul
Ballads* album, called "Cigarettes and Coffee."

"Cigarettes and Coffee" is set in the midnight hours. "It's early in the
morning, about a quarter till three," Otis sings as the guitar of Steve
Cropper plays off the swelling BarKays horns. This is Redding inside out

—at least so far as most know him. He isn't despairing or pleading, but speaking as plainly as possible. He doesn't preach, he confesses. Nor is he raging against infidelity or dissatisfaction; he's celebrating a profound contentment. (The lyric develops into a marriage proposal.) All the while, Al Jackson keeps time with stately accents, popping the one and virtually smothering all the other beats. And in the end, Redding's vulnerability is so great that it makes me accept my own a little bit better.

No one makes records like that anymore, maybe because the world has changed enough to make such peace of mind even less imaginable than it was fifteen years ago when Otis recorded the song. For a long time, anyone who still held on to such music seemed anachronistic or felt very, very lonely (part of the purpose, I guess). But in the last few months, soul music has begun to blossom again: Wilson Pickett, James Brown, Solomon Burke, Sam and Dave, Rufus Thomas, Junior Walker and the All Stars, Percy Sledge, Carla Thomas, Martha Reeves and Clarence Carter have all made appearances at New York clubs, from the tiny ones to the huge Ritz Ballroom, from reasonably likely venues such as the Peppermint Lounge to the anomalous Lone Star Café, a country bar.

In Japan and England, there are already substantial soul revivals, spearheaded by an exquisite reissue program in Japan, and in the UK by a number of good, solid soul-style bands, notably Dexy's Midnight Runners, Nine Below Zero and Paul Jones' The Blues Band. If trends operate as they usually do, that should make the spring of '81 just the moment for soul to reclaim some mainstream American attention. Already Solid Smoke, the San Francisco revivalist label, has released an album of fifties and sixties tracks by the obscure but marvelous Sheppards, a Chicago harmony quartet, reissued James Brown's masterpiece, *Live and Lowdown at the Apollo, Volume 1* and reportedly, has plans afoot to put out some new sides by a revived version of the Falcons, the venerable Detroit group, whose reincarnation includes original members Eddie Floyd, Mack Rice (author of "Mustang Sally") and Joe Stubbs (brother of the Four Tops' Levi) and possibly featuring guest appearances by erstwhile Falcons Pickett and Johnny Taylor.

I've seen only a couple of the soul shows that have hit New York, one by Pickett at the Lone Star and another at the much larger Ritz, which featured Sledge, Carla Thomas and Clarence Carter. The Ritz show was poorly attended, although the four or five hundred patrons might well have been only a hundred or so fewer than those who packed the Lone Star for Pickett's two sets. Thomas turned in a rather pedestrian set, which came to life only at the very end, when she soared into "Gee Whiz," her first hit. Sledge, the headliner, had disastrous problems with the band and retired after singing but one full song—but that was a heartfelt "My Special Prayer," and revealed that he remains in full command of his spectacularly huge and orchestrally mellow voice. Carter, second-billed, stole the show like the rapscallion he is, cutting through the bulk of his hits, tossing off casually terrific guitar solos, singing professionally, if not nearly so passionately as he did on his great records. Carter is blind, and perhaps it helped that he didn't have to confront the spectacle of the hall's empty spaces—indeed, his wholehearted enthusiasm for the crowd, sparse as it was, struck me as a model of soul artifice, that special capacity such singers have for bringing emotional conviction to the most specious material, the most dubious circumstances. That artifice is soul's special glory.

Wilson Pickett was another story, but then, he always has been. Pickett never had much subtlety, but he's learned more than a few tricks over the years and despite the fact that his best hits are nearly a decade behind him, the Lone Star performance convinced me that he is a surer, more intelligent singer than he was during his commercial heyday. Backed by a powerhouse band, which rocked mercilessly and set up a devilish groove, Pickett matched his best records lick for lick, opening with "Don't Let the Green Grass Fool You" and running through "In the Midnight Hour," "Mustang Sally" and about eight bars of "Ninety-nine and a Half (Just Won't Do)." Pickett was all sweat and leather, Stagger Lee incarnate, and although the audience was curiously apathetic—or maybe intimidated— he didn't hold back anything. In fact the lukewarm response he received seemed to spur the Wicked One on, and he pulled out "Hey Jude" for the set's final song.

I've never liked Pickett's recording of the Beatles' chestnut, because it served as a showcase for the weaknesses of both Pickett and guitarist Duane Allman. But on this night, the song was simply unmatchable, hard, stinging lick after lick, body punches that finally loosened up the crowd enough to share some of Pickett's frenzied energy. In those moments, when he was chanting "Hey Jude" over and over, Pickett not only beat his own version of the song, he topped the original. For that night, at least, he *owned* all of his material, and it was hard to believe that anyone anywhere was singing any better. Pickett's show was a minor revelation, a lesson to anyone who takes seriously the idea that youth is a prerequisite for musical intensity. He must be past forty by now, and it was hard to believe that Pickett had ever been more ferocious on any stage.

At first I thought that this ferocity explained the temerity of the audience. At his best, Pickett is a show business version of the urban black man most whites (and whites were 90 percent of the crowd) have been brought up to fear above all other things. (That makes Wilson Pickett the true counterpart of Jerry Lee Lewis, who represents to northerners all that they've been raised to fear about the redneck South.)

Yet Pickett was downright cordial (for Pickett) that night, at least until he became frustrated with the lack of feedback. Maybe, it later occurred to me, such audiences have simply forgotten, if they ever knew, what it means to respond to such audience/performer give and take. What Pickett wanted was something more than the idle bottom shaking and random huzzahs of a rock band's show—he wanted participation in the spirit of the moment and he wanted collective testimony to the power and presence of that spirit (like the gospel-trained singer he is).

But then, clearly that audience at the Lone Star wasn't particularly interested in saluting the spirit. At first I couldn't figure this out. Any experience of Pickett's show was colored, for me, by the fact that soul really didn't need to be revived, having never strayed far from my turntable anyway. Yet for most of the soul revival crowd, this music is not an emotional necessity—it's just a convenience. Like most revivals, soul's resurgence is more concerned with form than feeling. It's not insignificant that of all the performers I saw, only Clarence Carter offered any new or unfamiliar material. (And Carter's new tune was a song he's just recorded as a 45, and one that sounds like an outtake from his sixties sessions.) And I suspect that most of the audience would have been terribly uncomfortable if they'd been confronted with anything less predictable. You can't ignore the composition of those crowds, loaded as they are with just those whites who are most alienated from contemporary black pop. That is, the sort of music fan who still insists that disco sucks and has never made peace with post-Sly funk. The kind whose older brother once snubbed soul music in favor of the more "authentic" Chicago and Delta blues.

For just such reasons, pop music revivals are always untrustworthy. The revivalist cult invariably looks for reiterations of old-fashioned moves without much regard for old-fashioned motivation. Usually, this is the product of looking for an excuse not to deal with something contemporary and discomforting. Perhaps white hipsters are perennially destined to be wrapped up in black styles one or two convolutions behind current black taste, to forever be reviving Mississippi John Hurt just as Marvin Gaye and Eddie Floyd are hitting their stride, or rediscovering James Brown just when Bernard Edwards and Nile Rodgers are making dance rhythms and post-psychedelic funk fascinating once again. Unless the soul revival can create a universe wherein Smokey Robinson can coexist with Junie Morrison, it represents a failure of nerve and stands as an insult to the genuine creativity of both men.

If Otis Redding, by far the greatest soul singer, were still alive, he would sing "Try a Little Tenderness" only to deepen the meaning of his contemporary music. I'd also be willing to bet most of the soul revival fans wouldn't have stayed with him this long in any event. Ask Marvin Gaye. That doesn't mean I'd rather listen to the new Phillipe Wynne album than to Wilson Pickett's "634-5789" or that a lot of what passes for avant-garde in funk doesn't strike me as recycling the worst tendencies of acid rock. But somehow it seems valuable to struggle with what I don't like about those styles, to keep listening until I'm sure that I'm rejecting for the right reasons or can reach an understanding and an acceptance of what really is going on. Just dredging up the past won't do. When Wilson Pickett transformed "Hey Jude" that night, it was the only song he sang that *wasn't* part of the soul revival.

Musician, 1980

The Return of Mr. Dynamite (And Other Great Hits)

This is the most recently written piece in Fortunate Son. *It concerns some of the oldest music discussed here. Those two statements are probably a framework for the entire project, or so it seems now that it's almost completed.*

Listening to James Brown in the midsixties, besides marveling at his ragged-but-right vocals and his unbelievable sense of beat, makes me feel closer than I'd have expected to the funk stylizations represented by George Clinton's Parliament and Funkadelic. I've never liked that music much—it incorporates too much of what is meretricious in white rock and never came up with a singer to please me— but its inevitability is more striking when compared with the music on I Got You (I Feel Good) *and the other Brown albums discussed here. The limitation is mine, but the amplification those records offer is available to everybody.*

History does not wait for the idlers.
—Peter Kropotkin

In mid-January 1984, James Brown and his companions arrived at the Hollywood Palladium for an appearance on a network rock special, his first prime-time exposure in years. On the afternoon of the taping, Brown was looking blowsy and old. The effect was as disheartening as seeing Elizabeth Taylor turn corpulent—exaggerated, that is, by contrast with youthful beauty.

Still, there stood James Brown, a man with as much claim as anyone since the rise of rock to being a musical visionary: Godfather of Soul, Founder of Funk, Dance Master to a couple of generations. Watching him, one could not but hope for one last hour of grace, a final surge of his old spirit.

Clearly the chances of such a miracle were slim. In his tight blue shirt and slacks, Brown looked paunchy; his unruly hair and the age lines in his face made him seem tired. His rehearsal verged on self-parody—when he executed a kneedrop, he held on to the mike stand to brace himself and cushion the impact. Nevertheless he exhorted the crowd, insisting that the staff and stagehands pay him full attention. Through it all, Brown seemed more pathetically self-indulgent than fired up, more egomaniac than master showman.

But at the show that night, with a real audience and the cameras grinding—that is, with his career on the line—he was once again James Brown. He strutted out unbelievably bold, bobbing and weaving like the former boxer that he is, fancystepping through teenage break dancers who had no idea that they were performing routines this man suggested in stage shows done twenty years ago (and more). James Brown held the stage for perhaps twenty long minutes, playing snatches of one hit and another. He made a monarch's exit, not swathed in capes, but swaggering.

Always and forever, you begin with James Brown onstage, because that's where he redefined what was possible "in concert." Not that his shows were simple concerts, combining as they did elements of dance and dramaturgy, griot and Christian liturgy, sermonizing and romancing. It's hard to think of a well-known stage performer in any area of American music who doesn't owe a ton to the moves Brown developed.

James Brown on record is another story. In the wake of the funk revolution that he pioneered, Brown is accepted as a great bandleader whose sense of rhythm and ability to create (or just think up) licks is unparalleled. But Brown's talents as singer and songwriter are disre-

garded. As a result, one may almost be persuaded that his revolutionary music sprang full-blown from an inchoate, inarticulate primitivist
impulse.

Yet Brown's breakthrough was anything but accidental or improvised.
On the contrary, the one chord, choke rhythm sound he developed in the
midsixties was the logical product of the previous decade's recording and
performances, in which he toyed with blues, R&B, pop, gospel and
jazz ideas, tossing them up in the air and letting the pieces fall to the
ground, then picking through the rubble in search of a pattern that
could liberate him from the contradictory push and pull of R&B conventions.

The development of black music since World War II is exemplified by
its first crucial transitions: from the lush, cosmopolitan pop balladry of Nat
"King" Cole to the raw, basic gospel fervor of Ray Charles, and similarly,
from the sophisticated pop harmonies of Sonny Til and the Orioles to the
progressively more frantic expostulations of Clyde McPhatter and his
successors.

The tension between such styles wasn't only an overall pattern of black
pop (which it remains to this day: consider the career trajectories of Donna
Summer, Michael Jackson and George Clinton). That tension also transformed individual careers. McPhatter snapped R&B harmony loose from
pop restrictions, but in less than a decade he was singing nightclub ballads
himself. Charles pulled off some of the most exciting small combo recordings ever made, but within a few years he was cutting albums full of flaccid
big-band orchestrations.

James Brown became King of Soul by mastering that set of contradictions. Out of his dialectical resolution arose seventies funk and disco and
all of today's pop rhythm music. But for Brown in, say, 1964, the task was
simply to invent a single system that encompassed the energy of black
theaters like the Apollo and the polish of upscale white nightclubs like the
Copa. He didn't want to abandon one for the other, as McPhatter, Sam
Cooke and others had done; he wanted to junk the process that forced a
performer into such false choices in the first place.

The evidence of Brown's ambition, the foraging and tinkering that
resulted in his creative triumph can be found in the eight King Records
albums recently reissued by French Polydor. These albums include a hefty
slice of everything that Brown recorded between 1962 and 1967: *Mr.
Dynamite* (1962) was issued only a few months before his live masterpiece,
Live at the Apollo (missing from this batch but still available as a reissue
on Solid Smoke); *Prisoner of Love* (1963), *The Unbeatable James Brown*

and *Please Please Please* (both 1964) collect an assortment of tunes that include contemporary hits, fifties R&B misses, rummagings through jump blues and forties ballads and feints into the unknown; *Papa's Got a Brand New Bag* (1965), *I Got You (I Feel Good)* (1966), *Soul Brother #1* (1966) and *Cold Sweat* (1967) appear as if from the other side of a chasm, Brown's revolution exemplified.

The Polydor series isn't a complete summary of Brown's output in these years, but it's a more than adequate one. Brown was always a singles-oriented performer, as soul artists had to be, but more than most he used his recording time wisely, filling out his LPs with tributes to old heroes, instrumentals that have surprising staying power and schematics for future hits. The Polydor reissues include a great deal of material (the whole *Please Please Please* album, it would seem) that was recorded in the fifties and saw the light of day on LP only because King needed to release something while contesting Brown's move to Smash in 1964–65. But together with the omissions, this backtracking makes it impossible to point out a clear, linear progression in which the man and the group who cut "Please Please Please," "Think" and "O Baby Don't You Weep" arrived at "Cold Sweat," "Money Won't Change You" and "I Can't Stand Myself." But then, since pop radio listeners were also deprived of hearing "I'll Go Crazy" (which didn't even make "Bubbling Under the Top Hundred") as a bridge, it served you right to suffer, as the saying goes.

And then again, the fact that there was a progression doesn't mean that there was a clear and linear one anyhow—unless of course you believe that a sequence of R&B hits that goes from "Think" through "Prisoner of Love" and "Mashed Potatoes USA" to "Out of Sight" and "Papa's Got a Brand New Bag" has the same symmetry as one which arrives at "The Long and Winding Road" after creating "Yesterday" and "Michelle." James Brown was always an anomaly, never relied upon any logic other than his own.

This completely self-referential system is today—now that it no longer generates gold and platinum discs (for Brown)—commonly cited as evidence of his rampant megalomania. Maybe it is. But let's consider "Prisoner of Love," his first pop Top Twenty hit in 1963.

"Prisoner of Love" began life as a Russ Columbo ballad—Columbo was a dance band leader of the thirties, one of Bing Crosby's major, if mediocre, competitors. It was Crosby and the Ink Spots who first charted the song, in 1946. This is a song as jive and banal as anything Clyde McPhatter was ever swindled with by his white handlers at Mercury, more bathetic than most of what Columbia asked Aretha to sing, not any better than what Hugo and Luigi forced Sam Cooke to clean from his plate.

Yet in James Brown's hands, this tripe is not just redeemed, it is elevated, made radiant and sent soaring. From it, Brown fashioned a definitive soul ballad performance and he did it the hard way, not by paring the arrangement down to its guts (à la Percy Sledge's "When a Man Loves a Woman") but by introducing it with distant tympani thunder and a riffing violin section then setting his raggedy voice in the midst of a pool of echo. Taken together, those elements make the arrangement an absolutely perfect parody of nothing other than a Johnny Mathis pop tune. And Brown has the audacity to accentuate the resemblance by singing the first lines at the top of his skimpy range.

That is, in order to manufacture his first pop hit, James Brown first created an almost obscene parody of the worst hokum he could find, then completely personalized it. He accomplished this with a bass line that's the soul of doom, a chorus that screams white-bread harmonies in his ears and a lead vocal that defines control. It's one long crescendo, starting as a calm recitation of the facts and ending as a frantic, pained shriek that disfigures voice and transfigures song. "I'm just a prisoner," Brown proclaims— refusing to complete the title phrase, thus tightening the tension a further notch. "Don't let me be a prisoner."

Aside from Jerry Lee Lewis, there isn't another singer in the past forty years with both the chops and the imagination to pull off that kind of deconstructive tour de force, much less do it and make the result into a pop hit. And that's why James Brown, who had maybe the tenth best voice in soul music, was maybe the twelfth best writer and had the worst record label imaginable was nevertheless crowned King of Soul. Put the dude in a corner and he battles his way out—with grace.

It would be nice to say that all of the King albums are filled with such revelations. They aren't. On the other hand, if there's a single bad performance, or even the kind of sloppy one that mars his recent LPs, I've yet to locate it. The cliché is that soul singers didn't make good albums, but that's utterly exploded here.

Of the four pre-1965 albums in the French Polydor reissue series, the best by far are *Prisoner of Love*, for its diversity, and *Please Please Please*, for its incredible resurgence of jump blues drive. Cohesive as they are, these albums work because Brown labored over each of his singles, A side and B side: vanity has its advantages, and one is an awareness (or at least a suspicion) that posterity might pay attention. The records Brown made after his return to King in 1965 cohere for another reason: he planned them that way.

Before he could achieve his greatest work, James Brown, like all mythic figures, had to fight a battle. Before he could declare his independence from musical conventionality, he had to win his freedom from the restrictive conventions of the music business. Or at least he had to create a space within that business that had the appearance of freedom.

Of all the cheapskate, small-time record company owners in America, King's Syd Nathan may have been the meanest, the stingiest, the least respectful of the talent with which he dealt. (At least in lore, his only real competitor for any of these titles was Savoy's Herman Lubinsky.)

Nathan formed King and its subsidiaries, Starday, Federal and DeLuxe, in Cincinnati in 1945. He recorded the most diverse assortment of music of any independent label entrepreneur, everybody from Wynonie Harris, Bill Doggett and Tiny Bradshaw to the Stanley Brothers, Cowboy Copas and Moon Mullican. Even before Brown arrived, King and Federal had recorded two of his biggest influences, the Five Royales and Little Willie John.

That Nathan drove cruel bargains can perhaps be confirmed by this: When James Brown, with the encouragement of agent Ben Bart, decided to abrogate his King contract in 1964, a portion of his case rested upon the 14th Amendment, prohibiting slavery. And that is the portion of the suit that the Supreme Court upheld.

Meantime, Brown had signed with Smash, a subsidiary of Mercury, which had specialized in white cover versions of R&B hits since the fifties. Mercury had gotten away with its covers because it had clout in the white market, and that's what Brown was seeking. He'd had some pop success at King—a Top Twenty single, a No. 2 album—but he'd been unable to sustain it. At Smash, he had only one Top Forty hit, "Out of Sight," but he got exposure in the white media that was simply impossible to find at King. And he also was given more creative latitude than King's cantankerous Nathan ever granted. (Nathan had rejected several Brown proposals, and was so gunshy about making a live album that Brown finally paid for the Apollo recording himself.)

For all his frustrations, Brown returned willingly to Nathan's shop once he'd proved his point. (He continued to make instrumental albums for Smash.) Back at King, Brown had full autonomy, partly because he was just about the only hitmaker the label had left. The result was the amazing series of records that began with "Papa's Got a Brand New Bag" in 1965.

That hit set off a string that ran through 1971's "Soul Power," during which Brown scored twenty-seven Top Ten R&B singles, hit the LP chart Top Forty eight times and made six singles that hit the pop Top Ten: "Papa's Got a Brand New Bag," "I Got You (I Feel Good)," "It's a Man's Man's Man's World," "Cold Sweat," "I Got the Feelin' " and "Say It Loud—I'm Black and I'm Proud."

The simplest way to keep track of Brown's big hits in this period is the Solid Smoke anthology, *Can Your Heart Stand It* (1981). But you can't quite imagine how ubiquitous and dominant James Brown's presence was in those years from '65 to '71 unless you were listening to the radio—especially soul stations. Put it this way: His impact on his own was as great as the whole of Motown, and if urban contemporary operated the way AOR does, there might be all-day *James Brown A to Z* specials during Soultober in which only singles were played.

If Brown was Mr. Dynamite on soul radio, he was nothing less than the Atomic Bomb on Top Forty. With "Poppa's Got a Brand New Bag," he redefined what was possible in hit records. The choked, jangly guitar; the stunted horns blaring riffs cut off just as they started to soar, then blaring into illogical life in what passed for a chorus; the popping bass that pumped the tune into mania; the nasty, hoarse vocal and surreally sexual lyrics set "Poppa's Got a Brand New Bag" apart not only from everything else on the radio in 1965, but from anything else that had ever been there. In a way, this was exactly what the anti-rock forces of the fifties predicted: jungle rhythms come to life to terrorize mid-America. (I can still remember my father cursing the first time he heard it.) And succeeding records took Brown further: "Cold Sweat" is probably the *rudest* funk ever to hit the Top Ten to this day, since by then Brown had figured out how to work bass, drums, horns and guitars into a polyrhythmic series that was the only apt counterpoint to his raving vocal dementia.

To talk about this music as a defiance of pop and soul conventions is fatuous—it's accurate only to say that these songs are an abolition of every convention except the self-proclaimed (and often self-descriptive: "Ain't That a Groove" and its brethren *testify*) genius of James Brown.

Retrospectively, Brown's development of his new music can be seen in the tracks repeated from the pre–*Poppa's Got a Brand New Bag* albums. These are rarely the hits, just fragments of the basic James Brown repertoire, and in their later appearances they aren't revamped. Nevertheless, they fit perfectly alongside the recent stuff. For instance, the demolished Ray Brown jump blues "Love Don't Love Nobody" (which later formed the basis of "Licking Stick, Licking Stick") pops up on no less than three of these albums, and it makes even more sense on the later ones: What's anomalous if invigorating on *Mr. Dynamite* is of a piece with *I Got You (I Feel Good)*. Still, the essential tools—riffs, lines, patterns—are hardly altered.

The ballads hardly changed, and these pieces do sound dated—sometimes as with "I Stay in the Chapel Every Night," from *Poppa's Got a Brand New Bag*, deliberately so. The guitar riffs, often lifted whole from Lowman Pauling's work with the Five Royales, the horns sluicing the rhythm in waves that toss the beat back into the face of the melody, are the very R&B conventions that Stax and Motown shattered almost daily in those years. Yet Brown persisted in this old-fashioned ballad approach, even after "Poppa's Got a Brand New Bag."

Brown's great deconstructive soul ballad was of course the monumental, unforgettable, just plain bizarre "It's a Man's Man's Man's World" of 1966. This record parodies soul itself, which in a way means that it's Brown parodying Brown. (How self-consciously? The title derives from the comedy film *It's a Mad Mad Mad Mad World*.) The song takes the preaching, confessional style and stands it on its head.

Musically, "It's a Man's Man's Man's World" is nearly as skeletal as the dance numbers. It's composed of interwoven ostinato figures on bass, guitar, piano and strings, which overlap to approximate a melody. Like the Bob Dylan songs of the same era, the song has a chorus but no release: when Brown hits the title phrase, he again uses it to tighten the tension a notch, never to relax it. But rather than going over the top emotionally (which is the essence of soul cliché), he holds himself back. He sobs, catches himself, forces his voice back into the groove, keeps a handle on his emotions as he recites the lyrics. He emphasizes a word here and there —"Lost!"—but he never begins to rave and declaim in the grandiose fashion we've been led to expect. The result is a performance that redeems the camp macho of the lyric through an almost purely musical instinct.

Of all these albums, the greatest and most consistently fascinating is *Cold Sweat*. The title track, presented here in its extended version (parts one and two back to back, not chopped up as "Ain't That a Groove" was on *Soul Brother #1*), remains outrageous the hundredth time you hear it, incorporating both the dialogue between Brown and the band and part playing by bassist, drummer and tenor saxophonist that's among the most imaginative and free ever to top the charts. This is gutbucket, protean funk, so mind-expanding it might even deserve the epithet psychedelic.

"Cold Sweat" establishes James Brown's future—and soul's. James Brown uses the rest of the *Cold Sweat* album to establish the tradition in which he works and his dominance of it. It's hard to think of another singer, except maybe Presley or Lewis, who's had the sheer nerve to record such a breadth of material. Side one is filled out with R&B standards: "Fever," "Kansas City," "Stagger Lee," "Good Rockin' Tonight," each given definitively Brownian motion, readings that are so utterly personal they're almost possessive, though always reflecting a complete awareness of the original hits.

On side two, Brown stretches even further. This side rampages through the pop catalogue, fastening upon a pair of songs identified with Nat "King" Cole, "Mona Lisa" and "Nature Boy," a pair written by Johnny Mercer, "I Wanna Be Around" and "Come Rain or Come Shine" and most arrogantly, audaciously of all, George Gershwin's "I Loves You Porgy," before closing with an original instrumental, "Back Stabbin'," that evokes the wild R&B of side one and the futurism of "Cold Sweat" itself while thumbing its nose at the pop pieties Brown has just handled with great delicacy and surface respect.

There are undeniably rustic aspects to Brown's approach: his naive faith in the American Dream, reflected in his late sixties dalliances with LBJ and Nixon; his country mannerisms, including diction that is both extremely black and extremely Southern; the sheer grandiosity of his ambition and ego, which seem to completely obscure his sense of how his behavior really looks to outsiders. But anybody who hears him sing "I Loves You Porgy" will never doubt that James Brown knows exactly what he's doing when he steps to the microphone.

At first "Porgy" seems an ingenuous choice: Does he take this blackface caricature for a *compliment?* He does—it's a great song, and however removed from reality (what in Broadway history ain't?), deeply felt—and he doesn't: The title is listed as "I Loves You, Porgy," but Brown, whose diction can lapse into street patterns more easily than any other singer's, makes sure to sing the more grammatical "I love you," each and every time.

Brown removes the song from its old-fashioned, racist context and establishes it in his own milieu by surrounding the lyric with a Sinatra-style monologue. This Porgy is a street dude, trying to get his girl back. (Even though James gets the story so tangled up, he actually has Porgy singing about how much he loves himself.) Then he lets the music shine, caressing it gently and finishing with a homily that sums up his entire career: "And do you know what this means? This means that they are together, that they love each other. This means that you can go on and on and on. This means that *everything's all right."* And so he went, into uncharted territory: "I Can't Stand Myself," "Licking Stick, Licking Stick," "Say It Loud—I'm Black and I'm Proud," "Mother Popcorn" and its multi-part brethren, all the way through "Get Up, I Feel Like Being a Sex Machine" and "Super Bad."

But of course everything was not all right. And gradually James watched his fame and fortune slip away from him, went from a millionaire, set for life, with honor and respect from the White House on down, to a guy who is going to have to work joints the rest of his life just to make a living. The seeds of that downfall are also in these albums.

For in trying to balance his devotion to funk and the future with a respect for the past—all the past, not just a black or blackface fragment of it—Brown strayed into the most devastating minefield of American cultural contradiction. Artistry and vision had raised him above the station of his birth, but the particulars of his creations eventually clashed with the privilege and fame they brought him. It's no accident that "Say It Loud —I'm Black and I'm Proud" was a Top Ten hit—the timing was perfect —just as it is no accident that after it, James Brown never had another, despite four years of often brilliant recordings. And it's not surprising that at the end of those four years, he fell apart all at once, losing touch with his black listeners and flailing about in search of reasons why his white audience had abandoned him.

Brown wanted to pursue respectability offstage, while remaining uppity in his music. Since he was a millionaire and a success, given a solid quarter-hour in prime time, all by himself, on *Ed Sullivan,* the task looked easy. Performing at Nixon's Inaugural and his trip to Vietnam for LBJ and HHH lost him the loyalty of the hip white audience. And by making his aggressively black music, he guaranteed the loss of his place on the pop charts, for records like "Say It Loud—I'm Black and I'm Proud" sounded too threatening for more casual white listeners, who simply wanted some thoughtless stomp (which they were soon to have aplenty from other sources).

Having known crossover success, Brown was never again happy with more limited acclaim. Finally, frustrated, he became a house divided against itself, and did not stand any longer at the pinnacle, but dropped back and was half forgotten until contemporary funk made his indelible pioneering clear. And so he turns up now and again, a reissue here, a single there, at a special or an awards ceremony. Like his dear friend Elvis, he is overweight, misunderstood, probably to blame for much of his own disrepair—a shining example of what American music has wrought, a shameful reminder of how we neglect our greatest creators. These albums,

all eight of them, separately and together, illuminate a story that's instructive, inspiring and a little bit frightening: the tale of a man who went as
far as anyone in the race and ran into a brick wall. Pure dynamite, indeed.

Boston Phoenix, 1984

10

Love Is Strange

Introduction

I n the end, writing about music for me has been worthwhile not because it has provided a usual fulcrum for discussing so much of the rest of the world, but because I love the best of what I hear so deeply. And so this selection covers what have been and remain among my deepest passions. These are the performers and the songs to which I return in dead of night or when I wake up feeling groggy and need to hear something to stimulate me, make me feel like going back to bed to stay would be a grievous error. Which is another way of saying that in one way or another each of the performers and recordings discussed so avidly here has been a comrade. And so this unlikely volume reaches its conclusion, nestled—as all of us should be—in the arms of friends.

How Great Thou Art

The afternoon of August 15, 1977, I spent in an Indian restaurant in midtown Manhattan, with my colleague Robert Palmer. We were ostensibly discussing story ideas for Rolling Stone, *but somewhere between the mulligatawny and the thali, the conversation boiled down to Elvis. There was no particular reason for it—rock critics and musicians just talk about Elvis all the time. So we speculated about his condition for a while, and then headed back to work.*

I was sitting at my desk when an editorial assistant stuck her head in the doorway to say that word had come over the radio that Elvis

Presley was dead. In general, such rumors don't faze me—I had to be convinced that Keith Moon was dead, for instance. But there was no doubt in my mind that this one was for real.

For the next four days, I spent almost all my time locked up at home, with Elvis music playing constantly. A lot of tears were shed, not so much because Presley's death was a tragedy—his life was the tragedy—as because it was so difficult to figure out just what it all meant. A certain slice of meaning revealed itself to me right away. That night, on national television, speaking in a blur and fighting back tears, I said that the worst part for me was that Elvis was supposed to be around for much, much longer, as a sort of national treasure to be shared with my children and grandchildren.

In that sense, you can interpret Elvis Presley's ugly demise as a betrayal. Somehow, what seemed immediately apparent to me, and remains so even now, was that what happened to Elvis at the end was not nearly so significant as the incredible parable of his beginnings, and the astonishing reaction of the world to his achievements. And that is what this obituary, blasphemous and overwrought though it may be, tries to assess.

In Elvis Presley's penultimate filmed drama, *Change of Habit,* he plays a young doctor working in a ghetto clinic, a sort of urban Albert Schweitzer. A trio of nuns led by Mary Tyler Moore, working in street dress, without their habits, are sent to aid him, though their religious status is unrevealed. Moore and Elvis fall in love. Shaken, Mary returns to the convent, questioning her commitment to the church. But one day she is summoned to the chapel. Elvis stands at the altar, looking radiant. He is singing a hymn. The camera follows her eyes from Presley's face to Christ on the cross, back and forth several times. In the film's final shot, we see Mary's face. She looks perplexed. For her, there seems to be no difference between these two men.

This is the most supremely arrogant moment in recent cultural history, surpassing even John Lennon's "We're bigger than Jesus" wisecrack. For Elvis didn't just make a boast, he offered a practical demonstration. In our eyes, there isn't much difference either. And unless you understand that Elvis Presley was more than anything a spiritual leader of our generation, there's really no way to assess his importance, much less the meaning of the music he created.

Listen to his best songs; there is no mistaking it. Uniting opposites is the essence of religion, and Elvis did that in the most banal, pragmatic and sublime ways: he obliterated distinctions between musical forms, between races (for a while at least) and even between good and bad. Many singers of our era might have recorded bits of deviltry like "One Night" and "All Shook Up." No one else could also have made a hymn like "Crying in the Chapel" a convincing hit. It would not even have occurred to anyone else to try to span the gulf between those songs.

Elvis' fans surrendered to him instinctively, willing to take what he gave (no matter how silly), always confident that he could possess them completely any time he chose. Their faith, coupled with the complacency of his advisers, was both his glory and a plague. For if he was so great an artist in an environment where his mere presence was enough to incite riotous devotion, what might he have become in an atmosphere where creative challenge was fostered, risk encouraged, banality derided?

There's no denying that his final few years were depressing and humiliating—especially since their mediocrity followed the great moments of redemption, the 1968 TV show and the string of vital hits that surrounded it. "If I Can Dream," "Kentucky Rain," "The Wonder of You" and "Suspicious Minds" were among the greatest records he ever made. As depressing as the backsliding—perhaps more so—was the physical deterioration. From a lithe, athletic and infinitely sexual creature, Elvis became the antithesis of our dreams.

Still, many of us turned to each new record with expectations that must confound those who missed even the final glimmerings of his majesty. Why did we bother?

Because Elvis was unique. He had it all. Every element of the rock and roll dream was his—pink Cadillacs, beautiful women, untold wealth, true genius and inspiration—and that was a claim no one else could ever make. A few others might have had some hope of it, most notably Chuck Berry. Berry united his own set of opposites: black and white, adult and teenage, verbal and nonverbal. But Berry was also black, and though he too blazed a tough and glorious path, his race denied him the full honor due his genius.

In a way, though, it was Berry's story that Elvis lived out, because Berry wrote songs like "Johnny B. Goode" and "Promised Land," which came to stand as prophecies of Elvis, and finally as epitaphs for him. (It's especially ironic that those two songs were among the finest recordings of Elvis' final years.) "Johnny B. Goode" was a story Elvis, and Elvis alone, lived to the hilt. "Promised Land" must have seemed a plain fact to him —at least some of the time.

Perhaps I make too much of Elvis Presley—he was, after all, not a saint or a guru. But if any individual of our time can be said to have changed the world, Elvis Presley is the one. In his wake more than music is different. Nothing and no one looks or sounds the same. His music was the most liberating event of our era because it taught us new possibilities of feeling and perception, new modes of action and appearance, and because it reminded us not only of his greatness but also of our own potential. If those things were not already so well integrated into our lives that they have become commonplace, it would be simpler to explain how astonishing a feat Elvis Presley's advent really was.

Of course it's unquestionable that there would have been rock and roll music without Elvis Presley. But it's just as unquestionable that the kind of rock and roll we have—a music of dreams and visions, not just facts and figures or even songs and singers—was shaped by him in its most fundamental features.

His life must have been brutally lonely, for Elvis took the biggest chance of all and went it alone. One reason the Beatles did better, or at least lasted longer at their peak, was that they had learned from his mistakes and successes. Elvis had no such map to guide him, so he had to invent himself over and over, come up with new terms for dealing with each situation. In the process, he invented us, whether or not we all know it. We are a hero-worshiping, thrill-crazy mob, I suppose, but at our best one that's tuned into the heart of things—open, honest, unpretentious. Which is to say that he made us in his image.

Elvis was the King of rock and roll because he was the embodiment of its sins and virtues: grand and vulgar, rude and eloquent, powerful and frustrated, absurdly simple and awesomely complex. He was the King, I mean, in our hearts, which is the place where the music really comes to life. And just as rock and roll will stand as long as our hearts beat, he will always be our King: forever, irreplaceable, corrupt and incorruptible, beautiful and horrible, imprisoned and liberated. And finally, rockin' and free, free at last.

Rolling Stone, 1977

Wonderful One:
Marvin Gaye (1939–1984)

The murder of Marvin Gaye at the hand of his father provided the occasion for this piece. But my interest in Gaye preceded and exceeded any fascination with his death and its macabre circumstances. Spawned as it was in tragedy, every word of this not-exactly-an-obituary is heartfelt. There were few better performers than Marvin Gaye, and there were—and are and will be—none like him.

I used to think that Marvin Gaye was the most underrated soul singer of the sixties. Now I'd expand that judgment, not only because of his ugly, tragic death but because the music Gaye made in the last decade of his life warrants it. Gaye was the most underrated singer of the past *two* decades—and since "Sexual Healing" has been overwhelmed in public memory by *Thriller,* perhaps he would have suffered the same fate in a third.

Yet Marvin Gaye was a great singer, a great entertainer, and for my money, as great an artist as popular music has produced. My office is littered now with twenty albums spanning his career from the first Tamla hit, "Stubborn Kind of Fellow" (1962), through *Midnight Love,* the 1982 album that contained "Sexual Healing." These albums are Gaye's legacy. They include every style of music from the bluesiest singles ever created at Motown to Nat "King" Cole tributes, from doo-wop emulations to the slinky sexual syncopations of *Let's Get It On,* from duet triumphs with Tammi Terrell to the inconsolably solitary creations of the early eighties. Some of these songs are inalterably basic examples of the gospel-blues bedrock in which Gaye and producers Holland-Dozier-Holland specialized on his early hits. Others are among the most sophisticated pop music ever crafted, incoporating production electronics, post-psychedelic conceptualizing and Caribbean rhythms without ever making a gauche or foolish move.

For all its disparate elements, Gaye's music is held together from beginning to end by a sense of cool so complete that it's majestic, an awesome unflappability that is his trademark. Gaye's cool wasn't a matter of emotional distance or reserve (except when it needed to be). It was a matter of *control.* Even when he cuts loose, as in "Can I Get a Witness" and "Wonderful One," you can hear him building up to the peak, measuring the moment, modulating it, reining it in again. Other performers—even ones as great as Solomon Burke and Wilson Pickett—zoomed in on a target and pulverized it with saturation attacks. Gaye first surveyed every inch of the ground his trajectory covered, then homed in and pulverized with aplomb.

Gaye's talent couldn't be denied. It began with a three-octave tenor voice, and included a full range of effects from breathy falsetto to gravelly basso, an amazing ability to find a pocket in the beat and cruise in it, a sharp sense of how to get the most from his collaborators. But what's finally most striking about his work is that it's always intelligent, forever conscious of itself. Gaye was always probing, restlessly tinkering with shades of meaning even—or especially—during his best performances. What he did with "The Star Spangled Banner," when he sang the anthem to open the 1983 NBA All-Star Game, transforming the unwieldy words and old-fashioned melody into something contemporary that became a statement about the sentiment at the core of the song, about his own relationship to it, about the piece as a *work of art,* he did continuously and less obtrusively in his own albums and shows.

Even performers as great as Smokey Robinson and Stevie Wonder sometimes like to ride on instinct. Gaye never acquired that habit, so even when he was bored and annoyed—as he was through most of his last two Tamla albums—he couldn't fall back on craft and let himself glide. Instead, Gaye fashioned those albums, *Here, My Dear* and *In Our Lifetime,* as comments on his situation: the injustice of alimony in the first case, the tribulations of making music to finish off a contract in the second. He did this even though—or again, because—that meant that those albums were often tedious and irritating.

As a result of those traits, of the concreteness of his concepts, of the sweep of his ambition and the totality of his command, Marvin Gaye's approach has more in common with the smartest, most inspired white rock stars—Lennon, Townshend, Brian Wilson—than it does with such black performers as Wonder, George Clinton or even Sly Stone. Gaye shared with such white rockers the inclination to shape each album around an explicitly stated theme—and indeed, the inclination to mold his music in album-length rather than hit single formats in the first place. This cost him in the late seventies, when white-oriented FM radio banished black musicians from its precincts, while black-oriented radio never relinquished its hit emphasis.

Motown was set apart from the rest of black music, given its greater access to the pop mainstream, largely because of what it wasn't. Motown records were aware of blues and gospel, used them as tangible reference points, but first and foremost, Motown singers sang *pop*. Thus the label's appropriate patron saint was Jackie Wilson, with his big-band arrangements and Al Jolson tributes. But after his experience as a Wilson songwriter, Berry Gordy perfected a more balanced blend. If any one performer could be said to best express the artistry of that mix, it was probably Marvin Gaye.

Gaye had a background in doo-wop, R&B and gospel. When he needed to reflect it, he could summon it up as effectively, as authentically as the great Atlantic and Stax singers: "Can I Get a Witness" is cut from the same cloth as the hits of Solomon Burke, and records like "I'll Be Doggone" and "Baby Don't You Do It" echo Otis Redding and Wilson Pickett, without the former's rusticity or the latter's implied threat. Yet it's hard to imagine any other Motown star pulling off music so bluesy, so deeply rooted in gospel, as the Holland-Dozier-Holland hits of Marvin Gaye. The marvelous, gospel-like simplicity of "You're a Wonderful One," "How Sweet It Is (To Be Loved by You)," "Your Unchanging Love" and the other Gaye/HDH collaborations continually promise full-blown outbursts in the Stax-Volt style, but they're kept perpetually in check. The resulting tension, and the fact that it's never fully released, is uniquely Motown's. But it's hard to think of a singer who was so clearly suited to the style as the diffident and debonair young Marvin Gaye.

However unhappy and recalcitrant he may have been with the production process, Gaye had hits with every significant writer, performer and arranger in the Gordy group, and he fitted perfectly with four different duet partners (Tammi Terrell, Kim Weston, Diana Ross and Mary Wells). Unlike Stevie Wonder, Gaye's career didn't develop neatly, so you can't talk about periods in his music. He worked off and on with Holland-Dozier-Holland from 1963 ("Witness") through 1967 ("Your Unchanging Love"), after which HDH split the label. But he also worked with his onetime mentor, Harvey Fuqua, and Johnny Bristol on those shattering duet records, including the unforgettable, inimitable (ask Diana Ross) "Ain't No Mountain High Enough," "It Takes Two," "Ain't Nothing Like the Real Thing" and "If I Could Build My Whole World Around You." And during 1965 and 1966 he made three singles with Smokey Robinson that are so sassy, sophisticated, smooth and danceable that they seem like the truest progenitors of his seventies style: "I'll Be Doggone," "Take This Heart of Mine" and "One More Heartache," confessions more complete than any Smokey ever allowed himself, coupled with snaky, sensuous rhythms not months but years ahead of their time. This music all but demands the extension it received in *What's Going On* and *Let's Get It On*. But for the time Marvin was still chained to the Motown machine.

It was with the machine—indeed, with Norman Whitfield, probably the most mechanistic producer Motown ever saw—that he made his masterpiece, the single most enduring track he recorded: "I Heard It Through the Grapevine," a composite of four hundred years of paranoia and talking drum gossip distilled into three minutes and fifteen seconds of anguished soul searching. "Grapevine" is a great song, but Gaye's version is by far the greatest anyone has ever done, because his fretful, self-absorbed vocal so completely complements Whitfield's ominous arrangement. Bearing down on every word, making each syllable count, Gaye explored "Grapevine" as if the song were a lost continent of music and emotion, as if the plotters in the song were his true and personal demons, had in fact scorched his identity all but out of existence, as the music suggests. In those three and a quarter minutes, Marvin Gaye earned his independence from the Motown mill, in part by perfectly summarizing all of its splendors and delights. And as his final Whitfield collaborations, "That's the Way That Love Is" and "The End of Our Road," suggest, Marvin Gaye was going in his own direction anyhow. The suggestion of seventies funk in those two numbers is at least as much Whitfield as Gaye, but the intimacy, the degree to which they become dialogues between Marvin and the band (especially the bass), the suppleness with which the voice commands, is far, far removed from what happened in more typical Whitfield hits of the period: Compare them to the Temptations' "I Can't Get Next to You" or "Psychedelic Shack" sometime.

Whatever his eccentricities and indulgences—on the basis of his 1971 confessions to Ben Fong-Torres of *Rolling Stone*, his vices were many and carnal—Gaye's determination to break out of the Motown production mold was firm. His instinct about what to do with his talent was sure, and when he finally bartered a shot at producing himself out of a recalcitrant Gordy, the result was one of the great seventies albums, *What's Going On*.

What's Going On was a landmark in four areas. It opened black record production to the advances in technique made by white rock groups such as the Beatles. It expanded the music rhythmically by stretching the meter further than even Sly Stone had dared to do, and it upended the R&B song form, which had persisted basically unchanged through the soul years, by unraveling it, allowing a performer to explore nooks, crannies and nuances inaccessible within the more strictly blues-derived format. Finally, songs such as "What's Going On," "Inner City Blues," "What's Happening Brother" and "Save the Children" exploded the range of topics available to black songwriters, previously limited to (at most) making general salutes to brotherhood and expressions of anguish over discrimination. Gaye not only laid out the specifics of oppression in some detail but also made strong statements about returning Vietnam veterans and against nuclear warfare, at a time when such subjects were risky even for acid-rockers.

What's Going On and its successor, the less political and more sensual *Let's Get It On* (which nevertheless served the admirable function of moving black pop thematically past mere flirtation and teasing, into the sweaty passions and complexities of adult fucking), stand as the two most elegant, exciting and seamless records Marvin Gaye ever made.

Yet after making them, Gaye was embittered. He felt slighted when less groundbreaking music got the reviews and awards: In 1971, the year of *What's Going On*, Grammys went to Carole King, Isaac Hayes, Paul McCartney, Lou Rawls, James Taylor and Bill Withers. Marvin Gaye garnered nary a nomination.

His fragile ego never recovered from that snub, which colored the rest of his days as surely as the collapse of Tammi Terrell into his arms just before her death of a brain hemorrhage. Gaye would never again make innocent music after Terrell's death; he would never make music so ambitious, lean and intensely performed after the Grammys ignored him. It wasn't until "Sexual Healing" that he had another big hit. His last decade was marred over and over with tragedy, disruption, disintegration: the failure of his marriage to Anna Gordy (supposedly portrayed à clef in Elaine Jesmer's 1974 novel, *Number One with a Bullet*), stage fright that all but immobilized him, a drug habit (he's said to have once injected himself with an ounce of pure cocaine in a suicide attempt), back tax bills, expatriation in England and Belgium, bankruptcy. The records became stark, perverse and infrequent, though his shows (when he could do them) remained straightforwardly sexual enterprises.

Now Gaye is in danger of being swallowed up—for the time being—by the manner of his death. Filicide is a rare thing; the headlines are unavoidable. But that's not the substance of Marvin Gaye's life and career. The real story is the beauty and power of his recordings. When I hear "Pride and Joy" or "Distant Lover," "Hitch Hike" or "Got to Give It Up," when he and Tammi swing into the agonies and ecstasies of "Ain't No Mountain High Enough," the truth becomes clear. There was no one quite like Marvin Gaye in the history of popular music, and while that means

that he can never, ever be replaced, it also means that those of us who
loved him and what he did will never, ever let the world forget him.

Record, 1983

No Tears of Regret

*"Fortunate Son" is the title of one of Creedence Clearwater Revival's
greatest songs. It isn't all that surprising that it was a song written by
John Fogerty which gave me the title of this book, for in so many ways
what I have been trying to say in a sometimes fumbling fashion,
Fogerty was expressing with beautiful simplicity and clarity all
through Creedence Clearwater Revival's career. "Fortunate Son"
sums up the situation described in this book's introduction, and the
emotion surrounding such self-discovery, in phrases so pithy with
bitterness that to print them is to defile them: They must be* heard,
*snarling out of Fogerty's throat with a couple of generations' worth
of Irish-American working-class pathos and four hundred years of
Afro-American rhythmic interchange behind them.*

*John Fogerty is a quintessential American artist, akin in his fatalism
and workaday ethic to such determined but brilliant eccentrics as
Mark Twain and Joseph Cornell. Like them he reached for the sky
even when he seemed to be executing in miniature, and the years make
what he accomplished in his rather diffident style more and more
rewarding.*

Stuck in Phoenix on election night, the only East Coast radlibs in that part
of the desert, we planned to spend the evening holed up in front of the
hotel room TV, deciphering returns and fishing for omens. But the race
was over by check-in time.

Jesus, I thought, the sun's not even down yet. It was one of those nights
when I hope it will linger, for fear that once it disappears, light will never
return. It was sinking fast enough.

A song insinuated itself into the back of my mind just then, and as though it had ideas of its own, the music stayed around for the next few days: an insistent choogling rhythm propelling a flat voice wailing dimestore doom with rockabilly overtones. Cheap, nasty sentiments, the kind I ordinarily like but at that time wanted and needed to avoid. Somehow this music wouldn't let me avoid those thoughts. "I feel rivers overflowing," the song said. "I feel the voice of rage and ruin . . . There's a bad moon on the rise."

"Bad Moon Rising" is a John Fogerty song, and it's no surprise that it was one of his numbers that came to mind on the night America saddled itself with a Boraxo future. Fogerty's songs have always been equally clear and morbid, rock and roll's version of a balance of terror. The best Creedence Clearwater Revival hits strip the world down to its basics and then slowly rebuild its complexities, never relaxing the pressure. This they share with reggae, hillbilly ballads and the blues. It was John Fogerty's genius that made such songs, their portent continually awful, songs that were not just accessible but absolutely buoyant with dread. For beneath the exhilaration, there was always damage to be assessed; sometimes it was explicit ("Who'll Stop the Rain"), but just as often it was a subtle undercurrent, based on the knowledge that even the best times will soon enough give way to something dreary and painful ("Lookin' Out My Back Door").

These days, records as grand as *Blonde on Blonde* and as unvarnished as *The Rolling Stones Now* seem a little dated. Somehow, the very simplicity of Fogerty classics like "Bad Moon Rising," "Who'll Stop the Rain," "Have You Ever Seen the Rain," "Lodi" and "Fortunate Son" keeps them not only fresh but surprisingly relevant. At a time when even the Rascals, those wide-eyed soul innocents, were seduced by psychedelic flimflam, Fogerty never discarded the basic rock and roll schematic. The concerns of Creedence remain contemporary: rockabilly riffs, moody bass lines, posers and egalitarianism, paranoid vulnerability, the spaces between responsibility and apocalypse, snap-and-crackle rhythm. You can listen to a record like Rockpile's *Seconds of Pleasure* as nothing more than Creedence pastiche, or perhaps an outline of what that band might be doing if it had managed to hold itself together.

From the vantage point of a decade marred by his virtual absence, John Fogerty now seems the great lost American rock and roller. Creedence was virtually the only American band of the late sixties that didn't miss the point of the British Invasion, which was just that our national roots music was sufficiently exciting unto itself to provide almost endless opportunity for investigation and extrapolation.

At the beginning, of course, Fogerty was nobody's genius. For most, he was simply the most interesting voice on pop radio; the hipsters put their money down on the acid rockers across San Francisco Bay, middle-class kids who looked down on the working-class stability of El Cerrito, from which Creedence sprang. It's always been said that Fogerty's downfall was trying to prove himself the peer of the Dead and the Airplane, that his failure to make a really great extended jam drove him to all sorts of excess on the Creedence Clearwater Revival LPs. A nice theory until you check it against the evidence and realize that the eleven-minute Creedence workout on "I Heard It Through the Grapevine" now stands with Quicksilver's "Who Do You Love" as the only remaining listenable extended jams ever recorded by Bay Area groups.

For Creedence and Fogerty, the cycle now comes full circle, partly because today's critics, the arbiters of respectability, are a bit younger and wiser and full of fond memories of Creedence as teenage radio music, partly because hippie is in deep eclipse (from which it may never return, if we are lucky), but mostly because the Creedence approach was the only productive one right along. Speak your piece and shut the fuck up; pull no punches; respect tradition but not authority. So a record as marginally interesting as *The Royal Albert Hall Concert* (mistitled, since it was really recorded at home in the East Bay, in Oakland Coliseum) gets rave write-ups today, when it might have been dismissed or almost overlooked when it was first issued.

I don't think that the new album is much superior to the roundly (and wrongly) planned *Live in Europe*. Neither gives a fair picture of the band I saw at Detroit's Grande Ballroom in 1970, which had aggression stamped in every move, and played everything tightly, powerfully, above all LOUDLY. That night, at least, Creedence sounded exactly like its records (an accolade of major proportions) except when they extended the solos and breaks, repeating the same phrases until you thought the tension would snap not the song but the room.

That tension is at the heart of the revival of interest in John Fogerty's music. Pessimism, paranoia and puritanism (he's the perfect feminist male rocker, having never written about love relationships at all) are carried to such extremes in his work that it's easy to miss what really distinguishes the appearance of those attitudes: their offhandedness, as though such terminal inability to communicate was not a private problem, but a universal one.

In that regard, Fogerty was genuinely ahead of his time. His alienation is even more extreme than Elvis Costello's. Indeed, by comparison Costello's a bleeding heart who takes each betrayal personally—a sign that he retains some hope for the situation to reverse itself. Fogerty takes each betrayal for granted. "I pulled out from the platform, nobody raised they hand," he sings in "Crosstie Walker," recorded at the height of his success. "There were no tears of regret from that runaway train." Those lines are sung with an absence of outrage, even though they might be a capsule description of his career.

In her illuminating essay on Creedence in *The Rolling Stone Illustrated History of Rock and Roll*, Ellen Willis writes that such fatalism represents Creedence's greatest limitation. On the contrary, to me it is that fatalism which has made Fogerty almost timelessly relevant. In the happiest song he has ever written, "Lookin' Out My Back Door," Fogerty finally asserts that tomorrow will certainly (not even probably) be miserable. And even though he claims to be content within the moment, he's clearly lying— the way the music changes, opening up to reveal previously concealed dead spaces around the voice, denies the very possibility of contentment.

Fogerty is obsessed with the utter failure of human communication, which makes him a great deal like Costello. Just as surely, he disdains all forms of reformist and and revolutionary rhetoric. It is precisely his anti-utopianism which makes him such a quintessentially American artist. Yet Fogerty is incapable of anything like the anger expressed by the current generation of rock and rollers. Indeed, the only songs of recent vintage which I can imagine Fogerty having written are Bruce Springsteen's "The Ties That Bind" (which quotes him) and Neil Young's "Powderfinger." And Fogerty would never have written "Born to Run" or "Sugar Mountain," for he never knew that much hope.

It's hard to decide what tense one ought to use in talking about Fogerty. After Creedence Clearwater Revival split in 1973, he made two solo albums, *The Blue Ridge Rangers* in 1973 and one under his own name in 1976. Since then, he has woodshedded—I hear he's been working on his drumming, presumably the weak link in the one-man-band approach he adopted after his band (originally formed in high school in 1959) broke up. But I also hear Asylum has rejected a couple of albums. [Later on, after a lengthy lawsuit was settled, word had it that it was litigation that kept Fogerty away from the public eye.]

At a time when Tom Petty screams about the possible retail price of his albums and Johnny Rotten makes harassing and abusing record companies his favorite sport, it's typical that Fogerty never has spoken a word of public complaint. I wouldn't be surprised if he never again released a record—or if a new album arrived in tomorrow's mail. That's fatalism for you, and Fogerty's fatalism is about as complete as any American artist's since Mark Twain.

Yet he's ever present anyhow. Performers as diverse as Emmylou Harris and the Brooklyn reggae group Jah Malla have recently covered "Bad Moon Rising," as if to acknowledge that this song, written at the moment of Nixon's ascendancy, is in fact the perfect prelude to Reagan's regime. When he was recording prolifically it was said that Fogerty lacked the charisma to be a star of major proportions. In his absence, his magic has grown. I suspect that he could be a major musical force if he returned now.

But whatever John Fogerty does in the future, his music will be there. Only a month after Reagan's election, John Lennon was murdered. Even for a fatalist, that was an omen to reckon with. Two weeks later, during Bruce Springsteen's Madison Square Garden concert, Bruce stopped the band, took a deep breath and sang the only song I know that sums up my feelings about Lennon's murder:

> Long as I remember, the rain's been coming down
> Clouds of mystery pouring confusion on the ground
> Good men through the ages trying to find the sun
> And I wonder, still I wonder,
> Who'll stop the rain.

Springsteen didn't identify the song or explain it. He didn't need to. Like all of John Fogerty's music, it spoke for itself.

Musician, 1981

Lotta Goin' Nowhere Goin' On

There are those who would argue that the New York Dolls were too crude to be a great band, that their output was too limited (their second album was their last), their act too gimmicky, their playing too crude and dumb.

Those people simply haven't listened closely enough. It's not simply that the Dolls were five years ahead of their time, a sweeter Manhattan precursor of the Sex Pistols. It's also that the Dolls were rock's perfect amateurs, playing sloppily but with complete passionate abandon, the

great American inheritors of a tradition founded by the Who or the
MC5 or who knows, maybe some of the lost fifties rockabilly zanies
—Hank Mizell or someone like him—who could not have passed a
properly constructed rite of passage but who, for a shining moment,
extended as long as possible, broke free and rocked the planet itself.
  Or maybe you just had to be there. I was, and what happened in
their shows is captured just sufficiently on their records to revivify the
memory for me on a regular basis.

The New York Dolls' first album expanded their cult from New York to
the rest of hard-core, hard-rock America. As a result, *Too Much Too Soon*
is less specifically rooted in Manhattan, though its bluster and swagger are
no less urban. Rather than the specifically NYC "Subway Train" from
their self-titled first LP, there's "Babylon," the town on Long Island;
"There's Gonna Be a Showdown," the Philadelphia soul classic; and "Bad
Detective," with its Chinese accents. *Too Much Too Soon* is plainly about
moving a lot and not going anywhere. "All dressed up / Got nowhere
to go," sings lead guitarist Johnny Thunders, and he's aching for release.

Just as lead singer David Johansen's taunting "Do you think you could
make it with Frankenstein?" encapsulated the first album, Thunders'
"C'mon, gimme some lips" becomes this one's motif. The Dolls have
never lacked arrogance, which has earned them often invidious compari-
sons to the Rolling Stones. But now their self-assurance seems matter-of-
fact. "Frankenstein" defended their eccentricity—bassist Arthur Kane's
chemise, Thunders' feathery hair, Johansen's blaring New York accent.
"I'm a Human Being," which closes this set, isn't a taunt but a statement
of complicity: the Dolls have discovered the ways in which they aren't
really so different.

Onstage the Dolls' dynamism covers their rough edges. But their records work as well. *Too Much Too Soon* owes much to producer Shadow
Morton, who has shown the Dolls how to make those edges stand in relief
against the group's natural and undeniable talent.

Consequently, their nerviest attempts are among their surest successes.
For instance, Kenny Gamble and Leon Huff's "There's Gonna Be a
Showdown" is of interest not just because it's the album's strongest cut
but because it is built on Jerry Nolan's drumming. Nolan is the one Doll
who approximates the standard definition of musical competence. Critics
usually ignore the issue of musical competence with groups like the Dolls
—but that term simply has a different meaning in the context of such

groups. They are searching for effects, and it's to their credit that we only hear the best of them.

To that end, *Too Much Too Soon* makes it clear that the Dolls are not just David Johansen's backing band. Both Nolan and Thunders emerge as powerful forces. Thunders' "Chatterbox," which he wrote and sings, is a classic—his guitar work is as inventive as the most underrated of all punky metal guitarists, the MC5's Fred Smith. Meanwhile Johansen is a talented showman with an amazing ability to bring characters to life as a lyricist, in the songs he co-writes with Sylvain Sylvain.

Ultimately, the Dolls remind me less of other rock bands than of their hometown baseball team. Like the Mets, they are rising from deprecation to become champs. I think they're the best hard-rock band in America right now. As they say, "I can hold my head so high, 'cause I'm a human, a riffraff human being." And that's what it's all about.

Rolling Stone, 1974

Bruce and Bob/
Bruce Springsteen Raises Cain

Most of the reasons why I have continued to write about rock music, without becoming completely cynical or dispirited, are spelled out one way or another in Fortunate Son. *But there is another to which I eagerly admit, and it deserves a moment's recitation here, for to omit it would leave a gaping hole in the personal part of this story.*

By 1974, or thereabouts, anyone with any critical intelligence would have had to be dissatisfied with the state of rock and roll music. The singer/songwriters seemed to have established virtual hegemony over the serious American wing of the music; heavy metal had petered out into all-but-completely-coopted bombast; black pop was entering its mechanistic phase; what arrived from England was arty, archaic or just plain silly. These were the preconditions of the punk revolt in 1976, but the stasis and enervation that produced that revolt existed for many months before.

Around then, I began attending a remarkable series of shows by

Bruce Springsteen and his group, which reaffirmed almost all of what are for me the best parts of rock. It wasn't his lyrics, although he has a way with words. It wasn't his sense of tradition, though he worked with that tradition in such clever ways that he (and he almost alone) established that there was life in it yet.

But it was more than any of that that restored my enthusiasm. Bruce Springsteen offered not a single song, image or event that galvanized my passion and made me recall my roots, but a whole series of them, which in combination made me (I suppose) a fanatic for the first time since the demise of the MC5. For instance, by mid-1974, Springsteen was fronting a band with three black members and three white ones, and even in the wake of Sly Stone, that was an unusual thing. It was more unusual that he took it for granted, did not play upon it as a noble gesture but simply used his group as a single unit.

Furthermore, Springsteen had both an instinct for the buried gems and hidden treasures of rock and roll—the multitude of one-shots whose monument was his set-closing version of Garry "U.S." Bonds' "Quarter to Three"—and the ability to incorporate them into a personal style, using those songs not as "oldies" or some sort of sacred relics but as a storehouse of energy, rhythm and humor.

And I mean humor, not that spurious, corporate alternative "fun." By the midseventies, "fun" was something entertainers sold their audiences when they hadn't anything better to offer. Springsteen never offered his listeners a mere diversion, never turned his shows into commodities. He was intent and purposeful at every moment, and the part of his work that was funny and enjoyable grew out of that very serious mood, which by all bureaucratic standards should have been its "opposite."

In this sense, of course, Springsteen incarnated every critical principle I'd ever cherished. That he was also a rebel against shoddy musical values and corporate control but that he was not freaky, druggy or violent, that he was an all-American boy not a beatnik, just made him all the more relatable to me. And since the music that he made was rooted in pop radio music, not anybody's avant-gardism, I felt, seeing him burst out before me, like I'd finally arrived back home.

That doesn't mean that Springsteen's greatness was immediately apparent to me. In fact, the first time that I saw him, he seemed more strange and bewildering than enlightening. The record of my reaction is in the first piece that follows, a review which appeared in Newsday without censorship (meaning that the "pumps his way into his hat" *quotation went unremarked). The concept of seeing two figures as monumentally important to pop music in our time as Marley and Springsteen in a club which seated not more than two hundred patrons is still amazing and amusing to me. (I'd only lived in New York for about a month; maybe I thought that this was the way it would be all the time.)*

Springsteen wasn't great the first time I saw him, sad to say. But one of the things that attracted me to him in those early months was his capacity for growth. Though I didn't see him do an unforgettable show for several months, Springsteen, in his live performances, exhibited an early inclination to work his way out of difficult situations, to exceed his limitations, rather than letting the former fester and the latter drag him down. In many senses, a critic spends his time watching artists allow just those things to happen. Most performers, like most people, aren't especially eager to change, much less to change (and therefore confront) the weakest parts of their acts. Springsteen was, and this remains among his rarest qualities.

The second piece below, "Bruce Springsteen Raises Cain" represents Springsteen's act considerably cleaned up. He had shaved his beard and shed his scruffy (or was that scroungy?) stage image, the band (now with only one black member but still a hot group) was better incorporated into his compositions, and he had discovered how to make hit records and keep in some kind of direct contact with a segment of his audience and the person he had started out to be. I doubt that I have spent a more enjoyable week in my life. (You can confirm the veracity of my enthusiasm next time MTV broadcasts the video of "Rosalita," filmed at that Phoenix show in the story.)

Besides their concurrent appearance at Max's Kansas City, Bruce Springsteen and the Wailers, featuring Bob Marley, have in common a continuing battle with the English language. The Wailers are at something of a disadvantage in this battle of syntax, since they are Jamaican and therefore not expected to be familiar with the American idiom. Springsteen has no excuse half as good, but then, he doesn't need one; the profusion of metaphors, similes, allusion, alliteration and allegory that overflows his songs is so dazzling—not to mention dizzying—that it justifies itself.

Marley and the Wailers are the first big-time reggae stars to tour the United States. Marley is an excellent songwriter and when the band is performing Marley's better material, it's first rate. But when his material weakens, so does their performance.

The music business seems to be expecting a big reggae explosion. If that explosion is to happen, the Wailers should represent its first wave. But I doubt if reggae will become a major phenomenon, not because the music isn't better than most current American rock—which in the case of the Wailers and particularly the great Toots and the Maytals, it certainly is —but because it's too difficult for American ears and feet to pick up, memorize and dance to. If you're interested in reggae for its musical values —the beat, the rich lyric imagery—the Wailers' appearance at Max's is a rare opportunity to experience some of the best of the genre firsthand.

Marley is one of the most physically striking performers I've seen in some time. He is very short, hardly more than five feet tall, and his hair is wild in the Rastafarian manner. The general scruffiness of his dress gives a hint of what the Jamaican streets might look like.

If Marley is scruffy, Springsteen is absolutely scroungy. He looks somewhat like Bob Dylan during his motorcycle accident: a Lincolnesque beard, dirty T-shirt and jeans, wraparound sunglasses to go with his wraparound lyrics.

Springsteen plays what I would call Bellevue rock, without intending to be pejorative. His lyrics tread a fine line between the psychotic and the mildly demented, but I wouldn't want to have to judge where the point of demarcation lies. A typical couplet is: "Madman drummers bummers and Indians in the summer with a teenage diplomat / In the dumps with the mumps as the adolescent pumps his way into his hat." I don't know how seriously Springsteen takes himself, but behind this stream of unconsciousness must lie a reeling mind.

Surprisingly enough, for someone who in many ways fits into the singer/songwriter idiom, Springsteen is backed by a fine rocking band, equipped with such arcane (for rock) instruments as the tuba, accordion and flute.

This madness fits into a pattern that has only the visionary ramblings of Dylan and maybe Van Morrison as its precedent. I'm not quite sure whether what I saw is believable, but if it is, Bruce Springsteen is one of the most healthful signs of post-sixties rock: a polysyllabic punk who walks it like he talks it.

Newsday, 1973

Los Angeles, Tuesday, July 4, 1978
One of Bruce Springsteen's most popular early songs is "4th of July, Asbury Park (Sandy)." That he is spending this Independence Day on the

shores of the wrong ocean is an irony that escapes no one, least of all himself. LA is not terra incognita but Springsteen doesn't yet reign here as he does back east. Perhaps the time is auspicious for changing that. Although he's been up all night mixing tapes recorded at his most recent concert (Saturday night in Berkeley), Springsteen is at the pool soaking up sun by eleven A.M.

If God had invented a hotel for rock bands, it probably would look like the Sunset Marquis, where Springsteen and the E Street Band are staying. Nestled on a steep side street just below Sunset Strip, the Marquis is a combination summer camp and commune. Its rooms are laid out around the pool, and guests on the first floor use the pool terrace as a sort of patio. In the daytime the poolside is jammed, and at night it's easy to tell who's home by the lights shining through curtained glass doors. Springsteen, the band, their crew and entourage occupy thirty rooms, including all those around the pool.

At noon producer/manager Jon Landau, Bruce and I duck into Springsteen's room to hear the Berkeley concert mixes. There are also two mixes of an eight-minute live rendition of "Prove It All Night" which shatter the LP version, and one mix of an unnamed shorter instrumental, often called "Paradise by the Sea," which opens the second half of his concerts. Even on a small cassette player, it's clear that something considerable is going on.

For years people have been begging Springsteen to make a live album, and "Prove It All Night" shows why. The song is considered the lightest item on *Darkness on the Edge of Town,* his new album, but onstage it becomes what pianist Roy Bittan, for one, thinks is the most exciting song of the show, featuring a lengthy guitar and keyboard improvisation that sounds like an unholy alliance between the Yardbirds and Bob Dylan. When the introduction gives way to the melody of the song, "Prove It" is transformed from something potentially slight and dismissible into an emotional crucible. Hearing it, you may wonder if "Prove It All Night" is a hit single, but you *know* it's a great song.

"Paradise by the Sea" is its alter ego. Only Springsteen, touring behind a new album, would have come up with this previously unheard number to open the second half of the show: a five-minute instrumental featuring Clarence Clemons' sax and Danny Federici's organ. The song simultaneously evokes Duane Eddy and Booker T. and the MGs.

Clemons walks into the room with an unbelievably joyous look on his face, and when the tape ends, he takes Bruce by the arm and shouts, "Everybody into the pool!" The next sound is a series of splashes. In a few minutes, they reappear, Huck and Jim after a dip off the raft, bathing suits dripping, and listen again, then repeat the performance. Soon the tiny hotel bedroom is crowded with a half-dozen people dripping wet and exuberant.

At 6:30 P.M. Bruce is at KMET-FM to do an on-the-air interview with disc jockey Mary Turner. There are a couple of bottles of champagne, which may be a mistake: Bruce gets loose pretty easily. And in fact he is a little sloshed as the interview begins. Turner plays it perfectly, fishing for stories. She gets at least one winner.

"When my folks moved out to California," Springsteen begins in response to a question about whether he really knows "a pretty little place in Southern California / Down San Diego way," as he claims in "Rosalita," "my mom decided—see, my father and I would fight all the time—and she decided that we should take a trip together. She decided that we should go to *Tijuana* [he laughs his hoarse staccato laugh, reserved for all that he finds truly absurd]. So we got in the car and drove down there, arguing all the way. First I drove and he yelled at me, and then he drove and I yelled at him.

"Anyway, we finally got there, and of course my old man is the softest-hearted guy in the world. Within fifteen minutes some guy has sold him some watch that must've run for all of an hour and a half before it stopped. And then some guy comes up and says, 'Hey, would you guys like to have your picture taken on a zebra?'

"Well, we looked at each other—who could believe this, right? Zebras are in Africa. And so we said, 'Well, if you've got a zebra, we definitely want to have our picture taken.' So we give him ten bucks and he takes us around this corner and he's got—he's got a damn donkey with stripes painted on its side. And he pulls out these two hats—one says Pancho, one says Cisco, I swear—and he sits us on the donkey and takes our picture. My mother's still got that picture. But that is all I knew about Southern California at the time I wrote 'Rosalita.' "

This is the easiest I've ever heard Bruce speak of his father. "Adam Raised a Cain," from the *Darkness* album, may have exorcised a lot of ghosts. In some of the stories Bruce has told onstage about their relationship, however, his father seems like a demon—which of course he is not.

In fact Douglas Springsteen has lived a very difficult, often impoverished working-class life. For a great deal of Bruce's childhood, his family (he has two sisters, both younger) shared a house with his grandparents while his father worked at an assortment of jobs—in a factory, as a gardener, as a prison guard—without ever making as much as $10,000 a year. Later he moved the family from New Jersey to Northern California, where he is now a bus driver. Bruce says that the tales of their conflicts are true ("I don't make 'em up"), but that they're meant to be "universal." He is not exactly enthusiastic about discussing the relationship, although in a couple of songs that did not make it onto *Darkness,* particularly "The Promise" and "Independence Day," he has chronicled his preoccupation with fathers as thoroughly as did John Steinbeck in *East of Eden,* the novel that inspired the film that inspired "Adam Raised a Cain."

Bruce is so loose by now that when an ad for Magic Mountain's roller coaster—the largest in the world—comes on, he discourses upon great roller coasters he has known, and his desire to see this one. "Ya wanna date?" he asks Turner, in front of who knows how many listeners. She makes the perfect reply: "Only if we sit in the front seat."

After the interview, we head to the car and a Santa Monica beach house where there's a promise of food and fireworks. We race straight out Santa Monica Boulevard to the freeway like something out of a Steve McQueen movie. I haven't spent as reckless a moment as this one in years. But Bruce, who isn't driving, is determined not to miss the fireworks. "C'mon," he says over and over again, "I don't wanna miss 'em." He's like a little boy in his contagious enthusiasm, and the car whips straight into a terrific jam at the end of the Freeway, where we poke along, seeing hints of the fireworks—blue, red, gold, green—cascading out over the ocean.

It's a chill night and the party is outside. Band and crew members shiver on the patio, chewing on cold cut sandwiches and sucking down beer and soda. Bruce quickly determines that this won't do. He heads for the gate leading to the beach. "C'mon," he says to one and all, "let's walk up to the pier. I want a hot dog."

So a foursome strikes out down the beach. The pier is a mile south, far enough so that its lights are at first only a glow on the horizon. And covering the beach the entire distance are people shooting off their own fireworks, Roman candles and skyrockets. We haven't gone a hundred yards before the scene has become a combat zone. Bruce gives me a look. "C'mon, what's the worst that can happen? A rocket upside the head?" He giggles with joy and keeps trudging on through the sand.

The rockets are now exploding directly over our heads, and once in a while one comes closer than that. A rocket upside the head is not unimaginable. Bruce strikes out closer to the water, where the sand is more firmly packed and the walking easier. Down here there are other sorts of activity: lovers in sleeping bags and drinkers sitting in sand pits, nursing themselves with liquor against the chill. The rockets, fewer now, drift out into the water to die with a hiss or fizzle into the damp sand and Bruce Springsteen moves through it all, just another cloud in a hurricane, a natural force or maybe just a big kid out hustling adventure.

Two hot dogs with relish and an hour of pinball later, we walk back along the highway to our car and zip back to the hotel. Tour manager Jim McHale, David Landau (Warren Zevon's guitarist and Jon's brother) and booking agent Barry Bell are talking in Jon's room when Bruce bursts through the poolside curtains. His face is glowing. "We're goin' to make the hit," he shouts and ducks back out. McHale's jaw drops and he races from the room. "I think they're going to paint the billboard," says David.

The raid isn't a complete surprise. Sunday night, driving up the Strip on the way to see *The Buddy Holly Story*, Bruce had first seen the billboard looming above a seven-story building just west of the Continental Hyatt House. Billboards advertising new albums are a Hollywood institution—they're put up for every significant record release and concert appearance. This one uses a poorly cropped version of the *Darkness* cover photo to promote both the record and the band's upcoming appearance at the Forum. As we passed this enormous monument, Bruce groaned and slumped in his seat. "That is the *ugliest* thing I've ever seen in my *life,*" he declared.

The billboard is only a few blocks up the street from the hotel. According to all accounts, Springsteen, Clemons, bassist Garry Tallent and several crew members stealthily approached the office building on which the offending object was perched. Much to their surprise, the door was unlocked, the building wide open. An elevator took them quickly to the roof where McHale, perhaps figuring that cleverness could avoid a bust, quickly organized them. There were twenty cans of black spray paint available and Bruce, Garry and Clarence assumed positions on the paperhangers' ledge. Bell was positioned across the street to watch for cops.

At a signal from McHale, the painting began: PROVE IT ALL NIGHT spread across the billboard from edge to edge, the middle words nearly lost in the dark photo of Springsteen. Then Bruce climbed on Clarence's back, standing on his saxman's shoulders to paint a second legend above the first: E STREET, it read. As they were clambering down, a signal came—the cops. Some members of the entourage headed back for the elevator, but Bruce, Clarence and McHale left Cagney-style, down the exterior fire escape. It was a false alarm anyway.

In the hotel's lobby at quarter to three, Springsteen is exhilarated. "You shoulda been there," he exults, running over the event like a general fresh from a successful battle. Was he worried about getting caught? "Naw," he says. "I figured if they caught us, that was great, and if we got away with it, that was even better." He looks down at himself—hands black with paint, boots ruinously dusty from the beach—and laughs yet again. "There

it is," he says. "Physical evidence . . . The only thing is, I wanted to get
to my face, and paint on a mustache. But it was just too damn high." He
terms his paint job "an artistic improvement."

Wednesday, July 5
Last night, as we were getting into the car after the KMET interview,
Bruce began talking about the reviews *Darkness on the Edge of Town* has
received. It's a subject on which he qualifies as something of an expert:
more has been written about him—and about what has been written about
him—than any other rock performer of recent years, with the possible
exception of Mick Jagger. The scars hardly show. Springsteen just looks
at the press with exceptionally avid interest.

"It's a weird thing about those reviews," Bruce says. "You can find any
conceivable opinion in them. One guy says the record's exactly like *Born
to Run* and it's great, the next one says it's not like *Born to Run* and it's
great, the next one says it's not like *Born to Run* and it's awful." This
amuses him. The nearly unanimous opinion that the album is grim and
depressing doesn't.

It's the title, I suggest. "I know, I know," he says impatiently. "But I
put in the first few seconds of 'Badlands' [the album's first song], those
lines about 'I believe in the love and the hope and the faith.' It's there
on all four corners of the album." By which he meant the first and last
songs of each side: "Badlands" and "Racing in the Street," "The Promised
Land" and "Darkness on the Edge of Town." Springsteen is clearly dis-
tressed by what he sees as a misreading; he meant *Darkness* to be "relentless," not grim.

Later I ask him why the album lacks the humor that buoys his shows.
"In the show, it's a compilation of all the recorded stuff," he says in the
halting way he uses when he's considering something seriously. "If you go
back to *The Wild and the Innocent*, 'Rosalita' is there and all that stuff.
But when I was making this particular album, I just had a specific thing
in mind. And one of the important things was that it had to be just a
relentless . . . just a barrage of the particular thing.

"I got an album's worth of pop songs, like 'Rendezvous' and early
English-style stuff. I got an album's worth right now and I'm gonna get
it out somehow. I wanna do an album that's got ten or eleven things like
that on it. But I just didn't feel it was the right time to do that and I didn't
want to sacrifice any of the intensity of the album by throwing in 'Rendezvous,' even though I knew it was popular from the show."

The other criticism easily made of *Darkness* concerns its repetition of
certain images: cars, street life, abandonment of or by lovers, family and

friends. Those who like this aspect of Springsteen's writing call it style; those who don't say Springsteen is drilling a dry hole. But perhaps Springsteen's greatest and most repeated image is the lie.

"It's hard to explain without getting too heavy. What it is, it's the characters' commitment. In the face of all the betrayals, in the face of all the imperfections that surround you in whatever kind of life you lead, it's the characters' refusal to let go of their own humanity, to let go of their own belief in the other side. It's a certain loss of innocence—more so than in the other albums."

I drove out to the Forum this afternoon with Obie. She is twenty-five and has been Bruce Springsteen's biggest fan for more than a decade. When he was still just a local star, she waited overnight for tickets to his shows to make certain she'd have perfect seats. She's now secretary to Miami Steve Van Zandt, Springsteen's guitarist who is also manager/producer of Southside Johnny and the Asbury Jukes. This means that while Springsteen is on tour, Obie becomes the Jukes' de facto manager. But she's also something more. She makes some of the suits and jackets Bruce wears onstage. She is also something of a historian; there are a thousand Asbury Park legends stored behind her twinkling eyes. More than anything, Obie is a fan who counts the days between Springsteen shows. Her loyalty is repaid in kind. Whenever she comes to a show, in any town, the front-row center pair of seats is reserved for her.

It is partly this atmosphere that makes Bruce Springsteen so attractive: He is surrounded by real-life characters that form the kind of idealized community most of us lost when we graduated high school. One of the reasons Springsteen is such a singular performer is that he has never lost touch with this decidedly noncosmopolitan gang.

Part of the legend is the E Street Band. "Ya know, you can tell by looking at 'em," Bruce explains to me, "that this isn't a bunch of guys with a whole lot in common. But somehow the music cuts right through all that."

There's a lot to cut. Bassist Garry Tallent is a consummate rockabilly addict who looks the part. He's been known to use Brylcreem—recently. Organist Danny Federici has an angel face that could pass for the kind of tough guy Harvey Keitel portrays in *Fingers*. Roy Bittan, the pianist, and Max Weinberg, the drummer, are seasoned pros, veterans of recording studios and Broadway pit bands, and look that part. Miami Steve is a perpetual motion machine, a comic version of the Keith Richards' Barbary pirate act, with a slice of small-town boy made good on the side. And Clarence Clemons, last of all, dwells in a land all his own, not quite like the universe inhabited by the rest of us, though access to it is seemingly available to all comers. Clemons transforms any room he enters, as a six-foot-plus black man with the bulk of a former football player often can do, but even in his own digs at the Marquis, there's something special happening. His hospitality is perfect and generous, and it is in Clarence's room that the tour's inevitable all-night party is most likely to run.

Bruce stands distinctly apart from the group, outside it. "It's weird," he says, " 'cause it's not really a touring band or just a recording band. And it's definitely me, I'm a solo act, y'know." But there is also a sense in which Bruce Springsteen has never been able to mesh in any society, and it has a great deal to do with what makes him so obsessive about his music.

Before he landed a record contract, all of the Asbury Park musicians held day jobs. Garry Tallent worked in a music store, Clemons was a social worker, Van Zandt in the construction union, repairing highways. The exception, always, was Bruce, apparently because he could not conceive of doing anything except playing music. When he was eight years old he first heard Presley and lightning struck; when he picked up the guitar at thirteen, another bolt hit him. "When I got the guitar," he told me Wednesday night, "I wasn't getting out of myself. I was already out of myself. I knew myself and I did not dig me. I was getting into myself."

By fourteen he was in his first band; by sixteen he was so good that when he practiced in his manager's garage, neighborhood kids would stand on milk crates at the window, pressing their noses to the glass just so they could hear a bit. The only other things besides music that ever meant much to him, Springsteen says, were surfing and cars. But nothing—not even girls—ever got in the way of his obsession with making music. There is a certain amount of awe in the way that people who've known him for many years speak of Springsteen's single-minded devotion to playing. It's as if he has always known his destiny, and while this hasn't made him cold —he is one of the friendliest people I know, once you crack the ice—it has given him considerable distance from everyday relationships and ordinary lifestyles. One does not ever think of Bruce Springsteen married and settled, raising a family, having kids; that would be too much monkey business.

What keeps the band tight is the two-to-three-hour sound check before each gig. Today's began at 3:30 P.M.—the ticket says it's a 7:30 show— and didn't end until almost seven. In part, these are informal band rehearsals, with Bruce working up new material and going over old favorites: As we enter the hall at five, he's singing Buddy Holly's "Rave On," a number he's never performed live. But there's more to these sound checks than that.

On this tour, Springsteen's sound mixer is Bruce Jackson, a tall blond Australian who for several years performed the same function for Elvis Presley. Jackson is amazed at Springsteen's perfectionism. "At every date he goes out and sits in every section of the hall to listen to the sound," he says. "And if it isn't right, even in the last row, I hear about it, and we make changes. I mean every date, too—he doesn't let it slip in Davenport, Iowa, or something." Presley, on the other hand, was concerned only with the sound he would hear, which came from onstage monitors.

("Anybody who works for me," Springsteen says without a hint that he might be joking, "the first thing you better know is I'm gonna drive you crazy. Because I don't compromise in certain areas. So if you're gonna be in, you better be ready for that.")

Which maybe explains the consistently high quality of Springsteen's live performances. I must have seen forty over the years, and no two are alike. Even if the selection of songs is the same, which it hardly ever is, Bruce brings something different to every night. Tonight's show at the Forum is conversational—the loosest I've ever seen, and at the same time frighteningly intense in spots. He begins immediately after "Badlands," the opening number, by talking about the walk on the beach last night ("It's like a combat zone out there") and makes some self-deprecating remarks about his press attention, which has mushroomed this week: Robert Hilburn had written a rave advance notice in the Sunday *Los Angeles Times* and Ed Kociela had more than matched Hilburn's enthusiasm with a pair of pieces—an interview and a Berkeley concert review—in Monday's *Herald-Examiner.* In a way, Springsteen was taking Los Angeles by storm just as he had taken New York in August 1975 with the release of *Born to Run* and ten shows at the Bottom Line. There are some who must find such excessive praise threatening or suspicious—though only a fool would think that such enthusiasm could be manufactured—but Bruce defuses the type with ease: "See all that fancy stuff in the papers about me? Big deal, huh? I gotta tell you, I only levitate to the upper deck on Wednesdays and Fridays . . . Wednesdays and Fridays and I don't do no windows."

Perhaps the most nervy and nerve-racking antic Springsteen has retained in making the transition to hockey arenas is his trademark leap into the audience during the set's third song, "Spirit in the Night." He looks frail—at an extremely wiry and agile five foot nine, he is not—and one is always worried that his consummate trust in his fans is going to let him down, that he'll come back injured or ripped apart. But night after night he gets away with it. Somehow. Tonight the security force doesn't get the picture and tries to drag the fans off Bruce as he ascends an aisle deep in the loges. "You guys work here or somethin'?" Springsteen demands. "Get outta here. These guys are my friends." The crowd roars.

His parents have come down from their home near San Francisco for the show, and the evening's stage talk is sprinkled with references to them and his sister Pam, now sixteen. The stories Springsteen tells are always among the best moments of his shows, but what gets me tonight are the asides and dedications: he tells about the billboard ("We made a few improvements"), about asking Mary Turner for a date, and when he sings "For You," he dedicates the song to Greg Kihn, who recorded that song for Beserkley Records a year ago. And because Gary Busey is here, he spins a yarn about seeing *The Buddy Holly Story*. It's the perfect review.

"It's funny because I could never really picture Buddy Holly moving. To me, he was always just that guy with the bow tie on the album cover. I liked the picture because it made him a lot more real for me."

But the encores are the musical highlights of the evening. First, "The Promise," a quiet ballad that was one of the first things Springsteen wrote for the new album and was dropped from it only at the very last minute. In an earlier version, "The Promise" was taken by many listeners to be a metaphor for the lawsuit with former manager Mike Appel that delayed production of the *Born to Run* follow-up LP for more than a year. But tonight, with a new verse added in the studio, it's obviously about something more universal: "Now my daddy taught me how to walk quiet / And how to make my peace with the past / And I learned real good to tighten up inside / And I don't say nothin' unless I'm asked."

And then to top it all, he does his two most famous songs, back to back: "Born to Run" and "Because the Night," the latter in a version that shrivels one's memory of the Patti Smith hit. When the night finally ends, it's with "Quarter to Three," house lights up full and the crowd singing along as spontaneously as I've ever heard 14,500 people do anything.

Backstage, I run into Jackson Browne. "Good show, huh?" I say. He looks at me querulously, like I was just released from the nuthouse. "Uh-unh," Jackson says as if disgusted with such understatement. "Great show."

At midnight, local FM stations broadcast an announcement that Springsteen will play the Roxy, the 500-seat club and record company hangout on Sunset Strip on Friday night, one show only. Lines begin forming almost immediately.

Thursday, July 6

Walking through the lobby of the Marquis last night, just after two A.M., I ran into Bruce, who asked if I wanted to walk over to Ben Frank's for something to eat. On the way, I mentioned that there must be a lot of people in line at the Roxy, just up the street. Bruce shot me a look. "I don't like people waiting up all night for me," he said.

Springsteen ate a prodigious meal: four eggs, toast, a grilled-cheese sandwich, large glasses of orange juice and milk. And the talk ranged widely: surfing (Bruce had lived with some of the Jersey breed for a while in the late sixties and he's a little frustrated with trying to give a glimmer of its complexity to a landlocked hodad like me), the new album and its live-in-the-studio recording style ("I don't think I'll ever go back to over-dubbing," he said, mentioning that almost all of the LP was done completely live, and that "Streets of Fire" and "Something in the Night" were first takes). But mostly we talked, or rather, Bruce talked and I listened.

Springsteen can be spellbinding, partly because he is so completely ingenuous as he sails into a tale, partly because of the intensity and sincerity with which he has thought out his role as a rock star. He delivers his ideas with an air of conviction, but not a proselytizing one; some of his ideas are radical enough for Patti Smith and the punks, yet he lacks their sanctimonious and artsy rhetoric.

I asked him why the band plays so long—their shows rarely last less than three hours—and he said: "It's hard to explain. 'Cause every time I read stuff that I say, like in the papers, I always think I come off sounding like some kind of crazed fanatic. When I read it, it sounds like that, but it's the way I am about it. It's like you have to go the whole way because . . . that's what keeps everything *real*. It all ties in with the records and the values, the morality of the records. There's a certain morality of the show and it's very strict." Such comments can seem not only fanatical but also self-serving. The great advantage of the sanctimony and rhetoric that infests the punks is that such flaws humanize their zealotry. Lacking such egregiously sinful characteristics, Bruce Springsteen seems too good to be true when his world view is reduced to cold type. Nice guys finish last, we are told, and here's one at the top. So what's the catch? I just don't know.

At the end of every show on this tour, before the first encore, Bruce stands tall at the microphone and makes a little speech. "I want to thank all of you for supporting the band for the past three years," he concludes, and then plays "Born to Run." I wondered why.

"That's what it's about," he said. "Everything counts. Every person, every individual in the crowd counts—to me. I see it both ways. There is a crowd reaction. But then I also think very, very personally, one to one with the kids. 'Cause you put out the effort and then if it doesn't come through it's a . . . it's a breakdown. What I always feel is that I don't like to let people that have supported me down. I don't like to let myself down.

Whatever the situation, as impossible as it is, I like to try to . . . I don't wanna try to get by."

And so it was no surprise that, waking up this morning, I found that all hell had broken loose. Only 250 seats for the Roxy show were available for public sale, which meant that a great many of those who had waited up weren't going to get in. And Bruce wasn't just upset; he was furious. It was a betrayal, however well-intentioned the attempt to do a special sort of show had been, and the fact that another 120 of the tickets would go to fans through radio-station giveaways didn't mollify him. People had been fruitlessly inconvenienced on his behalf. It didn't matter that at most small club gigs, this proportion of public to industry seating is reversed. This was *his* show and it was supposed to have been handled properly.

Friday, July 7

Whatever bad blood had erupted from the overnight Roxy fiasco is gone. In its place, one begins to get a sense of Springsteen's impact on LA. Polaroids snap at the billboard remodeling job up on the Strip, and the band seems prepared to make the Roxy show a big night. At six P.M., there's a media first: Springsteen is interviewed on KABC-TV, the first time he has ever been on TV in any way, shape or form. He gives J. J. Jackson a good interview—"It's probably the thing that I live for. When I was a kid, I didn't only know nothin' about nothin' until rock and roll got into my house. To me, it was the only thing that was ever true, it was the only thing that never let me down. And no matter who was out there, ten people or ten thousand people, there's a lot to live up to . . . What happens is, there's a lotta trappings, there's a lotta things that are there to tempt you, sort of. It's just meaningless. And I just try to . . . I play Buddy Holly every night before I go on, that keeps me honest."

But even more striking are the filmed performances of "Prove It All Night" and "Rosalita" that accompany the interview. Even on this small screen, Springsteen is a visual natural, mugging like a seven-year-old and leaping like the rocker of someone's dreams. I now know why so many film directors, seeing him for the first time, have virtually drooled in anticipation.

After the Forum, the Roxy seems cramped. The broadcast is set for nine, but it's quarter past by the time the band takes the stage. The place is packed—even the balcony box above Roy Bittan's piano looks like it's holding twice the customers it was intended for. And while there are celebrities here—Cher and Kiss' Gene Simmons, Jackson Browne, Irving Azoff and Glenn Frey of the Eagles, Karla Bonoff, Gary Busey, Tom Waits —it remains mostly a crowd of kids and young adults.

The crowd rustles as Bruce steps to the mike, but he holds up his hand, asking silence. "I want to apologize to everybody," he says, "for what happened with the tickets to this show. It was my fault, and I'm really sorry. I wasn't tryin' to make this no private party—I don't play no parties anymore. Except my own." Then he steps to the mike and sings: "Well-a-well-a little things you say and do . . . " It's Holly's "Rave On" and the joint explodes. Garry Tallent, who loves this music as much as anyone I have ever met, is singing the choruses with a shining face. "I've always wanted to sing Buddy Holly onstage," he says later in his quiet way.

But "Rave On" is only the ignition spark. Having decided to play a special show, Springsteen goes out of his way. He dances on the tabletops as the crowd leaps to grab him. He adds "Candy's Room," a *Darkness* song he *never* performs, and halfway through the first set, he introduces a "new song that I wrote right after I finished *Darkness*. It's called 'Point Blank' and it's about being trapped." And he tells a story of a friend of his who has to work two jobs, as does her husband, to make ends meet and "they're" still trying to take the couple's house away. When he sings, it's very real, living up to that title: "Point blank, right between the eyes / They got you, point blank / Right between them pretty lies that they tell . . . No one survives untouched / No one survives untouched / No one survives."

Near the end of the first set, he tells this story: "Last summer I went driving out in the desert near Reno—we just flew to Phoenix and rented a car and drove around. And in the desert we came upon a house that this old Indian had built of stuff scavenged from the desert. And on his house there was a sign: THIS IS THE LAND OF PEACE, LOVE, JUSTICE AND NO MERCY. And at the bottom of the sign there was an arrow pointing down this old dirt road. And it said . . . " The biggest hand of the evening erupts as the band explodes into "Thunder Road."

The second half is, if anything, harder to believe. It begins, after the usual twenty-minute intermission, with Bruce striding to the mike and snapping: "All right, all of you bootleggers out there in radioland. Roll them tapes!" And he comes on with a performance that deserves preservation. Even when his guitar has to be sent backstage for repairs, he saves the moment with inspiration and finesse, calling a brief onstage conference after which the band takes two steps forward and surges into "Heartbreak Hotel," of all things. There's an encore performance of "Independence Day," another of those songs that didn't quite make *Darkness*, this one the most moving ballad version of the "Adam Raised a Cain" story that I've ever heard in any medium.

Three hours into the set, during "Quarter to Three," Bruce climbs to the balcony and sings a chorus before leaping ten feet down to the piano, miraculously landing uninjured. The houselights come up and the kids are on their feet, chanting "Broooce"—no one's going home. And even when the announcement that the band has left the building comes, no one moves. "Brooce," the chant goes on and on. "Bru-ce, Bru-ce." And suddenly the curtain rises and there they are, Max Weinberg with his head still wet from the shower. The E Streeters roll into "Twist and Shout" and finally, nearly four hours after it began in apology, the show concludes in ecstasy.

Los Angeles Times rock critic Robert Hilburn is at a loss for words. "How do I come back and review this show," he asks despairingly, "after I just said that the Forum concert was one of the best events ever in Los Angeles? Who's gonna believe me?" Maybe, I can only suggest, that's everybody else's problem.

Phoenix, Arizona, Saturday, July 8

My favorite comment on last night's Roxy show came from Max Weinberg on this morning's flight. "You know, I was thinking in the middle of the show that when I was twelve years old, this is exactly what I wanted to be doing."

Later, I ask Springsteen why he'd apologized. "It just seemed like the only thing to do," he says. "I couldn't imagine not. There was a little naiveté in thinking that the kids are gonna come and when somebody tells them that there's no more tickets, they're gonna go home. They're not. All I know is, it should've been done better."

Still, I suggest, he could have gotten away without an apology. "*I* couldn't have gotten away with it," he says, shooting me a look harder than the one he'd cast that night when I suggested visiting the kids standing in line. "That's all I try to do—live so I can sleep at night. That's my main concern."

Even with a clear conscience, sleeping's going to be a task tonight. It was 109 degrees when we got off the plane and into this oven, and a film crew has shown up to shoot tonight's performance for a possible TV commercial. They'll be at the sound check and they'll also have cameras and additional lights at the show, making the experience even sweatier than usual.

Springsteen seems more eager and open to the possibility of promoting *Darkness* than any of his other albums. Despite the massive amounts of ink he's attracted, Bruce has never been a particularly accessible interview, and with the exception of that quickie in LA the other night, he has never, ever appeared on TV. I wonder why the change.

"I always had a certain kinda thing about all those things—like the TV ad or this ad or that ad. But I realized shortly after this album came out that things had changed a lot since *Born to Run.* I just stopped taking it as seriously, and I realized that I worked a year—a year of my life—on somethin' and I wasn't aggressively tryin' to get it out there to people. I was super aggressive in my approach toward the record and toward makin' it happen—you know, nonrelenting. And then when it came out, I went, 'Oh, I don't wanna *push* it.'

"It's just facing up to certain realities. It was ridiculous to cut off your nose to spite your face. What it was, was I was so blown away by what happened last time, I initially thought of doing *no* ads. Just put it out, literally just put it out."

It is the first time I have ever heard Springsteen refer to the negative effect of the past three years of accusation, litigation and layoff. It's strange he's not more bitter, I suggest. "At the time that that went down," he explains, "I wasn't mentally prepared. I knew nothin' about it. It was all distressing to me. There were some good times, but what it was, was . . . the loss of control. See, all the characters [on the LPs] and everything is about the attempt to gain control of your life. And here, all this stuff, whether it had a good effect or a bad effect, I realized the one thing it did have was it had a bad effect on my control of myself. Which is why I initially started playing and why I play. That's what upset me most about it. It was like somebody bein' in a car with the gas pedal to the floor."

(I have only heard Springsteen explain his relationship with former manager Mike Appel more vividly on one occasion. "In a way, Mike was as naive as me," he told a group of European and Japanese journalists in Los Angeles. "His idea was 'You be Elvis and I'll be the Colonel.' Except he wasn't the Colonel and I wasn't Elvis.")

There are of course other reasons for the TV commercial: while Springsteen is enormously popular in certain areas, in others he is all but unknown. This is particularly true of the South. And it's especially difficult for people who live in the Northeast and Southwest, where Springsteen already is a star, to grasp his commercial limitations elsewhere. Anyone who sells out both the Los Angeles Forum and Madison Square Garden (three nights at the latter) ought to be a national star, but for a variety of reasons, Springsteen still isn't there. Most of this had to do with his lack of acceptance on AM radio—on that side of the dial, he remains virtually unheard. "Born to Run" made the Top Twenty, but "Prove It All Night" will be lucky to get that high, principally because both emphasize electric guitars, which the collective wisdom of AM program directors has currently banished from that side of the spectrum.

In Phoenix, however, all of these cavils can be forgotten. Phoenix was the first town outside of the New York/New Jersey/Boston/Philadelphia megalopolis where Springsteen became popular. In the everlasting idiom of Danny Federici: "This is the first place I ever felt like a star." It's hard to believe, driving past deserted desert streets at 7:30 on a Saturday evening, that the 10,000-seat Veterans Memorial Coliseum is sold out. But when the show is over, I know what Robert Hilburn felt the night before.

It's not just that it's another fantastic show. This is another goddamn event, and it goes farther than the Roxy, with all of that show's intimacy, innocence and vulnerability, but with an added factor of pandemonium. The Phoenix crowd is the sweetest-tempered I've ever been with, and at the same time, the most maniacal. Bruce dedicates the show to the town, in memory of the time "when this was about the only place I could get a job," and the crowd responds in kind. During "Prove It All Night," three extremely young girls in the front row hold up a hand-lettered sign written on a bedsheet. Quoting the song, it says, JUST ONE KISS WILL GET THESE THINGS FOR YOU. And Bruce gets them, during "Rosalita," one after another, as they race up to kiss him, lightly on the cheek. A fourth darts forward and just . . . reaches out and touches his hand, dissolving in giggly tears. Finally three more race up and bowl him over. ("This *little* girl, couldn't have been more than fifteen, and she had braces on her teeth," Springsteen later exclaims. "And she had her tongue so far down my throat I nearly choked.")

I've never seen anything like this in such a big hall. Before the encores are over, not seven but seventeen girls have climbed up to kiss him, and there are couples dancing, actually jitterbugging, on the front of the stage. The cameras are torn between filming Bruce, who's pouring it all out, and simply shooting the crowd, which is pushing him farther and farther into one of the great grandstand performances.

It is a perfect climax to a week of rock and roll unparalleled in my experience, so good that it lives up to the grand story Bruce told in the midst of "Growin' Up." The story has become virtually a set piece, but that night he gave it a special twist. For me, it fills in some of the cracks, explaining just why Bruce Springsteen pushes people to the edge of frenzy in his appearances.

The story began with a description of his family, house and home and of his perennial battling with his father. "Finally," he says, "my father said to me, 'Bruce, it's time to get serious with your life. This guitar thing is okay as a hobby, but you need something to fall back on. You should be a lawyer'—which I coulda used later on in my life. He says, 'Lawyers, they run the world.' But I didn't think they did—and I still don't.

"My mother, she's more sensitive. She thinks I should be an author and write books. But I wanted to play guitar. So my mother, she's very Italian, she says, 'This is a big thing, you should go see the priest.' So I went to the rectory and knocked on the door. 'Hi, Father Ray, I'm Mr. Springsteen's son. I got this problem. My father thinks I should be a lawyer, and my mother, she wants me to be an author. But I got this guitar.'

"Father Ray says, 'This is too big a deal for me. You gotta talk to God,' who I didn't know too well at the time. 'Tell him about the lawyer and the author,' he says, 'but don't say *nothin'* about that guitar.'

"Well, I didn't know how to find God, so I went to Clarence's house. He says, 'No sweat. He's just outside of town.' So we drive outside of town, way out on this little dark road.

"I said, 'Clarence, are you sure you know where we're goin'?' He said, 'Sure, I just took a guy out there the other day.' So we come to this little house out in the woods. There's music blasting out and a little hole in the door. I say, 'Clarence sent me,' and they let me in. And there's God behind the drums. On the bass drum it says: G–O–D. So I said, 'God, I got this problem. My father wants me to be a lawyer and my mother wants me to be an author. But they just don't understand—I got this guitar.'

"God says, 'What they don't understand is that there was supposed to be an Eleventh Commandment. I don't know why it didn't make it in. Actually, it was probably Moses' fault. He was so scared after ten, he said, this is enough, and went back down the mountain. You shoulda seen it —great show, the burning bush, thunder, lightning.

" 'So you see what those guys didn't understand was that there *was* an Eleventh Commandment. And all it said was: LET IT ROCK!' "

DAVE MARSH is the author of the best-selling *Born to Run: The Bruce Springsteen Story*, *The Book of Rock Lists*, *Elvis*, and a biography of the Who, *Before I Get Old*. A founding editor of *Creem*, a former *Rolling Stone* editor, and a co-editor for *The Rolling Stone Record Guide*, Marsh has contributed essays, articles and reviews to a number of newspapers and magazines. He currently edits *The Rock and Roll Confidential*, available by writing to Box 1073, Maywood, N.J. 07607.